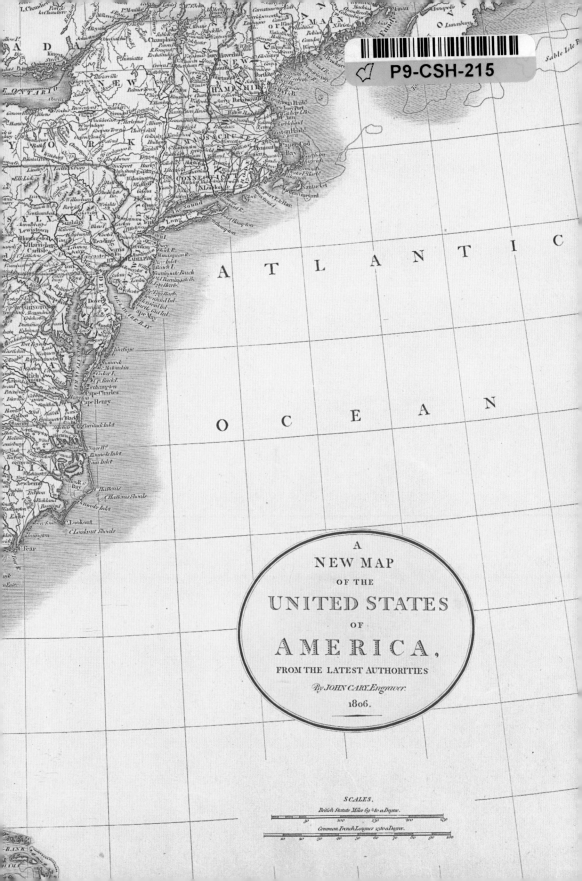

ATLANTIC

OCEAN

A

NEW MAP

OF THE

UNITED STATES

OF

AMERICA,

FROM THE LATEST AUTHORITIES

By JOHN CARY, Engraver.

1806.

SCALES.

British Statute Miles 69 ½ to a Degree.

Common French Leagues 25 to a Degree.

Also by A. Roger Ekirch

At Day's Close
Birthright
Bound for America
"Poor Carolina"

American Sanctuary

American Sanctuary

MUTINY, MARTYRDOM, AND NATIONAL IDENTITY IN THE AGE OF REVOLUTION

A. Roger Ekirch

Pantheon Books, New York

Endpaper maps courtesy of the New York Public Library Digital Collections

Library of Congress Cataloging-in-Publication Data
Name: Ekirch, A. Roger, [date] author.
Title: American Sanctuary : Mutiny, Martyrdom, and National Identity in the
Age of Revolution / A. Roger Ekirch.
Description: First Edition. New York : Pantheon, 2017. Includes bibliographical
references and index.
Identifiers: LCCN 2016015119. ISBN 9780307379900 (hardcover).
ISBN 9781101871737 (ebook).
Subjects: LCSH: United States—Politics and government—1797–1801. Adams,
John, 1735–1826. Hermione Mutiny, 1797. Nash, Thomas, –1799. Fugitives
from justice—Great Britain—Biography. Political refugees—United States—
Biography. Mutiny—Political aspects—United States—History—18th century.
Martyrdom—Political aspects—United States—History—18th century. Asylum,
Right of—United States—History—18th century. Nationalism—United
States—History—18th century.
Classification: LCC E321 .E38 2017. DDC 973.4/4—dc23.
LC record available at lccn.loc.gov/2016015119.

www.pantheonbooks.com

Jacket illustration: *The Cutting Out of HMS* Hermione, *24 October 1799*
(detail), by Nicholas Polock. © National Maritime Museum,
Greenwich, London / The Image Works
Jacket design by Janet Hansen
Map by David Lindroth

Printed in the United States of America
First Edition
2 4 6 8 9 7 5 3

For my sisters,
Cheryl Nancy Remley
and
Caryl Jocelyn Williams

Every spot of the old world is over-run with oppression. Freedom hath been hunted round the Globe. Asia, and Africa, have long expelled her.—Europe regards her like a stranger, and England hath given her warning to depart. O! receive the fugitive, and prepare in time an asylum for mankind.

—Thomas Paine, *Common Sense* (1776)

The unsuccessful strugglers against tyranny have been the chief martyrs of treason laws in all countries. Reformation of government with *our* neighbors, being as much wanted now as religion is, or ever was anywhere, we should not wish then to give up to the executioner the patriot who fails and flees to us.

—Thomas Jefferson, *Heads of consideration on the establishment of extradition treaties*, March 22, 1792

Contents

Preface

IT WAS THE BLOODIEST MUTINY in the annals of the Royal Navy, a horrific eruption of savagery during the most storied epoch in British seafaring history. At the height of the French Revolutionary Wars, when England stood imperiled by invasion, mutineers on a pitch-black night in September 1797 murdered the captain and nine other officers aboard a thirty-two-gun frigate, HMS *Hermione,* four thousand miles from home in the tropical waters of the Caribbean. Butchered by crew men brandishing axes and cutlasses, all ten officers, including a fourteen-year-old midshipman and a second lieutenant delirious with yellow fever, their skulls crushed by tomahawks, were heaved overboard ten leagues off the western coast of Puerto Rico. By morning light, except for a dozen shipmates, well over one hundred men had joined the uprising.

This book begins by following the fortunes of the *Hermione,* from the genesis of the mutiny and the crew's flight to the Spanish Main to the transatlantic dragnet laid by the Royal Navy. Very little has been written about the ill-fated frigate since the publication of Dudley Pope's popular narrative, *The Black Ship,* in 1963. Except for scattered historians and legal scholars, the mutiny remains largely unknown.[1] Unlike the South Pacific saga of the *Bounty* eight years earlier, the carnage aboard the *Hermione* generated few heroics. The tale is not easily romanticized, with little to match Captain Bligh's epic survival in a cramped launch or the nomadic adventures of the *Bounty*'s crew on the far side of the world. But the bloodbath in Puerto Rico's Mona Passage did have profound repercussions, especially for the young American republic, that have been widely ignored.

For the mutiny thrust upon the administration of John Adams, America's second president, already bedeviled by partisan opposition, a set of incendiary issues involving natural rights, American citizenship, and political asylum—a consequence of the purported presence of impressed American sailors aboard the *Hermione* and, in turn, their threatened extradition to Great Britain after seeking refuge in the United States. In sanctioning the surrender of a seaman named Jonathan Robbins—a native son, he claimed, of Danbury, Connecticut—Adams in the summer of 1799 ignited a political firestorm fanned in the following weeks by news from Jamaica of the sailor's hanging as the reputed Irish ringleader Thomas Nash. "No one circumstance since the establishment of our government," observed Thomas Jefferson, "has affected the popular mind more."

Not only did the aftershocks of Robbins's martyrdom powerfully influence the momentous election of 1800, the first full-blown presidential campaign, but they also helped to shape the infant Republic's identity—how Americans envisioned both themselves and the larger destiny of the United States. In drawing heightened importance to the principles of 1776, the *Hermione* crisis led directly to America's historic decision whether to grant political asylum to refugees from foreign governments, a major step toward fulfilling the magnetic promise of American independence, famously voiced by Tom Paine, to provide "an asylum for mankind."

A few studies, especially a long article by the legal scholar Ruth Wedgwood, have probed the affair's constitutional implications arising from allegations of judicial interference by Adams.[2] I am indebted to Professor Wedgwood's meticulous scholarship for helping me to navigate the crosscurrents of constitutional law. Less attention has been paid, particularly by historians, to the mutiny's impact on the early Republic's political culture, including the deepening rift between Federalists and Jeffersonian Republicans.[3] Perhaps as a consequence, recent studies of the Revolution of 1800 and biographies of John Adams have either minimized or, more often, entirely overlooked the controversy. Even so, I have profited greatly from scholarship that has of late centered on the young Republic, including the contested landscape of early national politics.

Sources for this book have been wide ranging, among them documents in the British National Archives at Kew. Especially critical were Admiralty dispatches, journals, logs, and muster books. Court-martial records graphically detail events aboard the *Hermione* before, during, and after the mutiny. Also vital were records at the National Archives in Washington, D.C. Manuscripts of key political figures proved revealing, not least those of Robert Liston, Timothy Pickering, Oliver Wolcott, Rufus King, and Edward Livingston, along with the correspondence of Adams and Jefferson. Electronic databases such as America's Historical Newspapers and the British Newspaper Archives offered an unparalleled opportunity to canvass innumerable papers published on opposite sides of the Atlantic. Highly influential at the turn of the eighteenth century, newspapers in the United States afford a particularly striking lens on public opinion as well as on national politics.

The book is a triptych, beginning with the mutiny on the *Hermione* and the ensuing manhunt for members of her crew. The second section recounts the arrival of a handful of mutineers, including Jonathan Robbins, in the United States before examining in depth the political crisis that engulfed John Adams and the Federalist Party. The final three chapters focus on the election of 1800 and the protracted consequences of Robbins's martyrdom during the years of Republican ascendancy. As late as 1812, Adams bitterly complained that "Robbins" was "a scandal that ought to have been killed before it died of old age"—"a more infernal, wicked, malicious, unprincipled, deliberate, and cruel scandal never stalked this earth." "Indeed," he rued, "I know not whether it be dead yet."

Quotations are set in the original spelling except when altered to improve clarity. Capitalization has been modernized and punctuation added when necessary. To avoid confusion, I have chosen to employ the name "Jonathan Robbins" to refer to the seaman whose extradition lies at the heart of this story. The decision to use the alternate name "Thomas Nash" only when invoked by Federalist partisans and the British is not intended to render a verdict on the contentious issue of Robbins's identity, which is among the larger of several mysteries that the book seeks to unravel.

Prologue

FIRST LIGHT ON THE TWENTY-SECOND of April 1769 brought frantic cries of an advancing man-of-war, its enormous foresail bellied out in the breeze. Any thought of escape was folly. Homeward bound for Marblehead, the merchantman was ill equipped to outrun, much less fend off, a twenty-gun frigate under full sail, the red ensign of the Royal Navy flapping from its stern. Closing quickly, HMS *Rose* bore down on the *Pitt Packet,* captained by Thomas Power, just four leagues off Cape Ann, a rugged granite peninsula north of Boston. Its hold brimming with lemons and salt from Spain, the New England brig also bore a small cache of contraband—sundry crates of wine and champagne in addition to three casks of gin—barely enough, once inspected, to warrant chalking the King's "broad arrow" on the mainmast.[1]

Two thunderous volleys of cannon fire forced the gently pitching boat to heave to, followed in short order by the approach of a cutter carrying Lieutenant Henry Panton, two midshipmen, and seven seamen bearing the telltale swagger of a press-gang. Clambering aboard, Panton lost no time in inquiring after the ship's company, only two of whom, both Americans, appeared before the mast. Besides Master Power, the vessel's log revealed a crew of six. "Here they are," exclaimed a sailor from the *Rose* upon opening a hatch. Beneath the deck huddled four Irish seamen barricaded in the forepeak, a small, ill-lit enclosure in the bow separated from the main hold by a wooden bulwark. Armed with little more than a musket and a harpoon, there they had decided to plant their flag, vowing to die as "freemen born free" rather than be "pressed" into the British navy.

It went badly. Going below with drawn swords and candles to light the way, Panton's men laid siege to the makeshift fortress, the lieutenant at first entreating, then commanding the band's surrender. "I'm the man who will bring you out," he declared. As the morning wore on, a squad of marines arrived from the *Rose.* Joining the gangsmen, they tore into the bulkhead with a crowbar and axe, cutting deep holes in the wooden planks. Tempers flared. "Fire if you dare," cried Michael Corbet, leader of the four sailors and likely a former seaman in the Royal Navy. "I will not go back, I will kill the first of you." In a blur, a pistol snapped, the flash scorching Corbet's face and bloodying his lip. Desperate to regain control, Panton grabbed the pistol from a young marine. It was too late. Through a breach in the bulkhead, Corbet drove a harpoon into the left side of the lieutenant's neck, severing the carotid artery and two jugular veins. Blood sprayed everywhere as Panton's face began to cloud. Rushed to the master's cabin—handkerchiefs vainly binding the gash—he was beyond saving. Within minutes, Panton lay stone dead at his men's feet.

Nor was this all. No sooner had the lieutenant been struck than a midshipman shot a second seaman in the arm. Three of the four were shortly seized and dragged to the main deck, where they learned of Panton's fate. Through his tears, Corbet, the last to surrender, glimpsed the callow marine who'd fired at him. "You are the rascal that is the occasion of this gentleman losing his life," he cried. As for the wounded shipmate, he survived the gunshot, no thanks to the *Rose's* doctor, who seethed, "Let the dog die and be damned."

Thus the grim case that fell to John Adams, at the age of thirty-three, on agreeing to defend the *Pitt's* Irish hands against the capital charge of murdering a lieutenant in the Royal Navy—all four seamen tarred with the same brush. A seasoned trial attorney, Adams had practiced law ever since graduating from Harvard and forgoing a career in the ministry. In 1768, the year of his family's removal from his native Braintree to Brattle Street in Boston, he appeared in over three hundred cases, approximately a third before the Massachusetts Superior Court. He had also become associated, by then, with escalating protests against British authority, beginning with his public condemnation of the Stamp Act.

Just a month prior to Panton's death, he had launched a newspaper column critical of British policies, including recent prosecutions in Boston for smuggling. Besides affording an opportunity to further his political career, *Rex v. Corbet* magnified Adams's gravest fears. Taxation without representation, greedy customs commissioners, trials bereft of juries, armed soldiers on Boston streets, and now, by all accounts, a shocking attempt to deprive free men of their liberty—inescapable evidence, in Adams's view, of a conspiracy in the highest echelons of the British government to snuff out American rights.

Predictably, the deadly fray became the talk of Boston. At first, the Patriot leader James Otis, famed for his political oratory and legal acumen, agreed to serve as co-counsel. But Otis's mental instability, reputedly compounded by bouts with the bottle, undercut his usefulness. With nowhere else to turn, Adams scoured his personal library—arguably the finest in Boston—for legal references and precedents pertaining to homicide, and to the deeply unpopular practice of impressment long employed by the Royal Navy to replenish its ranks with merchant seamen. Law, history, theology, and political philosophy all figured in his research, occasioning nights spent poring over tomes both familiar and obscure. Neither before nor afterward in his legal career did Adams devote so many hours with near bottomless energy to a single case. "I vainly thought as if I could shake the town and the world," he later confessed.

Perhaps. On Wednesday, June 14, inside a packed chamber on the second floor of the Boston courthouse—"no trial had ever interested the community so much"—Adams entered four pleas of justifiable homicide before a Special Court of Admiralty. Due to the denial of his motion for a jury trial, a panel of fifteen high-ranking crown officials heard the case the following morning, including the governors of Massachusetts and New Hampshire and the chief justice of Massachusetts, Thomas Hutchinson, fated to become the most hated man in America during his impending tenure as the colony's royal governor.

For the better part of three days, a stream of witnesses paraded before the court to recount the morning of Panton's death, among them seven crew members of the *Rose*. Although by law criminal defendants were forbidden to testify, the crew's unvarying testimony, to a man, combined with that of the master and two seamen from the *Pitt,* buttressed the defense's case. By any reckoning, the overriding purpose of the boarding party had been to impress able seamen, preferably any who hailed from England, Ireland, or Scotland. The prosecution's contention to the contrary, inspecting the brig for contraband had been an afterthought and the lieutenant's death the tragic consequence of a standoff in which the accused again and again affirmed their determination not to be pressed. The court also learned that the first pistol fired belowdecks had been unloaded, save for black powder. The marine, by hoping to cow Corbet into surrendering, had committed a fatal error. *Fire if you dare. I will not go back, I will kill the first of you.*

On Saturday morning, steeped in law and legal precedent, Adams stood before the hushed gathering to deliver his argument. To judge from his notes, he fully intended to claim self-defense. Shot point-blank in the face, Corbet had been forced to defend his person. What's more, Panton had committed an illegal act in boarding the *Pitt* for the purpose of pressing crew members. A little-known act of Parliament passed in 1707 during the reign of Queen Anne expressly prohibited the impressment of seamen in North America, no matter their native origins, save for deserters.

Adams's opportunity never arrived. Scarcely had he uttered a sentence before the chief justice arose from his chair to move that the judges adjourn to the council chamber. There, sequestered from the public, the panel deliberated for the remainder of the day and early evening, to the apprehension of much of Boston, not least Adams himself. Notwithstanding the week's testimony, he, like others, feared a conviction when the court reconvened, followed by the death sentence for all four defendants. "Never was a more gloomy assembly of countenances painted with terror and horror than appeared in the audience next morning," he recalled.

All the more astounding, then, once the prisoners had been summoned to the bar, that the president of the court, Governor Francis Bernard of Massachusetts, pronounced a unanimous verdict of justifiable homicide in necessary self-defense. And there, with no further explanation, the case of *Rex v. Corbet* rested. In a breathtaking reversal of fortune, it was over. Adams, for his part, was dumbfounded, writing long afterward that he still did not know whether "to laugh, or cry, or scold." Notwithstanding his delight, the trial's improbable conclusion had rendered his preparation moot, which for both personal and political reasons made the triumph, at best, incomplete. The court, Adams calculated years later, could not have returned a verdict favorable to impressment. "Such a judgment, would, at that time, have been condemned, reprobated, and execrated. . . . It would have accelerated the Revolution." Neither, however, could the court permit "a public exhibition of the law in all its details before the people," even less a full-throated attack of the sort that Adams envisaged.

On departing the courthouse, toward the bottom of the stairs leading to the foyer, he was met by the boatswain of the *Rose*. "Sir," the sailor volunteered, "we are all greatly obliged to you for your noble conduct in defense of those brave fellows." "This is the employment," he admitted, "in which I have been almost constantly engaged for twenty years, fighting with honest men to deprive them of their liberty. I always thought I ought to be hanged for it, and now I know it."

Oddly, in light of later events, it was an anecdote that John Adams long delighted in telling after his presidency.

PART ONE

Mutiny

I

Men-of-War

AT HIGH TIDE ON A September morning in 1782, not quite a year since Britain's humiliating capitulation at the Battle of Yorktown, His Majesty's Ship *Hermione*, her coppered hull slathered with grease, slid stern-first down a wooden slipway into the swollen waters of the River Avon, fed by the swift currents of the Severn estuary. A launch was no easy feat, nor was it free of peril, but the port of Bristol, England's "metropolis of the west," had been building ships since the thirteenth century. Before a rapt crowd lining the stone quay—sailors, shipwrights, and merchant princes—heavy ropes, tethered fast to the bow, were cast off with ceremonial fanfare. Slowly the tide-borne frigate began to slip away from the dry dock of Sydenham Teast, directly across the Avon from the elegant townhouses of Queen Square. With a surplus of warships at royal wharves waiting to be built or repaired, private docks such as Teast's reaped the rewards of government contracts.[1]

It was a promising start. Fitted out in a naval yard, the *Hermione* was commissioned for duty the following spring—too late, owing to a halt in hostilities that February, to enter the American War of Independence. Two-decked, three-masted, and square-rigged in the fashion of frigates, she was the first in a new class designed by Sir Edward Hunt, bearing a rounder midsection, much like the profile of a tulip, to lend stability. The clean-lined hull ran 129 feet in length with a beam of nearly 36 feet. Of 714 tons burden, she was notably larger than the slavers that Teast's shipyard furnished for Bristol's lucrative African trade, designed instead for a naval company of 220 men. Costs of construction, fittings, sails, rigging, and armament exceeded £16,000. In addition to six carronades, devised with a large caliber for firing at close range, the *Hermione* received 32 cast-iron cannons, among them 26 twelve-pounders for the main deck. Unlike larger, more powerful men-of-war that boasted two or even three gun decks, with lower ports vulnerable to ocean swells, the main battery of the *Hermione*, lying well above the waterline, promised greater versatility in heavy weather.[2]

In the annals of classical mythology, Homer tells of the "rose-lipped" Hermione, the only daughter of Menelaus, king of Sparta, and Helen, whose abduction ignited the Trojan War.[3] For many Britons, however, the frigate's name conjured halcyon memories of wartime riches and national glory. Years back, in May 1762, toward the close of the Seven Years' War, two British warships cruising off the southern coast of Portugal captured a Spanish treasure galleon named the *Hermione* just a day's sail from the port of Cádiz, home to Spanish fleets for nearly two centuries. Striking her colors before firing a single shot, the enemy prize had been en route from Peru with a glittering cargo of gold dust, jewels, and silver estimated at £700,000 to £800,000, the "richest capture" in the history of the Royal Navy. Such was the outpouring of joy in Britain that the name "Hermione" graced newborns and racehorses alike. In August, throngs gathered from Portsmouth to London, anxious to glimpse twenty heavily laden wagons transporting the treasure under military escort to Tower Hill. George III viewed from an upper chamber in St. James's Palace the convoy's arrival in the capital, which was followed by a marching band. "The air was rent with the shouts of the populace," described a newspaper. Less happily, major Spanish banking houses from Barcelona to Málaga collapsed; chaos reigned among Andalusian merchants; and the *Hermione's* captain, on returning home, forfeited his head.[4]

IN THE DECADE THAT FOLLOWED the Treaty of Paris of 1783—years that saw a resurgence of transatlantic traffic; the Royal Navy's startling expansion to keep pace with rival fleets; and the spiraling descent of the French monarchy, corrupted by debt and decay, into revolution—an anxious peace descended on Europe like a bank of dark, low-hanging clouds lit by fitful flashes of sheet lightning. In the course of losing most of its American colonies, England had acquired a host of familiar enemies nursing grudges old and new. More than once, the country teetered on the brink of fresh hostilities, in 1787 with France over rival claimants in the Netherlands, and three years later with Spain in the Pacific Northwest.[5]

As much as ever, the realm's safety depended upon naval superiority. During the Revolutionary War, control of the English Channel had been surrendered, sparking widespread fears of foreign invasion. Little wonder, with the looming prospect of peace, that the Admiralty, at the urging of England's fledgling prime minister, William Pitt the Younger, set about rebuilding the fleet with an aggressive program of extensive repairs and new construction. Already the country's largest industrial infrastructure, naval dockyards stretching from Deptford to Portsmouth resounded with newfound urgency. "The great naval preparations now making militate against every idea of peace," observed the *Reading Mercury* in January 1783.[6]

All the while, British warships plied the North Atlantic. With the Channel fleet guarding the homeland, frigates, prized for their speed, firepower, and maneuverability, played a pivotal role in projecting British power overseas—displaying the flag, keeping sea-lanes open, and escorting commercial convoys. First designed by the French in the late seventeenth century, frigates typically cruised the seas either alone, in pairs, or in small squadrons detached from battle fleets. Not uncommonly, they roamed out of signaling range from other vessels. Though smaller than line ships armed with "heavier metal," they were the most glamorous vessels in the Royal Navy, famed for their aura of adventure as well as for their autonomy and sailing prowess. "Star captains" was how an English poet described the small number of officers fortunate enough to receive a command.[7]

Adding to their allure was the prospect of prize money. Upon the capture of an enemy warship, merchantman, or privateer, everyone from the admiral of the fleet to the cabin boy, according to rank, reaped a portion of the spoils, with captains due a quarter share. In 1790, when war with Spain appeared imminent, a young officer, on hearing rumors of his posting to a frigate, immediately wrote his sister. Acknowledging the larger sums paid to captains of line-of-battle ships, he assured her, "If I can get her into the W't Indies, I will make the Dons pay me the difference once or twice a month."[8]

Besides periodic patrols of home waters and routine repairs in royal shipyards, the *Hermione* spent long spells cruising the Caribbean. When spring yielded to summer, it was not unusual to find her farther north—safe from hurricanes—policing British fishing banks off Newfoundland. Even then, uncertain trade winds, fickle currents, and mercurial weather could render familiar seas hazardous. During a harrowing trip from Halifax, Nova Scotia, to Ireland in 1789, fierce storms, exhausted provisions, and the deaths of ten seamen forced the *Hermione*'s crew to take refuge in the Spanish port of Corunna. Sixteen bedraggled survivors were left to die in a hospital as the stricken vessel beat on for Ireland.[9]

Only after extensive repairs at a cost in excess of £20,000 did the *Hermione* return to the West Indies three years later in a squadron of seven warships, arriving barely a month after the revolutionary government in Paris declared war against Britain on February 1, 1793. Tensions had mounted after French troops invaded the Austrian Netherlands, followed in January by shocking reports of the execution of King Louis XVI at the age of thirty-eight. Insofar as prospects for peace had grown bleak, the only surprise was that France, not Britain, first loosed the dogs of war.[10]

Although the greatest part of the bloodletting during the First French Revolutionary War (1792–1797) occurred in Europe, the Caribbean, for the Pitt government, became a critical theater of operations. For all the hurricanes and earthquakes, the stifling summers, the perils of disease to say nothing of the Lilliputian size of most islands—their plantation economies afforded European powers immense troves of wealth. For Britain, the loss of Barbados or, worse, the much larger island of Jamaica would have been devastating. If anything, France's colonies were dearer. Boasting eight thousand plantations, the French island of Saint Domingue (now Haiti) was the wealthiest colony in the Caribbean.[11]

Equally important, with France deprived of naval bases, British sea power in the North Atlantic would again "rule the waves." And with French troops on the march in Europe and much of the navy sidelined,

View of PORT ROYAL *and* KINGSTON HARBOUR *in the Island of* JAMAICA.

Anonymous, View of Port Royal and Kingston Harbour
in the Island of Jamaica, *1782*

the islands were all the more vulnerable to coastal raids and amphibious assaults. Hence the departure of a mammoth flotilla, months in the planning, in November 1793 under the seasoned command of Vice Admiral Sir John Jervis. Fitted out in Portsmouth and Cork, the expedition to the Caribbean comprised nearly one hundred warships and transports ferrying eight thousand unblooded troops tasked with bringing the French empire to its knees.[12]

Even before the fleet's arrival that January, life aboard the *Hermione* had quickened. Along with squadrons stationed from Newfoundland to East India, the Royal Navy maintained two bases in the West Indies: Port Royal, on the southeastern coast of Jamaica, once a pirate haven reviled as the most wicked town in the West, and Carlisle Bay, home to Bridgetown, the capital of Barbados, from which the *Hermione* under Captain John Hills routinely departed to escort merchant convoys to safer waters. Come fall, however, the *Hermione* had joined a squadron from Jamaica in landing troops in western Saint Domingue. Soon afterward, a small inlet at Cape Saint Nicholas Mole, on the northwestern tip of the island where the sandy coastline gave way to mountains and lush forests, was seized from the French. On the same spot on December 6, 1492, Columbus had landed during his first expedition to the Americas. Although notorious for yellow fever, the sheltered bay gave the British a strategic anchorage in the Western Caribbean second only to Port Royal and Kingston.[13]

In the months following Jervis's arrival in early 1794, Port-au-Prince, the capital of Saint Domingue, lying to the south, was taken after the fall of Martinique, Saint Lucia, and Guadeloupe, like so many dominoes, to British forces in the Eastern Caribbean. For several hours, the *Hermione*, lying directly opposite the capital, traded volleys of cannon fire with a French shore battery. Then one of the ship's main guns blew up, igniting a second explosion on the larboard (port) side of the forecastle. "We suffer'd very severely," a young officer later wrote of the eleven casualties, including five seamen mortally wounded. Despite the British victory, the interior of Saint Domingue, in the early stages of a slave insurrection resulting in Haitian independence, remained an elusive prize. And by year's end, in an abrupt reversal, heavy French reinforcements poured into the Caribbean, causing the British offensive to sputter.[14]

The military, hobbled by indecision, struggled to retain hard-won terrain. The bill was steep. As the fighting ground on, massive numbers of troops and seamen perished, owing less to hostile fire than to the deadly triumvirate of yellow fever ("black vomit"), malaria ("ague"), and dysentery ("bloody flux"). "In the *Hermione* alone," a junior officer attested, "we lost in three or four months, nearly half our crew; many from apparent good health, dying in a few hours."[15]

The *Hermione* persevered in the thick of the fighting, shelling and protecting ports from Saint Nicholas Mole to Cape Tiburon, at the southern tip of the island's western coast. She also tacked to and fro in search of merchantmen and other easy prey. Black with white molding, the frigate cut a forbidding figure. Not only were the commercial ships of belligerent nations subject to seizure but also neutral craft suspected of trading with the enemy, including the vessels of American merchants who enjoyed a lucrative commerce with the French islands. Profiting from the spoils, British commanders interpreted their instructions liberally. Frigates became notorious in the United States for their depredations. To the deep chagrin of George Washington's administration in

Philadelphia, by March 1, 1794, no fewer than 250 American vessels had been commandeered, with the lion's share ruled legitimate prizes by British Admiralty courts.[16]

The *Hermione* garnered a princely portion of the plunder. By late 1793, she had already snagged four American ships laden with sugar, coffee, cotton, and provisions. More seizures followed, among them a Boston schooner taken at anchor off Saint Nicholas Mole while its captain, on shore, scrambled to sell its cargo of lumber. More lucrative, potentially, was the capture of the *Rising Sun*, a twenty-gun U.S. merchant ship thought to contain "a great quantity of money" belonging to the French commissary on Saint Domingue. To little effect, an American in Kingston howled, "The property of real American citizens are waisting by endless vexations, and her most invaluable treasure, the lives of her virtuous citizens, are daily closed by illegal detentions. Nothing can equal the contempt and derision wherewith we are treated."[17]

Worst was the impressment of American sailors on suspicion of being either deserters, British citizens, or both, an estimated ten thousand men during all of the French Wars (1793–1815). Desperate to man their warships, the British had grown exasperated by the loss of seamen to an expanding American merchant marine. In the mid-1790s, no vessel earned a blacker reputation in American eyes than the *Hermione* under Philip Wilkinson's command. On July 4, 1795, she left Port-au-Prince for the remote outpost of Jérémie, 120 miles to the west. There, at anchor, lay twenty American ships, which members of the frigate's crew methodically boarded. Before the day was out, they had laid hold of nearly seventy seamen, practically all claiming to be native-born Americans. Kept aboard the *Hermione* without food for the better part of two days, they refused to enlist in the Royal Navy. Although five sailors were returned for being "unfit to serve king or country," the angry protests of American captains, unable to crew their vessels, went unheard. "The next thing we shall hear of this frigate, *Hermione*, perhaps," warned a New Jersey newspaper, "[is that she is] on our coasts, annoying not only our allies, but plundering our own vessels."[18]

ON THE TENTH OF FEBRUARY 1797, command of the *Hermione* fell to a twenty-eight-year-old naval lieutenant. Full-faced, with thin lips, a

Francesco Bartolozzi et al.,
"Hugh Pigott," 1802. One of
thirty-four miniature portraits
in Commemoration of the
Victory of June 1st, 1794.

strong chin, and a broad nose, Hugh Pigot bore an impeccable pedigree. Not only did he descend from prominent stock—"one of the first families in England"—but Pigot was also a child of the service. A nephew of the Duchess of Grafton, he was born in Staffordshire, the second son of Admiral Hugh Pigot (1722–1792), whose naval career included service during the Seven Years' War at both Louisbourg and Quebec. Although the admiral's political proclivities had precluded a command for most of the Revolutionary War—landlocked instead at Patshull, his country seat in Staffordshire—the fall of Tory rule in March 1782 brought new opportunities for Whig stalwarts. In truth, Pigot senior had never commanded anything larger than an eighty-four-gun ship, nor had he been at sea for nineteen years. Still and all, owing to the generosity of the First Lord of the Admiralty in Whitehall, he obtained a plum appointment as commander in chief of naval forces stationed at Port Royal. That May, at the age of twelve, young Hugh accompanied his father as they departed Plymouth aboard the *Jupiter*, a fifty-gun two-decker under Captain Thomas Pasley bound for Jamaica. Scarcely a day passed before father and son, still finding their footing, succumbed to seasickness. Pasley fretted that the admiral, whom he deemed "good company," was not up to his new post. The captain confided to his journal "fears when he comes to command so large a fleet: in that line he can have no experience, and from what I have seen, a change must be worked to cut a figure."[19]

Although the arrival of peace hastened his father's return to London, the boy stayed behind in the Caribbean, serving aboard four ships over the ensuing decade. Pigot's youth was not unusual. Most frigate commanders entered the service between twelve and fourteen years of age. Some, before becoming midshipmen, underwent an apprenticeship of three years as a captain's servant. Common, too, were family ties that powered officers' careers. Bloodlines in the military, as in church and state, brought enormous benefits, particularly for sons with high-ranking fathers. During the French Wars, nearly a quarter of all officers came from naval families. There was a great deal of truth to Horatio Nelson's observation that the "near relations of brother officers" were "legacies to the service."[20]

At the time of his lieutenant's commission in 1790, Pigot served aboard the *Colossus*, a 1,716-ton guard ship stationed at Portsmouth, Britain's largest and most important naval yard. By then, he was on his way to a promising career. Four years later, at age twenty-four, after postings in the Channel fleet and a brief stint as the commander of a fireship, he received his first warship, an eighteen-gun sloop named the *Swan*, anchored at Port Royal with a complement of eighty men. Almost from the start, however, there was trouble. Just two weeks after Pigot's appointment, in the course of escorting a convoy, his impatience with the slow progress of the *Canada*, a West Indiaman, led to his firing a shot across her bow. Later that evening, the two vessels collided. The damage was modest, and the uproar passed quickly, though Pigot, in defending his conduct to London officials, heatedly denounced the "insolent and provocative language" of the *Canada*'s master. The young lieutenant was "strongly of opinion" that the merchantman had "purposely" run afoul of the *Swan*.[21]

There is no knowing the true cause of the accident, but within four months, in September 1794, Pigot received command of the *Success*, a thirty-two-gun frigate twice the size of the *Swan*. His rise in rank owed much to the navy's sudden need for fresh officers. The availability of frigate commands escalated sharply after the outbreak of war with France. From none in 1792, the number of new commands rose to thirty-one in 1793 and fifty-four in 1794, the year of Pigot's posting. At no other time in the eighteenth century did opportunities for promotion expand so dramatically, with the consequence that the transition from lieutenant to captain averaged from seven to eight years. (Before the American Revolution, the interval had been twenty years.) Even so, Pigot at age twenty-five was exceptionally young for such a daunting assignment. Barely four years had elapsed since his commission, with fewer than four months in command of a warship. None of this would have been possible but for his father's influence. Nor, despite his death in 1792, was the admiral's older brother Sir Robert, a lieutenant general in the army, without connections.[22]

Over the coming months, the *Success* performed the routine tasks of scouting enemy islands and escorting troop transports. She occasionally captured a prize, among them the *Poisson Volant* in October 1795, a French privateer with a crew of eighty-seven, off Jamaica's northern coast. But the art of command did not come naturally to Pigot. Rather than affection, he was apt to inspire respect—or rather fear—in crew men. To enforce discipline, he relied heavily upon corporal punishment. Floggings were frequent, even by the standards of the Royal Navy, for which the cat-o'-nine-tails was the punishment of choice for petty offenses. Stripped to the waist, seamen were bound spread-eagled, often to the capstan, a revolving wooden drum with bars designed to be pushed by deckhands for winching ropes and cables. Made with a heavy rope handle, a "cat" had nine "tails," cords roughly two feet in length, each bearing three small knots. Administered by a boatswain's mate, a dozen lashes, normally the minimum, could inflict excruciating pain. In

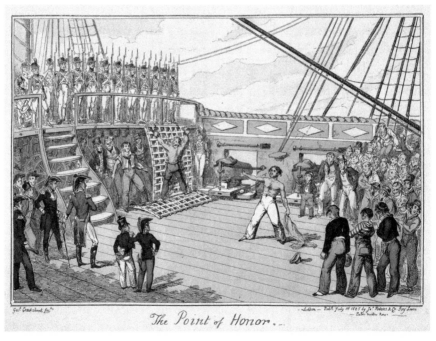

The Point of Honor.

George Cruikshank, The Point of Honor, *1825*

the event of open wounds, infection, even death, might ensue. Over a period of 49 weeks for which records exist during Pigot's command of the *Success*, whose crew numbered between 160 and 170 men, he ordered as many as 85 floggings, with 7 men receiving 3 or more floggings apiece. The number of lashes over those 49 weeks totaled nearly 1,400, an average of 25 lashes inflicted each week. By contrast, aboard the *Bounty*, with a complement of 46 men, Captain William Bligh, famously vilified for cruelty, ordered a total of just 30 lashes during a voyage of roughly 44 weeks to Tahiti: 24 to a seaman for insolence and 6 to a second hand for neglect of duty.[23]

According to American newspapers, Pigot also pressed United States citizens. To an American captain overtaken at sea, reported a witness in 1796, he vowed to conscript seven of his ten sailors. The captain protested that he would not be able to return home safely with just three seamen, prompting Pigot to press all ten, ranting, "You are yourself one of these damned *rebels*—go below!" That notoriety paled next to the debacle which erupted over the summer. The *Mercury* out of New York, captained by William Jessup, was one of several merchant vessels en route to Port-au-Prince escorted by the *Success*, pursuant to the terms of the Treaty of Amity, Commerce, and Navigation of 1794, which accorded protection by the Royal Navy to American merchant shipping. In the small hours of July 1, Jessup's brig struck the frigate's starboard beam dead-on, causing the *Mercury*'s jibboom to extend like a lance over the main deck. "Put your helm hard a' starboard or you will be on board of us," the master of the *Success* had shouted moments before impact. Remarkably, neither ship suffered serious damage. Jarred awake in his berth, Pigot was enraged. Amid the clamor on deck, he roared curses and instantly ordered the *Mercury*'s fore rigging cut away, along with a sail and "every thing" his crew "could lay their hands on." Jessup pleaded "For God's sake not to cut any more," but it did no good. That was not the worst of it. Brought aboard the *Success*, the American captain was stripped to the waist and given twenty stripes with a rope. "Flog him well!" Pigot ordered a boatswain's mate over the din.[24]

No one could have predicted the consequences, but Captain Jessup's painful humiliation set in motion a far-reaching train of events, beginning in the morning light with a formal complaint, upon the *Mercury*'s arrival in Port-au-Prince, to the American consul. With his assistance, Jessup penned a grievance to the capital's ranking British officer that not only detailed his flogging but also blamed the *Success* for the collision. "Your petitioner," he added, "made use of no offensive language whatever, nor any kind of resistance, but only begged they would have compassion on him." Attached was a certificate signed by the consul and thirty-seven of the town's "most respectable inhabitants" attesting to "the marks and lashing inflicted" on Jessup's back.[25]

And there, over the course of the summer, the petition languished. In the meantime, word of the incident prominently appeared by month's end in American newspapers, which caught the eye of Robert Liston, the British minister to the United States. A well-traveled Scottish diplomat at fifty-five years of age, Liston had originally studied at Edinburgh for the ministry. Following his arrival in Philadelphia in March 1796, the new envoy had grown increasingly apprehensive about American grievances arising from the West Indies, particularly in light of French efforts to court U.S. support. In August, he informed William Wyndham, Lord Grenville, the British foreign secretary, of the "deep impression" that had been "made upon persons of all ranks" of the "outrage offered to Mr. William Jessup," which, he reported, "has been published in every newspaper in the United States." The Massachusetts doctor Nathaniel Ames entered in his diary: "Captain Jessup, flogged on board Pigot's Frigate 'till he fainted, then vomited blood & just escaped with his life . . . so brutally shocking." At stake for Americans was less the collision's cause than the flogging of a fellow citizen, a sea captain no less, aboard a British ship. Better had he been shot, railed a contributor to the *Gazette of the United States*, than that "a high spirited, independent American" be "stripped and whipped like a thief." One widely reprinted story used the occasion to denounce Pigot's indiscriminate impressment of Americans, which he reportedly called "vexing the Yankees."[26]

Notified by Grenville, who had first informed the King, the Admiralty ordered a full review of the captain's "outrageous and cruel behaviour." En route to the Caribbean, the newly appointed commander in chief of the Jamaica station, Vice Admiral Sir Hyde Parker, fifty-eight years of age, was among the last to learn of the affair, finally arriving at Saint Nicholas Mole in late fall. Even so, the incident appeared at first to pose little more than a passing annoyance. The second son of a vice admiral dubbed "Old Vinegar," Parker, a naval officer for forty years, had a sharp, pointed nose, protruding eyes, and prominent jowls. Renowned for his courage, he had been knighted for breaking a blockade under heavy fire during the occupation of New York City in 1776. No stranger to adversity, he had served in stations around the world with the loss of just one ship (in the midst of a hurricane off Cuba in 1780). In later years, he served in the Mediterranean and the Baltic. He was both patriotic and opportunistic.[27]

John Chapman, Admiral Sir Hyde Parker, *1796*

Apart from formulating and executing military strategy, coupled with overseeing the performance of men and ships at his station, Parker was charged with convening judicial inquiries and, if necessary, courts-martial. In the course of setting a court of inquiry for January 1797, he warmed to the embattled commander, owing in part to his family's prominence, a quality shared by other favorites of the vice admiral. And unlike Robert Liston, Sir Hyde felt no sympathy for American complaints. Of efforts by U.S. envoys in Jamaica to locate impressed citizens, he was openly scornful, warning the Admiralty, "The squadron under my command will, by these evils, joined by sickness, be rendered wholly unserviceable." Perhaps most important, Parker admired young Pigot's aggressive temperament, as had his predecessor Vice Admiral Jervis. "A very promising officer and very spirited fellow," noted Jervis. The commander in chief, after all, received one-eighth of the value of every prize, and Jamaica, according to the First Lord of the Admiralty, was "the most lucrative station in the service." It was not entirely surprising, then, that Parker permitted Pigot to select the hearing's witnesses or that, in the end, he would be lightly reprimanded for his transgression by a panel handpicked by Sir Hyde himself. In his testimony, Pigot reluctantly apologized for acting "in the heat of passion," but he laid blame for the collision with the captain of the *Mercury*, a view strongly echoed by Parker and members of the court. In his report to the Admiralty, dated January 27, 1797, Parker trusted "that however unjustifiable [Captain Pigot's] conduct may appear to their Lordships, they will be of the opinion with me, that it is proved to be far, very far, more favourable than what has been represented"—including, he pointedly stated, the allegations of "Mr. Liston."[28]

By a quirk of fate, the *Success* was due in a matter of weeks to accompany a commercial convoy to England. Clearly, the warship had enjoyed better days. Once at Portsmouth, she would be repaired and refitted top to bottom at a cost of more than £6,000. For Parker, however, the timing of Pigot's departure was problematic. His arrival in England might result in a court-martial, conducted not in Port Royal but in Portsmouth. Inasmuch as no word had yet arrived from the Admiralty, his exoneration was not a foregone conclusion. Caught in a bind, the vice admiral was not one to dither. With breathtaking audacity, he abruptly ordered Pigot and Captain Wilkinson of HMS *Hermione* to exchange ships, notwithstanding the unsettling impact this could have upon their crews. In all respects but one—the *Success*'s disrepair—it was an even swap, with neither promotion nor punishment the purpose of the switch. Instead, Parker wished to shield his hot-tempered commander from Whitehall's grasp. In retrospect, not only were his fears misplaced (the Admiralty dropped the inquiry), but Pigot would no doubt have benefited from an extended leave. He suggested as much in addressing the men aboard the *Success*: "I should be glad to go home as well as you." Having served in the West Indies for nearly four years, he, like his warship, stood in need of repair. If Parker prized Pigot's pugnacity as a frigate commander, he would—for the time being—be rewarded by this feat of legerdemain. If, as well, Parker hoped to protect his young protégé from harm, he badly erred. Worse was to come.[29]

PIPED ABOARD THE *HERMIONE*, Pigot paraded across a sun-washed deck past a column of marines, smartly attired in red jackets, to the continuous beating of a drum ruffle. Resplendent in a blue coat with gold braid, white breeches, and a cocked hat, he read aloud, from a parchment scroll, his commission from Vice Admiral Parker, after which the crew, in turn, let loose with three cheers. Lest there be any doubt, the commission instructed "all the officers and company" to "behave themselves jointly and severally" with "all due respect and obedience" to the captain.[30]

Pigot inherited a complement of some 150 men, to which he added 23 crew members from the *Success*. Ordinarily, in switching ships, each frigate commander took his entire company with him. "I would wish to carry you along with me if you are agreeable," Pigot had informed just twenty-six men invited to his cabin. Included were his cook, coxswain, and a boatswain's mate, none of whom needed coaxing. Strange to say, despite soaring mortality rates and Pigot's penchant for corporal punishment, only three of the twenty-six men opted to return to England, a likely testament to the prospect of prize money that was temporarily entangled in court proceedings. Additionally, by returning to England, crew members stood to forfeit future opportunities for gain. Plenty of men, if not all, appear to have shared Sir Hyde's faith in Pigot's promise. And for mariners who took omens to heart, the *Hermione*'s own good fortune may have heightened expectations of plunder.[31]

According to the last surviving muster roll, dated July 7, 1797, members of the crew—men mostly in their twenties and early thirties—were strikingly multinational in their origins, a virtual Babel of unfamiliar accents and outlandish tongues. Barely half of those with known origins hailed from England, with a fifth from Ireland (north and south), and another fifth from elsewhere in Britain's Atlantic empire, including the North American mainland, Scotland, and the Caribbean. At least twenty men appear to have been Americans, among them mariners from Charleston, Norfolk, Philadelphia, New York, and Nantucket. Upward of a dozen countries on the Continent furnished "tars," from Scandinavia to the Iberian Peninsula. Two shipmates were identified as "Africans." As on other naval vessels, local and regional identities accentuated divisions. Among Englishmen, provincial loyalties were deeply rooted. A sailor aboard a man-of-war wrote of encountering "Irish, Welsh, Dutch, Portuguese, Spanish, French, Swedish, Italian and all the provincial dialects which prevail between Lands End and John O'Groats," a coastal village at the northern tip of Scotland. The *Hermione*'s company, like most, was at once cosmopolitan and narrowly parochial.[32]

It is tempting to attribute the international cast of British crews in the late 1700s to the broad appeal of naval service. For laboring men of meager means leading a hand-to-mouth existence, the Royal Navy afforded regular employment, food and shelter, and the possibility of prize money. A young surgeon's mate in 1790 likened a "ship of war" to "a refuge for the distressed" of both foreign and domestic origins. And while terms were shorter and wages higher aboard European merchantmen, the regimen on commercial vessels was more arduous owing to the smaller number of seamen. But the diversity of crews like the *Hermione*'s also reflected the navy's voracious need for manpower—all the more because England so frequently found itself at war, in nearly two of every three years between 1739 and 1815. Beginning in 1793, conflict was virtually continuous, with a changing cast of adversaries in addition to France, Britain's most tenacious foe.[33]

Apart from enlisting volunteers, from unskilled tradesmen to runaway apprentices, conscription offered the most reliable, if least savory, remedy. Rights celebrated by British citizens invariably gave way to the pressing priority of naval supremacy. Even before the Norman Conquest in 1066, English monarchs had required ports to supply ships and seamen. With the royal prerogative buttressed by parliamentary law, "impressment" (rooted chiefly in the Latin word *pressare*, meaning "to weigh down, afflict, or oppress") accounted for roughly 50 percent of all seamen in the Royal Navy by the second half of the eighteenth century, with the consequence that among all forms of forced labor in the British Empire, conscripted sailors stood second in number only to African slaves. In some years, the proportion of pressed sailors among crews may have approached two-thirds: "The floating sinews" of Britain's "existence," a sailor wrote of his fellow mariners. Moreover, some "recruits," as might be expected, enlisted to avoid the likelihood of impressment. Volunteers at least stood to reap bounty money and advance wages.[34]

At risk were all males from eighteen to fifty-five years of age who "used the sea." Most desirable, naturally, were deepwater mariners with skills and experience—able seamen—not vagrants and paupers. Although press-gangs still combed British port towns, a majority of conscripts were taken off foreign and domestic vessels at sea. Naval regulations, first published in 1731, authorized captains, on encountering a foreign

George Morland, The Press Gang, *1790*

ship, "to enquire if any seamen, who are his Majesty's subjects, be on board her, and to demand all such." Especially vulnerable during wartime were merchant convoys returning to British seaports from the West Indies and the South Pacific. Pressed hands were typically confined in the holds of tenders, small vessels likened to floating prisons, before being conveyed to a warship.[35]

Not only were seizures easier offshore, but they also hid from view the violent spectacle of impressment, associated in the public mind with involuntary servitude and state tyranny. Out of sight, out of mind. It was one thing to conscript freeborn Englishmen at sea; it was quite another to rip fathers, husbands, and sons from the embrace of their families. As even proponents grudgingly conceded, the legality of impressment was at best questionable. The Magna Carta, for one, roundly prohibited the arbitrary seizure of subjects without due process. For the eighteenth-century jurist William Blackstone, conscription, which violated the spirit of the British constitution, was "only defensible from public necessity."[36]

Even so, given its impact on seafaring families, impressment did not go unchallenged. Nor was popular opposition confined to ports. Newspapers contained heartrending stories depicting the evils of conscription, as did plays, ballads, and novels, among them Henry Fielding's *Tom Jones* (1749) and *Roderick Ransom* (1748) by Tobias Smollett. In his arresting painting "The Press Gang" (1790), George Morland depicted a young waterman as he is violently seized from a skiff, to the shock of his genteel passengers. Critics of impressment included David Hume and Voltaire as well as George II, who lamented the navy's reliance upon "force and violence." Put on the defensive, Sir Robert Walpole, England's first prime minister, in 1740 tartly condemned "popular affectations of tenderness for liberty." The government brooked no opposition, tirelessly preventing the constitutionality of conscription from being put before a jury, while legal decisions from the bench continued to uphold its legality.[37]

It is impossible to determine with any precision the number of impressed seamen aboard the *Hermione*. Although a series of muster books have survived, save for the last volume, commencing in July 1797, their value, as with those of other ships, is problematic owing to the erratic quality of entries and the number of men who may have volunteered under duress. Of the twenty Americans aboard the *Hermione* in July 1797, a slight majority appear to have received bonuses for "enlisting," with the distinct likelihood that the remainder had been pressed. On the basis of anecdotal evidence, there is no reason to suspect that the percentage of conscripts, at least half of the crew, differed markedly from that of other ships during the French Wars. Thus in 1795, John Slushing, a thirty-eight-year-old Prussian raised on the outskirts of Danzig, was pressed off a British merchantman in Port-au-Prince to serve as a sailmaker's mate; whereas John Brown was removed from the *Fingal*, a Scottish vessel. And the Irishman Lawrence Cronin, on shore leave in Port Royal, joined the *Hermione* only to evade capture.[38]

Whatever the proportion of conscripts, impressment was unpopular among mariners of all ranks and ratings. If resigned to the necessity of coercion, naval officers bemoaned the inevitable damage to shipboard morale, for impressment, above all, stripped merchant seamen of their liberty—the chance to enjoy periodic stints ashore at home and abroad, to embark aboard different vessels, or, if they chose, to jump ship in a for-

"Muster-Table of His Majesty's Ship the Hermione
between the 7th April 1797 and the 7th July following,"
a table containing the number of crew members aboard
the Hermione, *taken from the ship's last surviving muster*
book, dated July 7, 1797. For the ensuing weeks preceding
the mutiny, no book has survived.

eign port. By contrast, naval seamen during wartime enjoyed fewer occasions for shore leave and fewer opportunities to desert. Particularly for tars manning frigates, freedom was hard to come by. Even the frequency of dockyard repairs decreased after the introduction of copper-sheathed hulls during the War of American Independence. On top of everything else, there was no end in sight during wartime, week after week, month after month. Time at sea, in Samuel Johnson's memorable words, resembled "being in a jail with the chance of being drowned."[39]

Naval service strained sentimental ties to king and country. True, patriotic feelings gave way at sea to choruses of "Rule Britannia," and fracases rooted in British xenophobia occasionally erupted. English animosity toward the Irish and French, to name the two most obvious targets within a ship's company, was common enough (even so, as many as fifty-seven French seamen served under Nelson at the Battle of Trafalgar). But a speedy and safe passage home, along with the welfare of one's shipmates, invariably outweighed pangs of nationalistic fervor. According to the impressed seaman John Nicol, "We all wished to be free to return to our homes and follow our own pursuits. We knew there was no other way of obtaining this than by defeating the enemy. 'The hotter war the sooner peace,' was a saying with us."[40]

Alternately, the cosmopolitan cast of crews worked to erode national identities, as did the emergence of a common maritime culture distinguished by its own argot, values, and dress (a short jacket and trousers for easier movement aloft and on deck). Manly qualities included courage and strength, coupled with an intimate knowledge of seamanship honed by years of experience. Prevalent, too, was a working-class spirit of dogged independence, restricted aboard ship to outbursts of "ill language" and the excessive consumption of grog (rum diluted with water). During shore leave—typically the captain's prerogative—unruly tempers gave vent in dockside taverns to violence, sexual escapades, and binges of heavy drinking. "Their manner of living, speaking, acting, dressing, and behaving are very peculiar to themselves," remarked the London magistrate John Fielding, blinded in a naval accident as a youth. "Yet with all their oddities, they are perhaps the bravest and boldest fellows in the universe."[41]

At sea, fiddling, dancing, and swapping yarns filled idle hours— momentary sources of comfort to ease the harsh realities of crowded, sometimes damp quarters, bland food, and low wages (just above the six to seven shillings per week paid farmworkers), not to mention the perils of disease, enemy fire, and ill weather. With most of a ship's company divided into two watches, sleep at night was limited to four hours suspended in a hammock. Day-to-day tasks could be punishing and dangerous. Maintenance of sails and rigging was continuous. Masts and yardarms required periodic adjustment and fresh coats of tar. "Ship-shape" called for scrubbed decks, neat quarters, and well-swabbed guns, usually the responsibility of landsmen with scant time at sea. Training drills were routine.[42]

No wonder the want of liberty, which, in practical terms, meant shore leave, mattered most to crews. The anonymous poem "The Tender's Hold" decried:

> While Landmen wander uncontrol'd,
> And boast the rights of Freemen,
> Oh! view the tender's loathsome hold,
> Where droop your injur'd Seamen:
> Dragg'd by Oppression's savage grasp,
> From ev'ry dear connection;
> 'Midst putrid air, Oh! see them gasp,
> Oh! mark their deep dejection.[43]

On the sixteenth of April 1797, crews mutinied aboard seventeen ships lying just off Portsmouth at Spithead, resulting in the largest uprising in the history of the Royal Navy. Comprising England's Channel Fleet, they defied officers' orders to put to sea in a well-coordinated protest over low wages, poor food, and, among other grievances, insufficient shore leave. Widely thought nonnegotiable in wartime, impressment was a "smoldering grievance." From the start, the mutiny barely lived up to its name, assuming instead the trappings of a nonviolent strike. Prevailing fears of foreign invasion, however, gave the seamen's demands added force. After four weeks of tense negotiations, briefly interrupted by an admiral's precipitous decision to fire on the insurgents, killing several, the mutiny ended peacefully upon promises of better pay and full pardons.[44]

But by then a new, more radical uprising, inspired by the French Revolution, unrest in Ireland, and the turmoil at Spithead, had suddenly arisen among a handful of ships at the Nore, an anchorage near Sheerness dockyard where the Thames emptied into the North Sea.

Within two weeks, most of the North Sea squadron arrived to lend the mutineers support. Many of the official demands echoed the rhetoric at Spithead, but impressment loomed more prominently as a grievance. Not only did it arise in the songs and conversation of seamen, but a petition condemned those who "drag us by force from our families to fight the battles of the country that refuses us protection." Following threats to ally with France and the Admiralty's refusal to meet the mutineers' demands, a number of ships broke ranks and the mutiny crumbled. Executed were twenty-nine leaders, including the impressed seaman Richard Parker, "president" of the self-proclaimed Floating Republic.[45]

2

Hand 'Em Up

AS THE "GREAT MUTINIES" roiled home waters, the British offensive in the Caribbean, nearing its final throes, continued to founder. During the three years after the triumphant arrival of Admiral Jervis's fleet, France struck an alliance with Spain, British troops fell back to enclaves on the western coast of Saint Domingue, and an invasion of Puerto Rico in April 1797 ended ingloriously in a hasty evacuation—a casualty of overconfidence bred by Britain's principal success, the occupation of Trinidad, a target of smaller strategic value. Shortages of ships, money, and men sped British retrenchment, as did flagging morale. The defense of Jamaica from foreign invasion became the navy's uppermost priority. The British war minister wrote that he would "much rather hear that 15,000 men were landed in Ireland or even in Great Britain" than in Jamaica. With news of the Spithead mutiny arriving in July, Sir Hyde Parker and senior officers could at least draw comfort from the absence of discord in the tropics. The commander in chief of the Leeward Islands station, Rear Admiral Henry Harvey, reported in July "not the least appearance" of trouble. Not quite. Later that month, sobering news arrived that the crew of the English schooner *Maria Antoinette* had inexplicably thrown two officers overboard and fled to a small French port on Saint Domingue.[1]

For the crew of the *Hermione*, hopes ran high during the first months of Captain Pigot's command. Instructed in March to patrol the Mona Passage—the channel running between Santo Domingo and the western coast of Puerto Rico—they discovered thirteen prizes taken by French privateers, including a brig from Bremen. After silencing a shore battery and putting twelve ships to the torch (already stripped bare by the French), the *Hermione* towed the brig to Port Royal. "She is laden very deep and is a very valuable vessel," Pigot reported to Admiral Parker. Just weeks later, Pigot led a small squadron at night in cutting out nine ships, loaded with provisions, from a French inlet south of Saint Nicholas Mole.[2]

The next cruise, in May, was less fortunate. While sailing off the Spanish Main in search of prizes, the *Hermione* in the dead of night briefly struck a reef while a second frigate, the *Ceres,* ran aground on a shoal closer to shore—both ships the victims of an unexpectedly strong current in the Gulf of Trieste, west of the Venezuelan port of La Guaira. While some of the *Ceres's* crew broke into the spirit room, seven others—purportedly Americans—fled in a boat to the coastal harbor of Puerto Cabello, where they claimed the protection of the United States consul. Only after torrid days spent making repairs and lightening the vessel's load by removing masts, booms, rigging, provisions, and guns, was she saved. It was no easy feat. In a letter to Parker, the commander of the *Ceres* pointedly commended not his own crew but the "uncommon exertions of the *Hermione's* men, Captain Pigot himself constantly assisting in person."[3]

Pigot was not without ability. During his first months as captain of the *Hermione*, more than once he displayed his skill. As a squadron commander, he had become Parker's favorite choice to cut out prizes from beneath the enemy's nose. Exposed to hostile fire, he took pride in suffering minimal casualties. He also shared credit with subordinates—"whose service," he reported to Parker in April, "was attended with much risk and fatigue, and executed with the greatest chearfulness, spirit, and good judgment." No preening coxcomb, he had become an able tactician of marked physical courage.[4]

Even under the best of circumstances, however, life aboard the *Hermione* was destined to be troubled. Many of the ship's company had served in the Caribbean from two to four years, with few opportunities for liberty (shore leave encouraged runaways, or "run men," as they were listed in muster books). As to the next leave, no one could say for

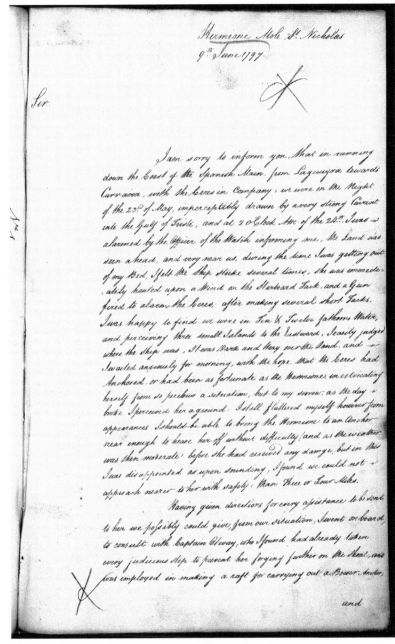

Hermione Mole St. Nicholas
9th June 1797.

Sir.

I am sorry to inform you, that in running
down the Coast of the Spanish Main, from Laguayra towards
Curracoa, with the Ceres in Company, we were on the Night
of the 23rd of May, imperceptibly drawn by a very strong Current
into the Gulf of Triste, and at 2 o'Clock AM, of the 24th, I was
alarmed by the Officer of the Watch informing me, the Land was
seen ahead, and very near us, during the time I was getting out
of my Bed, I felt the Ship strike several times, she was immediately hauled upon a Wind on the Starboard Tack, and a Gun
fired to alarm the Ceres; after making several short Tacks,
I was happy to find we were in Ten & Twelve fathoms Water,
and perceiving three small Islands to the Eastward, I easily judged
where the Ship was, It was Dark and Hazy over the Land, and
I waited anxiously for morning, with the hope that the Ceres had
Anchored, or had been as fortunate as the Hermione, in extricating
herself from so perilous a situation, but to my sorrow, as the day
broke I perceived her aground: I still flattered myself however from
appearances I should be able to bring the Hermione to an Anchor
near enough to heave her off without difficulty (and as the weather
was then moderate) before she had received any damage; but in this
I was disappointed as upon sounding, I found we could not
approach nearer to her with safety, than Three or Four Miles.

Having given directions for every assistance to be sent
to her we possibly could give, from our situation, I went on board,
to consult with Captain Otway, who I found had already taken
every judicious step to prevent her forging further on the Shoal, and
was employed in making a raft for carrying out a Bower Anchor,

and

Letter of Captain Hugh Pigot to Admiral Sir Hyde Parker, Hermione, Mole Saint
Nicholas, *June 9, 1797. Pigot's description of efforts to save the* Ceres *off the Venezuelan
coast: "I waited anxiously for morning, with the hope that the* Ceres *had Anchored,
or had been as fortunate as the* Hermione *in extricating herself from so perilous a
situation, but to my sorrow, as the day broke I perceived her aground."*

certain, much less when the *Hermione* would return to England. Upon the arrival of summer, the days grew hotter, more humid, and riven with pestilence. As hurricane season wore on, prizes were scarce, limited chiefly to a Spanish schooner, the spoils from which the *Hermione*'s company was forced to share with other crews. Pickings were slim.[5]

And this was not all. These hardships might have been more tolerable had the air not been thick with revolutionary rhetoric from abroad. Notwithstanding the enormous impact of American independence, it was the French Revolution and the Reign of Terror, driven by radical aspirations of social equality, that threatened to topple Europe's established order. Already Britain's domination of Ireland stood imperiled by the tide of insurrection. Republican organizations, notably the United Irishmen (Protestant) and the Irish Defenders (Catholic), steadily gained strength, fueled by hopes of French assistance. Anglo-Irish authorities arrested dissidents by the thousands in the mid-1790s, many of whom found themselves consigned to lives at sea aboard ships in the Royal Navy, including those in the Channel Fleet. With Whitehall reeling from the Great Mutinies, the American minister to Britain wrote the U.S. secretary of state, Timothy Pickering, in early June 1797, "The times have been feverish and critical, and men of all, including the most subordinate, conditions have heard so much of the Equality and Rights of Man." As did British tars serving in the West Indies, a major nexus of Atlantic shipping, rubbing shoulders with men of all beliefs and backgrounds, in port and at sea. Captured off the western coast of Saint Domingue by a British brig, the crew of a French privateer serenaded their guards with republican songs all the way to Jérémie.[6]

So it was in the summer of 1797. And yet, for all of the pestilence, the hardship, and the revolutionary fervor, there was nothing inevitable about the ensuing events. Tempting as it is to view the *Hermione*'s fate through the prism of the Great Mutinies, things would have turned out differently had its captain enjoyed the trust of his crew. Whereas Pigot's father had been affable by nature, young Hugh was a quick-tempered, at times impetuous, commander, seasoned by neither age nor experience. Most of all, he lacked a close affinity with the ship's company, including a majority of his officers, a vital bridge to men of the lower deck. According to Lieutenant Frederick Hoffman, when his own crew aboard

Lieutenant Gabriel Bray, Sketch Between Decks, *1775.*
Midshipmen taking a meal

HMS *Hannibal* in the West Indies received news of the Nore mutiny, there was, at first, a "disaffected spirit." "However, by reasoning with the petty officers and the best seamen," he later wrote, "it terminated without open mutiny or bloodshed." The absence, by contrast, of a strong rapport between Pigot and his crew, especially within the cramped confines of a frigate, made it all the more necessary that his orders, from the beginning, be thought judicious for the sake of discipline and morale.[7]

But already the arrival of sailors from the *Success* had fueled disturbing rumors. It was said by veteran "Hermiones," as they were called, that Pigot played favorites in meting out punishment and granting shore leave. However exaggerated, there was merit to the allegations. In April, after arriving in Port Royal, seamen from the *Success* not only garnered overdue prize money, but they alone received a day's liberty onshore. A former quartermaster's mate from the *Success* recalled, "There was a continual murmuring among the *Hermione*'s ship's company concerning his [Pigot's] followers, and the usage they [the Hermiones] had before Captain Pigot came on board."[8]

To make matters worse, Pigot's mood over the course of the summer became increasingly erratic. Toward all crew members, including officers, his behavior was frequently unpredictable. And he was easily

Anonymous, Lieutenant David O'Brien Casey (ca. 1775–1853), *nineteenth century. Shown here in his full-dress uniform as a first lieutenant, Casey continued to serve in the Royal Navy for some five decades after the mutiny.*

provoked. Few had benefited as much from the captain's generosity as Lieutenant David O'Brien Casey, on whose court-martial board, for negligence of duty aboard the frigate *Ambuscade*, Pigot had sat in February. Although demoted to the rank of midshipman, Casey was immediately invited to serve aboard the *Hermione*. There, he later wrote, he was treated "with mark'd attention and kindness." Commended that spring by Pigot to Sir Hyde Parker for his "exertions," including having played an essential role in saving the *Ceres*, Casey was promised another lieutenancy within the year.[9]

All the more surprising, then, was Pigot's behavior on a warm evening in September. While a handful of seamen reefed (that is, shortened) the topsails for the night, Pigot, who had been drinking freely, ranted that the sails were not as "smart as usual," unleashing a torrent of curses at Casey, who had been supervising the men from the maintop. When the midshipman attempted to defend his character, Pigot bellowed, "Silence Sir, or I will instantly tie you up to the gun and flog you." Confined to his berth, Casey was summoned to the captain's cabin, where Pigot and three officers stood waiting. Noting that the others had given Casey "the highest character possible," Pigot allowed that he, as well, had drawn "the greatest satisfaction" from his past conduct. Indeed, he had treated the midshipman "like one of his lieutenants." But unless he knelt on the quarterdeck the following morning to beg Pigot's pardon, Casey would be flogged.[10]

Despite attempts by several officers to persuade the midshipman to avoid the disgrace of a flogging, he declined his friends' entreaties. They "appeared greatly in dread" of Pigot, Casey subsequently noted. And so, under a climbing sun at the usual hour of punishment, eleven o'clock, marines brought him to the quarterdeck before the entire ship's company. The Articles of War (the Royal Navy's regulations) having been read aloud, Pigot issued his demand. Casey denied having harbored any "intention of offering him the slightest insult." He begged Pigot's pardon but remained erect. Repeatedly ordered to kneel, he grimly refused, provoking the captain to confess that he would have despised him for doing so. And there the exchange stopped. True to his word, Pigot ordered Casey stripped of his shirt and bound to the capstan, at which he received twelve lashes from the boatswain, the petty officer tasked with managing the deck. After the last stroke, the midshipman was ordered, at the first opportunity in port, to quit the ship. In the following days, Pigot was often heard to claim that "no circumstance in his life" had "given him more real pain" than Casey's punishment.[11]

By now, the *Hermione* had returned to the Mona Passage in order to support troops on Hispaniola as well as to patrol for prizes. Together with the brig *Diligence* (sixteen guns), they threaded their way through the strait's perilous sandbars and shifting currents. Known for high waves and strong winds, the passage in places was more than three thousand feet deep. Another ship, the *Renommée*, with two masts "shivered to pieces" by lightning, had been forced to limp back to Saint Nicholas Mole, escorted by the *Hermione* on September 11.[12]

Among frigate commanders, Pigot was a breed apart. On Thursday the twentieth, six days after Casey's flogging, a squall in the early evening threatened to engulf both vessels. Almost immediately, a handful of topmen scrambled up the masts to reef the sails from footropes and yards. If not shortened before the wind kicked up, the canvas might be shredded or, worse, the ship could capsize. Annoyed by their slow progress, Pigot shouted to the men on the mizzenmast yard, "I'll flog the last man down!" In their haste, three topmen, in the blink of an eye, plunged fifty feet to their deaths. No bulging sails lay beneath the yard to break their fall. At least two of the seamen lost their grip in leaping to the topmast rigging. Peter Bascomb, a black youth, fell atop the ship's master, Edward Southcott, before hitting the quarterdeck. There was nothing to be done. Despite the respect topmen enjoyed for their courage and skill, Pigot barely paused, barking, "Throw the lubbers overboard," invoking a derogatory epithet for inexperienced seamen. A chill swept the deck. Nor was that the end of it. Still seething as their corpses vanished in the ship's wake, he ordered the boatswain's mates to ascend the masts to "start," with knotted ropes, topmen still aloft. The final act played out the next morning, marked by a dreary rain, when more than a dozen men were flogged for their tardiness. "A very severe punishment of several men, I believe twelve or fourteen, took place in the usual way," Casey later wrote.[13]

The day's savagery was just beginning.

AT DUSK, AS THE *HERMIONE* veered north off the western coast of Puerto Rico, Pigot signaled the *Diligence*, four miles to the lee side, to give chase to a privateer. The brig's sails disappeared in the dying light—gone with the wind—as boatswain's mates aboard the *Hermione* piped "down hammocks," followed, in turn, by "lights out." After 10 p.m., only a few lanterns remained aglow to assist the helmsman and a handful of sentries, the lights barely piercing the thick darkness blanketing the main deck. "The weather extremely dark and gloomy," recalled Captain Robert Mends, commander of the *Diligence*.[14]

It was time to settle scores. In the seconds it might have taken Pigot, bleary-eyed from sleep, to grab his sword, a half-dozen seamen, brandishing cutlasses and tomahawks, burst into his cabin around half-past ten, first knocking a sentry senseless before bashing in the door. Rising from his cot, the captain gripped a dirk as his assailants, barely visible in the dark, charged, roaring curses. In the forefront were the Kent topman David Forrester, scarcely seventeen years old, with light hair and boyish freckles; Thomas Nash, an Irish boatswain's mate with a flowing black mane; and Patrick Foster, also from Ireland and the captain's coxswain. In a frenzy, they descended on Pigot, whom Forrester slashed at least twice. More men arrived. Calling for help, the besieged captain managed to draw blood, stabbing Forrester in the foot and another seaman in the hand. To no avail. His blood-soaked nightshirt in tatters, Pigot lay dying against the barrel of a cannon as the men rushed outside to join a larger party that had cornered Third Lieutenant Henry Foreshaw.[15]

As officer of the watch that evening, Foreshaw had assumed his station on the quarterdeck, lying above Pigot's cabin. On hearing the commotion, he ordered the master's mate, William Turner, a thickset man of medium height, to inspect below. "If you want to know, you can go down yourself," Turner shot back. Turning immediately to Thomas Osborn at the wheel, Foreshaw shouted, "Put the helm up, wear the ship, and steer for the *Diligence*!" "I'll see you damned first," responded Osborn. Knocking the helmsman to the deck, the lieutenant found himself encircled by no fewer than a dozen men soon joined by Pigot's assailants. "Heave the bugger overboard," shouted Thomas Nash. There was little enough mercy. Pleading for his life for the sake of his wife and three children, Foreshaw was grabbed by Forrester, prompting others "to chop at him with tomahawks and bayonets" as he vainly tried to flee, only to disappear over the side of the ship.[16]

The night's business was not done. As a familiar signal of protest, conspirators hurled balls of double-headed shot about the main deck. Access to a cask of rum compounded the chaos, causing one band of mutineers to brawl among themselves. Returning to the cabin, Nash, Forrester, and other ringleaders discovered Pigot still alive. "You bugger, aren't you dead yet," yelled John Farrel, a forecastleman from New York. "No you villain, I'm not," Pigot struggled to answer as he waved the dirk, forcing his attackers to pause. "What, four against one and yet afraid?" goaded William Crawley, an Irish lad with a face deeply pitted by the pox. "Here goes then!" he exclaimed on striking Pigot with a tomahawk. Others hastened to join in the slaughter, burying their bayonets in the captain's gut as he tried to right himself. "You've showed no mercy yourself and therefore deserve none," shouted a Swiss topman, Joseph Montell. Hauled toward the rear of the cabin, his body and clothing awash in blood, Pigot murmured, "Forrester—are you against me too?" With a final stab of his cutlass, the young seaman replied, "Yes, you bugger," before he and others, using bayonets, pushed Pigot's body out the starboard cabin window. A few men later swore to hearing a distant cry. Tapping John Jones, the captain's distraught steward, on the shoulder, Forrester boasted, "I have just launched your bloody master overboard. The bugger—I gave him his death wound."[17]

There was no end. Pandemonium, by then, had broken out below-decks toward the stern of the ship, which contained the gun room, a mess room for officers surrounded by private quarters. Awakened in his cabin, Samuel Reed, the first lieutenant, tried to climb through a skylight to the main deck, only to tumble backward after being slashed from above with a handspike in the face and arm. "Hughey's overboard! The ship is ours!" men shouted aloft. The hunt for the second lieutenant, Archibald Douglas, now commenced, led by his fourteen-year-old servant, James Allen. "Here he is! Here he is!" Allen cried, on finding the lieutenant clad in a bedgown beneath his cot. A marine later testified, "There were twenty tomahawks, axes and boarding pikes jagged into him immediately in the gunroom." Among the assailants was young Allen, who exclaimed, "Let me have a chop at him! He shan't make me jump about in the gunroom anymore!" Captured, too, was a fourteen-year-old midshipman, Thomas Smith, who'd had a hand, the day before, in the flogging of the able seaman John Fletcher. After suffering multiple blows to his head and back from bayonets and tomahawks, the boy collapsed beside Douglas. "Hand the buggers up! Launch the buggers," a crowd at the top of the hatchway ladder chanted. By the light of a single lantern, one by one Douglas and Smith were dragged to the main deck—"as tho' they had been two dogs"—to be stabbed again and again. And chopped. Crawley broke the ash handle of his tomahawk after a crushing blow to Douglas's skull. Both bodies were forced through a gunport, young Smith's by Fletcher. With revenge the currency of choice, grudges were dispatched in short order.[18]

As luck would have it, Lieutenant Foreshaw, in falling overboard, had landed on top of the mizzen chainwales, a narrow ledge on the side of the hull. Only the rigging had saved him. Severely wounded, he slowly made his way back to the main deck through a porthole, appearing in the dark as if a ghost, while blood streamed down his ashen face. "Good God," he pleaded with hands clasped, "what harm have I ever done to any of you?" Despite pledges of mercy from the stunned crew, Thomas Nash descended from the quarterdeck to grab his right wrist. For Nash, the lieutenant's fate was never in doubt. "Foreshaw, you bugger," he exclaimed, "are you not overboard yet? Overboard you must go, and overboard you shall go!" And with that, the lieutenant was thrown off the larboard gangway. Entangled once more in the rigging, he struggled to crawl through a port. There he encountered the American John Farrel, who chopped off his hand just above the wrist before Foreshaw plunged overboard.[19]

And then, as if to catch their breaths, the carnage stopped. In little more than half an hour, facing scant resistance, the mutineers had murdered Captain Pigot, two lieutenants, and a midshipman. There, possibly, the killing might have ended. Such, at least, was the view of Midshipman Casey. Their thirst for vengeance slaked, some of the original mutineers, he later wrote, tried to stanch the bloodletting. With three senior officers slain, there were limits, he hoped, to the men's ferocity. "Striking for liberty," as one described their aim to rid themselves of Pigot's oppression. Casey, who despite his flogging deplored the mutiny, was himself protected from harm by Nash and Farrel. As was Master Southcott. John Elliot and three others guarded his cabin door as he lay injured from Bascomb's fall the day before. Lieutenant Reed, attacked earlier, received a visit in the gun room from an able seaman named Richard Redmond, who in shaking his hand said that "they did not intend to hurt him, who never hurt them." Would that it had been so.[20]

The violence had tapped a deep wellspring of hatred pent up for much of the summer, if not longer, among former crew members of the *Success*. Whatever their reasons for following Pigot to the *Hermione*, at least twelve of the twenty-three *Success* shipmates became active mutineers. Ill feelings between them and the Hermiones had faded in the face of Pigot's brutality. Making matters worse, rum flowed freely once the spirit room was breached (a thousand gallons had been locked away). Only the leaders, determined to keep their wits, remained sober in the event renewed violence flared. "A great part of the crew, many of whom were not concerned in the commencement," remembered Casey, "[were] much worse than the original mutineers." His own life was condemned at least twice during the night.[21]

The lull was brief. Scarcely three hours after Pigot's death, thirty-five-year-old Lawrence Cronin from Belfast leapt atop a table in the gun room crammed with shipmates. Still others, on the quarterdeck, peered below through a large skylight covered by a grating. Formerly an able seaman, the surgeon's mate was a man of some education, and now, his voice rising over the throng, Cronin exhorted his comrades to new feats of bloodshed. With the aid of a lantern, he read from a paper pulled from his pocket, beginning with the proud boast, "I have been a republican since the war." Declaring "they were doing very right, a very good thing," he echoed a growing call for every officer's death, followed by shouts from aloft, "Hand 'em up! Pass the buggers up! Kill them all!"– an imperative to which most of the original leaders now resigned themselves. "[We] might as well be hung for a sheep as a lamb," one reluctantly admitted. More than that, by defying the popular will, they stood to lose control of the uprising, including any chance, by setting the ship's heading, to avoid a hangman's noose, much less the swipe of a shipmate's tomahawk. The tide of violence, showing few signs of ebbing, had yet to run its course, a witch's brew of hatred and vengeance.[22]

It was over quickly. Taken first was the purser, Stephen Pacey, after he had been ordered to sit by the mizzenmast. Stabbed repeatedly, he was cast into the ink-black sea, followed shortly by Hugh Sansom, the surgeon. Previously punished for stealing from Sansom, his fourteen-year-old servant taunted the surgeon mercilessly with choruses of "Hand them up! Hand the buggers up!" Next to be flung over the side, his skull split by an axe, was Lieutenant Reed, notwithstanding Redmond's earlier assurance. Not to be outdone, Redmond, tall and lean with a "swarthy complexion," seized the boatswain, John Martin, who had brought his wife, Fanny, aboard the ship with Pigot's blessing. "By the Holy Ghost," exclaimed Redmond, "the boatswain shall go with the rest!" "My God," Martin declared to his attackers, "what have I done to you? I have been only six months with you!" Dragged to the main deck, he put up a ferocious struggle, protesting that he would not die "like a dog." Bathed in blood, his knees buckling, Martin was hurled into the sea. (Fanny by then had fainted. Her life spared, she was forced for the remainder of the night to share a cabin with Redmond.) Not even a marine lieutenant named McIntosh escaped the mob's wrath. In the final spasms of yellow fever, he was carried aloft in a blanket—"out of his mind"—and thrown over the starboard gangway by a marine dubbed "Happy Tom."[23]

Spithead, the Nore, even la Terreur, it was not.

THE FIRST GLIMMER OF LIGHT stole across the sea. Racing the dawn, the *Hermione* quit the Mona Passage under full sail, just within sight of the Puerto Rican coast.[24] Prospects were far from certain. Unlike the remote reaches of the South Pacific, the Caribbean contained few island hideaways of the sort that sheltered fugitives from the *Bounty*, whose numbers were markedly smaller. Nor did Bligh's crew, in taking up arms, claim any lives, let alone heave ten officers overboard. All the less likely, should the *Hermione*'s hands seek asylum, that pleas for clemency would fall on sympathetic ears. Or that the Royal Navy would give up the hunt.

European states reviled mutinous crews as international pariahs meriting swift retribution. Like the crime of piracy, the specter of armed rebellion, whatever the ship's colors, imperiled all seafaring nations. By absconding aboard the *Hermione*, its crew had committed both piracy and mutiny. "Every European power," a British newspaper observed, "[is] equally interested" in punishing "traitors and assassins" lest "they mean to expose themselves to the same atrocities."[25] But these were not ordinary times, nor in the current conflict were Europe's warring states wont to honor enemy requests for extradition. Then, too, with no other witnesses to the uprising, word of the carnage, for the time being, remained under wraps.

Several proposed destinations had stirred debate during the night. From the mutineers' perspective, forced to decide on the run, the Caribbean colonies of France and Spain afforded plausible sanctuaries, as did the United States, which continued to pursue a course of neutrality between combatants. Despite the proximity of Saint Domingue and Puerto Rico, British warships periodically patrolled both coasts, as they did other shorelines. Otherwise, Spanish Cuba, with little chance of falling into British hands, must have seemed a natural haven. To the south, however, with the exception of the neutral Dutch island of Curaçao, lay a vast expanse of open water—and beyond Curaçao, the Spanish Main at a distance of five hundred miles from Puerto Rico, less than a week's sail with fair winds. Not only was the coast of Venezuela familiar to the *Hermione*'s crew, but France's ally, Spain, they no doubt hoped, would be reluctant to surrender either them or their ship to Britain. As for betraying king and country, high treason, for mutineers and pirates, was the least of their worries. So they resolved, in the early morning darkness, to make a dash for La Guaira, colonial Venezuela's largest port, a fortified city founded in 1577 and the gateway of its capital, Caracas, to the Caribbean—the safest course if not the shortest, with little except for wind and waves to hamper their flight. (Had a British warship

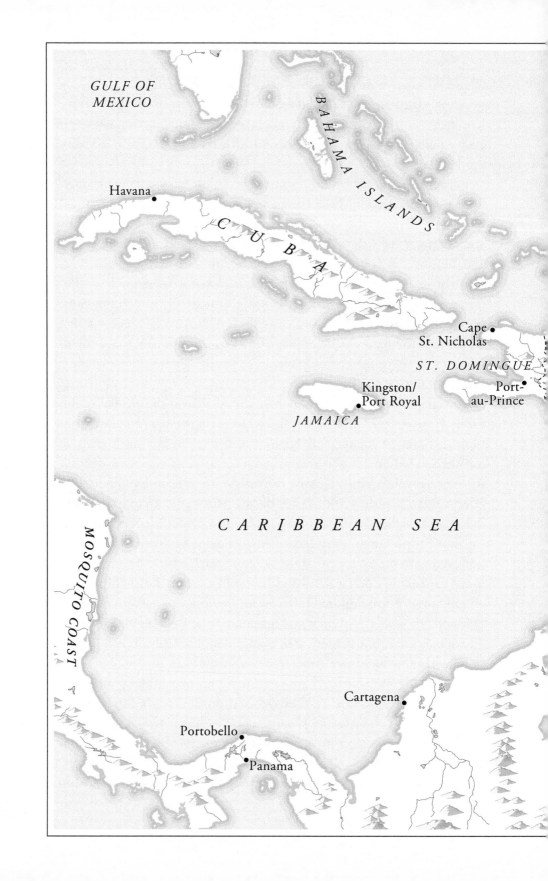

The Caribbean in the Late 18th Century

0   MILES   400

0   KILOMETERS   400

N
W   E
S

ATLANTIC OCEAN

HISPANIOLA

SANTO DOMINGO

• Santo Domingo

MONA PASSAGE

PUERTO RICO

Virgin Islands

St. Croix

St. Eustatius

St. Kitts

Nevis

Montserrat

Anguilla

St. Martin

St. Bartholomew

Barbuda

Antigua

Guadeloupe

Marie Galante

Dominica

Martinique

St. Lucia

St. Vincent

The Grenadines

Barbados

Grenada

Aruba

Curaçao

Tobago

TRINIDAD

Puerto Cabello •

La Guaira •

• Caracas

LAKE MARACAIBO

SPANISH   *MAIN*

appeared, leaving no path of escape, would the crew have surrendered? It seems likely that they would have shot a volley of cannon fire across her bow. Whether they would have shed the blood of fellow tars, there is no knowing.)[26]

As the morning hours wore on, most of the crew were afoot, gathering by noon around the mainmast. Rum and wine flowed freely. Sleep had done nothing to tamp the rage of scattered firebrands wishing to clear the decks, quite literally, of officers, including Master Edward Southcott, a senior warrant officer. But "the principal ringleaders," Southcott later described, intervened by asking the crowd "if they saw any occasion to put me to death in cold blood after they had got the ship so long." Then the leaders called for a show of hands from those who favored sparing Southcott's life. After the briefest of moments, not only did "a great part of them" raise their hands, but, to the shipmaster's astonishment, they let loose with three cheers. Unknown to Southcott, the night before, his young servant had gone "through the ship crying and begging of the crew most piteously that his life might be spared." Apart from his value as a navigator (they could ill afford to plot the wrong course), much of the crew's fury had begun to ebb. Also reprieved were Midshipman Casey and two additional warrant officers, the gunner Richard Searle and Richard Price, the ship's carpenter. To their advantage, Searle and Price had only recently been promoted; whereas Casey, himself a victim of Pigot's cruelty, remained under the protection of his countryman Thomas Nash. The Irish seaman commanded widespread respect among the crew by reason of his role in the deaths of Pigot and Foreshaw. "Nash above the rest," a shipmate recalled, "was most forward for bloodshed," with Casey the inadvertent beneficiary. Despite trying valiantly, however, Casey had been unable, at no small risk to his own life, to prevent the deaths of the surgeon and the purser.[27]

Once the early morning violence had ceased, Nash had hastily turned to more pressing priorities, calling members to their stations and ordering that the ship be put about. Besides designating master's mate William Turner the ship's captain, he urged Casey to become first lieutenant, which the midshipman firmly refused. The bulk of high-ranking posts fell to ringleaders, among them John Luxton, a gunner named captain of the hold; Robert McCready, captain of the maintop; and Richard

Redmond, captain of the forecastle. "The same as the real officers in every station," Southcott later noted. All appeared to adapt easily to their new ranks. Of Thomas Leech, formerly an able seaman, a marine corporal recollected, "I saw him act as an officer." The most telling sign? "The people obeyed him."[28]

If anything, the morning's display of mercy aroused fears in case any of the four prisoners ever be called to testify against members of the crew. In the afternoon, Cronin, the Belfast republican, administered an oath on deck to bind every person on board, officers included. Whether willing or not, all were required to swear "not to know one another in any part of the globe, man or boy, if they should meet, nor call each other by their former names." "This is my oath and obligation," they swore in unison, "so help me God." As best one can determine, probably fewer than a third of the crew, some 50 to 60 men, had actively partici- pated in the mutiny, with at most some 25 of those having hatched the conspiracy. On the other hand, more than 150 men, an overwhelming majority of the ship's company, ultimately supported the uprising, if only tacitly. According to Southcott, hands were "continually drunk, and all appeared unanimous." For the duration of the voyage, members of the crew followed orders, if not always briskly; and they moved freely about the ship. No longer under Pigot's thumb, the men acquired a fresh taste for liberty that would not soon leave them. Besides the four remain- ing officers, only six shipmates refused to support the mutiny, includ- ing the elderly cook, William Moncrieff, the *Hermione*'s longest-serving crew man. Unlike the others, who were confined to quarters, Casey and Southcott received permission to walk the main deck, albeit under strict orders not to converse privately.[29]

Left was the task of dividing the small trove of valuables belonging to Pigot and his subordinates. The crew shared much of the clothing. David Forrester was quick to don a shirt and a pair of stockings from Pigot's chest, and young James Allen claimed boots and a shirt from his late master, Lieutenant Douglas. Having taken over the captain's cabin, twenty leaders kept the bulk of the booty for themselves, including a total of $448 ($80 of which was Pigot's), five watches, a gold ring, and numerous items of silver, among them a teapot, a pair of mugs, shoe and knee buckles, fifty spoons, and two "silver-mounted" pistols, all of which was distributed on the quarterdeck. Afterward, Forrester was heard to grouse "that he had not received what he deserved," as "he was a principal in the murders."[30]

With the aid of charts and logbooks gathered from Southcott's cabin, the *Hermione* continued its southern course. Hours fell way to music, dancing, and drinking rum fetched from the hold. Steward Jones was ordered to play his flute. Most of the men were in fine fettle—"Making merry," Southcott subsequently remarked. A marine, John Pearce, hurled his uniform, complete with belts and gaiters, into the sea. Boasts added to the festive mood. William Crawley, for one, bragged of having killed Midshipman Smith, whereas Henry Poulson, a forecastleman, claimed to have had a hand in pushing Pigot out his cabin window.[31]

Small wonder that the few surviving officers continued to fear for their lives. According to Casey, "The ship was in the greatest possible confusion during the passage, many of the crew continually in a state of drunkenness and frequently fighting." "But for the steady good conduct of some of the principal mutineers," he wrote, "we must have suffered." "A general scene of riot, drinking, and confusion," a crew member remembered. De facto authority had quickly devolved upon a small clique of a dozen or so men, Thomas Nash first among them. Others included Turner, Redmond, Forrester, Crawley, Leech, and John Elliot, a forecastleman from Kent (just five feet six but "very stout"). Of Forrester, Southcott recalled, "He always looked on me with contempt and appeared to be one who wanted to murder me."[32]

On Sunday, the twenty-seventh of September, shortly past dawn, the rugged high ground of northern Venezuela appeared at last. Five days after leaving the waters of Puerto Rico, dead ahead lay the port of La Guaira, its streets just beginning to stir for the feast day of Saint Damianus. With a population in excess of five thousand, the city resided along a narrow coastal plain, the massive Cordillera de la Costa looming in the background. Nineteen miles to the south through a well-trodden pass stood the city of Caracas, three thousand feet above sea level and capital of the captaincy general of Venezuela. La Guaira's highest-ranking official was the governor, Don José Vásquez y Tellez, in whose hands the immediate fate of the *Hermione* and her crew lay. With great care Cronin again put pen to paper to plead their case. By his own admission, the crew had mutinied against their officers owing to the brutality of the British captain. This was the crux of their defense. Ill fed, harshly disciplined, and not paid for four years, they had no choice, claimed Cronin, but to take up arms. What's more, rather than exact retribution, they had placed all officers, along with their personal possessions, in a shallop amply supplied with provisions thirty miles off the Puerto Rican coast.[33]

Sent that afternoon as "delegates" in a jolly boat under a white flag to deliver the petition were Turner, Elliot, and Leech, all of whom first requested the steward Jones to shave their faces and tie their hair. Joining them was a fourth crew man, Antonio Francisco, a native of Spain, to act as interpreter. The meeting with Don Vasquez went well. The governor expressed not a whiff of skepticism about the story that Cronin had stitched together, nor did the captain-general of Caracas, Don Pedro Carbonell, upon consenting to asylum soon afterward. Royal approval appeared to be a formality. By the terms of the negotiations, crew members were placed under the protection of the Spanish government as subjects of the king; and, at the conclusion of the war, they would not be given up to Great Britain. All received liberty to travel about La Guaira, and Vasquez awarded twenty-five dollars to each man as "a present to subsist on" ("blood money," the British would call it). Following word

Anonymous, La Guaira on the Spanish Main, *n.d.*

of royal approval, they would be free to leave the province. Meanwhile, Spanish tobacco and fresh beef arrived on board the frigate, and Turner even sold a cargo of soap that Pigot, weeks earlier, had confiscated from a prize.[34]

What, then, of the *Hermione*? At a time when the Bourbon kingdom of Charles IV stood in urgent need of warships, she became Spanish property, along with all documents, correspondence, and signal codes belonging to the Royal Navy. It was a tariff that the crew gladly paid. Within days, the harbormaster of La Guaira took command, piloting the ship to an anchorage beneath the heavy guns of a nearby fort. As the crew saluted, sailors hoisted the red and yellow colors of Spain. The ship was renamed the *Santa Cecilia*, after an early Roman martyr whose uncorrupted remains, discovered in Sicily in 1599, were thought a special sign of holiness.[35]

3

Dragnet

ON THE TWENTIETH OF OCTOBER, twenty-nine days after the *Hermione*'s mysterious disappearance from the Mona Passage, its consort, the brig *Diligence,* the last vessel to glimpse the frigate, sighted a Spanish schooner in the pale morning light. Only after a three-hour chase and several shots across her bow did the *San Antonio* heave to, slightly windward of Alto Velo, a small, mountainous island south of Hispaniola. "The chase hauled down her colors," Master Charles White entered in the brig's log. Bound for the port of Santo Domingo with a cargo of cheese, soap, and cocoa for Spanish troops, the *San Antonio* was eight days out of La Guaira.[1]

Brought aboard the brig, the Spanish captain eagerly related details of the *Hermione*'s surprising arrival off the Venezuelan coast. If anything, his account of the mutiny was exaggerated beyond its true proportions. As many as forty lives were lost, he reported to Captain Robert Mends of the *Diligence,* including Captain Pigot, most officers, nearly all the marine guards, and six women. Certainly Spanish authorities in La Guaira no longer suffered any illusions about the uprising's resolution. The ship had been towed, unrigged, to nearby Puerto Cabello for repairs, Mends was told, and her guns as well as her stores brought ashore lest British raiders cut her out. Of the mutineers, they were "held in the utmost detestation, . . . the scorn and contempt of everyone," including, evidently, the *San Antonio*'s captain. All this and more Mends put in a dispatch to Sir Hyde Parker.[2]

Nearly as chilling was the Spaniard's advice to Mends to "take care." For seamen aboard the *Diligence,* he claimed, had conspired with ring-leaders on the *Hermione* to mutiny the same evening. Stunned by the disclosure, Mends immediately summoned his "people" to the main deck, whom he had always thought "truely gallant" and "good tem-pered." Not only was the crew visibly shocked by the commander's revelations, but they became indignant over allegations of collusion, a charge otherwise unsubstantiated. The paternalistic Mends, after all, was no Pigot. Thirty years of age, his right arm lost at the Battle of York-town, he had long enjoyed the respect of his men. In his report, he took pains to assure Parker that had his small brig been nearby at the time of the mutiny, they "would have retaken the *Hermione* or perished along-side of her." They almost got their chance, not once but twice. Just past midnight on the twenty-second, after the initial tumult, Master White of the *Diligence* glimpsed a distant sail, bearing east-southeast, that he took to be the *Hermione.* No signal of distress, however, appeared in the darkness. "Lost sight of the sail," White jotted in his log around 1 a.m. Hours later, in the half light of dawn, he again sighted the puz-zling silhouette of a ship far to the southeast. Of greater sailing speed—a frigate, perhaps—by noon she had long outrun the *Diligence,* which at last gave up the ghost.[3]

It remained, of course, to alert Admiral Parker. The *Diligence* was far from home. Against stiff headwinds, the ship logged more than three hundred miles in ten days to reach Saint Nicholas Mole, where Parker and HMS *Queen* had remained since mid-April. Arriving at 2 a.m. on October 31, Mends roused the admiral from bed to hand deliver his report. Already Parker had been in an uneasy state of mind. A week ear-lier, a veteran of the Nore uprising had been court-martialed at the Mole and executed for a threatening outburst. Two other suspects, owing to insufficient evidence, were on Parker's orders put ashore by a launch and stranded "near some Spanish settlement." As might be imagined, he was horrified by Mends's dire news, not least due to the loss of young Pigot. Apart from avenging the officers' deaths, swift and severe retribution, in Parker's opinion, would be essential to check the contagion.[4]

What could be done? Confident of London's blessing, he quickly opted, against the odds, to bargain with Spanish officials while they

Remarks, &c.

Moderate Sea breezes; Preparing my Dispatches for the Admiralty & other Naval Boards.

Little Air & very sultry weather.

Do. weather; Gave Lt. Kent, Agent for Transports, Orders for his Guidance during my Absence. — Issued several Orders for Surveys, &c.

Light winds with rain; A.M. Made the Signal & unmoor'd.

Do. weather; At 2 A.M. Arrived the Diligence, with an Account of the Hermione having been carried by her Crew into La Guira, after killing their Captain, Officers, Women & Boys, upwards of 40 in number. — Wrote to the Admiralty thereon. Ordered Captn. Mends to proceed with my Dispatches for Captain Ricketts, between Altavilla & Cape Roxo; the S.W. end of Porto Rico, and follow his Orders for his further Proceedings. — Wrote to the Governor of La Guira, demanding the Crew of the Hermione; — Enclosed it to Captn. Ricketts, with Orders to proceed thither and use his utmost endeavours to procure the Company of that Ship, and in case of success, to distri- bute them on board his Ships & join me off Monte Christe, or, in case of failure, to dispatch the Diligence to me with an Account of his Proceedings. — Ordered Captn. Cochet, to proceed, after completing his Provisions, to Port au Prince. Ordered Captn. Jenkins of the Ambuscade to take the Princess Royal Pacquet under his Convoy, and after seeing her 15 leagues to the Northward of the Great Caicos, to join me between Monte Christe & the Grange. — Ordered Captn. Bowen of the Carnatic to relieve the Brunswick as soon as possible, and acquaint the Rear Admiral I am on my passage up. — Wrote several Letters to the Admiralty and other Naval Boards, and left them with the Storekeeper to be sent by the Princess Royal Pacquet.

October 31, 1797, Journal of Sir Hyde Parker, 1797–98. Details of Captain Mends's early morning arrival at Saint Nicholas Mole with news of the mutiny.

still held the crew. With precious time already lost, he composed a letter to the governor of La Guaira that was by turns pointed and polite. Although recovery of the *Hermione* was to ask the impossible, he bluntly demanded the crew's surrender for having committed the crimes of murder and piracy against their officers. It fell to the intrepid Mends to deliver the letter promptly to Captain William Ricketts, commander of the *Magicienne,* a thirty-two-gun French prize, and to accompany him in the *Diligence* to La Guaira. At the time, Ricketts, a nephew of Admiral John Jervis, Earl of St. Vincent (formerly Sir John Jervis), was patrolling the Mona Passage. Parker's instructions were terse: Ricketts was to "use his best endeavours to procure the company."[5]

A more painful dispatch, sent to Evan Nepean, secretary of the Board of Admiralty, delivered news of the mutiny. Included was a copy of Mends's report. Not long afterward, Parker wrote with further reflections. "It being of such importance," he stressed, "to the salvation of the naval forces of Great Britain that the cruel perpetrators of the piracy should be brought to condign punishment," that the government should "make it a particular object with the Court of Spain to have the villains delivered up." Still, he was not hopeful. Harboring an innate skepticism of Spanish cooperation, Parker fretted that the crew had by then started to scatter, going their separate ways. "It is impossible," he asserted, "for the perpetrators of that horrid act to be at rest, and therefore most probably will ship themselves on board neutral vessels to America and these islands." An erroneous report in American newspapers had already alleged that men were "dispersing in every direction as fast as they could."[6]

It was a measure of Parker's anxiety that he dispatched to each British governor in the Caribbean, from the Windward Islands to the Bahamas, not only a narrative of the mutiny but also a letter suggesting the offer of rewards, even pardons, for seamen willing to turn King's evidence against the principal "perpetrators." No quarter should be given, at least not to the original conspirators. Also contacted was Britain's minister to the United States, Robert Liston, with whom Parker had crossed swords over Pigot's role in the Jessup affair. In his darker moments, the admiral, on some level, must have rued the painful irony of subsequent events, including his abrupt decision to award Pigot, his aggressive young officer, command of the *Hermione.*[7]

As Parker anxiously awaited a reply from La Guaira, his first letter reached London in early December. Beginning that month, newspapers steadily circulated reports of the carnage. It would be difficult to exaggerate the country's outrage. Words such as "atrocious," "horrid," and "inhuman" came quickly to English tongues. Papers fanned the uproar with fresh dispatches from the Caribbean that were widely reprinted throughout Britain.[8] Rumors ran wild. Besides La Guaira, reports placed the *Hermione* at either Havana or Guadeloupe. Others declared that the ship had been dismantled, not in La Guaira, but in Puerto Cabello. Or, more alarmingly, the Spaniards had put her, newly manned and refitted, back out to sea. The crew, according to one story, was mostly French or, described another, a "mixture of several nations." There was also word that the original company was en route to Spain to be surrendered to British authorities. Enthused a London paper, "The Spaniards have given an example of great wisdom and justice as well as magnanimity towards our nation."[9]

Most newspapers put the death toll at forty victims, including six women, as Mends had originally reported. The *Hereford Journal* of December 27 cited the loss of nine women, whereas that same month the *London Packet* claimed an excess of forty fatalities. Another paper inexplicably reported the loss of twenty-seven officers. Nor was this all. The coxswain had allegedly cut off Pigot's head as he slept. By spring, it was thought that others, too, had been beheaded. "The fate of the officers of the *Hermione*," declared the *True Briton*, "is melancholy in the extreme—We are certain there is not a British tar but must feel the utmost horror and indignation." Mindful of recent unrest at Spithead and the Nore, the *London Chronicle* drew a cautionary lesson from the tragedy. "This event, we trust, will prove to British sailors the danger of listening to the advice of men, who in the end involve them in the horrid crime of murder."[10]

Calls for retribution resounded across the nation, first and foremost in Whitehall, where the Admiralty announced plans to destroy the Bristol dock at which the *Hermione* had been built. In its place, a monument would forever proclaim abhorrence of her murderous crew. Despite problems at home and abroad ranging from war and a soaring national debt to a brewing rebellion in Ireland, pursuit of the crew became a pressing priority for the government of Pitt the Younger, anxious to deter further unrest. And, Parker's advice notwithstanding, not just the ringleaders, who naturally excited the greatest opprobrium. Under military law, any seaman who failed to oppose the uprising was complicit. Thus the maxim embraced by naval commanders, "The man who stands neuter is equally guilty with him who lifts his arms against the captain."[11]

For the crime of mutiny struck at the very foundation of military authority, not to mention Britain's hierarchical social order. Rooted in the Latin *motus* (movement, disturbance), "mutiny" in recent centuries had come to signify collective resistance as European states struggled to impose discipline on their expanding armies. By the late 1600s, naval forces, in turn, had adopted articles of war to punish organized disturbances. Whether at sea or on land, military leaders feared, in the absence of obedience, the collapse of all discipline, the very rule of law in confusion and chaos, as portended by recent events at home and abroad. Indeed, for the moral reformer Josiah Woodward, crews were to "avoid all murmurings and mutinies, not only because the well-being of society depends thereupon, but because it is the command of your GOD." And never more so than aboard ships at sea to ensure the success of naval operations. "British seamen," emphasized the "Seaman's Friend" in 1797, "owe their fame, success, and national character to vigor, union, discipline, and subordination." "Without them," the author declared, "the Navy is like a ship in a storm, without masts or rudder." Never was mutiny justified, and only in rare circumstances might a defendant be pardoned. No matter how imperious their behavior, superiors required obedience. According to Article 19 of the Royal Navy's Articles of War drafted in 1749, "If any person in or belonging to the Fleet shall make or endeavour to make any mutinous assembly upon any pretence whatsoever, every person offending herein, and being convicted thereof by the sentence of the Court Martial shall suffer death." Even seditious speech earned a death sentence unless the court recommended otherwise.[12]

Naval uprisings customarily resulted in high conviction rates and swift hangings, typically from the yardarm of a warship, though senior officers, in deference to their rank, were to be shot. Corporal punishment, in the case of mitigating circumstances, included the agony of being flogged around the fleet in a launch. Shuttled from one vessel to another as a drummer played the "Rogue's March," the victim typically received a severe lashing before each ship's company. If he survived the horrific ordeal—his back "lacerated" to "a bleeding pulp"—the seaman, according to a contemporary account, forever remained "a ruined man—broken in spirit." Although intended to discourage would-be insurgents, flogging was not always successful. Shortly before her final cruise, the *Hermione*'s crew, anchored at Saint Nicholas Mole, happened to witness two men being flogged around the fleet for mutinous speech voiced en route from Britain. Pigot, in August, had served at their court-martial, which ended in a sentence for each seaman of three hundred lashes.[13]

The mutiny on the *Hermione* was beyond words. Unlike events at Spithead or even the Nore, it was a full-blown insurrection rather than a strike or a protest. It had erupted not in port or in home waters but at sea, with greater risk to the ship and its crew, and not in peacetime but in the midst of a war, resulting in the surrender of the vessel to one enemy, Spain, at the same time as another, France, threatened a cross-channel invasion. The crew had violated every unwritten rule governing naval disobedience. Worst was the bloodshed. "An unprecedented barbarity," exclaimed the *Hampshire Chronicle*—"the most daring and sanguinary mutiny that the annals of the British navy can record." Especially for Britain's upper class, the gruesome deaths of Pigot and other young officers struck close to home. As Lady Hester Stanhope observed, "All the lords and the ladies began to tremble for their sons and nephews." As did numerous officers for their lives. Invited to command a ship with an unfamiliar crew, Cuthbert Collingwood demurred the honor, "for I know and am known here, which, in these ticklish times, I hold to be of much consequence."[14]

Not for weeks did word arrive from La Guaira, reaching Vice Admiral Parker in Jamaica. During his short stay on the Venezuelan coast, Ricketts had performed his duties as courier ably. Delivered by Captain Mends, the well-manicured reply came from Captain General Carbonell himself. It contained no great surprise. Dated the seventh of December, the letter related the mutineers' original account. Insofar as instructions had not yet arrived from the king, any decision, Carbonell related, would be premature, though the admiral would be kept informed with all due dispatch. "Everything that comes within my power," pledged Don Carbonell, "your excellency may command." Unknown to Parker, the captain general also rebuffed, about the same time, an envoy from Rear Admiral Henry Harvey, commander of the Leeward Islands station on the eastern rim of the Caribbean. The one glimmer of encouraging news, from Britain's perspective, lay in Carbonell's assurance to Parker that the crew yet remained in the province of Caracas. In early December, that at least was mostly true.[15]

Parker, however, would have none of it. So much dead paper, in his view—a "false policy," he decried to the Admiralty in February 1798, "which has actuated the Government of that country in the protection of these atrocious villains." Even before news arrived from La Guaira, the commander of British troops in Saint Domingue, Major General John Whyte, as well as the governor and assembly of Jamaica, had each pledged rewards of one thousand dollars for producing any of the ringleaders. Whyte's proclamation held out the prospect of pardons, "principles [sic] excepted," as Parker had originally proposed. A bitter, if necessary, pill. Copies blanketed the British islands, posted in Jamaica alone in fifteen cities and towns. Translations were distributed there and elsewhere in Spanish and in French. By raising the specter of further delay, Don Carbonell's anemic response only intensified Sir Hyde's alarm. Many of the leaders, he feared, had begun to abscond from La Guaira—"dispersing themselves to different parts," he wrote in February. The hunt was on.[16]

PARKER WAS RIGHT TO WORRY. On Governor Vasquez's orders, most of the crew had come ashore within days of their flight to La Guaira. Several men entered a local hospital due to injuries or illness, and Fanny Martin, widow of the boatswain, received permission to board a ship to New York. The four surviving officers, plus Moncrieff the cook and the steward Jones, insisted on being treated as prisoners of war until released to Britain. Four royal marines, untainted by the mutiny, subsequently joined them, including the sentinel attacked outside Pigot's cabin. Less credible were denials of culpability by Richard Redmond, who asked the ship's carpenter "what the Master [Southcott] and Midshipman [Casey] had to say against him." No more fortunate was James Parrott, having oft declared to Southcott after the bloodletting "what big rogues" the ten slain officers had been. For Redmond and Parrott, as in fact for the bulk of the crew, there was no turning back.[17]

A majority took up temporary quarters in barracks, while twenty-five shipmates, including the ringleaders Nash, Turner, and Farrel, volunteered to help take the *Santa Cecilia* to Puerto Cabello. By one account, Nash, following his arrival, resided with a few others "in great affluence," having sold "many valuable articles" pillaged from the ship. In the meantime, Spanish soldiers marched the remainder of the crew from La Guaira to Caracas, where they each received lodging and two royals a day. Venezuelan officials, mindful of the navy's need for mariners, repeatedly encouraged them to enter the Spanish service. Their entreaties netted but one recruit, the Irish master-at-arms Alexander McDougal, who enlisted as a musician. Only after three weeks did the rest obtain permission from the captain general to find other employment, so long as they remained in the province pending instructions from Spain.[18]

Work was hard to come by, compounded in most cases by a want of skills and ignorance of Spanish. Crew members found themselves in a tropical land that was heavily agrarian, known for producing tobacco, indigo, sugar, and cacao, in addition to raising cattle in the south. The hot-tempered Lawrence Cronin resumed his trade as a surgeon in La Guaira, and a few others, there and in Puerto Cabello, enlisted in the Spanish army. A marine corporal "sett up as a carpenter." Two men became cooks. In Caracas, the purser's steward, William Anderson, found employment as a painter, and Thomas Riley took up shoemaking. But for most, opportunities were limited to hard labor, either carrying rocks uphill to complete the construction of a fortress overlooking the port or pounding rock salt three miles to the east in the village of Macuto. Not only was the work unforgiving, but wages were paid in food, not cash, with no provision for shelter. More profitable was the opportunity to refit the *Santa Cecilia* at Puerto Cabello. Although laborers stood to receive up to twelve dollars a month, it was no small irony that they had to be "pressed" by soldiers in La Guaira. Brought to Puerto Cabello, some refused to board the ship. Sailors were a superstitious lot, and the frigate was not wanting for ghosts. But more compelling, in all likelihood, were the greater opportunities in La Guaira for enlisting aboard an outbound vessel. John Barton's stay in Puerto Cabello was brief. Barely two hours after arriving, the fifteen-year-old boy absconded to Macuto to resume his job as a "salter," hoping in due course to take passage abroad.[19]

There was no holding them. It was far easier for Spanish officials to impose travel restrictions than to enforce them. Although an untold quantity of men elected to remain in Venezuela to elude apprehension, and several others were lost to disease, by February mounting numbers were looking to abandon the coast. It was no secret that the prime period for finding passage extended from spring to early summer when merchant convoys appeared in advance of hurricane season. Thus began, slowly but inevitably, the Atlantic diaspora of the Hermione's crew. To say that they disbanded would be to impute lingering feelings of solidarity that few shipmates shared. Once free of Pigot, there was little left to bind them, least of all an oath requiring anonymity should their paths one day cross. "Every man for himself" was their new cri de coeur.[20]

For runaways, traveling separately or in isolated parties, the Atlantic offered no shortage of havens. Bounded by four continents, home to diverse cultures, nations, and empires, its breadth was enormous, all the more so in the absence of modern transportation and instant communications. It was an age of impostors and charlatans, when not just names but wholly new identities could be fabricated overnight. For sailors the task was easy enough in the absence of passports, whereas vital records (certificates of birth and marriage) were difficult to check under the best of circumstances, much less at sea. Nor, naturally, were there dental or fingerprint records to examine, or DNA samples. No photographs to consult, nor did mariners, many of them unlettered, leave behind specimens of handwriting. And unlike seamen in the South Pacific from the Bounty, the crew of the Hermione could expect to blend more easily into the multiracial populations ringing the North Atlantic. Then, too, due to the manning needs of merchant ships and privateers, mariners could work their passage from one port to another, usually with no questions asked. So ravaged were crews by disease that ships in Caribbean ports almost always had empty berths.[21]

From today's perspective, it is hard to imagine how any members of the crew, in the end, were caught. And yet, however immense its expanse, the breadth of the Atlantic by the late eighteenth century had effectively shrunk, growing more intimate, more interconnected, and less mysterious. As crossroads of international trade, seaports attracted rumors and information along with people and commodities, all of which circulated more quickly than in years past. For fugitives, the ocean was as much a curse as a blessing, heightening the risk of capture while speeding their flight. Never were they more vulnerable than at sea. This would not have been a problem had it not been for another. The Royal Navy proved unflagging in its pursuit, determined to scour the Atlantic before crew members who quit Venezuela could run to ground on foreign coasts. Boarding parties were relentless. Traditional ploys used by deserters to elude capture—such as proffering bribes or hiding in cargo holds—were futile. Naval stations from Halifax to the Leeward Islands were alerted to the likelihood of flight from La Guaira, as were warships patrolling familiar sea-lanes. In the Caribbean, enemy ports received special scrutiny from frigates offshore. Additional bounties were pledged by the colonial assemblies of Saint Vincent and Grenada. Meanwhile, the Admiralty continued to hope, in vain, for the extradition of any mutineers still in Venezuela.[22]

The first sailor caught was John Slushing, alias "John Henson," a forty-two-year-old Prussian. A reputed leader, Slushing had absconded from La Guaira as early as November, bound for Spain on the schooner *Casualidad* (the Chance). On the seventeenth of January, a British boarding party from the *Aurora,* a frigate belonging to the Lisbon fleet of Lord St. Vincent, captured him at sea, not far from Cádiz. Brought on board, Slushing wrote a four-page confession detailing the murders. In what was otherwise a straightforward, candid account, he neither admitted nor denied a hand in the bloodshed. In a matter of weeks the Admiralty ordered Slushing's return for what would be the first in a series of courts-martial and executions at the Portsmouth Naval Yard.[23]

AS EVENTS UNFOLDED ABROAD, vice Admiral Parker turned to spending long hours at sea, cruising aboard the *Queen,* accompanied by two ships of the line, the *Carnatic* and the *Valiant.* At the sight of an unfamiliar sail in the early afternoon of March 1, he signaled the *Valiant,* commanded by Captain John Crawley, to give chase. After five hours, the sixteen-gun French corsair *La Magicienne* (not to be confused with the frigate commanded by William Ricketts) lowered her flag in submission. The ship's company of eighty-eight men contained no fewer than five former crew members of the *Hermione,* one of whom, John Mason, a carpenter's mate from Belfast, stepped forward to identify himself and four shipmates, three of whom were traveling under aliases: Pierre D'Orlaine, a French native; the Kent forecastleman John Elliot; Antonio Marco of Genoa; and the Swiss foretopman Joseph Montell, prone to boasting of having given Pigot a final shove.[24]

From La Guaira, Mason had caught a Spanish schooner to Curaçao. Lying 150 miles northwest of the Venezuelan port, the Dutch island, with a population in excess of twenty thousand, was a profitable plantation colony and a commercial hub overflowing with seamen of all nationalities, hues, and political beliefs. Smuggling between the island and Venezuela was widespread. Much of Curaçao lay in a state of ferment. Not only were its political loyalties divided owing to events in Europe, but as recently as 1795 a slave revolt had erupted, followed in 1796 by a coup d'état. Amid the uncertainty and intrigue, seamen looking to sign on to a ship provoked negligible concern, and numerous Hermiones flocked there from the mainland. Joined by Elliot, whom Mason had first met aboard the *Success,* the pair enlisted in the harbor of Willemstad on *La Magicienne,* which upon reaching the Spanish port of Santo Domingo took on Montell, Marco, and D'Orlaine, all of whom had recently arrived on another privateer. Each man, for his labor on the French corsair, received an advance of twenty-four dollars coupled with a share in future profits.[25]

At last, Parker's first catch. It had been a long wait. All five men were transported aboard the *Valiant* to Saint Nicholas Mole, where the *Queen* lay at anchor. Mason supplied a detailed confession, the first account of the mutiny since that furnished five months earlier by the Spanish captain of the *San Antonio*—or so Parker thought. Pelted with questions, Mason left few unanswered, identifying by name the ten slain officers, the four officers yet languishing in La Guaira, and five of the crew's leaders, among them Nash and Turner—not an exhaustive list, but a start.

Claiming to have been inside a cabin with the injured Southcott, Mason denied firsthand knowledge of the murderers, though he had heard "repeated groans and screeches." Later, he observed "a great quantity of blood in the [captain's] cabin window and at the after hatchway, leading from the gunroom." Nearly as disturbing was Mason's testimony that "the whole ship's company," after Pigot's murder, cheered that "they had possession of the ship." A number of the crew, he stated, besides those still in Venezuela, had departed for Curaçao to find passage elsewhere. As to the cause of the mutiny, Mason did not say, other than to note toward the end of his confession the fall of three men, the day before, from the mizzentop yard. "There was punishment," he added, "for several days previous to this and no appearance of mutiny."[26]

On March 17, a court-martial convened aboard the warship *York*. Not one of Mason's shipmates spoke or otherwise offered a defense. With his testimony front and center, their presence during the uprising went undisputed. Less clear, in the absence of positive proof, were their roles, though circumstantial evidence, if strong, was permitted. And the five judges, each a naval commander, were in no mood to quibble in handing down convictions for murder as well as mutiny. Two days later, at 9 a.m., a yellow flag was hoisted aboard the *York* as four guns fired and the sailors, Mason excepted, were run up a yardarm, their death throes partially obscured by the smoke. Pursuant to the sentence, each body was taken ashore and hung from a gibbet in chains. Later that day, Parker received a statement dictated by Montell an hour before his execution. Confessing his role in the deaths of both Pigot and Lieutenant Douglas, Montell absolved D'Orlaine of guilt and wrote that Elliot had "saved the life of the Master of the *Hermione* [Southcott], standing sentry over him sick in his berth."[27]

A broadsheet announcing the court-martial appeared throughout the British West Indies. Armed with fresh evidence, Parker drafted a letter to the governor of La Guaira demanding the immediate extradition of the "principal actors and murderers" named in Mason's confession. The punishment of such "atrocious villains," he declared, was in the "general interest of all nations." Professing surprise at Spain's intransigence—a "nation so marked in history for its national honor and justice"—he further insisted upon the release of the British prisoners of war. Lending force to his demands was a curious report dated March 17 from Halifax, Nova Scotia, later to appear in the *London Chronicle*. On the basis of letters from Saint Nicholas Mole, the Halifax report claimed that a British expedition was "on foot" to attempt an exchange of Spanish prisoners for the *Hermione*'s crew. Unless Venezuelan officials cooperated, the account warned, the squadron of five warships—a flagship boasting 108 guns and four consorts with 74 guns apiece—would lay siege to La Guaira. A British gambit intended for Spanish eyes, however circuitous the route? Or an operation that died on the drawing board? Idle threat or not, all five ships identified in the story lay moored, if needed, at Saint Nicholas Mole.[28]

AT A COURT MARTIAL

Assembled and held on Board His Majesty's Ship *York*, Mole Saint Nicholas, on the Seventeenth Day of March 1798.

PRESENT

GEORGE BOWEN, Esquire, Captain of His Majesty's Ship *Carnatic*, and Third in Command.

PRESIDENT.

CAPTAINS.

EDWARD TYRREL SMITH.   JOHN FERRIER.
MAN DOBSON.   JOHN CRAWLEY.

THE Court, in pursuance of an Order of the fifteenth of March 1798, from Sir *Hyde Parker*, Knt. Vice Admiral of the Red and Commander in Chief of His Majesty's Ships and Vessels employed and to be employed at and about *Jamaica*, &c. &c. addressed to *George Bowen*, Esq. Captain of His Majesty's Ship *Carnatic*, and Third in Command, being first duly sworn, proceeded to try *Anthony Mark*, alias *Antonio Marco*, *John Elliot*, *Joseph Mansell*, and *Peter Delany*, alias, *Pierre d'Orlanie*, upon an information contained in a Letter from Captain *Mends*, of His Majesty's Sloop *Diligence*, of the 27th of October 1797, to the Commander in Chief, and one from Captain *Crawley*, of His Majesty's Ship *Valiant*, dated the 8th of March instant, and also the deposition of *John Mason*, late carpenters Mate of His Majesty's Ship *Hermione*, taken in the presence of the said Captain *Crawley*, and Lieutenants *Philpot* and *Hancock*, of the *Valiant*, dated the 2nd of the said month of March, representing that the said *Anthony Mark*, alias *Antonio Marco*, *John Elliot*, *Joseph Mansell*, and *Peter Delany*, alias *Pierre d'Orlanie*, were a part of the Crew of the French Privateer *la Magicienne*, captured by the said Ship; and also a part of the Crew of His Majesty's said Ship *Hermione*, and were actually on board His Majesty's said Ship *Hermione*, at the time the Mutiny, Murders and Piracy were committed on board her; and for being taken in arms against His Majesty. And having heard the Evidence produced to identify the Persons of the Prisoners, and very maturely and deliberately weighed and considered the several circumstances in the Letters, and Paper abovementioned, and

the Prisoners having no Evidence to produce, or any thing to offer in their own defence, THE COURT is of opinion, that the charges of Mutiny, Murder and running away with His Majesty's said Ship *Hermione*, and delivering her up to the Enemy; And being found actually in arms against His Majesty and His Subjects, on board *la Magicienne*, a French Privateer, are fully proved.

THE COURT do therefore adjudge the said *Anthony Mark*, alias *Antonio Marco*, *John Elliot*, *Joseph Mansell*, and *Peter Delany*, alias *Pierre d'Orlanie*, to be hung by their Necks until they are dead, at the Yard Arms of such of His Majesty's Ships, and at such times, as shall be directed by the Commander in Chief.

And as a further Example to deter others from committing, or being accessory to such shocking and atrocious Crimes; that when dead, their Bodies be hung in chains upon Gibbets on such conspicuous points, or head lands, as the Commander in Chief shall direct. And they are hereby sentenced to be so hung until they are dead, and their Bodies gibbetted accordingly.

(Signed)   GEO. BOWEN.
EDW. TYRREL SMITH.
JN. FERRIER.
MAN DOBSON.
JN. CRAWLEY.

W. PAGE, *Deputy*
Judge Advocate.

Anonymous, AT A COURT MARTIAL Assembled and held
on Board His Majesty's Ship *York,* Mole Saint Nicholas,
on the Seventeenth Day of March 1798

Fueling Parker's impatience was a fresh instance of naval unrest. During the first week of March, while cruising off Cuba, the captain of the frigate *Renommée* caught wind of a plot—"as that of the *Hermione*"—designed to carry the ship into Havana following every officer's murder. Disclosed by the *Renommée's* carpenter, it was alleged that up to forty members of the crew had sworn themselves to "death or liberty." For the next two weeks at sea, each officer kept armed watch and slept with a brace of pistols. "We never went to rest," one reported, "without expectation of having our throats cut before the next morning." There were also hints that various seamen aboard the *Ceres,* accompanying the *Renommée,* had joined the conspiracy. Both vessels returned safely to the Mole escorted by a twenty-four-gun post ship, the *Porcupine.* One day after the execution of the four Hermiones, four seamen from the *Renommée* were court-martialed and all but one sentenced to hang.[29]

Six months after the September mutiny, the navy's manhunt was gathering momentum. No sooner had Parker's letter left Saint Nicholas Mole than Governor Vasquez placed the British prisoners on board a schooner, *La Bonita,* bound for the British island of Grenada. Unknown to Parker, Admiral Harvey of the Leeward Islands station had negotiated an exchange of Spanish prisoners with Vasquez. Transferred to a British ship after reaching Grenada, Southcott and Casey, who were among them, joined Harvey aboard the *Prince of Wales* at Fort Royal, on the western coast of Martinique, on April 11. Almost immediately, their release proved a windfall. Imprisoned on Martinique were two men suspected of having served on the *Hermione,* able seaman Joseph Leech and foretopman William Mason (no relation to John), both captured at sea by the frigate *L'Amiable.* Identified by Southcott, they were tried on the first of May 1798. With all ten of the La Guaira prisoners enlisted to testify, witnesses were not wanting. Their testimony portrayed Mason's conduct during the mutiny sympathetically, as animated more by fear than by malice. By contrast, a pile of evidence pointed to Leech's leadership, from the attack in Pigot's cabin to the *Hermione's* arrival at La Guaira, where he went ashore to negotiate terms. Mitigating testimony backfired. Leech, Southcott recalled, had entered his cabin "with arms" shortly before midnight to say that he "should not be hurt by the ship's company." On May 3, the able seaman swung from a yardarm alone.

MUTINEERS OF THE HERMIONE.

———

SAINT JOHN's (ANTIGUA), 14th APRIL, 1798.

It is hoped that all such Attrocious Villains may be brought to the punishments they merit, and that Humanity and Virtue will call forth the most strenuous exertions, not only of all his Majesty's Subjects, but also of all civilized Nations, to bring them to Justice ; and it is recommended, that Copies of the following Description be circulated in the different Islands and especially in all Cruizing Vessels.

THE Following is a Description of the Men, as given by two Seamen late belonging to the *Hermione*, now Prisoners on board His Majesty's Ship *Beaver* ; who were the Ringleaders and Promoters of the Mutiny that took place on board His Majesty's Ship *Hermione*. in the night of the 21st of September, 1797, off *Mona-Island*, the North End of *Porto-Rico* ;—In which Captain Pigot, Mr. Richards, the First-Lieutenant, Mr. Douglas, the Second-Lieutenant, Mr. Foreshaw, the Third-Lieutenant, Mr. ——————, the Lieutenant of Marines, Mr. Smith, Midshipman, Mr. Martin the Boatswain, Mr. Sampson the Surgeon, Mr. Pacey the Purser, with several of the Crew, were murdered and thrown over-board.

Mr. Southcoate the Master, ⎫
Mr. Price, Carpenter, ⎬ Saved.
Mr. Melcher, Midshipman, ⎭

Mr. Searl Gunner, since dead at the Hospital at la Guira.

———

A N T I G U A.

Printed at the Journal Printing-Office, *At the Expence of* Walter Colquhoun, *Esq.*

Anonymous, Mutineers of the *Hermione,* Saint John's
(Antigua), 14th April, 1798

Rather than transport Leech to England, Harvey decided that "an example" was more desirable in the Caribbean.[30]

By then, Mason and Leech had provided detailed descriptions along with the identities of leading mutineers far in excess of the handful of names that John Mason, the carpenter's mate, had supplied at the Mole or Slushing had furnished aboard the *Aurora.* It was this information that resulted in a nine-page list of thirty-three ringleaders. Printed April 14 on Antigua, the pamphlet circulated widely. Titled "MUTINEERS OF THE HERMIONE," the document's preamble called for "the most strenuous exertions, not only of all his Majesty's Subjects, but also of all civilized nations." It also urged that "all cruizing vessels" acquire copies of the circular. Topping the list was Thomas Turner, described as "a master's mate, about 5 feet 8 or 9 inches tall, of a dark complexion, black hair, rather thick-set, and well-made." He was said to have commanded the ship after the mutiny and to have adopted the alias of "Captain William Rhodes." Commonly included in each profile were the seaman's former rank and duties, nationality and alias, his last-known location, and a physical description. In lieu of other means of identification, information relating to height, hair color and length, build, and complexion (e.g., "ruddy," "fresh," or "pale") was vital, particularly reports of scars, injuries, and tattoos. The Yorkshireman John Smith, alias "Richard Appleby," bore, among other tattoos, a tree on his right arm, a cross on his left, and a mermaid.[31]

Of the twenty-four fugitives of known nationalities, ten hailed from England, as many as nine from Ireland, and various others from Scotland, the Netherlands, and Switzerland. Besides those still in Venezuela, most of the leaders were thought to be headed to Curaçao to sign on to outbound ships. Puerto Rico and Cuba were rumored points of interest, as was, for several, the Spanish seaport of Cádiz, a portal to the European continent. Irish gunner James Bell had reportedly embarked on a Spanish schooner from Barcelona, a coastal town over two hundred miles east of La Guaira, hoping to reach either Cádiz or "any port they could make in the Mediterranean." And the Irishman Thomas Nash? It was said that the most notorious mutineer had left Puerto Cabello aboard either a Spanish or an American schooner.[32]

Although it is impossible to gauge the pamphlet's impact, at the least it deprived more than thirty fugitives of their anonymity. While false identities often went undetected in the absence of modern technology, an individual's physical appearance, if widely circulated, was difficult to change. Height, bone structure, and complexion were for the most part unalterable, except for the gradual toll exacted by age. Nash, for one, was said to be "remarkably hairy" on his arms and chest. Distinguishing marks such as scars, blemishes, and tattoos were not only irreversible but also hard to hide or disguise. As were accents. In the pamphlet's profiles, regional origins—in some instances the names of cities or counties—appeared for English fugitives (only one of whom reputedly came from London).[33]

With the aid of British privateers, the navy's dragnet snagged sundry crew members. A number had boarded foreign merchantmen—chiefly Spanish, French, and American carriers. In April off the coast of Puerto Rico, a Scottish privateer discovered John Holford, a cook, and his thirteen-year-old son on a Spanish xebec loaded with cocoa for Cádiz. That same month, the crew of a British privateer, the *Benson,* boarded a merchantman and found a young Scottish maintopman named John Brown, an even greater catch. Taken to Kingston, Brown made a full confession. More than that, his detailed knowledge of the crew, including their names and whereabouts at the time of his departure from La Guaira, was invaluable. In the absence of the *Hermione*'s last muster book, officials compiled a full roster of the ship's company, 177 names in all, including those of 10 victims and 10 loyalists. Despite occasional inaccuracies and omissions, the compilation added immensely to the navy's small storehouse of information. Brown also turned King's evidence against three suspects, already imprisoned at Saint Nicholas Mole, during a court-martial on May 5. All three were executed, including able seaman William Herd, who, according to Brown, had broken into Pigot's cabin during the attack.[34]

The fugitive Richard Redmond, on board a Spanish schooner, fell into British hands hours from reaching the port of Vigo, in northern Spain. More circuitous was the flight of John Coe, an East Anglian native, who embarked from La Guaira on *La Fleur de Mer,* a French privateer. After capturing an American brig on her way from New York to New Orleans, the French captain ordered Coe to assist in taking the prize to a French port on Santo Domingo—only to be intercepted days later by a British frigate. Coe joined a handful of shipmates in a short-lived attempt to escape in a jolly boat. More desperate was an English fugitive aboard a French privateer off Jamaica that was seized by a British schooner. Moments before royal marines boarded, he shouted, "If I am taken, I shall be hanged, so here goes!" Promptly jumping overboard, he vanished beneath the swells.[35]

At least one member of the crew returned to England. A merchant seaman from Liverpool for twenty-five years, John Williams had been impressed aboard the *Hermione* in Kingston less than three months before the mutiny. He later claimed to have been laid up with a lame leg at the time of the uprising. From La Guaira, where he was hospitalized, he signed aboard a Danish brig that was shortly seized by a British privateer. Taken to Tortola, some sixty miles to the east of Puerto Rico, Williams succeeded in boarding the *Mona,* a merchantman bound for Liverpool. Upon arriving, he sought out the father of Lieutenant Foreshaw, "to whom he faithfully related" the details of his son's death "that came to his knowledge." After a five-day stay in a hospital, he delivered himself up to the mayor of Liverpool. With Southcott and Casey confirming the bulk of his account, a court-martial in Portsmouth acquitted Williams.[36]

Old habits dying hard, a few fugitives pushed their luck at sea. Twenty-six-year-old Thomas Charlton and Adam Lynn, more than twenty years his senior, should have known better. After working their passage from La Guaira to Boston on an American brig, they left New England aboard a schooner for Barbados, pushed on to Trinidad, and, finally, they hoped, headed back to Boston. But on the last leg, a French privateer overtook their ship, the *Two Friends,* and just three weeks later, with Charlton and Lynn still aboard, the privateer surrendered to the *Resolution,* a British warship out of Nova Scotia.[37] The two were executed at Port Royal in August aboard the *York.*

IN THE TWELVE MONTHS AFTER word first reached London, news of the mutiny and its aftermath continued to stir public attention, notwithstanding military reports of far greater consequence from Europe and the Mediterranean. Descriptions of shipboard executions from the West Indies were eagerly received. "These execrable wretches behaved with a hardiness of villainy scarcely credible," declared London's *Evening Mail* of the four mutineers hanged at Saint Nicholas Mole in March. Equally welcome was the arrival from Martinique of the four officers, who returned home to serve as witnesses (the marines stayed behind to testify at trials in the Caribbean). On August 9 at a court-martial at Sheerness, in northern Kent, a board of ten senior officers, including Captain William Bligh, formerly of the *Bounty,* exonerated all four men for their conduct during the mutiny. Midshipman Casey, who had suffered dearly at Pigot's hands, immediately garnered an invitation to join the Channel Fleet. Not only was the board's verdict well received in the press, but on a practical level, it lent added weight to the men's credibility as witnesses.[38]

Public speculation about the whereabouts of the *Hermione,* as might be expected, persisted in the wake of her removal to Puerto Cabello. More than once, papers erroneously reported that she had put to sea. On the basis of reports from Jamaica, *Lloyd's Evening Post* in London declared that the *Santa Cecilia* was set to embark in early April, manned by a crew of three hundred, mostly landsmen, in addition to fifty mutineers, including William Turner, the former master's mate. "As the information is known to our cruizers," stated the paper, "it is hoped the whole gang of these pirates and assassins will be taken." Although the *Acasta,* a formidable forty-gun frigate, prowled offshore, its prey never left port.[39]

Few had as much invested in the crew's capture, personally and professionally, as Sir Hyde Parker. Even as the British army found itself fighting a rearguard campaign on Saint Domingue—forced in October to abandon the island altogether—for Parker, the hunt remained a major preoccupation. He routinely kept the Admiralty abreast of new courts-martial, most ending in executions and the defendant's corpse hung in chains. It was all the more surprising, then, when a Kingston trial in late May 1798 acquitted John Holford and his son of assisting in the insurrection. The board recommended a third defendant, James Irwin from Limerick, "as a proper object of mercy." He was transported not long afterward as a convict to Australia. Rear Admiral Richard Rodney Bligh, Parker's second in command and a distant relation of William, presided over the court-martial. It did not help that Bligh and Parker had clashed just a year earlier over apportioning blame for the grounding of the *Ceres* off the Venezuelan coast. Livid at the lenient verdicts, Parker unsuccessfully urged Bligh's reassignment. In a caustic dispatch to the Admiralty, he condemned Bligh's "supineness" when "it becomes more than ever necessary for officers' exertions to subdue the licentiousness and bloodthirsty ideas of seamen." Essential "at this momentary crisis," he implored, was the "terror of exemplary punishment."[40]

By late 1798, some seventeen Hermiones had been apprehended, fourteen of whom were convicted of one or more offenses, from murder, mutiny, and piracy to taking up arms against the King, and eleven hanged. Still others awaited trial, one of whom was among the thirty-three leaders publicized in the Antiguan pamphlet of April 14. And yet for all the navy's tenacity, well over one hundred men were still at large, including the likes of Thomas Nash, William Turner, and David Forrester. Worse, Parker remained convinced that most had already eluded British pursuit—not, however, by remaining in La Guaira or Puerto Cabello. Believing just the opposite, he no longer held to any hope of cooperation from Venezuelan officials. Instead, the vice admiral continued to worry that untold numbers had absconded to the United States. As early as November 1797, he had warned the Admiralty of this danger, knowing that once on shore the "pirates and murderers" could only be apprehended by means of diplomatic entreaties from London. Anecdotal evidence later culled from confessions augmented his fears. "Unless sound policy induces the United States of America to exert their power in apprehending these principals," he wrote the Admiralty in February, "I much fear that they will escape that punishment which the heinousness of their crimes so justly merits."[41]

PART TWO

Martyrdom

4

Receive the Fugitive

BY THE LATE EIGHTEENTH CENTURY, America had long afforded a refuge for Europeans in flight. Religious dissenters, land-hungry families, men on the make all flocked to the New World in search of freedom and economic opportunity. As early as 1584, the English clergyman Richard Hakluyt promoted the North American wilderness as a humane remedy for overpopulation and mounting poverty. Petty thieves and vagrants might one day "be raised againe." Although a dumping ground, in time, for British convicts, the American colonies, for burgeoning numbers of Europeans, embodied a land alive with possibilities, where neither church nor state ruled with a whip hand. A massive influx of immigrants from continental Europe, Ireland, and Scotland in the 1700s, some persecuted for their faiths, attested to the colonies' far-flung reputation as the "best poor man's country" in the world.[1]

Not until the War of Independence, however, did multitudes at home and abroad increasingly view America as an asylum for liberty, besieged by the same sinister, tyrannical forces that had oppressed free peoples throughout history. To an unprecedented degree, America's exceptionalism acquired profound political significance. "For while the greatest part of the nations of the earth are held together under the yoke of universal slavery," exclaimed Reverend Samuel Williams of Massachusetts, "the North-American provinces yet remain *the country of free men.*" That the American wilderness stood as a beacon of liberty testified to its physical isolation—uncontaminated, as yet, by "the fatal arts of luxury and corruption." More, this uncharted, primitive land with its vast forests bred a spirit of simplicity, self-reliance, and individual initiative—all prerequisites of a liberty-loving people—while affording newcomers the means to achieve propertied independence.[2] It was this uplifting vision of America's unique role in a world of larger, more dangerous nations that defined the broader purpose of its struggle for self-determination. At stake for future generations, as for the revolutionaries themselves, was the very survival of freedom. "In our destruction," declared a Philadelphia patriot, "liberty itself expires, and human nature will despair of evermore regaining its first and original dignity." With liberty's preservation, America would offer sanctuary to the oppressed in foreign tyrannies. In Thomas Paine's climactic words, "Freedom hath been hunted around the globe. . . . Receive the fugitive, and prepare in time an asylum for mankind."[3]

Implicit in America's mission was the revolutionary conviction that victims of oppression would flock to its shores, forsaking Old World allegiances to become naturalized citizens, removed from the venality of Europe. America, an essayist affirmed in 1786, "invited the persecuted of the earth to her open bosom, there to be safe from the despot's rod of wrath." In the view of the Founders, citizenship was volitional, not the indelible consequence of birth ("perpetual allegiance," as the British insisted). Equally axiomatic in the afterglow of independence was the belief that émigrés would embrace the ideals of republicanism. According to Tench Coxe of Pennsylvania, they would assist in forging not only a new nation but also "a political fellowship" of and by the people dedicated to advancing civil and religious liberty. In the public mind, Americans already stood united, not by ancestry or tradition but by the "choice of freedom over tyranny."[4]

In the early Republic, with a white population of just over three million in 1790, immigration assumed heightened importance, as much for its impact on the nation's principles as for its contribution to an expanding country. Nearly one hundred thousand Europeans landed in the United States during the 1790s. Few issues were thought as vital to shaping the nation's destiny, or to the preservation of liberty. One of the charges laid at the feet of George III in the Declaration of Independence had been that he obstructed "the laws for the naturalization of

foreigners; refusing to pass others, to encourage their migration hither."
During the first year of George Washington's presidency, Congress gave
broad support to a comprehensive naturalization law, among the most
important of its legislative accomplishments. In keeping with the spirit
of revolutionary idealism, ports stayed open to "free white persons" of
all nationalities and creeds, as did citizenship. After just two years, naturalized aliens stood to receive the full rights and privileges of native-born
Americans, aside from being eligible to seek the presidency. Tragically,
nonwhites, as might be expected, were excluded due to deep-seated
racism; but for Europeans, the law welcomed victims of government
oppression. Even so, there were opponents of any probationary restrictions. "We shall be inconsistent with ourselves," complained Congressman John Page of Virginia during a debate on the House floor, "if, after
boasting of having opened an asylum for the oppressed of all nations . . .
we make the terms of admission to the full enjoyment of that asylum so
hard as now proposed."[5]

And yet, once the initial euphoria of the Revolution faded, attitudes
toward European immigration grew perceptibly ambivalent. Even before
passage of the Naturalization Act of 1790, Thomas Jefferson, for one,
had feared the inundation of uprooted aliens untutored in republican
values. Later, in 1795, pangs of uncertainty led to a new law extending
the residential requirement for citizenship to five years, a compromise in
lieu of a more stringent proposal favoring ten. The act insisted on proof
of the applicant's "good moral character" and fidelity to the principles of
the Constitution. It also required newly minted citizens to renounce all
prior allegiances and, at the insistence of the fledgling Republican Party,
all titles of nobility. Without comment, President Washington approved
the bill, notwithstanding his professed hope at the beginning of the year
"to render this country more and more a safe and propitious asylum for
the unfortunate of other countries."[6]

Not, however, until the full-scale emergence of political parties
coupled with spreading concern over both the French Revolution and
unrest in Ireland did nativist sentiment intensify. And more and more,
the most strident voices belonged to members of the Federalist camp,
aghast by the prospect of a sudden influx of French Jacobins. Every bit as
licentious, in Federalist eyes, were newly arrived emigrants from Ireland.

With thousands disembarking each year, they, even more than French radicals, progressively fueled nativist fears. Notwithstanding widespread prejudice toward Catholics, it mattered not that most newcomers were Presbyterians from Ulster. Having embraced England as a bastion of civil order during France's Reign of Terror, Federalists, whose strength lay centered in New England, identified the Irish with poverty, drink, and crime. They became reviled all the more for their growing insurgence, with French aid, against British occupation. In the meantime, the "wild Irish," settled in western Pennsylvania, were thought to have played a major role in the Whiskey Rebellion of 1794 before its collapse in the face of an army led by Alexander Hamilton and Henry "Light Horse Harry" Lee. By contrast, Jefferson, despite his earlier qualms, increasingly championed the plight of Irish immigrants, whom he and other pro-French Republicans considered victims of British oppression in need of America's shelter. If Republicans' motives were principled, their support for Irish Americans was no less shrewd, since Irish votes gave the party new grounds for hope in seeking to expand its predominantly southern base.[7]

Fresh from winning the presidency in 1796 and control of both houses, Federalists grew more xenophobic. It did not help that party stalwarts blamed Irish American voters for John Adams's narrow margin of victory. Thus commenced a concerted effort in Congress to impose additional impediments to naturalization, designed not only to deter citizenship but to discourage immigration altogether. The imposition of a $20 federal fee on naturalization certificates in 1797 barely failed after a robust debate in the House of Representatives. The Federalist representative from Massachusetts, Harrison Gray Otis, railed that he did "not wish to invite hoards of wild Irishmen, nor the turbulent and disorderly of all parts of the world, to come here with a view to disturb our tranquility, and who after unfurling the standard of rebellion in their own countries, may come hither to revolutionize ours." Nephew of the Revolutionary hero James Otis, he favored a new naturalization act lengthening, yet again, the residence requirement for citizenship. "There was a moment of enthusiasm in this country," Robert Goodloe Harper of South Carolina remarked, "when we were not satisfied with giving to immigrants every blessing which we had earned with our

blood and treasure, but admitted them instantly to the rights of citizenship." Proposing instead the abolition of any path to citizenship apart
from birth, Harper flatly declared, "We were wrong."[8]

THE UNITED STATES HELD A powerful allure for members of the *Hermione*'s crew quitting the Spanish Main. America's material prosperity,
breadth, and proximity, let alone its Caribbean shipping connections,
made it an inviting haven. With English the predominant language,
the mainland colonies had long been a favorite destination for deserters from the Royal Navy, nearly fifteen thousand seamen during the
Revolutionary War alone. In the spring of 1798, the nation's political
neutrality only heightened its appeal. An ever-widening war, by contrast, engulfed much of Europe, including the Low Countries, which
had afforded foreigners a refuge since the sixteenth century. Alternately,
the fragility of the infant U.S. government made it ill equipped to monitor newly arrived seamen virtually indistinguishable in appearance and
speech from American mariners, many of whom were themselves British émigrés. Nor, presumably, did authorities have cause to expel foreign fugitives. Was America not, as Tom Paine pledged, an asylum for
mankind? A land of liberty, not least for victims of British oppression?
"Here in happy America," boasted a South Carolina planter in 1792 to
a Scottish baronet, "we find the end of Governt completely answered in
the freedom & happiness of the people." No wonder that Vice Admiral
Parker thought the United States a natural refuge, or that the mutineer
Joseph Montell, who left La Guaira no later than February 1798, volunteered, when caught, that as many as ten shipmates may already have
departed for the American mainland.[9]

At around the same time, the American schooner *Hannah,* out of
Santo Domingo, dropped anchor in the harbor of Wilmington, Delaware. A bustling port boasting six hundred homes, predominantly
brick and attractively laid out, Wilmington rested on a small rise beside
the Delaware River fewer than thirty miles south of Philadelphia, the
nation's capital. Among the crew on board the merchant ship was an
Italian seaman named Simon Marcus, who'd blurted to a shipmate that
he had served aboard the *Hermione.* An idle boast perhaps, but Mar-

Gilbert Stuart,
Sir Robert Liston, *1800*

cus was immediately detained on shore. In a strange twist, word of this reached Fanny Martin, widow of the slain boatswain, who had arrived in New York City from La Guaira in late December. On February 16, she swore out a deposition before a notary attesting to her "certain knowledge" of Marcus's presence during the mutiny. At five feet nine or five feet ten in height, the seaman, according to Martin, bore a slender frame, a "swarthy" complexion with facial scars from smallpox, and "remarkably long and thick black hair." Ringleaders, she added, had included "Dick Redman, a West Country man," "Thomas Nash, an Irishman," "Jack Smith, a young man with a fair complexion, marked with the small pox," and "one [H]arry Croker, gunner's mate," who had murdered her husband. As a prosecution witness, Martin was a mixed blessing, having by then blamed Pigot's cruelty for the mutiny in a widely reprinted newspaper story.[10]

Within days, a copy of the affidavit reached the hands of the British envoy, Robert Liston, in Philadelphia. Though he was no friend of Sir Hyde Parker, his own zeal in pursuit of the *Hermione*'s crew nearly matched the admiral's. An adroit diplomat who spoke ten languages, Liston was a faithful servant of the crown. In a painting by Gilbert Stuart in 1800, he possessed a long, ruddy face with a pleasing smile. Since arriving in Philadelphia with his bride, Henrietta, he was thought an improvement over the previous ambassador, George Hammond, whose prickly demeanor had alienated much of the capital. "A sensible, pleasant, easy, and agreeable man," observed a Federalist politician of Liston in May 1796—"much superior in fullness of character to the former minister." Henrietta reported to her uncle in Scotland, "People seem disposed to entertain of Mr. Liston." A frequent guest at dinner parties, he assiduously cultivated ties to leading figures in the Washington and Adams administrations, none more promising or powerful than the secretary of state, Timothy Pickering.[11]

A native of Salem, Massachusetts, and a graduate of Harvard College, Pickering had served as quartermaster general for Washington's Continental Army during the last years of the Revolutionary War. Tall in height and ramrod stiff, with an angular nose, balding pate, and piercing eyes, he was a conservative Federalist, albeit with little pretense to elegance or wealth to indulge the trappings of aristocracy. Before serving in a succession of federal posts, he nearly went bankrupt in 1790. Nor had his sympathies long favored Great Britain. Initially supportive

Gilbert Stuart, Timothy Pickering, *ca. nineteenth century*

of the French Revolution, even after the executions of Louis XVI and Marie Antoinette, Pickering was said by George Hammond in 1795 to exhibit "a most blind and undistinguishing hatred of Great Britain." By then, however, the secretary's attitudes were shifting, chiefly because of his unwavering support for the Treaty of Amity, Commerce, and Navigation as an alternative to war with Britain. In 1794, Washington had dispatched John Jay, chief justice of the Supreme Court, to London to negotiate terms pertaining to a number of issues straining relations between the two nations. Ultimately approved by the Senate in June 1795 with Washington's belated support, the British Treaty, as it was known, as much as any single controversy gave rise to America's first political party system. The treaty was a bargain with the devil, in the view of critics. So revolted was Pickering by the ferocity of Republican opposition that he feared for the government's stability at the hands of "Jacobins" in league with the French.[12]

But Pickering, as secretary of state, also endeavored to halt the worst abuses of the Royal Navy, which he rightly thought the major cause of persistent opposition to the treaty. A "continual irritation in the public mind," he confided to Thomas Pinckney, the U.S. minister to Britain. No problem proved more urgent than the impressment of American seamen, which the accord had failed to address. "While they remain subjected to impressments, even against proof of their citizenship," Pickering wrote Robert Liston in June 1796, "conciliation will be a visionary idea." He repeatedly complained of the flagrant disregard for American rights shown by officers under the command of Vice Admiral Parker, who, the secretary wrote, "from the very beginning has thrown obstacles in the way." "What is worse, and past enduring" was that American seamen "were brought to the gangway and whipped" for writing U.S. officials. Even more appalling to Pickering was the flogging of Captain William Jessup in July 1796. Instructing Rufus King, the new minister in London, to protest "the tyrannical and inhuman conduct of Captain Pigot," Pickering expressed his astonishment "at the quiet submission of Captain Jessup and other American citizens, victims of the frequent tyranny and cruelty of British officers, and that some of them do not take instant vengeance on the ruffians who thus put them to the torture."[13]

Despite strong differences at times with Pickering, Robert Liston was not unsympathetic to American grievances and often expedited the secretary's inquiries into the impressment of U.S. citizens. Liston, of course, had also clashed with Parker over Jessup's mistreatment. Both in their early fifties, Liston and Pickering dealt with each other on an equal footing, enjoying a working relationship that was even at times good humored and warm, rooted perhaps in their shared middle-class origins as well as in their enmity for France. Pickering, Henrietta informed her uncle in July 1797, "is an honest good man, more the true Republican in figure, manners and mode of living than any man I have seen in America." The following March the Listons invited Pickering and his wife, Rebecca, to dinner. Replying that although he would be pleased to accept the invitation, Pickering reluctantly declined. "Congress do not allow persons with executive offices under the United States (unless they possess private fortunes) to have any convivial intercourse with foreign ministers. . . . It is deemed honor enough for executive officers to toil without interruption for their country and indulgence enough to live on mutton, mush, and cold water."[14]

On receiving Fanny Martin's affidavit in February, Liston immediately busied himself with notifying Pickering. In a letter dated the nineteenth, which he hand delivered, Liston requested the arrest "without delay" of Simon Marcus, "an accomplice" to murder, in anticipation of his extradition to Britain in keeping with the terms of the recent Anglo-American treaty.[15]

Favored as a means of avoiding conflict by such prominent scholars of international law as Hugo Grotius and Emmerich de Vattel, extradition went back at least to the thirteenth century B.C., when the Egyptian pharaoh Ramses II negotiated a treaty with the Hittites. Beginning in the 1500s, however, Britain had grown wary of surrendering residents to foreign powers, though it remained eager to retrieve criminal suspects from abroad. No less an authority than the jurist Sir Edward Coke was deeply skeptical of extradition, citing not only the Magna Carta but also Deuteronomy, which cautioned, "Thou shalt not deliver unto his master the servant who is escaped from his master unto thee." The Habeas Corpus Act of 1679 stipulated that *"no inhabitant"* or *"resident"* could be sent "beyond the seas" to a foreign country against his will. Britain made an exception in its treaty with the United States in light of their shared legal heritage and the accord's specificity. According to Article 27, in the event of flight from one nation to the other after the commission of murder or forgery, the suspect was to be returned to the home country, "provided that this shall *only* [my italics] be done on such evidence of criminality as according to the laws of the place where the fugitive or person so charged shall be found would justify his apprehension and commitment for trial, if the offence had there been committed." It was on the insistence of Lord Grenville, the principal British negotiator, that "only," for added emphasis, was inserted before the clause mandating probable cause.[16]

Amid escalating tensions between Federalists and Republicans over the British Treaty, Article 27 had provoked scant concern, even though the Washington administration had previously resisted extraditing fugitives to France "upon reasons of law and magnanimity." A pro-Federalist newspaper in New York proclaimed, "By the ref[u]sal of refuge to murderers and forgers, we add security to life and property," a sentiment seemingly shared by most Republicans. In the view of Congressman William Branch Giles of Virginia, a staunch opponent of the treaty on other grounds, the article "was not objectionable." Only the Revolutionary poet Philip Freneau of Philadelphia wrote publicly in opposition, declaring unconstitutional the article's denial of trial by jury in an American court. Thomas Jefferson, as George Washington's secretary of state, had privately voiced misgivings about extradition as early as 1792. Underlying his unease was a harsh appraisal of foreign courts. Cer-

tainly, suspects accused of treason, Jefferson believed, should not be surrendered. "The unsuccessful strugglers against tyranny," he wrote in a
diplomatic memorandum, "have been the chief martyrs of treason laws
in all countries. . . . We should not wish, then, to give up to the executioner the patriot who fails and flees to us." More broadly, he feared
that fugitives, once returned, would not receive just trials in their own
countries. "The evil of protecting malefactors of every dye is sensibly felt
here as in other countries; but until a reformation of the criminal codes
of most nations, to deliver fugitives to them would be to become their
accomplices."[17]

On receiving Liston's request of the nineteenth, Pickering immediately informed President John Adams. Ordinarily, the secretary reported,
Adams would "with promptitude" cause Marcus "to be apprehended
and delivered up to justice"—by which Pickering appears to have meant
a British rather than an American court. But he relayed the president's
apprehension that Fanny Martin's affidavit had not implicated the seaman in the murders or in any violence aboard the *Hermione*. (Then, too,
unknown to Pickering and Adams, Marcus now claimed from his jail
cell that he had left the ship weeks before the mutiny.)[18]

Liston barely had time to lick his wounds before learning that three
additional members of the *Hermione*'s crew had been seized on board the
Relief from Santo Domingo on March 10. The brigantine lay anchored
in the harbor of Amboy, New Jersey, a small port just across a tidal strait
from Staten Island, New York. Tipped off by the vessel's master, Yellis
Mandeville, officials confined the seamen to the Middlesex County jail
in nearby New Brunswick, a modest market town settled by the Dutch
that lay on the King's Highway connecting New York and Philadelphia.
Whether or not the trio arrived in the United States in search of asylum
is not known. All three suspects, John Evans, Joannes Williams, and
William Brigstock, had been traveling under aliases. A local alderman
charged each with "feloniously murdering on the high seas the captain
and other officers of his Britannic Majesty's ship the *Hermione*" and
"piratically delivering up the said ship *Hermione* to the officers of the
king of Spain, now at war with his said Britannic Majesty." Besides Article 27 of the British Treaty, the arrest warrant cited Article 20, denying
protection to pirates.[19]

The shipmates freely admitted to having served on board the *Hermione* at the time of the mutiny. They also confirmed the veracity of Simon Marcus's absence, thereby freeing the young sailor from his Wilmington cell. All three men, nonetheless, denied having any hand in the uprising. Little is known of Williams, apart from his Swedish ancestry. Neither he nor the others appeared on any list of ringleaders. Bedridden with scurvy on the night of the mutiny, Evans, an Englishman, had been treated by the ship's surgeon, Hugh Sansum, shortly before he was thrown overboard. Brigstock, an American citizen, was pressed aboard the *Success* in Kingston prior to joining the *Hermione* as a boatswain's mate. Unknown to British and American officials, Brigstock and Evans had accompanied John Elliot, one of Pigot's murderers, to Curaçao on the first leg of their journey from La Guaira.[20]

On the twenty-ninth of March, Liston requested that the three sailors be delivered up to Great Britain. Enclosed in a letter to Pickering was a fresh affidavit, just three days old, from Fanny Martin attesting to Brigstock's "active part" in the officers' deaths. Noting that a magistrate had examined the seamen, Liston asserted that not "a moment's doubt" should arise regarding the "propriety" of their surrender. By then, Secretary Pickering had inquired of Charles Lee, the attorney general, whether there was sufficient evidence among the documents, which included an affidavit from Master Mandeville of the *Relief*, to charge the suspects. If so, Pickering informed Lee that the men should be turned over to the British in accordance with the treaty.[21]

Lee's assent was not certain. A moderate Federalist, he was a staunch critic of the French. But he was no one's footboy, least of all Great Britain's. The younger brother of Henry Lee, the famed Revolutionary cavalry officer, Charles had practiced law in Virginia since 1781. Named attorney general in late 1795 by Washington, he had retained the post under Adams. Possessing a healthy respect for the American legal system, Lee promptly informed Pickering that the United States had no obligation to surrender the suspects. The alleged murders had not occurred within British jurisdiction, as the treaty required. No nation's territorial authority, in his view, extended to the high seas. Nor should the United States voluntarily honor Liston's request. Brigstock, Lee emphasized to Pickering, was an American citizen—as were, possibly, Evans

Cephas Thompson,
Charles Lee, *1807*

and Williams—currently "in the custody of our laws for trial." Whether citizens or not, he wrote, "I believe it more becoming the honor, justice, and dignity of the United States that the trial should be in our courts."[22]

FROM THE FIRST REPORTS IN November 1797, Americans had kept abreast of the mutiny, followed by British efforts to apprehend the *Hermione*'s crew. Major cities along the Eastern Seaboard, in fact, often received news from the Caribbean more quickly than did London or Bristol. Unlike newssheets prior to independence, papers by the end of the century, owing to a sharp rise in political consciousness, devoted more ink to substantive news and commentary, often of a highly partisan nature, as the breach between political parties widened.[23]

Early coverage of the mutiny was straightforward. Minor inaccuracies arose, but none of the gross distortions that littered British newspapers. Neither Pigot's cruelty nor the crew's violence was omitted from a preliminary account that appeared in papers extending from the Carolina lowcountry to northern New England. With winter's arrival, however, Republican newspapers tilted sharply in favor of the mutiny, notwithstanding its heavy loss of life. As Republicans had already shown in their response to the French Revolution, violence, even indiscriminate carnage, afforded a legitimate weapon against tyranny. In the struggle against despotism, it was altogether necessary at times to rely upon popular vengeance—what Jefferson referred to as the "arm of the people, a machine not quite so blind as balls and bombs, but blind to a certain degree." Outraged by British depredations in the Atlantic, Republicans overwhelmingly identified with the mutineers. Memories of the *Hermione* only shook the hornet's nest. The ship's notoriety was compounded by a widespread hatred of Pigot—the "same Captain Pigot," emphasized the *City Gazette & Daily Advertiser* of Charleston, South

Carolina, "that so inhumanly abused Capt. Jessup of the American ship *Mercury.*" A large number of Pigot's crew, the paper erroneously pointed out, "were impressed Americans." Besides Jessup's humiliation, the *Bee* of Hartford, Connecticut, also reminded readers of Pigot's impressment of American seamen: "The cruelty of tyrants sometimes recoils on their own heads."[24]

Still, no commentary matched the vitriol spewed by the *Aurora and General Advertiser* of Philadelphia less than a week after the arrest of the three Hermiones in New Jersey. Fiercely Republican, the paper had been founded in 1794 by Benjamin Franklin Bache, Franklin's grandson, also known as "Lightning Rod Junior." Noting that the *Hermione* was "one of the frigates that did the greatest mischief to American trade by the impressment of American seamen," a correspondent confessed feelings of "intense satisfaction" on learning of the "extirpation of the officers of this execrable corsair," which "every man must feel who wishes for the liberty of American seamen." United States authorities, the writer urged, should refrain from "apprehending the actors of this most laudable enterprise," whereas every British ship guilty of impressing seamen, whether Americans or not, deserved the *Hermione's* fate. Rather than imprisonment, he declared, those who fought British oppression merited a pension or a gold medal.[25]

On Thursday, the fifth of April, a grand jury convened in the U.S. circuit court in the New Jersey city of Trenton. Lying across the Delaware River from Pennsylvania, just thirty miles from Philadelphia, the state capital contained fewer than three thousand inhabitants. "The streets are commodious, and the houses neatly built," noted a visitor, with the best homes, constructed of brick, fronting the main road. A market, four churches, and sundry inns in addition to the courthouse joined the statehouse, a "heavy, clumsy edifice."[26]

Only Fanny Martin testified before the grand jury. Indicted the following day, the three seamen—Brigstock, Evans, and Williams—were each charged with "turning pirate," betraying "the trust in them reposed as mariners," and "run[ning] away" with a ship valued at $50,000. Stolen, too, were a gold watch ($100) along with a silver tankard ($50) and spoon ($2). In addition, the court indicted Brigstock—"not having the fear of God before his eyes, but being moved and seduced by the instigation of the devil"—with wielding a tomahawk to inflict a "mortal bruise" on the right side of Lieutenant Henry Foreshaw's skull. All of which, the court claimed, was "against the peace of the United States," despite the ship's nationality and its location, at the time, off the coast of Puerto Rico. The indictment identified Brigstock as "a citizen of New York, one of the United States of America," and "late of the kingdom of Great Britain." His two shipmates were also said to be "late" of Great Britain. Hopeful of the outcome, specially in regard to Brigstock, Liston wrote Pickering from New York: "If, after hearing the testimony of Mrs. Martin, the Grand Jury shall find against him [for murder], there will then no longer be any possible doubt but that he is strictly within the terms of the treaty; and I beg leave to repeat my request that he may in that case be without delay delivered up."[27]

Pickering had not told Liston of Lee's judgment, and President Adams, if kept informed, did nothing to curtail the trial. In addition to convening in New Jersey, the U.S. Circuit Court for the Middle Circuit, by virtue of the Judiciary Act of 1789, typically sat twice a year in Virginia, Maryland, Delaware, and Pennsylvania. On Monday, it assembled in Trenton with Supreme Court Justice Samuel Chase presiding. Just days shy of his fifty-seventh birthday, Chase, a native of Maryland, had been a fervent anti-Federalist at the time of the Constitution's ratification, but he had grown steadily convinced of the need for a strong central government. Beside him on the bench sat Robert Morris, who at age forty-five had been nominated by Washington for the federal district court of New Jersey. A co-counsel joined the district attorney for New Jersey, Lucius H. Stockton, while the defense marshaled two attorneys of its own.[28]

Other than a brief appearance by Martin, six defense witnesses testified, all of them, presumably from New York, on behalf of Brigstock's character. The trial consumed eleven hours, but the jury of twelve men required only twenty minutes before the foreman, Ellet Tucker, at one o'clock in the morning, in a resounding verdict, declared the defendants not guilty of the charge of piracy. Their presence aboard the *Hermione,* in the absence of more compelling evidence, did not confirm their participation in the mutiny. Nonetheless, the court ordered Brigstock remanded to custody to answer the charge of murder.[29]

It was left to Pickering to inform Robert Liston of the acquittals. In a letter of April 13, he explained that the evidence had failed to prove that "they had any agency in the horrible deed, excepting Brigstock, against whom it is said the proof is strong." The secretary of state also reported the attorney general's opinion that Article 27 of the British Treaty did not extend to the open sea. With Evans and Williams already discharged, Brigstock would again face trial in a U.S. court. Equally disheartening from Liston's perspective, Pickering wrote of the seaman, "He is a citizen of the United States whose friends live in New York, and probably he was impressed on board the *Hermione*."[30]

John Wesley Jarvis,
Samuel Chase, *n.d.*

But the letter was never delivered. "The original remains in the office," Pickering noted in the margin. The explanation for his reluctance is not hard to find. Almost certainly, Pickering did not wish to put the United States on record endorsing Lee's narrow interpretation of the British Treaty. Notified informally, Liston wrote Lord Grenville in early June, "[President Adams] has been embarrassed by the contrary opinion of the Attorney General, which goes to a direct disapprobation of the surrender."[31]

No less curious was a letter written by Brigstock on April 23 from the New Brunswick jail. "Loaded with Irons," he addressed the note to Edward Livingston, a congressman from New York City, while the House was meeting in nearby Philadelphia. Probably Livingston was the seaman's representative. More important, in 1796 he had spearheaded passage of an act for the "Relief and Protection of American Seamen" from British impressment; and the following year, he had chaired a committee to investigate changes that the law had implemented in the distribution of protection certificates to mariners. Sailors, Livingston declared in Congress, were "a very important and meritorious class of men, whose value seemed to be overlooked, and whose dearest rights were either shamefully neglected, or ignominiously surrendered."[32]

Letter from William Brigstock to Edward Livingston, April 23, 1798. "Sir I am in Brunswick Gaol at this Present Time Loaded with Irons By being So Unfortunate as To belong to His Majesties Frigate the Hermione.*"*

For all of this and more, Brigstock could not have selected a more fitting champion. Born in 1764 at Clermont, situated south of Albany in Columbia County, the youngest of eleven children, Livingston belonged to one of the state's most prominent landed families. Educated at the College of New Jersey (now Princeton University), he married and practiced law in New York City before entering politics. Elected to the House in 1794, he was a true-blue Republican, a turncoat to his class, with no interest in warming a backbench. If not handsome, his prominent features—a sharp

Anonymous, Edward Livingston, *nineteenth century*

nose framed by large eyes, topped by a crop of unruly black hair—left an indelible impression. It was said that Edward lived "like a nabob" but talked "like a Jacobin." And talk he did, beginning in 1796 in vociferously opposing both British impressment and funds for the British Treaty. As a freshman congressman, he surprised elder members of his party by calling on the president to supply documents pertinent to the treaty, a request that George Washington refused and the *Aurora* in Philadelphia applauded. By the following year, Livingston had earned the antipathy of Federalists as well as a reputation for giving three-hour speeches. But "Beau Ned" was no demagogue. During his tour of the United States, the Duke de La Rochefoucault Liancourt deemed him "one of the most enlightened and eloquent members of the opposition party in congress."[33]

In his letter, Brigstock identified himself as a native of New York who had been "press'd" aboard the *Success* in Kingston, Jamaica, before joining the *Hermione*. Referring to Evans and Williams, he stated, "I have had two of my shipmates tried and acquitted that is ready to appear in my behalf at any time what ever to convince the public of my innonency." His mother, he explained, who had arrived at the jail to lend comfort, urgently wanted to know "how to forward a Special Court"—by which he evidently meant a special court of oyer and terminer, a state court occasionally convened to try serious crimes. Whether Brigstock hoped to delay his May 1 trial in a federal court, perhaps in order to garner public support, is not known. Otherwise, there appears to have been little to distinguish one court from the other, apart from the judges. In both courts, guilt or innocence was to be determined by a jury, and murder in each qualified as a capital offense. On the other hand, Brigstock and his mother may not have known that benefit of clergy, a privilege in Anglo-American law dating to the Middle Ages that had previously allowed first-time offenders to escape the death penalty, had been abolished just two years earlier by the New Jersey Assembly, as it had already been in federal courts.[34]

Whether Livingston replied to Brigstock's appeal became moot when events took an unexpected turn. Without warning, the case unraveled. Following a delay in the trial, Pickering wrote the New Jersey district attorney on June 8 to request the court to discharge the prisoner by "special command" of the president. Liston had received news from Vice Admiral Parker a week earlier impeaching the credibility of Fanny Martin. Fresh evidence also confirmed that Simon Marcus, the first to be arrested, had indeed been discharged from the *Hermione* prior to the mutiny. More than that, Parker reported that Brigstock had incurred the wrath of leading mutineers for his refusal to join in the bloodshed. And as punishment, the seaman had been forced to swab the decks. For all the disappointing news, Liston, in writing Lord Grenville, tried to make a virtue of necessity. "By this means," he stated, "an innocent man will be released from unmerited punishment, and we shall avoid the estab-lishment by precedent of an unfavourable interpretation of the Article [27] in question." Yet another dividend, Liston explained, accrued to President Adams. In words reminiscent of Pickering's unsent letter, he reported that Brigstock's conviction "would have been very unpopular with a large portion of the publick; for Brigstock is a American born, has a family at New York, and was pressed on board Captain Pigot's ship, who," he related with unsparing candor, "is supposed here to have treated his ship's company with unusual severity." Left unsaid, though surely known by Liston, was that the state of New York, as in the presi-dential election of 1796, would be critical to Adams's chances for reelec-tion in the coming year. The *New-Jersey Journal*, in reporting Brigstock's release from jail, wrote of "his numerous and respectable connexions now living in the city of New York."[35]

Under the circumstances, a fortuitous outcome all around.

STUNG BY THE EMBARRASSMENT TO Britain, the *Gazette of the United States,* the prominent Federalist newspaper in Philadelphia, blamed Brigstock's botched prosecution on the testimony of Widow Martin—"an infamous and abandoned woman"—all the while ignoring more perplexing problems threatening British attempts to extradite members of the *Hermione*'s crew. Plainly, Attorney General Lee could not be relied upon to expedite future requests when, as seemed likely, they again arose. Pickering, notwithstanding his hostility to impressment, remained London's most loyal ally in the administration. This was all the more important given the uncertainty of President Adams's reading of Article 27. One matter, at a minimum, was indubitably clear. American jurors, if permitted during a trial to render judgment, would invariably acquit seamen whom they viewed as victims of British oppression, whether or not they were U.S. citizens.[36]

Scarcely had the three Trenton prisoners regained their freedom when another fugitive was chanced upon. It was not in New Jersey but in Virginia that British persistence paid off. That August, the American frigate *Constellation,* the first U.S. naval vessel to put to sea, lay moored near the port of Norfolk after her maiden voyage. The captain, Thomas Truxton, a highly respected naval officer during the Revolutionary War, read aloud to his crew descriptions received from Jamaica of the mutiny's ringleaders. Not long afterward, an officer noticed a seaman by the name of Hugh Williamson "in a tremor." On being questioned, he quickly gave up his real name, John Watson, and admitted to having been a quarter gunner on the *Hermione.* Having learned that a shipmate on the *Constellation* was going to inform on him for reward money, Watson confessed so that "his blood might not be sold by one of his companions." It was later said at his court-martial that in the days following the mutiny, he was "always stupid with liquor." From La Guaira, he had made his way to Curaçao and then to Norfolk, whose vessels carried on a flourishing trade in provisions, tobacco, and timber to the Caribbean. Once in port, Watson had signed aboard the *Constellation*.[37]

Norfolk lay on the right bank of the Elizabeth River just south of its juncture with the James and the Chesapeake Bay. On August 20, Watson was escorted ashore under the supervision of the British consul, Colonel John Hamilton, a North Carolinian who had served as a Loyalist officer during the Revolution. Once labeled a "blockhead" by General Charles Cornwallis, Hamilton, short and stout, was a controversial figure in the politically polarized port. He was widely despised by local Republicans, though embraced by British merchants and naval officers as well as by former Loyalists. (While visiting Norfolk in late 1797, Liston and his wife resided at Hamilton's home at 118 Main Street, where, according to Henrietta, "all is kindness, ease & cheerfulness.") During the Revolution, much of the town had been burnt to the ground due to the torching of Loyalist homes and British naval bombardments. In later years, the community rebounded to become the state's busiest port, home to some eighty deepwater ships. But it also fell prey in the summer to yellow fever, and the rebuilt town ranked among Virginia's ugliest, suffering from unpaved streets (either dusty or muddy depending on the weather), makeshift houses, and the noxious smell of open sewage ditches best crossed on wooden planks. Wharves and warehouses crowded the riverfront. Surrounded by mosquito-infested swamps filled with brushwood and pine trees, Norfolk contained a population of three thousand. Qualified magistrates were notoriously scarce, and the jails "small and ill conducted," according to a visitor in 1797.[38]

It was a borough magistrate, Dr. John K. Read, who saw to Watson's confinement. After questioning the "scoundrel" in his shop, Read ordered him sent to jail under British custody. By then a crowd, from curiosity, had assembled outdoors. On leaving the shop, Watson, according to an eyewitness, "declared that he was an American impressed on board the *Hermione,* and that if the thing was to do over again, he would act in the same manner rather than be confined on board a British vessel."[39]

Informed of Watson's incarceration pending transport to Jamaica, Liston notified neither Secretary Pickering nor the Republican governor of Virginia, James Wood, who was less than one hundred miles distant in Richmond, the state capital. Never mind that neither Read nor the jailer possessed authority to surrender Watson. Jailhouse procedures were indeed lax. Questioned more than a year later, the keeper John Brannon recalled that he had been seriously ill at the time of Watson's detention, whose crime he "never knew." "To officiate" during his absence, he had "procured an English gentleman," who happened to room near the jail. Of the prisoner, the keeper never learned "what became of him, or who committed him." And though he later searched the jail's files for a warrant of commitment, "it could not be found."[40]

5

United States v. Nathan Robbins

FOR MORE THAN A CENTURY, the Caribbean islands helped to shape the destiny of the renowned Carolina lowcountry. The undulating currents of West Indian life flowed northward, not unlike the mighty Gulf Stream, toward the city of Charleston, a flourishing port on the outer rim of the greater Caribbean. Lying on an isthmus between the Santee and Cooper Rivers, linking the hinterland to the coast, Charleston was blessed with a protected deepwater harbor. Dominated by slave-owning planters from Barbados, the settlement of "Charles Town," from its founding in the 1670s at Oyster Point to its emergence as the richest city on the Atlantic Seaboard, remained closely connected to the changing fortunes of its island neighbors. By dint of wars, migration, and commerce, not to mention the impact of earthquakes and tropical storms, the Caribbean played a vital role in the city's shifting fortunes.[1]

The aftershocks felt in Charleston from the mutiny aboard the *Hermione* unfolded over many months, especially in the fractious arena of popular politics, climaxing finally in the selection of presidential electors during the election of 1800. No incident, however, was more consequential than the arrival of an American schooner out of Santo Domingo on February 1, 1799. It had been six months since the apprehension of John Watson in Norfolk. Among the crew of the *Tanner's Delight* was an illiterate eighteen-year-old eager to locate a magistrate, the British consul, or both. William Portlock had a story to peddle.[2]

According to an affidavit that young Portlock swore on February 20, it

Thomas Mellish, A View of Charleston, South Carolina,
ca. eighteenth century

was during Christmas night, on board the *Tanner's Delight* in the harbor
of Santo Domingo, that he overheard a conversation between a handful of "French privateersmen" and a shipmate who went by the name
of Nathan Robbins. In appearance, described Portlock, Robbins was
"a tall man, middle size, had long black hair, dark complection, with a
scar on one of his lips." During the exchange, he claimed to have been a
"boatswain's mate of his Britannic Majesty's frigate *Hermione,* when she
was carried into the port Cavilla [Puerto Cabello]." Also incriminating,
"sometimes when he was drunk," Portlock continued, Robbins "would
mention the name of the *Hermione,* and say, bad luck to her" as he
clenched his fist. (Left unsaid by Portlock was the likelihood that Robbins was in drink at the time of his conversation with the privateers.)[3]

Nathan, or more commonly Jonathan, Robbins would not have been
the first sailor to spin yarns to impress fellow tars, even tales of a mutiny.
That misstep had landed Simon Marcus behind bars, as it did briefly a
London seaman, James Brown, who in a state of intoxication bragged
of having belonged to the *Hermione's* crew. Notwithstanding the under-

standable hubbub, the mayor of London, armed with testimony from the ship's former steward, concluded that Brown had embellished his service aboard a prior ship commanded by Hugh Pigot. Two months later, after repeating his confected claim in Portsmouth, Brown was again arrested.[4]

Almost immediately, Robbins, at twenty-seven years of age, found himself in a Charleston jail at the request of Benjamin Moodie, the city's British consul. Invoking Article 27 of the British Treaty, Moodie urged the suspect's extradition to stand trial in Jamaica. Despite the legal outcome in New Jersey months earlier, British hopes ran high. Such was the confidence of Vice Admiral Parker, on receiving word in Port Royal, that a cutter departed in March to collect the prisoner. When the *Sprightly* under the command of Lieutenant Robert Jump dropped anchor in Charleston harbor ten days later, among those to disembark was a young naval lieutenant, John Forbes, who had served on the *Hermione* as a midshipman. To his good fortune, he had been transferred to the *Diligence* just three weeks before the mutiny. Robbins, the lieutenant declared after visiting the Charleston jail, was none other than Thomas Nash, the notorious Irish ringleader who'd had a direct hand in the murders of both Captain Pigot and Lieutenant Foreshaw. Nash, whose apprehension was a pressing priority for the Admiralty, had last been seen a year earlier aboard a schooner leaving Puerto Cabello. Forbes, however, could not swear to Nash's actions during the mutiny, let alone to the offense of murder that would facilitate his extradition by virtue of the treaty. His knowledge was secondhand, the product of having read court-martial transcripts. Moreover, due to the passage of nearly two years, and given the size of the ship's company, how could Forbes be certain that Jonathan Robbins was, in fact, Thomas Nash?[5]

Charleston was not Norfolk, and whatever his failings the federal district judge, Thomas Bee, was not for hire. A wealthy planter, a member of the American Philosophical Society, and a former delegate to the Continental Congress, Bee had been a "furious Liberty Boy" in the years approaching independence. Appointed by George Washington in 1790 to the federal district court in Charleston, he was mentioned for a Supreme Court appointment in 1791. In late 1795, his name surfaced as a potential secretary of state until Alexander Hamilton, yet a close confidant of the president, informed Washington, "I do not know Judge Bee. I have barely thought of him." A staunch Federalist, Bee, however, was no zealot; and by temperament, despite his radical youth, he was a cautious jurist not known for voicing bold opinions from the bench.[6]

So it was not surprising, on being approached by the consul Moodie, that the judge declined to grant his request to surrender Robbins. In attendance during their meeting was the U.S. district attorney for Charleston, Thomas Parker. Robbins, after all, promised to be a "new case," the first requiring extradition by virtue of the British Treaty. Further, both Bee and Parker, as Moodie shortly wrote Sir Hyde Parker, were "under an opinion that the 27th Article of the Treaty does not contemplate the case of the prisoner, in as much as it extends only to persons charged with forgery or murder committed 'within the jurisdiction' of either of the contracting parties." Their understanding, as such, was identical to Attorney General Lee's opinion in regard to William Brigstock *et al.* in New Jersey. Britain's jurisdiction did not extend to the open sea. Even so, there remained grounds for hope. Bee and the U.S. district attorney recommended "an application to the Executive of the United States." Although the *Sprightly* returned to Kingston empty-handed—except for a French schooner seized en route—Robbins, related the consul, would remain in jail, if necessary, until October.[7]

From his cabin aboard the *Queen,* Parker, more resolute than ever, wrote Secretary Evan Nepean in London. Although "the lawyer's [*sic*] opinion went against this villain being given up," Parker intended to send the *Sprightly* back to Charleston to "again claim Nash." As a precaution, he had alerted Minister Liston in Philadelphia of his "fear there would be difficulties." More to the point, Parker requested Liston to "use his interest with the Executive Government to remove them." In order to speed communications, an armed vessel was designated to carry dispatches back and forth to the mainland.[8]

Early in May, Liston informed Pickering of Judge Bee's opposition to the prisoner's surrender. The judge, he reported vaguely, had "not deemed it proper" to deliver him up. A formal letter followed, in which Liston elaborated that Bee and the district attorney "were of the opinion that he could not with propriety be delivered up without a previous requisition on my part made to the Executive Government of the United

States." Omitted from Liston's letter was any reference to the real reason for their reluctance to accommodate Britain's request, their concern over the applicability of Article 27. By eighteenth-century standards, this degree of diplomatic deceit was not uncommon, but neither was it the rule. "May I therefore request, Sir," continued Liston, "that you will be pleased to lay this matter before the President and procure his orders that the said Thomas Nash be delivered up to justice." Fortunately for Liston, neither Bee nor Thomas Parker appears to have written to Pickering. Not that candor would have mattered much, aside from forcing the secretary's hand. Would Pickering, in the end, have disregarded the misgivings of a federal judge and a district attorney? An awkward course, but one that he almost certainly would have taken. There is every reason to believe that he supported Britain's interpretation of Article 27 and, as a consequence, Jonathan Robbins's extradition. Indeed, in sharp contrast to the case of the three Trenton defendants, Pickering did not share Liston's request with Attorney General Lee, much less solicit his opinion.[9]

Instead, Pickering wrote to President Adams, who since mid-March had taken up residence at Peacefield, his beloved farm, with its "grass and blossoms and corn," in Quincy, Massachusetts, as was his habit upon Congress's adjournment. Bucolic Quincy was infinitely more to his liking than Philadelphia, above all during the summer months, when yellow fever posed a threat; the epidemic of 1793 had claimed upward of five thousand lives. Still, friends and political allies fretted that ambitious cabinet officials in the capital might exploit Adams's absence for their own ends. Boston, after all, lay three hundred miles, more than a week's travel, from Philadelphia, even in a coach managing eighteen hours a day. In late April 1799, the president's confidant Uriah Forrest warned, "The public sentiment is very much against your being so much away from the seat of government. . . . The people elected you to administer the government. They did not elect your officers." Another loyalist remonstrated to Rufus King in London that the president was governing "by fits and starts—without the advice of his friends around him—nay without even consulting them."[10]

In his letter of May fifteenth, Pickering told Adams, "Mr. Liston informs me, that on information rec'd by Admiral Sir Hyde Parker, of one of the mutineers and murderers of the officers of the British frigate *Hermione* being at Charleston So. Carolina. The Admiral sent thither a vessel on purpose to receive and carry the culprit to the fleet to be tried: but that the district judge had not deemed it proper to deliver him up." Why Bee had thought it improper went unmentioned. Pickering then turned to the prior case in New Jersey in which the administration had followed Attorney General Lee's advice against extradition. "The only legal question," wrote Pickering,

Gilbert Stuart, John Adams, *1800–1815*

"was whether an offence committed on board a publick ship of war on the high seas was 'committed within the jurisdiction' of the party demanding the offender on a just construction of the 27th article of the treaty. Upon a further consideration of the subject, I am inclined to answer in the affirmative."[11]

The secretary of state offered two reasons for his opinion, neither of which cited legal precedents or texts apart from the treaty itself. The first was pragmatic. "I suppose the offence committed on board the *Hermione* to have been a most atrocious act of <u>piracy</u> accompanied with <u>murder</u>; that all nations having jurisdiction in this case, if the pirates be found within their dominions, any of them may try and punish them; but wanting the full evidence for that purpose, it would seem reasonable and essential to the due administration of justice that the culprits be delivered up to the country to which they belong [according, that is, to the nationality of the vessel]."[12]

In addition, he repeated Britain's position that "on the high seas, her officers have and exercise a particular jurisdiction on board of their own ships," a view that directly contradicted Lee's reading of international law and, for that matter, the initial inclinations of Judge Bee and District Attorney Parker, all of which went unmentioned. On what basis Pickering reached his conclusion, he did not say. Nor did he address whether Robbins was an American citizen and, perhaps, the victim of a British press-gang, which for Pickering was irrelevant anyway according to Article 27 of the British Treaty. "I respectfully submit my opinion," the secretary concluded, "that the Judge of the District of South Carolina should be directed to deliver up the offender."[13]

An ardent Federalist, Pickering believed deeply in the prerogatives of the executive branch, particularly in foreign policy. He had also become, by then, a fervent anglophile, though he was not quite, as some claimed, Liston's "bosom friend." With party tensions rising, he remained heavily invested, politically and emotionally, in the success of the British Treaty. The implementation of Article 27 had assumed symbolic significance for both the Adams administration and Great Britain. Equally important, Pickering recognized the urgency that the British attached to apprehending renegade mutineers, not least the murderous Thomas Nash.[14]

Pickering's letter reached Adams in less than a week. Replying the next day, May 21, the president does not appear to have been unduly burdened or distracted, that same day writing just one other letter, to the secretary of the navy. Nevertheless, Abigail was still on the mend after having been bedridden with "melancholy," insomnia, and fever; an unusually torrid spell of weather in May had nearly provoked a relapse. Moreover, Adams was cut off from legal and political advice from trusted advisers like Lee. Pickering was a poor choice for either, having briefly served as a country lawyer and never having held elective office above the level of delegate to the Massachusetts General Court. "I have no doubt," Adams stated straightaway, "that an offense, committed on board a public ship of war, on the high seas, is committed within the jurisdiction of the nation to whom the ship belongs. How far the President of the United States would be justifiable in directing the judge to deliver up the offender is not clear." Even so, in one of the most fateful decisions of his presidency, he concluded, "*I have no objection to advise and request him to do it* [my italics]."[15]

Adams did not inquire about Robbins's citizenship or, equally surprising, the origins of his naval service. For one who, thirty years earlier, had been eager to defend the right of an Irish seaman off the coast of Massachusetts to kill the commander of a British press-gang, it was a curious oversight. To be sure, Adams, in arguing the case of *Rex v. Corbet*, had intended to invoke a law prohibiting conscription in the

American colonies. But he was under no illusions about the evils of impressment, either in 1769 or afterward. In 1787, as the U.S. minister to Britain, he had protested to London the "practice, which has been all too common, of impressing American citizens, and especially with the aggravating circumstances of going on board American vessels, which ought to be protected by the flag of their sovereign." Why, then, did Adams, after little apparent reflection, consent to Pickering's request without inquiring about Robbins's identity? Among other reasons, perhaps like his secretary, the president was anxious to flex the executive's authority in foreign affairs, with the added dividend of executing a treaty provision that had suddenly grown very dear to the British. At the time, goodwill between the two countries was in short supply. Besides the thorny issue of impressment, negotiations had deteriorated over competing compensation claims arising from the American Revolution, and Adams had abruptly chosen the path of peace rather than escalate America's quasi-naval war with France, which had broken out in July 1798 after French emissaries, in the XYZ debacle, had endeavored to extort not only money from a United States delegation in Paris but also an apology in the wake of America's treaty with Britain. But in mid-February 1799, the president announced to Congress, to the shock and vexation of orthodox Federalists like Pickering, the nomination of a minister plenipotentiary to France in order to negotiate a new treaty. Outraged, Congressman Robert Goodloe Harper of South Carolina privately expressed the wish that Adams might break his neck during the arduous trip to Quincy. Whatever Adams's misgivings, Robbins must have seemed like a minor price to pay to help regain the trust of both Britain and recalcitrant members of his own party.[16]

On June 3, around the start of hurricane season in Charleston, Pickering sent a letter to Judge Bee. Noting that the president considered the offenses of piracy and murder alleged against "Thomas Nash" to have been committed within British jurisdiction, Pickering reported that Adams had instructed him to communicate "his advice and request that Thomas Nash may be delivered up" to the British—"provided such evidence of his criminality be produced, as by the laws of the U. States or of S. Carolina would justify his apprehension and commitment for trial, as if the offence had been committed within the jurisdiction of the U.

States." That judgment would now be left to Bee and the federal district court of South Carolina. By referring to Jonathan Robbins as "Thomas Nash," Pickering, wittingly or not, had, of course, revealed to the judge his own predilection.[17]

Sir Hyde Parker was elated by the news. "The executive government," he notified the Admiralty, "has determined to give up Thomas Nash." Overlooking the need to establish probable cause, Parker reported, "I have therefore again sent the *Sprightly* Cutter to Charleston to receive that atrocious villain."[18]

OWING TO YELLOW FEVER and debilitating heat as well as to the threat of tropical storms, summers in Charleston were punishing. Experiencing 101 degrees Fahrenheit in the shade, the Englishman John Davis deemed it one of the "hottest places on earth," with the sun's rays only partially blocked by the elegant homes lining the city's narrow streets. Another visitor deplored the stench that emanated from cemeteries and animal carcasses besieged by turkey buzzards. Mosquitoes were everywhere. Wealthy planters customarily fled the city until cooling temperatures announced the arrival of fall. Only then did Charleston reclaim its reputation for southern elegance: balls, gaming, dinner parties—all sustained by transatlantic trade and immense fortunes generated by the bone-crushing labor of lowcountry slaves. "If festive and polite society is your object," a prominent planter counseled an Irish friend, "perhaps Charlestown affords as much of both as any part of the continent."[19]

Beginning in 1792, the federal district court convened on the second floor of a large Palladian building at the central intersection of Broad and Meeting Streets. The newly renovated Charleston County Courthouse had been South Carolina's capitol before being gutted by fire in 1788. Constructed of brick plastered with stucco, it featured a grand staircase that ascended from the ground-floor lobby to two courtrooms on the second of three floors. Judge Bee's courtroom, with its yellow walls, measured nearly seventeen feet from floor to ceiling, crowned by a twelve-inch cornice. The neoclassical windows in the front initially looked down upon a marble statue of the English statesman William Pitt, "The Great Commoner," a strong supporter of American griev-

Charles Fraser, A Scene in the Theatre—Charleston, *ca. 1792.*
The intersection of Broad and Market Streets, with a statue of
William Pitt the Elder standing between the Charleston County
Courthouse and Saint Michael's Church.

ances before the Revolution. Pitt's figure was dressed in a toga, with one
hand holding the Magna Carta. Erected in 1770, the statue was finally
removed from the intersection as a public nuisance in 1794, having been
damaged during the British siege of Charleston in 1780.[20]

On the first of July, Bee ordered that "Thomas Nash" be brought
to court on a writ of habeas corpus from the cell in which he had languished since February. Owing to "strong evidence of his criminality,"
he was to be immediately delivered to the British pursuant to Article 27
of the British Treaty, as the judge recounted later that day in a letter to
Secretary Pickering. Ordinarily, that would have been the end of Jonathan Robbins; but the *Sprightly*'s return voyage was prolonged when
Parker ordered Lieutenant Jump first to collect dispatches from a British
general last thought to be in "Gonaives, Port-au-Prince, or any other
port in St. Domingo." With the cutter still en route to Charleston, Bee
approved Consul Moodie's request that the prisoner temporarily remain
in the city jail.[21]

The delay proved costly. Earlier that May a stranger had paid Robbins
a visit. Abraham Sasportas was a grand juryman instructed to report on
the jail's condition. Until 1793, he had served as a mercantile agent for

the French government. Seeing Robbins in chains, he asked the reason for his imprisonment, only to learn that the seaman professed to be an American citizen who'd been impressed by the British navy. Shown a "protection" attesting to his citizenship, Sasportas retained an attorney, Colonel Alexander Moultrie, on Robbins's behalf. But before the two had even met, Moultrie abruptly resigned. As he later related, "When I was first called on in Robbins's case, I considered it generally; and gave my opinion that I thought such was the prevailing influence of opinions and sentiments of those in power, that every effort would be in vain. . . . I gave it but a short consideration, and soon determined, and thought no more of it."[22]

By Tuesday morning, July 23, when Judge Bee again convened court to surrender the prisoner to the British consul on a writ of habeas corpus, Robbins had a new attorney to fight his extradition. An honors graduate of the College of New Jersey in 1790, William Johnson had been Speaker of the South Carolina House before being named to the Court of Common Pleas in 1798. That did not keep him from representing Robbins, at least long enough to request a one-day adjournment, having "only a few minutes engaged as council with the prisoner." So that Johnson might be able "to examine into the nature of his case," Bee instead granted a two-day delay.[23]

It was all the more surprising, then, that on Thursday, Moultrie, not Johnson, suddenly appeared on Robbins's behalf. Along with a new attorney, Robbins had gained a fresh defense. In recent days, Moultrie later claimed, he had learned that Robbins was an American citizen, writing, "I was struck and alarmed that I had deserted him." Because Moultrie had never met, much less conversed or corresponded, with his former client, Robbins had to be singled out when court convened on the twenty-third. Whatever ensued during their brief conversation led to the resignation of Johnson, a future Supreme Court justice, and Moultrie's reappointment. Joining him at the last minute was Samuel Ker, an attorney from the upland town of Newberry.[24]

At first glance Moultrie, at forty-nine years of age, was a promising choice. The younger brother of William, a Revolutionary War general who later served as governor of South Carolina (1785–1787, 1792–1794), Alexander had received his legal training in England. He, too, was a veteran of the war as well as the state's first attorney general, from 1776 until 1792. But the following year saw him impeached and convicted for embezzling public funds to invest in land speculation. He was also prohibited from serving in public office for seven years. Nevertheless, in addition to his extensive legal experience, he was a fervid Republican well equipped to argue the constitutional implications of Robbins's plight. For Moultrie, whose banishment from office would shortly expire, the politically charged case afforded an opportunity for redemption.[25]

Equally unexpected was an affidavit that the defense introduced in court. That morning, Robbins had declared himself a native of Connecticut, born in the western town of Danbury. Some two years earlier, according to the statement, he had been a mariner on the brig *Betsey* out of New York, under the command of a Captain White, bound for Saint Nicholas Mole. But at sea, Robbins was reportedly pressed aboard the British frigate *Hermione,* commanded by Captain Philip Wilkinson. Present during the mutiny, he denied any hand in the bloodletting. In lieu of other physical evidence (some American seamen, hoping to avoid impressment, bore tattoos of eagles and American flags), Moultrie introduced the protection document shown Sasportas in May. Signed on a printed form by John Keese, a New York City justice and notary public, on May 25, 1795, it affirmed that "Jonathan Robbins, mariner," five feet six inches in height, aged about twenty-three years, was a Connecticut native and a citizen of the United States. At least those were the facts to which Robbins had reputedly sworn, with God as his witness. Insofar as he was "liable to be called in the service of his country," the certificate stated that he was "to be respected accordingly, at all times by sea and land." Lending credence to both documents, Robbins's two signatures matched. And so began, with a flourish, the case of *United States v. Nathan Robbins alias Nash* on a blistering day in late July.[26]

Samuel Ker rose first from his chair to address the bench. At the crux of the case, which, he stated, embraced "great constitutional principles," was whether an American citizen should "be tried by his country or be delivered up to a foreign tribunal." The prisoner's protection and affidavit, Ker insisted, were proof of his impressment. Then, notwithstanding Robbins's denial of having mutinied, Ker addressed his client's right of resistance, fearing perhaps incriminating evidence from the prosecution.

Having been forcibly conscripted, Robbins, he stated, enjoyed a natural right of self-defense according to *The Law of Nations,* a learned treatise on international jurisprudence by Vattel. The defendant was "warranted by the most sacred rights of nature, and the laws of nations, to have recourse to violence in the recovery of that liberty, of which he had been unjustly and lawfully deprived." Even had his conduct been criminal, Ker reasoned, America shared concurrent jurisdiction on the open sea with other countries, and no citizen within the jurisdiction of the United States could be deprived of his constitutional right to a jury trial attended by fellow citizens versed in the country's political principles.[27]

Moultrie, joining in Robbins's defense, also began on a lofty plane, speaking at length on the primacy of the Constitution, the "very foundation of our government and guardian of our liberty." Treaties, by contrast, being fashioned by legislatures, were "derivative" and, as such, wholly subordinate to "the supreme code of the law of the land." In time, Moultrie, like Ker, expanded upon the issue of concurrent jurisdiction at sea, followed by the question of Robbins's citizenship. The certificate from New York plainly was genuine, he asserted. Moultrie invited skeptics to consult crew lists for the *Betsey* in the New York City Custom House. By contrast, the affidavits of Portlock and Forbes were "vague, uncertain, and ascertained no specific charge against the defendant." They "amounted to nothing more than mere suspicion." He also contested the chief executive's interference in a matter reserved for the courts. The president, in advising the defendant's surrender, "had no right to control this court."[28]

Representing the British government, the attorney John Ward dismissed the issue of constitutionality, because Congress had already approved the British Treaty negotiated by the executive branch. Moreover, lest the treaty deprive any citizen of his right to a jury trial, Ward voiced the bold principle that a "treaty made by the powers pointed out for the purpose in the constitution, is co-ordinate with the constitution itself, and even paramount to it." The court, he continued, "had only to consider whether the prisoner is, or is not, comprehended in the meaning of the 27th article of the treaty." That Britain enjoyed jurisdiction aboard its ships at sea, he insisted, was clear. Hence an infant born on a British vessel would automatically be deemed a British subject. Besides, asserted Ward before returning to his seat, "If the prisoner was really the American he pretended to be, he would have been able, before this time, to have made it appear more clearly." His certificate of protection, by itself, was insufficient.[29]

It was a telling argument. Why had Robbins not divulged his citizenship sooner? To a degree, the defense had anticipated Ward's point. Ker had already suggested that Robbins, "an obscure character," was "as destitute of friends as if he were on the opposite side of the globe." Whether Robbins himself thought it fruitless to enlist witnesses or placed excessive faith in his certificate, sworn under oath, is unclear. At the least, he had informed Abraham Sasportas of his citizenship two months earlier. To little effect, Ker in his opening remarks had endeavored to shift the burden of proof to the prosecution, which had a duty to demonstrate "by the ship's articles, or by any other legal testimony," that Robbins had "entered voluntarily into their service."[30]

Adjourning for the afternoon, the court reconvened the following day at 1 p.m. Bee, in delivering his judgment, lost no time in deriding the defense's principal points as "warm and pathetic appeals to the passions" made "on some of the old grounds of opposition to the [British] treaty." This, he reminded the defense, had been ratified according to the provisions of the Constitution. On the question of jurisdiction, on the constitutionality of the treaty, on the right to a jury trial in the United States—indeed, on every matter—Bee ruled firmly in favor of the prosecution, utterly deaf to the defense's entreaties. Jury trials, he asserted, were suspended in "the land and sea service, or even in the militia when in actual service, in time of war or public danger." They were not an inviolable right. "It is remarkable," he chided the defense, "that in the midst of all the warmth against the treaty, at its first publication, the 27th article was one of the few that was never excepted to." He further declared that it made no difference to the prisoner's extradition "whether the offense" was "committed by a citizen or another person." Were Robbins an American, he would still be remanded on the charge of murder to British custody, despite allegations of having been impressed. Even so, Bee could not resist ridiculing Robbins's claim to citizenship after having lain "in jail here five or six months." "I do therefore order and command the marshal," the judge declared, "to deliver the body of the said Nathan Robbins, alias Thomas Nash, to the British consul." Almost immediately, upon the court's adjournment, Robbins was placed in irons and handed over by constables to a small detachment of federal troops. Stationed for the duration of the hearing outside the courthouse, they in turn surrendered the prisoner to Lieutenant Jump. "A trial of vast magnitude," a newspaper declared afterward.[31]

No shortage of blunders had marred Robbins's defense, beginning with Moultrie's erratic behavior, not the least of which was failing to meet with the defendant or to ask for a continuance with just two days to prepare his case. Why did he not cite the failed Brigstock prosecution in New Jersey, assuming that he was aware of it? Most damning, none of the defense attorneys—Moultrie, Johnson, or Ker—bothered to verify whether their client was an American as his certificate indicated. That alone was reason enough to request a delay in order to investigate Robbins's purported upbringing in Danbury and to visit the New York Custom House to examine shipping records for the *Betsey*. Perhaps even to locate John Keese, prominent at one point in both the antislavery movement and in a New York City charitable society assisting immigrants. At the time of the trial, he maintained a law office in lower Manhattan on Water Street, opposite the well-known Tontine Coffee House. Bee's ruling to the contrary, confirmation of Robbins's citizenship would have been difficult for the court to ignore, as it would have been for President Adams. Instead, much of the defense's argument, despite occasional bursts of eloquence from Moultrie and Ker, was contradictory—denying Robbins's participation in the mutiny, yet claiming that he enjoyed the right of self-defense as an impressed seaman. The *Philadelphia Gazette* reported that Moultrie and Ker had "exerted themselves in his behalf with great skill, much eloquence, and an abundant variation of reasoning"; whereas the *New Hampshire Gazette* added that the "arguments on both sides" had been "lengthy and ingenious."[32]

Still, most of the blame belonged to Bee. The judge's initial reservations regarding British jurisdiction vanished by the wayside once Adams and Pickering joined the fray. Instead, in this instance and in others, he toed the Federalist line. Notwithstanding his contempt for Robbins's notarized protection from New York (even if it were legitimate evidence, it would "prove little or nothing"), he attached surprising weight to the words of a British lieutenant unable to tie the defendant to a single act of violence aboard the *Hermione,* much less the commission of murder. A firm believer in the authority of the government, Bee possessed an innate skepticism regarding the popular will, including the wisdom of juries. Of his demeanor, a fellow delegate to the Continental Congress wrote in 1781 that he had "a cruid restive temper, not eloquent but of a harsh & disagreeable dilivery; consiquential in his deportment and conceited in his notions—very desirous of order in the House, but most apt to transgress it himself."[33]

THE MORNING OF SATURDAY, JULY 27, found Robbins, fettered in shackles, at sea aboard the *Sprightly* as the city of Charleston slowly receded from sight. By the time of his arrival at Port Royal two weeks later, he had long since assumed, in the eyes of the Royal Navy, the infamous identity of the Irish mutineer Thomas Nash. His court-martial got under way on the morning of Thursday, August 15. A gun sounded as the Union Jack was run up the mainmast of the *Hannibal,* a seventy-four-gun ship under the command of Edward Tyrrell Smith, who presided over a board composed of the commanding officers of six other vessels, each selected by Sir Hyde Parker. In full-dress uniform, they sat at a long table on either side of Smith. One, Captain Man Dobson, had participated in all eight of the courts-martial held by then in Kingston harbor for crew members of the *Hermione.*[34]

Grounded in myriad conventions of English common law, naval courts-martial accorded defendants many of the prerogatives of due process typical of criminal trials, including rights against self-incrimination and double jeopardy. Drumhead justice this was not. The accused was deemed innocent until proven guilty, whereas imprecise or erroneous charges could result in a case's dismissal. Besides calling witnesses of their own, defendants enjoyed the right to question hostile witnesses, who were sworn to tell "the truth, the whole truth and nothing but the truth." Despite the logistical problems encountered by the navy, particularly during wartime, testimony was given viva voce. Only rarely were sworn affidavits admissible. Questions needed to be precise, neither leading nor open-ended, though parties enjoyed greater latitude during cross-examination. If sentenced to death, a defendant had the right to appeal, except in cases of mutiny.[35]

Still, courts-martial remained, in the end, tribunals subject to military exigencies and traditions. First and foremost, defendants were not tried by a jury of their peers but instead by a board of senior officers acting as both judges and jury, thereby preventing, in the view of the navy, acquittals arising from sympathetic shipmates. Nor did the accused possess the right to legal representation or the same opportunity as the prosecution to summon witnesses, especially if months, even years, had passed since the commission of a crime. The time and the location of a court-martial was the navy's choice, best suited to accommodate the prosecution's needs and convenience, not those of the defendant.[36]

From the outset, strict formality governed the choreography of a court-martial. Besides enhancing the majesty and strength of the law, as in civilian trials, this instilled greater respect for naval discipline. For this reason and for the appearance of fairness, proceedings occurred in the "*forenoon* in the most public part of the ship," the main deck. John Delafons, in his *Treatise on Naval Courts Martial* (1805), wrote of "that awe and dread which such a tribunal is calculated to impress on the minds of seamen, and by which they will continue to be influenced, so long as men are brought to trial on assured grounds; the punishment inflicted becoming a beacon to warn and deter others from pursuing the same course, and getting aground on the shoals of disobedience."[37]

In a strong, somber voice, the charges against "Jonathan or Nathan Robbins, alias Thomas Nash" were read aloud: desertion to the enemy, absconding with the HMS *Hermione,* delivering her up to the Spanish at La Guaira, and murder. Beside Robbins stood the provost marshal with a drawn sword.[38]

Close on the heels of the first witness, Lieutenant Jump, who briefly described the means by which he had conveyed Robbins to Jamaica, the tribunal heard from John Mason—the carpenter's mate aboard the *Hermione,* who in March 1798 at Saint Nicholas Mole had been the prosecution's star witness against four shipmates. After identifying the defendant as Thomas Nash, a member of the *Hermione*'s crew, Mason held fast to his previous testimony professing ignorance of the murderers other than to repeat scuttlebutt implicating Nash. More damaging was his rec-

*Court-Martial Proceedings of "Jonathan or Nathan Robbins,
alias Thomas Nash," August 15, 1799*

ollection that the accused, following the uprising, had been "esteemed an officer" [that is, a leader] by the ship's company. Robbins, desperate to sow doubt, asked whether Mason had saved his life after the mutineers overheard him discussing a plot to retake the ship. "I cannot recollect any thing of the kind," replied the carpenter's mate.[39]

More helpful to the prosecution was John Brown, who at another court-martial had, like Mason, turned King's evidence against former crew members. After certifying Nash's identity, Brown spoke of the initial, unsuccessful attempt to murder Lieutenant Foreshaw. "Heave the bugger overboard," Nash had reportedly shouted. Moreover, thought Brown, Nash had received a watch from among the officers' effects. Although Robbins repeated his earlier line of questioning, with no greater success, the prosecution up to this point had been less than overpowering in tying him to the murders of either Pigot or Foreshaw, the surest path to a death sentence.[40]

Left to testify was John Holford, Sr., the former cook whose Kingston acquittal in May 1798, it should be remembered, had outraged Sir Hyde Parker. At the time, Parker had railed to Secretary Evan Nepean that Holford was among those "implicated most indubitably" in the mutiny and, as such, deserved the death penalty. Now, in an odd turn of fate, the prosecution's charge of murder rested on Holford's testimony. Certainly, his was the most damning evidence. Asked by the court to relate what he knew "of the prisoner's taking any part of the mutiny and the murders committed on board the late Hermione," Holford recounted the early moments of the uprising. He then described Foreshaw's startling resurrection after being forced overboard. The cook's testimony was worth the wait.

> When I saw Foreshaw come in at the port,
> the blood was streaming down his face from his
> forehead. . . . He clapped his two hands
> together and said "Good God men, what have I
> done to harm you that I should be treated in
> this manner?" Some of the men made out that
> they would speak to the ship's company and
> endeavor to save his life. Just upon those words being

spoke, I saw Thomas Nash come running
down the ladder from the quarter deck.
He advanced toward Lt. Foreshaw immediately
and caught him by the right wrist, and said,
"You bugger Foreshaw. Are you not overboard
yet? Overboard you must go, and overboard you
shall go." . . . He led him to the lanyard
gangway ladder. . . . They got him upon the
gangway and immediately hove him overboard.[41]

And with that, the prosecution rested. As did the defendant, who
had neither witnesses nor evidence to produce. With the trial abruptly
adjourned, the board retired to deliberate. Saturday morning, the verdict
of guilty was read aloud, followed immediately by Robbins's sentence.
Oddly, the court still referred to "Jonathan or Nathan Robbins, alias
Thomas Nash." The prisoner was to "suffer death by being hung by
the neck until he is dead at the yard arm on such of his Majesty's ships

at the port as the Commander-in-Chief
shall think proper to direct. And his body
to be hung in chains." Placed in the custody of the provost marshal, Robbins's
detention was brief. On the back of the
verdict was the penned instruction "This
sentence to be carried into execution
Monday morning."[42]

Two days later, on a gray morning
amid strong breezes, crews in port bore
witness to the terror of British justice. To
the report of a lone bow gun, Robbins was
hauled up the fore yardarm of the frigate
Acasta—blindfolded and hands bound
behind his back—by members of the
crew. The haste with which they pulled
the rope governed whether he escaped
with a broken neck rather than endure a
slower death by strangulation. To confirm

Captain Kidd Hanging in
Chains, *n.d. suspended from
a gibbet beside the Thames,
following his execution in 1701*

the execution, the crew hoisted a yellow flag atop the mainmast. Not far away, on one of the small islands just beyond the natural breakwater forming Port Royal, stood more than a dozen weathered gibbets, each constructed of a wooden post at either end connected by a crossbar—a hideous spectacle for the crew of any vessel entering the harbor. As dusk thickened, Robbins's corpse joined the moldering remains of shipmates girdled in iron bands, their rusted hinges screeching in the breeze.[43]

6

Martyr to Liberty

EVEN FOR A MIDSUMMER MORNING, July 4, 1800, dawned unusually warm in the western Connecticut town of Danbury, the reputed birthplace of Jonathan Robbins. Of no known relation, Reverend Thomas Robbins was a recent graduate of Yale College. A schoolteacher as well as a minister at just twenty-three, he looked forward to a full day of celebration, highlighted by an afternoon parade honoring the anniversary of America's independence. Daylight, however, brought a shocking, if unfounded, report. "We had news of the death of Mr. Jefferson," Reverend Robbins scribbled in his diary. "It is to be hoped that it is true."[1]

Thomas Jefferson, the architect of the Declaration of Independence, had by then assumed, in Federalist minds, the persona of a radical atheist, a leveling democrat sworn to overthrowing—by Jacobin violence if necessary—all order, both divine and human. Nearly as sinister was the Republican image of John Adams, cast as a haughty monarchist whose despotic presidency, bound by the tentacles of British influence, had betrayed the cause of American liberty. Both men no doubt believed themselves victims, in Adams's description, of "the most envious malignity, the most base, vulgar, sordid, fish-woman scurrility, and the most palpable lies." Less than a decade after the inauguration of George Washington, these two friends from the Revolution had become standard bearers of opposing political camps, bitterly at odds over the scope and size of the federal government at home and, increasingly, the preservation of American honor abroad. Except for the Civil War, the years immediately preceding the tumultuous election of 1800—the "Revolution of 1800," as Jefferson would call it—were the most rancorous and divisive in the history of American politics. "Neither reason nor justice can be expected from either side," observed La Rochefoucauld, "and very seldom strict morality with respect to the means employed to serve the favourite cause; one cause alone appears good; every thing besides is deemed bad, nay criminal." From his vantage in Philadelphia, British Minister Robert Liston wrote toward the tag end of 1799, "The Country offers the spectacle of a perpetual struggle between two parties."[2]

Tensions still simmered over the financial program of Alexander Hamilton and the government's suppression of the Whiskey Rebellion; but for the remainder of the decade it was the relentless war between Britain and revolutionary France that profoundly shook the political landscape. News of the British Treaty, followed in the spring of 1795 by an angry ratification fight in the Senate, quickly spilled over into the streets. Up and down the Eastern Seaboard, from Savannah to Boston, riots erupted as copies of the treaty went up in smoke, to the glee of cheering throngs. Some in a crowd of hundreds reportedly pelted Hamilton with stones as he spoke in New York City, and there was even scattered talk of Washington's impeachment. Jefferson, his former secretary of state, thought the treaty "infamous," a devil's bargain. Any number of provisions were galling to Republicans, among them restrictions on American trade goods sent to the British West Indies, despite the promise to permit British imports into the United States. Differences relating to prewar debts and territorial boundaries were deferred to joint arbitration commissions. Among the worst grievances was the failure of John Jay's mission to secure Britain's pledge to respect U.S. neutrality by ceasing to impress American seamen on the high seas while confiscating ships and their cargoes. That France, too, was guilty of seizing vessels scarcely lessened the enormity of British transgressions, particularly at a time when American ships, as neutral carriers, stood to reap the rewards of filling wartime demands for provisions in Europe and the Caribbean. Given the intensity of partisan passions, Washington vainly condemned political parties in his Farewell Address, published on September 19, 1796, as instruments of "cunning, ambitious and unprincipled men" designed "to subvert the power of the people and to usurp for themselves the reins of government." In the presidential contest that year, John Adams, representing Washington's Federalists, narrowly defeated the Republican Jefferson, who was forced to settle for the vice presidency.[3]

These infant parties, despite their burgeoning power, bore a pale resemblance to modern political organizations. Highly elitist, they functioned in the absence of conventions, formal platforms, and staffs. The vast apparatus characteristic of political parties today, connecting the nation's capital to states and local communities, did not exist in the late eighteenth century. Then, also, individual personalities, together with their friendships and feuds, still played a large role in political life irrespective of party allegiances. Personal relationships, governed by a code of honor among gentlemen, still mattered, much as they had before the Revolution.[4]

For a brief period, no better example of their influence existed than the friendship that resumed between President Adams and Jefferson. For more than twenty years, these two "founding brothers" of the Revolution had married their prodigious talents, first in the cause of national independence during the Second Continental Congress, followed a decade later as commercial envoys in Paris for the infant republic. Adams and Jefferson, as diplomats in London and Paris respectively, kept in contact, as did their families. And as secretary of state, Jefferson joined Vice President Adams in George Washington's first administration. Both were powerful intellects: Jefferson the philosopher, scientist, and Virginia planter, every bit as visionary as he was, at times, inscrutable; Adams the "Atlas" of independence in 1776, with a well-earned reputation for vanity, integrity, and a deep hunger for adulation. "He is vain, irritable, and a bad calculator of the motives which govern men," Jefferson noted in 1783, but "this is all the ills which can possibly be said of him."[5]

As president, Adams early on spoke forcefully against "that fiend, the Spirit of Party." He also, in response to a warm letter from Jefferson, replied in kind. "Mr. Adams," Jefferson assured James Madison, "speaks of me with great friendship and with satisfaction in the prospect of administering the government in concurrence with me." And yet, however sincere Adams's sentiments, they were overtaken in March 1798 by news of the insulting treatment accorded American diplomats in the

XYZ Affair. As relations with the French Republic rapidly deteriorated, Congress that summer passed the Alien and Sedition Acts, which only deepened party divisions. While the Sedition Act threatened critics of the government with fines and imprisonment, the lapping tide of Federalist xenophobia crested in the Alien Acts. With the failure of the Bill of Rights to explicitly address the prerogatives of foreign nationals, the Alien Acts granted the president the unprecedented power to deport émigrés without due process of law. Before being expunged, a provision threatened any who returned to the United States with hard labor for life, which Jefferson thought "worthy of the eighth or ninth century." No less controversial was a draconian naturalization act extending the minimum period of residence for citizenship to fourteen years. It passed the House by a single vote. Whereas deportation, insisted Federalist lawmakers, was designed not to muzzle alien critics but to expel foreign subversives, there was no mistaking the aim of the naturalization law. Ever more threatening to domestic peace than French Jacobins, in Federalist eyes, were thousands of newly arrived Irish immigrants, whose numbers swelled after the abortive Rebellion of 1798 against British rule, in which forty thousand people may have died. The new law promised not only to dramatically delay the naturalization of Irish Americans but, as a consequence, to discourage future émigrés. A supporter of both measures caustically observed, "The Irish patriots, after having set their own country on fire, are running away by the light of it as wharf rats." Dead, in the view of Federalists, were visions of America's special role in the world as a beacon of liberty. "All that other states throw away, we are to take, and say thank you. Their offal is to be our aliment."[6]

All the while, barely beneath the surface of party conflict, smoldered the persistent problem of impressment, which for Americans violated the personal liberty of seamen and the nation's sovereignty. During the period since Robert Liston's appointment as minister to America, these affronts had grown more vexing, with the Caribbean, as in past years, the chief trouble spot. In September 1798, a Kingston magistrate who represented U.S. interests in Jamaica estimated that some 250 Americans currently served on board ships under Vice Admiral Parker's command. The Admiralty refused to recognize the right of British subjects—in a number of instances reputed deserters—to become American citizens;

and naval officers, ever in need of mariners, commonly disregarded notarized protections certifying their bearers' nativity. Protections could be acquired from magistrates in U.S. ports by virtue of false affidavits and bribes, the British were quick to claim.[7]

Secretary of State Pickering continued to deem impressment the principal danger to both public acceptance of the British Treaty and, more generally, peaceful relations with Great Britain. Notwithstanding his diplomatic efforts, Republicans blamed not only the British but also the Adams administration for its seeming indifference. In fact, Pickering may have hoped that Jonathan Robbins's extradition, as an expression of goodwill, would be reciprocated by British steps to curb the seizure of seamen from American ships. With dispatches flying back and forth over the fate of Robbins, Pickering on May 7, 1799, sent Liston a strongly worded appeal. In American opinion, he wrote, British naval officers were thought "more intent on gain than glory." Later, "in a private letter" to Liston, which the minister quoted at length to Grenville, Pickering complained of "horrible abuses in the impress of American seamen, by the ships under Sir Hyde Parker's command." In June, with a son of his own in the American navy, Pickering even proposed reciprocating in kind to Rufus King in London. "There is no principle by which they can justify taking by force, even from an American merchant vessel, even a deserter from their navy or army, much less private seamen. If they have the right, we have the same. I know not whether the exercise of it would not be useful to us." Citing the large number of British merchant ships vulnerable to boarding, Pickering lamented that President Adams considered "the measure as destitute of principle."[8]

TO JUDGE FROM CHARLESTON's leading newspaper, local reaction to the trial of Jonathan Robbins was at first tepid. Published by Seth Paine and Peter Freneau, the younger brother of the Revolutionary poet Philip, the *City Gazette*'s sympathies normally tilted Republican. Although the editors recognized the likely importance of the trial, it was two days before the *Gazette* printed a brief overview of the outcome. And while they hoped to provide the attorneys' arguments "on this interesting question" in the future, these were preempted in the next issue by "late

European news." Finally published in full on July 31, a transcript of the trial was followed a day later by the odd assurance that "the editors indulge the hope that the public will believe they had no other motive in giving publicity to the case of Robbins in yesterday's paper, than a conviction that it was a case which would be interesting to their readers." Such was the potentially explosive nature of the proceedings that the counselor for the British consul enlisted Judge Bee to submit a correction in the same issue, seconded by each of Robbins's attorneys. Rather than having asserted in court that the British Treaty was "paramount" to the Constitution, John Ward had argued, Bee claimed, that it was "coordinate." Clearly, the editors did not wish to be faulted for igniting Republican passions. "Over cautious," the lowcountry Republican, Pierce Butler, once complained of the paper, a quality that the Sedition Act likely reinforced. Equally important, Freneau and Paine were the public printers of laws and other documents in South Carolina for the federal government as well as for the state, and they were understandably reluctant to jeopardize either contract.[9]

More eager to toll the fire bell was the nation's leading Republican paper, the *Aurora* of Philadelphia. Scheduled to be tried for sedition, its editor, Benjamin Franklin Bache, had died a year earlier at age twenty-nine during an outbreak of yellow fever. Still the paper retained its partisan edge under Bache's successor, William Duane, the son of Irish immigrants who had acquired printing experience during stints in Calcutta and London, only to face British persecution for supporting the French Revolution. Arriving in Philadelphia in 1796 at thirty-six years of age, Duane found himself "wretchedly poor and friendless." His highly critical "Letter to George Washington" not only secured him a position at the *Aurora* but also confirmed his credentials as a radical republican. Besides receiving the editorship after just two years, he married Bache's widow, Peggy, in 1800 and assumed the title of publisher.[10]

No sooner had word reached Philadelphia than the *Aurora* reported Bee's ruling on August 6. In addition to printing a transcript of the trial, Duane let loose his first salvo on August 12. Citing reports that the president had authorized the surrender of "an impressed citizen" to a "foreign belligerent power," he denounced the notion, whether propounded or not by the British consul's attorney, that the British Treaty was "paramount" to the Constitution, all the while lamenting America's descent into despotism. If anything, the next issue of the paper was more vociferous. "Let them [the American people] consider the violation of the constitution in the delivery of an American citizen, impressed on board a British man of war, to the fangs of those tyrants, when the constitution secures to every man a trial by jury." Worse, the *Aurora* warned, "What was the cause of Robbins yesterday, may be yours tomorrow."[11]

By then, the news had spread up and down the Eastern Seaboard, as other newspapers weighed in. Remarkably, the *Gazette of the United States* acknowledged Robbins's American citizenship plus the likelihood of his impressment. Even so, in light of the treaty's constitutionality, neither mattered, insisted the author of "The Case of Jonathan Robbins, Candidly Considered." Vastly more vocal was the Republican press. Public anger built quickly. In the slipstream of the *Aurora,* the August 17 issue of the *Alexandria Times* decried "that a native citizen of the United States, born and educated among us, and sailing with an *American* protection in his pocket, should be impressed," then to be denied a jury trial for trying to regain "that freedom and birthright of his countrymen." In Hartford, Connecticut, the weekly *American Mercury* ran a searing letter from Albany dated August 12. Punctuated by allusions to the "cruelty of impressment" and the "torture of the lash," the letter exhorted, "If we calmly and deliberately consent to his [Robbins's] being suspended from the *yard arm* of the frigate in which he was formerly tortured and imprisoned, what becomes of the natural, not to mention the political, rights of an American Citizen?" No American seaman, it warned, would be safe from impressment. Papers in Newark, New York, and New London sounded a similar refrain, while still others faithfully reprinted a steady stream of condemnation from the *Aurora,* a "common reservoir," described a New Jersey editor, "from which many aqueducts [are] continually replenished." Under the pen name "Robert Slender," Philip Freneau devoted several "letters" in the *Aurora* to "poor Robbins," the victim of British "sea-robbers." In the homespun language of a simple farmer, Slender dispensed with subtlety, favoring instead righteous indignation. "Is it possible," he wrote, "that any freeborn republican who loves, or ought to love his freedom more than his life, can condemn his equal in rights and in liberty for breaking the chains with which he

Reader
if thou art a Chriftian and a Freeman
confider
By what unexampled caufes,
it has become neceffary to conftruct
This monument
Of national degradation
and
Individual injuftice
which is erected
To commemorate a Citizen of the U. S.
JONATHAN ROBBINS, Mariner,
A native of Danbury in the pious and
induftrious ftate of Connecticut,
who
Under the PRESIDENCY of JOHN
ADAMS,
And by his advice
When Timothy Pickering was Secretary of State,
Was delivered up to the British Government,
By whom he was ignominioufly put to death
Becaufe
He was an American Citizen
who
After having been barbaroufly forced
into the fervice of his country's worft enemy,
And forced to fight
Againft his confcience and his country,
On board the British frigate Hermione,
Commanded by a monfter of the name of Pigott
Bravely afferted his right to freedom
as a man, and boldly extricated
himfelf from the bondage of
his tyrannical oppreffors.
After devoting them to merited deftruction.
If you are a Seaman
Paufe,
Caft your eyes into your soul
and afk
If you had been as Robbins was
What would you have done?
What ought you not to do?
And look at Robbins
Hanging at a British Yard-arm!
He was your comrade
And as true a tar as ever ftrapped a block;
He was your fellow-citizen
And as brave a heart as bled at Lexington or Trenton;
Like you
He was a member of a Republic,
Proud of paft glories
and
Boaftful of national honor, virtue, and independence;
Like him, you one day may be
Truffed up to fatiate British vengeance
your heinous crime
Daring to prefer danger or death
To a bafe bondage.
Alas poor Robbins!
Alas poor Liberty!
Alas poor humbled and degenerate country!

Indeed faid my friend, I fee you have wrought yourfelf up to a very ferious ftate of mind; but I much fear as the fcripture fays, that this cafe of poor Rob-

"To commemorate a Citizen of the U.S. JONATHAN ROBBINS, Mariner," Aurora and General Advertiser, *September 3, 1798*

is unjustly bound?" Again and yet again, Slender excoriated the Adams administration and Judge Bee for his ruling. "The people of America felt more alive to the public affront that was offered to them in the person of Jonathan Robbins," Slender declared, "than in any thing that has happened since the era of Independence." In early September, the *Aurora,* in expectation of Robbins's execution, printed Slender's epitaph for the seaman who, having "been barbarously forced into the service of his country's worst enemy," had "bravely asserted his right to freedom as a man"—"as brave a heart as bled at Lexington or Trenton." Bordered in black, the memorial implored, "Cast your eyes into your soul and ask, if you had been as Robbins was, what would you have done?"[12]

By 1799, newspapers had acquired unprecedented influence in the public arena. Not a single continuously published newssheet existed before the founding in 1704 of the *Boston News-Letter,* a two-column, two-sided broadside. It was the first of many. By the end of the century, the number of papers had swollen to some two hundred, more than twice the number only a decade earlier. Not just in the East but also in western settlements, newspapers flourished. In Kentucky, the towns of Lexington and Frankfurt boasted two papers apiece. Printed on durable linen rag paper and normally four pages in length, most were weekly and biweekly papers, though dailies thrived in cities such as Boston, New York, and Philadelphia. Whereas circulation was modest, limited to a few thousand copies for popular urban papers, issues passed through countless hands in taverns and reading rooms. And it was not uncommon for news to be read aloud. In 1800, a French visitor observed, "A large part of the nation reads the Bible, all of it assiduously peruse[s] the newspapers. The fathers read them aloud to their children."[13]

Crammed with advertisements, foreign news, and shipping notices, newspapers also featured columns and letters devoted to national politics, often reprinted from like-minded publications in other cities and states. For there emerged, beginning in 1789 with John Fenno's decidedly Federalist *Gazette of the United States,* followed two years later by Philip Freneau's *National Gazette* (encouraged by Jefferson and Madison), an increasingly vocal press, propelled by a handful of highly politicized publishers. Soon enough, rival networks of papers crisscrossed the country, with many unabashedly ideological. While it might have taken two to four weeks for copies of the *Aurora* to traverse the mountainous countryside of western Pennsylvania and Kentucky, sites as distant as Raleigh, North Carolina, and Pittsfield, Massachusetts, required just a few days. No other means of political communication had such a decisive impact in the heated battle for public opinion, providing voters, as Alexis de Tocqueville later commented, "some means of talking every day without seeing one another and of acting together without meeting." By the Adams presidency, Republicans steadily dominated efforts to reach a popular audience, having been the first to recognize the potential importance of papers. Nor was it the Republicans who promulgated the Sedition Act of 1798, thus commencing the administration's "reign of terror" against a free press. By then, however, government repression was too late. In founding the Baltimore *American and Daily Advertiser* in 1799, the publisher affirmed, "A new impulse is communicated to public curiosity; enquiry is everywhere afoot, [and] knowledge anxiously sought for by every description of persons." Claimed a foreign visitor, "The opinions of all classes arise entirely from what they read in their newspapers; so that *by newspapers the country is governed.*"[14]

Albert Rosenthal, Charles Pinckney, *nineteenth century*

FOR ALL THE INFLUENCE of the *Aurora,* arguably the most forceful broadside against the extradition of Robbins appeared, fittingly, in Charleston's *City Gazette.* Though late to the fray, on September 6, the paper published a lengthy essay written by a "South Carolina Planter." Over the coming year, no one, not Jefferson, not Madison, not even Edward Livingston or Albert Gallatin in Congress, would do more than Charles Pinckney, the "Planter," to exploit Robbins's death for partisan advantage. Dubbed "Blackguard Charlie" by his enemies, he brought equal measures of passion, ambition, and skill to the cause. Five months after his essay's appearance, Robert Liston still railed about the alarming impact of Pinckney's "malignant publication." By then, it had achieved widespread renown as the first of *Three Letters, Addressed to the People of the United States, Which Have Lately Appeared Under the Signature of "A South Carolina Planter."*[15]

The son of a wealthy Charleston lawyer and planter, Pinckney, who also studied law, won unanimous election in 1779 at age twenty-two to the South Carolina House of Representatives on the basis of just two votes. So foul was the weather on election day that only he and the supervisor of elections appeared at the poll. Or so he was wont to claim. A militia officer, Pinckney was taken prisoner by the British after the loss of Charleston in 1780. Service in Congress six years later led to representing South Carolina at the Constitutional Convention in 1787. Although the youngest delegate, he did not shrink from the debate, speaking on more than one hundred occasions over the summer. Serving three terms as state governor, he was a leading Republican in the South. At the time of Robbins's extradition, Pinckney had been elected a U.S. senator for South Carolina the preceding year.[16]

Tom Paine, he was not. More than eight thousand words in length, Pinckney's tract appears to have been composed in haste, ready for the printer a month after the trial's conclusion. Rather than a well-crafted

THREE LETTERS,

WRITTEN, AND ORIGINALLY PUBLISHED,

UNDER THE SIGNATURE OF

A SOUTH CAROLINA PLANTER.

THE FIRST,

ON THE CASE OF

JONATHAN ROBBINS;

DECIDED UNDER THE TWENTY-SIXTH ARTICLE OF THE TREATY WITH GREAT-BRITAIN,
IN THE DISTRICT COURT OF THE UNITED STATES,
FOR SOUTH CAROLINA.

THE SECOND,

ON THE RECENT CAPTURES

OF

AMERICAN VESSELS BY BRITISH CRUISERS,

CONTRARY TO THE LAWS OF NATIONS, AND THE TREATY BE-
TWEEN THE TWO COUNTRIES.

THE THIRD,

ON THE RIGHT OF EXPATRIATION.

By CHARLES PINCKNEY, ESQUIRE,

SENATOR IN CONGRESS, FOR SOUTH-CAROLINA.

TO WHICH IS ADDED,

AN APPENDIX,

CONTAINING SUNDRY DOCUMENTS CONCERNING JONATHAN ROBBINS.

PHILADELPHIA:

AURORA-OFFICE,

1799.

*Charles Pinckney, "Three Letters, Written, and
Originally Published, under the Signature of
A South Carolina Planter," 1799*

polemic, it resembled at times an indiscriminate litany of allegations critical of Robbins's surrender. Addressing the essay to his "fellow citizens," Pinckney warned that the Robbins case involved "the dearest and most valuable rights of every man in the United States"—"the most indigent" as well as the "elevated and opulent." His words were those of a Carolina aristocrat not given to the plain speech of Robert Slender. Even so, Pinckney's arguments reflected a keen intellect with a gift, at the least, for raising troubling questions and sowing deep furrows of doubt.[17]

A key theme was judicial negligence. This was, by Judge Bee's own admission, the "first instance" of "a demand under the British treaty in the United States." All the more reason, Pinckney declared, for Bee to have weighed more carefully the existence of evidence of murder or forgery, which under the terms of the treaty would "justify the sending of any man, claiming to be a citizen, and not disproved as such, from his country, to be tried by a foreign tribunal"—worse still, a court-martial acting "without a jury, in the most summary manner."[18]

In Pinckney's view, so meager was the evidence that it did not justify a trial in America, let alone overseas. He dismissed Portlock, the ship-mate aboard the *Tanner's Delight,* as "an illiterate sailor lad" who had not been asked in open court to swear positively to Robbins's identity. The incriminating words quoted in Portlock's affidavit ought to have been received with deep skepticism, voiced as they were by Robbins "in the *unguarded hours of boasting dissipation.*" Yet more flawed was Lieutenant Forbes's testimony implicating the defendant, which was based heavily on hearsay not admissible in an English court in any trial threatening either life or limb. Then too, Bee, and by implication the defendant's own attorneys, failed to recognize more tangible evidence, such as the disparity in height of Robbins, who stood five feet six, according to his protection certificate, whereas the Antiguan handbill printed in 1798 put the height of Thomas Nash at five feet ten (inexplicably, Robbins's height was not measured in Charleston).[19]

None of this information would have afforded a grand jury sufficient proof to indict Robbins, either in America or in England, contended Pinckney in quoting a "learned English judge" who observed that "slight, trivial surmise, suspicion, and hearsay evidences, are not suf-ficient." At a minimum, the court should have awarded the prisoner an opportunity to prove his citizenship by seeking corroboration in Con-necticut or New York City. Had not the British been allowed additional time to retrieve the witness Forbes from Jamaica?[20]

Nor were Adams and Pickering free of blame. Pinckney did not question their motives in response to Bee's letter. "They probably never heard" of Robbins's "claim of citizenship," and both were "anxious, on the part of government, faithfully to execute the treaty." But however innocent the president's intentions, no impression "more dangerous to a community can be entertained, than that of a wish of the executive to influence the judicial. It weakens the confidence of the public in both." And while Pinckney denied any effort to question the constitutionality of the British Treaty, he did challenge the extension of British territorial jurisdiction to the open sea. "If the space a ship covers *on the ocean was completely its territory,* . . . the British could have no more right to search or seize our vessels on the open sea, than in our harbors." Precisely.[21]

All this and more, every root and branch. Reserving the topic of impressment for the denouement, he wrote passionately about the plight of America's seamen:

> Can it be supposed because they are seamen,
> they have no families, no tender connexions,
> no comforts to endear their homes to them?
> Rough and boisterous as is the element they
> traverse, and laborious as are their lives,
> among none of our citizens are to be found
> more true independence and generosity, or more
> ardent attachment to their country. If then they
> have those passions, that impatience of
> insult, that invincible thirst for revenge,
> which indignities like impressment and tyranny
> never fail to provoke, are they to be punished
> for using opportunities to exercise them? Are
> they to submit to the manicle and the lash,
> without a murmur, because they fear their
> country, however possessing the means, may not
> have the inclination to protect them?[22]

So wrote South Carolina's junior senator. To speed the tract's circulation, Pinckney mailed copies to Jefferson and Madison in Virginia. Noting that Judge Bee's ruling was already making a "great noise," he asked Madison to have his words "republished in your state papers." Jefferson replied that he was "both pleased and edified by the piece on Robbins," predicting that it would "run through all the republican papers, and carry the question home to every man's mind." Sure enough, in addition to the *Aurora,* numerous newspapers printed "The Case of Jonathan Robbins"; and by late October, a Baltimore paper was advertising bound copies for twelve and a half cents. Such was its impact that issues of the

Aurora containing Pinckney's indictment, which in October appeared twice, were reportedly destroyed at a handful of federal post offices. Not long afterward, much as the publishers of Charleston's *City Gazette* had feared, the administration canceled their government printing contract. According to Pinckney, "immediately on the appearance of Robbins's *Case*," Secretary Pickering personally awarded "all the publick printing of the United States" in Charleston to a rival newspaper—"one of the most high toned and abusive federal papers in the Union."[23]

It would be hard to overstate the outpouring of anger following Robbins's extradition, augmented by fresh newspaper attacks throughout the fall. Their impact, coupled with Pinckney's tract, was far reaching. As early as September 5, Liston reported to Lord Grenville that Robbins's case had created "a topic of abuse against the government and of irritation among the lower classes." Charleston's British consul also acknowledged the "very great opposition to the delivering up" of Robbins. From Monticello, Jefferson wrote James Callender, editor of the *Richmond Examiner*, "The delivery of Robbins to the British excites much feeling and enquiry here." Another Virginian on the eleventh reported to a friend, "As far as I can learn, there is not scarcely such a thing as a dissentient voice from the general reprobation of Judge Bee." The more balanced *Centinel of Liberty* in the Potomac port of Georgetown noted in October, "This affair has excited considerable invective and discussion in the United States." And the following month, a report from Baltimore echoed, "The surrender of Jonathan Robbins has given rise to much clamor in various parts of the United States."[24]

Thrust on the defensive, Federalist newspapers vainly tried to weather the tempest by arguing the legal merits of Robbins's extradition. The prominent Virginia attorney John Marshall, enjoying a wave of national popularity from his service as a U.S. commissioner during the XYZ Affair, penned the most cogent rebuttal, which appeared anonymously in the *Virginia Federalist* of September 7. Having read law under George Wythe at the College of William and Mary, Marshall had been a leading Federalist in Virginia ever since his enthusiastic advocacy of the Constitution's ratification. Applauding Judge Bee's "excellent speech" in surrendering Robbins, he confined the bulk of his remarks to a methodical defense of the British Treaty and President Adams. Marshall's rebuttal, however, fell wide of the mark, for at no point did he address the allegations surrounding Robbins's citizenship and impressment.[25]

Therein lay the problem. Equally deaf to Republican outrage was the author of a rebuke to Pinckney's broadside in Charleston's Federalist paper, the *South-Carolina State Gazette*. Besides ridiculing, as Bee had, the authenticity of Robbins's protection, a self-styled "Friend to Propriety" dismissed the relevance of his citizenship. Invoking Pinckney's "idea that Americans should not be delivered up," he cited the treaty stipulation that "all" suspects charged with murder or forgery undergo extradition. "Upon what dictionary," he asked of Pinckney, "did you obtain the meaning of the word *all*? All in your idea signifies all men except Americans." No more deft was a piece in the *Hudson Gazette* in which the author denied Robbins's constitutional right to a trial by jury on the grounds that his crimes had not occurred in "a state or district" of the United States. Legally sound, perhaps, but at best politically obtuse, given the sanctity of jury trials in the public mind. As was the argument that "civilized nations" traditionally extradited serious criminals to neighboring countries. Aping the legal traditions of Europe, let alone consigning a citizen of the United States to military justice, held little appeal for Americans mindful of the exceptionalism of their fledgling republic.[26]

More sensitive to prevailing sentiment was a small minority of the Federalist party critical of Robbins's surrender. Already beset by opposition from doctrinaire Federalists over the prospect of peaceful relations with France, the administration faced fresh dissent from moderates, including Attorney General Charles Lee, irate over Pickering's subterfuge. In November, with Congress set to convene, Brigadier General James Wilkinson urged his close friend Alexander Hamilton to hasten to Philadelphia: "Your influence and your conciliation may I fear become necessary to prevent a dangerous schism in the ad[ministration]. The Attny. Genl. is vociferous in his reprobations of the surrender of Robbins." Pickering was even rumored, incorrectly, to have superseded President Adams's instructions in order to curry British favor.[27]

In the midst of the cabinet rift, an anonymous pamphlet titled "Letter from a Federalist" appeared. The author was John Steele, a thirty-five-year-old North Carolina politician appointed comptroller of the U.S. Treasury by President Washington in 1796. Noting that Robbins's extradition had "afforded anxiety to the better kind of Federalists," Steele recited Republican complaints with equal if not greater fervor. Judge Bee, in his eyes, was "a stain upon the justice of the United States" for having denied the prisoner a trial by his peers in an American court. Equally at fault were "violent Federalists who in the rage of party spirit admit nothing to be wrong when sanctioned by the Administration." No less critical was the editor of the vaunted *Virginia Federalist*: "If this ill-fated seaman was a native American, and his impressment on board the British frigate *Hermione* can be authenticated, his surrender to the nation from whose fetters he had escaped is an act not more calamitous to himself, than dishonourable to his country."[28]

For his part, Minister Liston relied upon an English émigré to counter the anti-British polemics. Arriving in Philadelphia in 1793 after a brief taste of the French Revolution, William Cobbett was a self-educated journalist who wrote under the pen name "Peter Porcupine." Fervently pro-British, by 1798 he had attracted a devoted following of readers. And enemies. Charged by Republicans and the French with financing Cobbett's columns with Secret Service money, Liston informed Grenville, "I need not assure your Lordship that I have not had the imprudence to pay publickly for the publications in question. But the fact is, and it is but justice to this extraordinary man to declare the truth, that I never have paid for them at all. I have not done so because I found it unnecessary." In time, however, "Porcupine's" columns proved too fiery even for Liston. On being successfully sued for libeling the eminent Philadelphia physician Benjamin Rush, Cobbett fled, first to New York to escape a judgment of £8,000, then to England in 1800.[29]

BUOYED BY THEIR PROSPECTS, Republican leaders in the early fall of 1799 looked forward to the season's marquee election. In Pennsylvania, set to face off for the governorship on October 8 were James Ross, age thirty-seven, a U.S. senator since 1794 who was wealthy and a rising star in the Federalist firmament, and Thomas McKean, of Scots-Irish origin, still feisty at sixty-five years of age and the state's chief justice since 1777. A signer of the Declaration of Independence and an energetic supporter of the Constitution's ratification, McKean had parted with the Washington administration over the British Treaty and Hamilton's financial policies.[30]

Along with the customary perquisites of power and patronage due the victor, the election's outcome, for both symbolic and practical reasons, held immense portent for the presidential contest of 1800. The struggle in Pennsylvania anticipated a political season that threatened to be nasty, brutish, and long. As early as July 1799, a Federalist wrote President Washington, "This state is greatly agitated by the approaching election of Governor." In September, Liston informed Grenville that the coming contest "much engrossed" the public. The most populous of the mid-Atlantic states, Pennsylvania, which Jefferson had narrowly carried in 1796, remained vitally important. Like other states, it retained the right to determine the mode of selecting presidential electors, whether by popular vote or legislative appointment. The latter alternative could open a Pandora's box of possibilities. The new governor would wield considerable power in influencing both the selection process and its implementation, including the right to veto any legislative decision. "The effects then of the election of governor will be incalculable," predicted the *Gazette of the United States.* To complicate matters, the members of both houses of the legislature, currently controlled by Federalist majorities, were themselves up for reelection.[31]

For weeks, no shortage of issues had framed the gubernatorial contest. Overwhelmingly, the most important of these were national in scope, with the British Treaty and the Alien and Sedition Acts dominating the debate, all of which Ross, an inveterate anglophile, had supported in the Senate. In a state whose Irish and German immigrant populations had grown ever larger in recent years, the Naturalization Act prolonging the probationary period for future émigrés proved worrisome for Federalists. They tarred McKean as both a Jacobin and a supporter of the United Irishmen, plenty of whom had fled to Pennsylvania after the failed Rebellion of 1798. McKean's election, warned the *Gazette,* would turn the "whole state" into "a filthy kennel of Jacobinical depravity." The campaign, Liston wryly noted, was "carried on by both sides with uncommon activity and zeal."[32]

The news of Jonathan Robbins's surrender, received in mid-August, set Pennsylvania Republicans ablaze. Catching Federalists off guard, papers like the *Aurora* inflamed partisan passions by portraying Adams, Pickering, and Bee as tools of British influence. In an unleavened assault published in the *Herald of Liberty* in the western town of Washington, "An American" lashed out at "mercenary sycophants" serving "under the immediate influence of the government of Great Britain" who had surrendered "a citizen of the United States, impressed from on board an American vessel to fight the battles of the Tyrant of Great Britain." "Beware who you appoint to the office of governor," he warned. "Let Thomas M'Kean be the man of your choice." Another writer, lamenting Robbins's extradition, instructed readers that Ross had energetically supported the British Treaty. In Germantown, the chairman of a "committee to promote the republican ticket" in a letter to "the Electors of Philadelphia County" alternately attacked Ross while lauding McKean, concluding his long epistle by reminding his "fellow citizens" of "Jonathan Robbins, a free American citizen, who had extricated himself from the worst of bondage," only to be "delivered up to be tried by a British court martial, and hanged (if it be their pleasure) at the yard arm." And Robert Slender exhorted, "Let Porcupine [William Cobbett] growl, Liston pet, the long list of English agents, speculators, approvers of the fate of Jonathan Robbins, tories, and refugees, gnash their teeth in vain. . . . LIBERTY AND M'KEAN."[33]

Pennsylvania's contest afforded an early litmus test of the Robbins controversy, which turned more acidic upon news from Jamaica of his execution. For Ross and other Federalist candidates, the timing could not have been less fortunate. Long after body and soul had separated, the *Aurora* in Philadelphia printed word of the hanging just three days before voters flocked to polling stations. Included in the same issue of the paper was a "last letter" from Robbins, dated July 30, purportedly composed at sea en route to Kingston. Though a fraud, the words were no less poignant, and pointed—from his joyful flight to America after months of Pigot's "barbarity" to the cruel consequences of the treaty with Britain. "The treaty could never intend a pressed man should be delivered up—we press no men." "You must excuse this scrawl," "Robbins" wrote, "as I am still in irons—Adieu—God bless you." What significance rival camps attached to the use of French, by a seaman no less, can only be imagined.[34]

Come the election, turnout was unprecedented, despite an outbreak of yellow fever in Philadelphia. According to estimates, upward of 60 percent of eligible voters cast ballots, more than double the number who had voted in the last gubernatorial contest. For the Federalists, the day went badly. Not only did McKean win handily—by some 5,000 votes out of 70,000 cast—but Republicans captured the lower house of the legislature and almost took the state senate as well. Narrowly controlling the upper chamber gave Federalists thin satisfaction. "Such a fire has been lighted up in Pennsylvania as will consume the Federal Union," despaired John Fenno of the *Gazette*.[35]

Pennsylvania bore witness to the political potency of Robbins's execution. On that much, opposing partisans agreed. There was considerable truth in Jefferson's observation that "Robbins's case" had "a great effect" on McKean's victory. More generally, he wrote Charles Pinckney from Monticello on October 29, "I think no one circumstance since the establishment of our government has affected the popular mind more." Meanwhile, on November 5, Guy Fawkes Day, Liston reported to Grenville, "The Jacobin party have on this occasion received no small assistance from the case of the seaman of the name of Nash," adding darkly that the election in Pennsylvania had "inspired the anti-federal and French faction with a degree of spirit and courage, which may in the future be attended with unfavourable consequences."[36]

At festive suppers across the state, Republicans commemorated their triumph at the polls. Wine, brandy, and hogsheads of beer flowed freely. Of Federalists, a song composed in honor of McKean's election, "The Republican Triumph," proclaimed, "They would talk of spoliations committed by France, / Yet were silent when Britain made poor Robbins dance." Toasts highlighted the celebrations, followed intermittently by music and volleys of musket fire. As Jeffrey L. Pasley has written, "Political banquet toasts served, and were intended to serve, as informal platforms." Numbering a dozen or more, Pennsylvania's postelection toasts typically wished ill to monarchists as well as to domestic and foreign enemies of liberty, all the while lauding patriotic Republicans, from the newly elected governor to Vice President Jefferson and "the fair daughters of Columbia." Such mainstays as the Constitution, the state of Pennsylvania, jury trials, and a well-armed militia all received their due during the merriment. As did the memory of "poor Robbins" at an elegant dinner following McKean's recital of the oath of office. Robbins invariably became the "skeleton at the feast" as a somber reminder of British oppression. Elsewhere, in Lancaster, 412 citizens sat at a table 300 feet in length, amid a thousand pounds of beef, turkey, and ham. The mood turned solemn when guests raised their cups to salute "the midnight visits" of Robbins's "departed spirit, to those whom the 'Recording Angel' shall point out, as his betrayers and murderers." Similarly, "a day of jollity and recreation" in Roxbury concluded with a toast "to the memory of Jonathan Robbins who fell a martyr to British tyranny." No less impassioned was the tribute at a smaller affair in the Philadelphia neighborhood of Kensington: "May the foul stain which our country has received in this man's martyrdom be avenged in the disgrace of those who made him a sacrifice."[37]

In the days following the election, victory in the Keystone State intensified opposition to the Adams administration, all the more as reports of Robbins's execution spread. The Dedham, Massachusetts, doctor, Nathaniel Ames jotted bitterly in his diary, "Infamy of Judge Bee So' Carolina causing murder of Jonath' Robbins by delivery to British under Jay's treaty—confirm's even by the British account. Why is not Judge Bee denounc'd to the President an alien, to be banished." In Baltimore, a subscription fund got under way for construction of a monument commemorating the seaman, who, in the words of the editor of the *American*, "was delivered up a human victim to the maw of a merciless monster." Federalists expressed disbelief over news of a statue to perpetuate the memory of a "murderer." The "murderous monument," one called it. "It is really surprising what a pretty tale the democrats have trumped up of this unfortunate wretch," railed a letter from Charleston.[38]

More than ever, the Republican press printed a withering onslaught of attacks. Some columns roundly criticized the constitutionality of Robbins's extradition, warning, on multiple grounds, of an imperial presidency with an unslaked thirst for power. Thus the British Treaty, notwithstanding the Senate's ratification, yet required congressional legislation to implement Article 27 in the absence of judicial procedures to execute extradition requests. Underlying this complaint was Republican anxiety, should the treaty instead be deemed "self-executing," that the role of the people's House in foreign affairs, already severely restricted, would be further eroded. More alarming was the undiminished belief that Adams had violated the independence of the judiciary by replying to Bee's request for counsel. However temperate the president's response, popular anxiety over executive interference long antedated the American Revolution—on both sides of the Atlantic—conjuring up visions of corrupt ministers and judicial malfeasance. Nor did the recent conduct of federal judges allay Republican fears. Among others, Supreme Court justices Samuel Chase and Bushrod Washington, the president's nephew, had become notorious for giving occasional pronouncements pregnant with partisan portent, both on and off the bench. "No instance is more alarming," declared a resident of the District of Columbia, than when "the Secretary of State writes to a *Judge,* that the *President* wishes a *certain decision* in a *criminal case* depending!!" Opponents also continued to dispute Adams's interpretation of Article 27, pointing out the inconsistency in prosecuting three defendants in New Jersey before extraditing Robbins on the grounds that his alleged crimes at sea had occurred on British territory. "Conformably to this doctrine," declared the *Centinel of Freedom* in Newark, "what must we think of the innumerable insults, flagellations, and impressments, which have been committed by the British on board our vessels?"[39]

What made matters worse, in critics' eyes, was Robbins's claim to American citizenship. By sacrificing a native son "on the altar of foreign domination," Adams and Pickering had violated the "spirit of the laws" of both Britain and the United States. Extradition had deprived Robbins of his sacred right to a trial by a jury of his peers, consigning him instead to a military tribunal without the opportunity of "procuring witnesses or other means of defense," a Virginian condemned.[40]

That Robbins's crime lay in resisting British tyranny magnified the pathos of his execution. Time and again, Republican partisans decried the injustice of his fate as a galley slave. Torture and imprisonment were the bitter consequences of his impressment. Liberty, against which "British arms could not prevail twenty years ago," was again under assault by America's "natural enemies." As if Pigot's command aboard the *Hermione* had not been appalling enough, "A Lover of Justice" described a floating chamber of horrors. One of Robbins's mates, on having his back and sides "lacerated" to the bone, was reputedly hoisted overboard on the captain's instructions to "pickle the Yankee." Not that Pigot's cruelty, in Republican eyes, was unique. Other cases of rough usage invariably surfaced. A Boston writer insisted that "British vengeance" against Americans had led to Robbins's impressment. "Ill-fated man, to be born in this country!"[41]

Had Robbins unquestionably been a British subject, charged on the basis of compelling evidence with an act of murder or forgery of no political consequence, public opposition would have been significantly muted—certainly nothing comparable to the ensuing furor. The first test of Article 27 would have been successful and a constructive precedent established for future exchanges. But in fact it would be difficult to imagine a more daunting set of circumstances for the article's implementation: a purported American, who had been impressed by the Royal Navy, surrendered by the federal government in the absence of probable cause for committing a crime that enjoyed widespread support in the United States.

For Republicans, Robbins's extradition, with the intensity of a lightning bolt, irradiated critical differences between Britain and the United States—from the role of jury trials to the stunning failure of the British Treaty to guarantee American neutrality on the high seas, with impressment far and away the gravest consequence. Jonathan Robbins represented countless victims of British abuse, whether at sea or on land, with Hugh Pigot the personification of unbridled cruelty.

If in fact a year earlier, as Robert Liston hinted, Adams had failed to extradite the three Trenton defendants for fear of inflaming popular opinion in William Brigstock's home state of New York, the president badly misjudged the repercussions of surrendering a "poor friendless Connecticut sailor" from South Carolina. For in death, Robbins became a national "martyr to liberty"—quite literally, a larger-than-life symbol dedicated to the cause of republicanism. Or, as a Federalist printer wrote contemptuously in the aftermath of his hanging, "St. Jonathan Robbins ranks as first martyr on the democratic calendar!"[42]

EARLY ON, TIMOTHY PICKERING, no less a Republican target than Adams, attempted to defuse the escalating crisis. Alive to its galvanizing impact, in early September he had written at length to a town elder in Danbury, Connecticut, the stronghold of Federalism that Robbins had named as his birthplace. "You have doubtless seen in the newspapers a lengthy argument . . . ," Pickering began his letter to James Clarke. Clearly troubled by Robbins's claim, he continued, "I suppose it was not true. I suppose he was a British subject. But the *Aurora* and other democratic papers, the constant vehicle of slander & lies, make a handle of the circumstances to vilify the General Government." Citing the description of Robbins in the notarized affidavit of 1795, Pickering asked Clarke to inquire whether such a person as Nathan or Jonathan Robbins had been born in the community. If not, Clarke was requested to obtain a certificate to that effect signed by the town selectmen. Besides emphasizing its potential importance to the Adams administration, Pickering requested no such document in the event of evidence confirming Robbins's birth. Finally, he instructed Clarke that the certificate, which was to be transmitted directly to him, should "state the plain facts only, without any reference to my request."[43]

It was several weeks before Pickering received the document, signed by the town's four selectmen. Ranging in age from forty-five to fifty-seven years, the officials denied ever having known a resident by the name of Jonathan or Nathan Robbins; nor did the former town clerk, who had kept Danbury's records from 1771 to 1796, recollect such a person. With the secretary of state's assistance, both affidavits were printed in a variety of Federalist and Republican newspapers beginning in November. "It is now incontestably proved," proclaimed New York City's *Daily Advertiser*, that the government "did not betray the right of American citizenship." About the same time, a letter dated September 9 from Sir Hyde Parker to Robert Liston appeared in Federalist papers. Reporting the court-martial and execution of "Thomas Nash," Parker disclosed that the prisoner had at last "acknowledged himself to be an Irishman." (A second witness, the squadron commander on the day of the hanging, related that Nash, minutes before his death, had urged other seamen "to take timely warning by his fate," but not a word was reported of his nativity.) The *Massachusetts Mercury* in Boston rejoiced, "Columns on columns, and paragraphs on paragraphs have appeared in the Jacobin Papers, . . . when lo! the poor blundering fellow in his dying confession

> Danbury, September 16th 1799.
>
> We the subscribers, select-men of the town of Danbury in the State of Connecticut, certify, That we have always been inhabitants of said town, and are from forty five to fifty seven years of age, and have never known an inhabitant of this town by the name of Jonathan or Nathan Robbins, and that there has not been nor now is any family, by the name of Robbins within the limits of said town.
>
> Certified by   Eli Mygatt
>   Eben.r Benedict
>   Justus Barnum
>   Benj.n Hickok
>
> ────────────────
>
> Danbury Sept.r 16th 1799.
>
> The subscriber, late Town Clerk for the Town of Danbury in the State of Connecticut, certifies that he kept the town records twenty five years, viz. from the year 1771 until the year 1796, that he is now fifty six years of age, and that he never knew any person by the name of Robins born or residing in the said town of Danbury, during that term of 25 years, before or since.
>   Major Taylor

Affidavits signed by Danbury, Connecticut, officials,
September 16, 1799

'acknowledges himself to be an *Irishman,*' and thus all the democratic labour is lost, oil, ink and papers wasted."[44]

But the Federalist counterattack, while giving a boost to party morale, shortly stalled, bogged down by allegations of partisanship and British propaganda. Many Republicans continued to affirm Robbins's American citizenship, whether by birth, as he had claimed, or by naturalization. Given his notoriety as the impresario of impressment, the claim of Vice Admiral Parker—"a twin brother of Piggott's in disposition"—was highly suspect. As was that of Federalist officeholders in Danbury amid rumors that families bearing the name of Robbins had resided within the vicinity of the town on either side of the New York border. On top

of everything else, protested a Pennsylvanian, "The principles of tolera-
tion, and the variety of sects, has rendered it almost impossible to obtain
accurate returns of the births & deaths, even in the smallest villages,"
particularly in the case of seamen and transients. (Later it would come
to light that in 1777 Danbury's records had been burned, along with
much of the town, by British troops.) Skepticism was rampant. Nor did
the "news" from Danbury, if true, excuse the failure of either Judge Bee
or the Adams administration to investigate Robbins's origins before surrendering him. A resident of New London, Connecticut, noted in late
November, "It is a curious method of administering justice to enquire of
town clerks, &c to prove a man's nativity *after he has been gibbetted two
months*. It is treating him like an *Irishman* indeed."[45]

As Robbins almost certainly was—and not just any Irishman, but
the notorious leader Thomas Nash, whose role in the deaths of Pigot
and Foreshaw had been seared into the British consciousness. He was
Thomas Nash not because of claims made by Danbury officials orchestrated by Pickering. The census of 1790 indicates, in fact, the presence
of two Robbins families in nearby Dutchess County, New York. Nor
because of Jonathan's last-minute confession, which Parker could have
contrived. But less easy to dismiss is the testimony of three former shipmates during Robbins's court-martial, all of whom identified him as
Nash, as had Lieutenant John Forbes, the midshipman who had served
aboard the *Hermione* shortly before the mutiny. Moreover, no surviving records, either muster rolls or the roster of crew members compiled
with the aid of the maintopman John Brown in the spring of 1798, contain the name of "Jonathan Robbins," though they do that of "Thomas
Nash," a native of Waterford, Ireland, who enlisted on December 21,
1792, upon receiving a bounty of three pounds and joined the *Hermione*
in late January. Most important, no one arguably was more anxious to
see the mutineers of the *Hermione* brought to justice than Vice Admiral
Parker and the officers under his command. There was nothing to be
gained from hanging the wrong seaman, especially if the real Thomas
Nash remained free as a consequence. The Royal Navy was absolutely
convinced that it had apprehended the right man, as in all likelihood
it had.[46]

In contrast to "Jonathan Robbins," Thomas Nash made an unlikely

Bounty Paid	Nº	Entry	Year	Appearance	Whence and whether Prest or not	Place and County where Born	Age at Time of Entry in this Ship	Nº and Letter of Tickets	MENS NAMES	Qualities	D.D. or R.	Time of Discharge
£5	161	1 Jany	93	Jan 14	Nemesis Volr	Bristol	26		John Quintrell	Ab		
£ 1/10		8				Canterbury	23		Wm Atkins	LM		
£ 1/10						Canterbury	20		John Atkins	LM		
£5		9			Cockatrice Volr	Newry Irdd	28		Thos McGee	Ab		
£5	5	15		15	Sheerness Lewisshp Volr		20		Henry Hume Spence 20 Jany 93 then Midn	Ab		
£2		17 Decr	92	Jany 14	Sandwich Volr	Leith	21		Thomas Smith	Ordy		
£3		20			Do	Dundee	23		Thos Chambers	Ab		
£1					Do	Foules Zetld	23		Thos Besler	LM		
£3		18			Do	Perth	21		Jas Fraser	Ab		
£5	170	7 Jany	93		Do	Edinburgh	22		Jas Lockart	Ab		
£3		15 Decr	92		Do	Undoresk Pennt	25		Geo McGile	Ab		
£ 2/10		19 Jany	93		Sheerness Volr	Kingsbury (Wales)	21		John Jones	Ordy		
.		23		23	Nemesis Pay List		21		Walter Gordon	Midn		
£1		19 Decr	92	28	Childers Mayor Randol	Margate	22		James Sagg	LM		
£2	5				Do	Canterbury	21		James Blaxland	Ordy		
£2		22			Do	Neilgurt London	29		Geo: Herman	Ordy		
£2		23			Do	Tarzin County Fermagh	28		Henry Thompson	Ordy		
£3		21			Dover Do Cork		34		John Conley Febry 93 2 Mast Mate	Ab		
£3					Do	Waterford	25		Thos Nash	Ab		
£3	180				Do	Dublin	22		Michl Maney	Ab		

(9)

"Muster-Table of His Majesty's Ship the Hermione," December 1, 1792–October 1, 1794. *The name of Thomas Nash, who enlisted in Dover on December 21, 1792, appears second from the bottom.*

martyr. Leaving aside his hand in Pigot's death, the violence he visited upon Foreshaw exceeded the ferocity of his shipmates, many of whom appear to have been willing to grant the lieutenant's plea for mercy following the initial attempt on his life. Nash's compassion was limited instead to Midshipman Casey, a fellow Irishman who, like others on board, had fallen victim to Pigot's wrath. Had the British released the minutes of Nash's court-martial, which Parker insisted would violate naval regulations, testimony describing Foreshaw's death—"You bugger Foreshaw. Are you not overboard yet? Overboard you must go, and overboard you shall go"—might have diminished, at least in some minds, the Irishman's prominence in the pantheon of republican martyrs.[47]

If anything, the uncertainty surrounding Robbins's identity gave forceful impetus to the simmering issue of alien rights left unsettled by the framers of the Bill of Rights. Had he been an Irish native, he would still have been entitled, in the view of Republicans, to such basic blessings, under the Constitution, as due process and trial by jury. At the heart of the party's affinity for the prerogatives of foreign immigrants lay a strong belief in natural rights as enunciated in the preamble to the Declaration of Independence. Federalists, too, recognized the existence of rights derived from natural law, but Republicans increasingly argued that they superseded civil rights that emanated from government. Whereas the latter's scope was limited, natural rights were broad and expansive. Critics of Robbins's extradition spoke of "natural rights" and "the rights of mankind." In the view of "Manlius," in a printed letter addressed to John Marshall, the possibility that Robbins "may have been a foreigner neither patronizes or changes the principles upon which Judge Bee acted." The seaman's extradition remained "a most horrid deed!" "A blacker outrage," he protested, "could not have been perpetrated on the rights of humanity."[48]

Further, in the eyes of a small but growing clutch of Republican partisans, more important than Robbins's birthplace was his defense of republican principles in the face of British tyranny. A Baltimore writer mourned the loss of "this unfortunate victim to British ferocity, whom bloody-minded barbarity has doomed to expire on a gibbet, for asserting those rights to which he was entitled to, by the laws of God and man"—"the first sacrifice under the horrid operations of that scandalous instrument, the British Treaty." In the *Aurora's* fictitious letter from "Robbins" en route to Jamaica, the author had written, "It has been said I am an Irishman, but you know I am an American—suppose I was from that country—where is there braver or better men than the Irish—should they be pressed, beat, and abused, by a set of rascals & not endeavour to gain their liberty, or when they have done it, be delivered up to be slaughtered!"[49]

From a Republican perspective, few people were thought to be more devoted to the cause of liberty than the Irish, with whom Americans, after all, had shared a common enemy. In 1775, John Adams himself had declared both peoples victims of Britain's "iniquitous schemes of extirpating liberty from the British empire." Irish leaders reciprocated by boldly voicing support for American independence, and Irish Americans fought side by side with other colonists in battle. Proclaimed an Irish American memorial submitted to Congress in 1799, "We glory in the belief that of the Irish residents in the United States, a greater *proportion* partook of the hazards of the field, and of the duties of your independent republican councils, than of the native Americans."[50]

Over the course of the 1790s, a handful of Irish American radicals had rallied to the principle that republican convictions merited, at the least, de facto United States citizenship, including constitutional rights prior to naturalization. Although most Irish immigrants, including prominent exiles like Naper Taper and Archibald Hamilton Rowan, forswore political agitation in their new homeland, other outcasts actively adopted the cause of achieving political equality. On arriving in Boston in 1796, the United Irishman John Daly Burk immediately declared himself a *virtual* citizen. "From the moment the stranger puts his foot on the soil of America, his fetters are rent to pieces," he publicly affirmed. Naturalization, in the view of these émigrés, required loyalty to the cause of democratic-republicanism rather than a probationary period of residence.[51]

In the wake of Robbins's extradition, Republicans had begun to conceive of citizenship and alien rights along similar lines. Even before the doubts sown by Danbury officials, critics of the administration had started to question the relevance of his nativity. Surely not all of them, as suggested by the fictitious letter in the *Aurora* lauding Irish republicans, had accepted his protestations of American citizenship at face value. In their eyes, birthplace, in contrast to political convictions, was arbitrary and accidental, not a deliberate or personal choice. More telling ultimately was not that Robbins may have lied or even that he might have been the fierce mutineer Thomas Nash. What mattered most was that he had valiantly resisted British oppression, for which he had sacrificed his life. In late November, a Massachusetts Federalist went so far as to report, "Some suppose that the Jacobins have been always aware that Robbins was an Irishman, and for that reason gave him their pity and friendship; for they have ever talked more of the rights of Aliens than of the rights of native Citizens." The *Albany Centinel* derided "their lamentations over the *murderer* Nash as a republican lost to the cause."[52]

Most Republican followers, to be sure, remained convinced of Robbins's Connecticut origins. But reports from Danbury encouraged evolving attitudes toward aliens and citizenship. And not purely for reasons of political expedience, among them the benefit of Irish American votes. Far from a poison pill, as Federalists had hoped, Robbins's uncertain background would encourage growing numbers to rethink traditional notions of national identity.

PART THREE

National Identity

7

Seignor Galatini and His Gang

NEARLY AS IMPORTANT TO THE British government as the apprehension of her mutinous crew was the recovery of the *Hermione* from the Spanish navy. A festering wound in the nation's psyche, the benighted frigate also posed a menace to British shipping. As the *Santa Cecilia,* she had reputedly been refitted with heavy ordnance. If not reclaimed from enemy hands, she would need to be found, holed, and sunk.

Despite rumored sightings elsewhere in the Caribbean, the vessel still lay moored in the Venezuelan harbor of Puerto Cabello. Word received by the Spanish that HMS *Acasta* was "cruising in that neighborhood" had kept her in port. Dashed hopes that she might be intercepted at sea in April 1798 only deepened British frustration. But the following year, in late summer, the Royal Navy caught wind of news that Admiral Don Juan de Langara in Cuba had ordered the *Santa Cecilia* in a matter of weeks to weigh anchor for Havana, more than two thousand miles to the northwest. Unknown to the British, she was to join a naval squadron assembled to attack commercial convoys. From his flagship in Port Royal, Jamaica, Sir Hyde Parker on September 17 entered in his journal:

Strong breezes and squally. Ordered Captn.
Hamilton to proceed with the Surprise and
cruise between the Aruba and Cape St. Roman
(taking care to prevent his station being
known at Curaçao) and use his utmost endeavours

to capture the Hermione frigate loading at Porto
Cavallo and intended to sail in early October
for the Havana.[1]

Just twenty-seven years old, Captain Edward Hamilton had first gone
to sea in 1779 with his father, a baronet and the captain of the *Hector,*
for a period of two years in the West Indies. After attending school and
serving in a variety of stations upon reentering the navy in 1787, shortly
after arriving in Jamaica in July 1798 Edward received command of the
Surprise, a thirty-two-gun frigate seized from the French. Five months
later, he sat on the court-martial board that condemned the mutineer
John Coe to hang in chains. In a little over a year, the *Surprise* sank, dis-
abled, or captured more than eighty ships, including several warships,
netting an estimated £200,000 in prize money. That feat alone made
Hamilton a natural choice to intercept the *Santa Cecilia* in the strait
between Venezuela's northern coastline and the tiny Dutch island of
Aruba, visible on a clear day just fifteen miles offshore.[2]

According to Parker's calculation, the Spanish captain would cruise
westward, hugging the coast, before breaking for open water and sailing north-northwest to Cuba. Prior to setting sail on the nineteenth,
nearly two years after the mutiny, Hamilton reportedly suggested the
more brazen strategy of cutting out the *Santa Cecilia* before the frigate
left her mooring at Puerto Cabello, but Parker thought the plan "too
desperate." Left to cruise eastward off the Spanish Main, the *Surprise*
plundered several vessels en route to Aruba, finally arriving in the channel on October 14. After capturing a Dutch schooner, the *Lame Duck,*
that evening and days later a Spanish ship, Hamilton, still well supplied
with water and provisions after twenty-seven days at sea, having mulled
over his options impetuously defied Parker's orders and pressed on to
Puerto Cabello. Arriving offshore after first frightening off a Danish
carrier with a shot across the bow, the *Surprise* could not afford to linger.
With the masts of the *Santa Cecilia* sighted from afar, Hamilton decided
to attack in the small hours of Friday the twenty-fifth.[3]

Prospects for success were daunting. The Spanish frigate, boasting
forty-four guns and a complement of nearly 400 officers, seamen, and
infantry, lay anchored within a protected lagoon that opened to the

west. Hamilton was alive to the risks. With a crew of 180, the *Surprise* was outgunned and outmanned. Additionally, the British had to overwhelm the enemy and gain control of the ship in order to cut her out, all within close range of three shore batteries fortified with two hundred cannons. The danger that Spanish artillery officers might open fire on their own men made the element of surprise even more imperative.[4]

Small wonder, then, that Hamilton's mission has been hailed as no less courageous than the mutiny on the *Hermione* was scandalous. Dressed in blue clothing, just over 50 seamen set out in three launches, barely visible in the darkness, with three more joining them en route. "Britain" was their password, and "Ireland" the countersign. Following Hamilton's lead, they stormed aboard the ship. Already alarmed by the fire of a guard ship, most of the Spanish crew scrambled to man the vessel's guns on the main deck, thus abandoning the upper decks to the boarding parties. Heavily armed with cutlasses, tomahawks, axes, and pikes, along with muskets and pistols, the British forced the captain to surrender after first slaying 119 crew members and infantrymen and wounding another 97. Quite possibly, a few were former Hermiones who had enlisted in Puerto Cabello as soldiers. The inability of the Spaniards either to fix bayonets or to reload their muskets put them at an impossible disadvantage. By 2 a.m., an hour and a half after the assault commenced, the

Roffe, The Boarding & Capturing of His Majesty's Late Ship, *Hermione* (Now *Retribution*) of 32 Guns . . . , *ca. eighteenth century*

ship was in British hands. Remarkably, Hamilton's raiders suffered just one fatality, a lieutenant, and twelve others received wounds, including the captain, who sustained a severe blow to the head from a musket stock. By 5:30, under her own sails, the *Hermione* had joined the *Surprise,* which was waiting four miles offshore. Together they arrived in Port Royal on a cloudy afternoon eight days later.[5]

"I have a peculiar satisfaction in communicating," Parker wrote the Admiralty on November 4, "that his Majesty's late ship Hermione is again restored to His Navy, by as daring and gallant an enterprise as is to be found in our Naval Annals." (Never mind that Hamilton had disobeyed orders.) While the captain recuperated from his wounds in Jamaica, a wave of rejoicing swept Britain in the wake of news reports. Besides garnering prize money in excess of £4,000, Hamilton was showered with gifts, including a sword from the Jamaican assembly and a gold box from the City of London. Not least was the knighthood and the Naval Gold Medal bestowed by the King. In the words of an Edinburgh newspaper, he "immortalized himself by the recapture of the Hermione," which was renamed the *Retribution.* As for the crew of the *Surprise,* Hamilton lavished profuse praise. "Every officer and man on this expedition behaved with an uncommon valor and exertion," he reported to Parker. The contrast between their patriotic service and the treachery of the mutineers could not have been more stark. "British seamen," hailed a paper, had displayed "their wonted superiority and irresistible bravery."[6]

IN THE UNITED STATES, news of Hamilton's heroics arrived in late fall, amid the political uproar over Robbins. Just the same, it was remarkable that Republican newspapers overwhelmingly ignored the *Hermione*'s dramatic capture. Apart from the *Bee* in New London, Charleston's *City Gazette,* still striking an independent course, published details contained in a letter from Jamaica, which recalled the grisly deaths of Pigot and his junior officers. Federalist editors seized upon the news from Puerto Cabello to pay homage to British fortitude. Few, however, reminded their readers of Pigot's cruelty or even the murderous role played by the "famous *Danbury* Irishman, *Thomas Nash,* alias *Jona-*

than Robbins"—better presumably to reap political dividends from the *Hermione's* capture without adding fresh fuel to the uproar engulfing the Adams administration.[7]

The sudden death of George Washington at Mount Vernon from an infection of the larynx on December 14 occasioned little more than a fleeting hiatus from the Robbins controversy. Partisanship receded briefly as newspapers, bordered in black, joined in mourning the nation's loss, and thousands participated in a National Funeral Procession in Philadelphia. Beginning at dawn on a clear, temperate day, more than a dozen cannons fired every half hour in salute. In his eulogy, printed in the *Aurora,* no less, Adams spoke of Washington as a "model citizen" whose virtues transcended ideological differences. Less gracious was the diehard Republican Nathaniel Ames of Massachusetts, who jotted in his diary, "In all the funeral pomp at Washington's death, it is hoped a thought will be bestowed on poor Jonathan Robbins!" Still in New York, the polemicist William Cobbett lamented to a friend in England that "universal *sorrow*" over the general's passing had, in some instances, given way to funeral orations branding George III a "tyrant."[8]

More ominous for Adams supporters was talk that Republicans in the Sixth Congress, having convened on December 2, intended to launch an investigation into Robbins's surrender despite Federalist majorities in both chambers. As early as August, a report had circulated that the House would likely pursue the case, and by late December, Robert Slender was urging a thorough inquiry. "I trust this affair will not be suffered to sleep in silence. Our Representatives are acquainted with it, it was not done in a corner. It calls loudly for a close investigation."[9]

The Sixth Congress was the last to meet in Philadelphia. Construction of public buildings was already under way in the new capital of Washington, on the northern bank of the Potomac. Fin-de-siècle Philadelphia, though bedeviled, like Charleston and Norfolk, by outbreaks of yellow fever, was at the time America's largest city, with a cosmopolitan population exceeding sixty thousand. In the words of a French visitor, included were the "inhabitants of every country, men of every class and of every kind of character—philosophers, priests, literati, princes, dentists, wits, and idiots." Founded in 1682 at the confluence of the Delaware and Schuylkill rivers, the city had quickly become a major seaport.

William Russell Birch, one of the
"Views of Philadelphia," 1799

In recent decades, Philadelphia had not only served as the capital of the Revolution but had also become the young nation's premier cultural center. Besides the American Philosophical Society, it was home to two theaters, a university, a public library with fifteen thousand volumes, and a natural history museum, not to mention more than a dozen newspapers. The city had been famously laid out in the shape of a rectangle, with streets crisscrossing at right angles. Owing to its stately brick buildings and cobblestoned avenues lined by gutters, brick pavements, and Italian poplars, a traveler pronounced it "one of the most beautiful cities in the world."[10]

The House of Representatives met on the lower floor of Congress Hall, a small, handsome brick edifice of Georgian design with white molding conceived by the architect Samuel Lewis. Located at the corner of Chestnut and 6th Streets, it had originally been constructed as the Philadelphia County Courthouse in the period 1787–89. It was here that the Constitution's Bill of Rights had been ratified, the presidential inaugurations of Washington (his second) and Adams had transpired, as well as congressional passage of the British Treaty, laws authorizing the Bank of the United States and the U.S. Navy, and the Alien and Sedition Acts. Whereas heavy red drapes, dark green walls, an elegant carpet, red leather armchairs, and secretary desks adorned the Senate chamber

Interior of House of Representatives, Congress Hall, n.d.

upstairs, the House, befitting its role as the people's voice, convened on the ground floor in a simpler, more modest setting: three semicircular tiers of long mahogany tables and leather chairs, a rostrum for the Speaker as the presiding officer, a nondescript carpet, white walls, and dark green valances topping more than a dozen large windows.[11]

When the House convened, Federalists controlled sixty-three seats and Republicans forty-three. Though dominant, Federalist members embodied a spectrum of political convictions complicated by conflicting loyalties to party elders. Due to mounting dissatisfaction over Adams's decision to pursue peaceful relations with France, hard-line Federalists had begun to rally around Alexander Hamilton, who after his resignation from Washington's cabinet remained active in party politics while practicing law in New York. Then, too, the most recent House election had returned a dozen moderate Federalists, among them forty-four-year-old John Marshall from Virginia, who had reluctantly agreed to run at Washington's behest. A Republican congressman from Georgia wrote a friend, "The disposition of the present Congress appears at present to be much more temperate than that of the late. There are in the majority many moderate men, who will not support any violent party measures, if any such should be proposed."[12]

On December 3, a Tuesday marred by overcast skies, President Adams delivered his opening address to both bodies of Congress in the House chamber. "It was," he began by noting, a "critical and interesting period." His tone was alternately hopeful—a prospering economy and renewed relations with France—and cautionary, as befitted a nation struggling to preserve its neutrality in time of war. Notwithstanding references to a tax revolt among German farmers in southeastern Pennsylvania (the Fries Rebellion), projected alterations to the federal judiciary, and plans for the new capital in Washington, foreign affairs dominated his remarks as he described prospects for a treaty with France in addition to a recent breakdown in debt negotiations with Britain. Such was the uncertainty of the times, Adams warned, that a strong national defense was essential: "Unsafe and precarious would be our situation, were we to neglect the means of maintaining our just rights." On a more optimistic note, he affirmed to Congress his wish that their "mutual labors" would "serve to increase and confirm union among our fellow citizens and an unshaken attachment to our Government." Controversies past and present went unmentioned, including prevailing opposition to the Alien and Sedition Acts and the surrender of Jonathan Robbins.[13]

One decade after the First Congress convened in New York's Federal Hall on March 4, 1789, little, apart from formalities, had become routine in the House's business. Precedents remained to be set, prerogatives clarified, traditions established. During the weeks following Adams's address, all manner of problems confronted House members, from setting census standards to debating an appeal from free blacks to ameliorate the plight of fugitive slaves. For much of early January 1800, the size of the regular army, newly raised for the nation's defense, occupied members. "Business proceeds slowly here," a Republican representative reported to a North Carolina constituent on January 10. With federal expenditures rising and prospects for war receding, Republicans pushed to disband most of the regiments, infantry and dragoons alike. Though unsuccessful, they prevailed in prohibiting further enlistments. Having escaped the "polluted atmosphere of the Hall," Harrison Gray Otis of Boston predicted in a letter to his wife that it was "the only pitched battle that will be fought," which would be followed, at worst, by "slight skirmishes" during the remainder of the session.[14]

Owing to party divisions and Washington's death, the Philadelphia social season during the winter suffered—there was a "cessation of gaiety," Otis reported to his wife. Illness, coupled with heavy snows, further diminished the number of parties and dinners, though neither obstacle deterred Robert Liston's wife, an intrepid hostess. Noting the dreadful weather, Henrietta wrote her uncle of being "obliged to entertain a room full of people when laboring under colds and headaches." The paucity of gatherings could only have contributed to feelings of malaise among congressmen already looking to adjourn early. Otis, for one, wrote home expressing the hope of returning to Boston as soon as possible.[15]

But on February 4, a Tuesday, the New York congressman Edward Livingston presented a pair of resolutions for consideration. The first urged Congress to establish proper procedures to implement Article 27 of the British Treaty, which, in its flawed execution, declared Livingston, had been found "unjust, impolitic, and cruel." A "citizen might be dragged from his Country, his connexions, and his friends, and subjected to an unrelenting military tribunal." A second motion went further by requesting President Adams to provide the House with papers relating to Robbins's apprehension and extradition, including correspondence between the executive branch and Judge Bee. The resolutions, predicted a newspaper, were "likely to produce long and warm debates." Already an omen had descended from the storm gods. A violent squall had struck Philadelphia the day before—first snow, then torrents of rain and fierce gusts lashed the city, the storm's strength mounting after dark. "Raining and blowing very hard," a Quaker matron scribbled in her diary. "I would as willingly set up as go to bed."[16]

In the months since the alleged mutineer William Brigstock had written Livingston from a New Jersey jail cell in the spring of 1798, the congressman had enhanced his reputation as a brash insurgent, a new breed of Republican intimidated by neither political opponents nor party elders. To his brother Robert, Edward early on expressed impatience with James Madison's caution as a congressional leader: "His great fault as a politician appears to me a want of decision and a disposition to magnify his adversaries' strength." In early 1799, Jefferson nonetheless

James Sharples (the Elder),
Albert Gallatin, *ca. 1796*

thought enough of Livingston to canvass him about founding a new Republican newspaper in Philadelphia. Along with the likes of Albert Gallatin, a sharp-witted Swiss native from Pennsylvania, and John Nicholas of Stafford County, Virginia, Livingston belonged to a rising generation of Republican representatives. Too young to have served during the Revolution, they were no less committed to the advancement of republican ideals—or outspoken in their defense. A poem titled "A View of Congress Hall" in April 1799 hailed all three: "Sir GALLATIN, the illustrious sage," and "Sir NICHOLAS AND LIVINGSTON, firm advocates of virtuous freedom, and firmest, too, when most we need 'em."[17]

Least well known today of the three, Nicholas was the son of the wealthy tidewater planter Robert Carter Nicholas. First elected to Congress in 1793, he was a Republican floor leader in the House who had to be coaxed in 1799 to seek another term. According to William Hill, a Federalist congressman from North Carolina, Nicholas possessed a "strong mind" and a "strong voice," though he suffered from a "bald, ill-shaped head, a squalid figure, and the loss of an eye, all of which undercut the power of his oratory." On the other hand, noted Hill, Gallatin, though slight in figure with a foreign accent, was as formidable an intellect as any in Congress "for clearness of thought, precision of argument, equanimity, and penetration."[18]

Livingston, for his part, remained in the forefront of Republican opposition to Federalist legislation, including, most recently, the Alien and Sedition Acts. Having in April 1798 been reelected to Congress for a third term, he attacked the Alien bill that June as an "engine of oppression" in direct violation of the Constitution. Ridiculing the threat, sounded by Federalists, that immigrants posed to the government, he drew on the history of free republics, like Venice and Switzerland, lost to despotic rulers. Rather than having succumbed to invasion, such republics were sundered, he insisted, by "domestic faction." "If any instruction was to be gained from those republics, it would be that we ought to banish, not the aliens, but all those citizens who did not approve the executive acts."[19]

Federalist control of the House, notwithstanding the party's divisions, rendered prospects poor for passage of Livingston's resolutions. Adams's reelection loomed, with Thomas Jefferson, his vice president, the leading Republican candidate. In December, barely a week into the new session, the Speaker of the House, Theodore Sedgwick of western Massachusetts, reminded a party loyalist, "In all our measures, we must never lose sight, of the next election of President." By the following month, a South Carolinian reported, "Parties are already at work for the election of a president." The first votes in the presidential contest of 1800, whether for members of the Electoral College scheduled for December or for state legislators delegated to choose members, were due to be cast in New York in late April. With Adams's conduct the target of House Republicans, party loyalty acquired added importance. From Philadelphia, Jefferson on February 2 wrote his son-in-law, Thomas Mann Randolph, Jr., "Robbins' affair is perhaps to be inquired into. However, the majority against these things leave no hope of success."[20]

Jefferson was too coy by half. Whatever the resolutions' fate, the ensuing debate would afford Republicans an opportunity to berate the administration, with the ghost of Jonathan Robbins center stage. In championing the president's vindication, Federalists could ill afford the taint of obstructionism. Further, there existed the chance, though slim, that moderate members of the Federalist caucus might strike an independent course at their party's expense. On February 28, the fiery Vermont representative, Matthew Lyon, wrote a fellow Republican, Andrew Jackson of Tennessee, "Administration have a more decided majority than ever before, but they have about a dozen in that majority who are not willing to go all lengths with them. This cools them. The Affair of Jonathan Robbins has nearly taken up this week & it is but just enterd upon [?]. The Aristo. Party are determined to justifie Mr. Adams at any rate but it gives them much trouble I can assure you."[21]

And what better forum for the opposition than the House floor? It was a revolutionary age in which political oratory reflected a heightened sensitivity to public opinion. Fully cognizant that debates, normally open to the public, often found their way into newspapers, representatives framed their arguments with increased care. Speeches expanded in length and frequency, provoking Benjamin Goodhue of Massachusetts to complain early on of "needless and lengthy harangues" by representatives "actuated by the vain display of their oratorical abilities."[22]

On Thursday, February 20, Livingston upped the ante by formally charging Adams with having advised and requested a federal judge to surrender to Great Britain a seaman "without any presentment or trial by jury." Nor had there been "any investigation of his claim to be a citizen of the United States" who had attempted to "regain his liberty from illegal imprisonment." Said actions, constituting "a dangerous interference of the Executive with Judicial decisions" and a threat to the "independence of the Judicial power," deserved the chamber's "suspicion and reproach."[23]

Why, we might ask, did Livingston and other Republicans choose this field of battle on which to attack Adams? Certainly, other administration policies, notably the Alien and Sedition Acts, hotly condemned as unconstitutional, offered handy bludgeons. Besides the fact that both houses of Congress were culpable in passing the legislation, no issue in the early months of 1800 resonated more deeply than Robbins's extradition. Other policies, though sharply criticized, produced no figure nearly as compelling as the American seaman spurned by his native country, only to be executed for resisting British oppression—from which, to make matters worse, the United States had failed to protect him. He had become a tragic, indeed the most tragic, victim of impressment—far and away the gravest grievance that Americans bore against Great Britain, one that could easily be reduced to inflammatory slogans. Although none of this was directly germane to Livingston's indictment, if in the public mind the president was to be censured for violating the independence of the judiciary and denying Robbins a jury trial, that would be good enough. "The president has been violently attacked for delivering up the murderer Thomas Nash," an observer wrote from Philadelphia. "Mr. Livingston presented the resolution to the House charging him in direct terms with 'a dangerous interference with the judiciary,' and the Demos with crocodile tears almost wept at the fate of the villain."[24]

By then, the Adams administration had supplied the House with relevant documents (pertaining to "Thomas Nash," not "Jonathan Robbins"); after which the Federalist James Bayard, Delaware's lone congressman, introduced a competing resolution approving the president's conduct. Rather than appoint a select committee, the House had designated itself a committee of the whole, as it often did to promote a free exchange of ideas, less bound by the etiquette of formal proceedings. Debates, as a consequence, grew more prolonged. Little had changed since Fisher Ames likened such deliberations to "a great clumsy machine . . . applied to the most delicate and slightest operations."[25]

Federalists were outraged by Livingston's move to censure Adams. "A direct road to an impeachment of the President," Representative Robert Goodloe Harper of South Carolina charged. This fear, though premature, was not irrational. For most of Washington's presidency, impeachment inquiries into the conduct of federal officials had generally been nonpartisan. But with the hardening of party lines during the British Treaty controversy, the prospect of impeachment became a political weapon to harass unpopular opponents. Prosecutions, to be sure, were more often threatened than initiated, not least against Alexander Hamilton and Washington himself. Elbridge Gerry, tarred for his timid, allegedly pro-French conduct as a U.S. commissioner to France in 1798, faced the wrath of Pickering and other arch-Federalists, only to be saved by Adams, an old friend. More successful was the campaign, again waged by Pickering, albeit with bipartisan support, to remove Senator William Blount, a former North Carolina Federalist turned Tennessee Republican. Charged with conspiring with British agents in 1797 in a military conspiracy to wrest control of Louisiana and Florida from Spain in order to advance the interests of land speculators like himself, Blount escaped impeachment only because the Senate first approved his expulsion.[26]

Just three days after the triumphant election of Governor McKean in Pennsylvania, the *Aurora* declared, "If the case of Blount did not furnish a disgraceful precedent of the inefficiency of an impeachment, we should think that Judge Bee & the writer of the letter who 'advised and requested' the delivery of a citizen into the murderous talons of the British government, should be arraigned at the bar of the nation, and fairly tried for their acts in that lamentable deed." As a practical matter, impeachment, of course, was highly unlikely in light of Federalist control of Congress. The Republican publishers of the *Albany Register* saw fit to write Livingston, "As the Constitution now stands, and as Executive favours are and have been dispensed, it would be the height of folly to attempt to impeach the President, let him even so far outdo his usual outdoings." Republicans, in fact, refused even to speak of impeachment for fear of overreaching.[27]

Still, Adams stood to be severely censured should his opponents in the House prevail, thus crippling his chances of reelection. "Had not this subject been talked of for eight months past," demanded Harper on the House floor, "and pasteboard figures of Jonathan Robbins been exhibited at every election ground in the United States?" The Virginia congressman Leven Powell later wrote his son, "Many ill natured and ill founded assertions were made calculated for out of door purposes." More plainspoken was Abigail Adams in telling her sister, "Electioneering purposes are answered by the gloss put upon the transaction by the Jacos, which is carefully retaild in all the democratic papers."[28]

Debate of the resolution, commencing on Tuesday the twenty-fifth, quickly bogged down in a procedural morass. When Livingston, in his opening statement, began to quote from a copy of the deposition given by Robbins before Judge Bee, Bayard immediately questioned the veracity and pertinence of this and other documents from Charleston attesting to his citizenship. Deemed the finest orator in the House by William Hill, Bayard expressed no doubt that Livingston's purpose was to legitimate Robbins's falsehoods. To the chamber's astonishment, Livingston shot back that, in fact, he "did not believe a word" of Robbins's affidavit. In his view, the sailor was an Irishman who had voluntarily entered on board the *Hermione* and committed every crime imputed to him. Still, Livingston did not "surrender one point" of his resolution, which he vowed to substantiate. The crux of the debate, for him at least, remained the independence of the judiciary and the sanctity of jury trials for citizens and aliens alike.[29]

As if in disbelief, for a brief moment neither side responded to Livingston's outburst, prompting Albert Gallatin to interject that Robbins had claimed to be an American citizen, which the member from New York had a right to note. In full agreement was Henry "Light Horse Harry" Lee, a newly elected Federalist from Virginia's northern neck.

("Elegant in his language but not powerful in his argument" was the verdict of Hill.) Only with open debate, Lee argued, would "the whole truth" appear. At that point, having heard enough, Speaker Sedgwick, a disciple of Alexander Hamilton, ruled against Livingston; but in the day's final surprise, enough Federalists crossed over to defeat his peremptory decision by a vote of 48 to 39.[30]

Notwithstanding their aristocratic mien, many Federalists recognized the necessity of open deliberations lest majority control make them vulnerable to charges of duplicity. At one point, John Rutledge, Jr., of South Carolina observed that "the minds of the people had been raised to the highest pitch of expectation" by "certain public prints." "The friends of the Administration would act a very unfriendly part," he warned, "if they should agree to smother the business." A viewing gallery packed with visitors afforded a daily reminder of public interest. On the other hand, some members, fearing the investigation incapable of resolution, urged its abandonment. Thomas Davis, a Kentucky Republican no less, calling it a "very disagreeable and irsksome business," declared himself unprepared either to "criminate" or to "applaud."[31]

For most Republicans, the answer to Davis's dilemma lay in obtaining additional evidence. John "Jacky" Randolph of Virginia urged the acquisition of "authentic copies of all the papers within the reach of the Government," beyond those previously supplied by the administration. He reminded his Federalist brethren that "the public mind" was "very uneasy upon the subject, and this state of disquiet was not to be eluded." At the least, Henry Lee stated, to discontinue or postpone the investigation to the succeeding session in November threatened to stain Adams's record, with the presidency in the balance—an outcome, many Federalists believed, that Republicans secretly preferred. Loath to prolong the inquiry farther into the election season, administration supporters wished to bring it to a conclusion by defeating Livingston's resolution as quickly as possible. Still, the appearance of obstruction was not without risk, and on Wednesday evening just fourteen representatives, including Representative Davis, voted to terminate the investigation.[32]

Left unresolved was the need for additional evidence. The following morning, Davis, chastened by the vote, abruptly called for copies of court proceedings from South Carolina in the matter of *United States*

v. Nathan Robbins alias Nash. Bayard immediately challenged their relevance, especially if Davis sought to prove Robbins's citizenship. Livingston, after all, Bayard declared with relish, had already acknowledged
the seaman's falsehood.[33]

For the Maryland Republican Samuel Smith, that was enough. A
hard-nosed veteran of the Revolutionary War who in 1814 would command the defenses of Baltimore during the British assault on Fort
McHenry, Smith for two days had wanted to correct Livingston's earlier
outburst. Disregarding the question of relevance to the resolution at
hand, Smith declared it vital to determine the authenticity of Robbins's
claims. In light of Bee's failure to ascertain his citizenship, the acquisition of Robbins's protection certificate, for one—signed and notarized
in New York—was essential to uncover "the whole truth." John Nicholas followed with a rebuke aimed at both Livingston and Bayard. "The
gentleman from New York, to be sure, had declared his satisfaction with
the facts that had been produced to the House, but did the gentleman
from Delaware know that this was the case with any other gentleman in
the House?"[34]

The wrenching debate consumed the entire day. Charges and coun-
tercharges filled the air. Not even estimates of the time required for
retrieving documents from Charleston yielded a consensus. John Marshall warned that their procurement could consume as much as a month.
Less fearful of public backlash than others in his party, he pushed for a
prompt vote on Livingston's censure resolution. Scarcely able to contain
his anger, Rutledge, notwithstanding his initial caution, was more blunt
in decrying the "monstrous clamor" that had been "raised about this
business." "We know," he continued, "that great pains have been taken
to make the people believe that their fellow-citizen has been torn from
his country." Further delay would suggest that the president had "been
grossly delinquent in his duty." "We say, if he has offended, punish him;
if he has not, discharge him from censure!"[35]

Republicans advanced two reasons for the pertinence of the Charleston proceedings. Davis and Nicholas both spoke to the necessity of
determining whether the president's intervention had occurred after
Bee's court had assumed jurisdiction over the case by indicting Robbins. If so, it would constitute interference of a deeper dye. (Accord-

ing to the minute book for the May 1799 term of the South Carolina federal district court, no such indictment was sought.) James Jones, a Georgia Republican, on the other hand, like Smith before him, felt unconstrained by the narrow scope of Livingston's resolution, deeming it immaterial whether Robbins was in truth a "Turk, a Hottentot, or a native-born American." More troubling was that Bee had deemed his citizenship to be irrelevant ("It is of no importance whether you are, or are not a citizen"). Until Robbins's claim, supported by evidence, was proven false, he was "a citizen to all intents and purposes" and thus "entitled to all the privileges of a citizen." That he had not been accorded those privileges, insisted Jones, jeopardized the safety of every American in similar circumstances.[36]

The member from Georgia acknowledged that evidence from Charleston was not, in all likelihood, critical to a resolution of censure. But, he added in a striking departure from the debate, the issue of Robbins's citizenship could prove material "to another charge or implication against the President." If the papers revealed that Adams had known of Robbins's claim, he would be as culpable as Bee for not investigating further. Even then, Jones was not through. Expressing annoyance over the "unworthy motives" frequently attributed to Republican representatives, he noted that they were innocent of one charge that applied directly to their antagonists. Certainly none could pretend, he declared, that the conduct of any Republican "was designed to throw themselves within the benign beams of Executive patronage." Salting the wound, he could "perceive no other object which could induce gentlemen to declaim so frequently and earnestly."[37]

And with that, the day's forensics neared their conclusion, with members pausing long enough to thwart by a vote of 57 to 44 the motion to procure additional records from South Carolina. Mindful of the public's interest, Henry Lee, along with three other Federalist representatives, sided with the minority.[38]

GIVEN THE PRESS OF BUSINESS, not until late Monday, March 3, did the House return to the Robbins controversy. Only Livingston spoke at length, nearly three hours before the Speaker adjourned for the day—time enough for the congressman to introduce a record of the New Jersey Circuit Court that in 1798 had acquitted William Brigstock and two other Hermiones. In highlighting obvious differences between the outcome of their arrests and Robbins's apprehension, Republicans hoped to uncover the reason for such an "extraordinary change" in Adams's conduct, as Livingston put it.[39]

Of Livingston's speech, Vice President Jefferson wrote the next day to James Madison that Federalists in the House "feel its pressure heavily, & tho' they may be able to repel L's motion of censure, I do not believe that they can carry Bayard's of approbation." Jefferson, of course, sat one floor above the House in Congress Hall as the presiding officer of the Senate. Although there is no evidence to indicate that he was more than an interested observer, it is implausible that he was not directly involved, at the least by dispensing advice to Livingston and other party leaders in the House. Although Jefferson preferred to project a disinterested persona prior to the election, his chambers at Marache's boardinghouse in Philadelphia had already assumed the role of a campaign headquarters.[40]

The following morning Gallatin hurriedly made a motion for the acquisition of all communications from any executive department relating to the commitment, trial, and acquittal of all three Trenton defendants, including germane correspondence between the administration and the British government. "One call for this, another for that, and there would be no end to their calling," declared Rutledge. Republicans, alleged Federalists, having found themselves unable to substantiate Livingston's charges, had grown desperate, all the while determined to damage the president. But it was Federalist rhetoric that turned shrill. The following day, Robert Goodloe Harper avowed that he never accepted advice from an "enemy" whose pen was "dipped in gall." Republicans had mounted "wretched arguments" born of "morbid imaginations." "Can it be supposed that the President would be guilty of such a boyish trick," he complained, "as in a few months, to put a different construction upon one and the same action?"[41]

Livingston, newly invigorated by the dispute, put the matter bluntly. "What inference can be drawn by the people of the United States," he demanded, "but that there is something rotten in the business, that would bear too hard on the President to be made public?" He also alleged that administration supporters had been in contact with the Department of State. "Might it not be inferred, for their subsequent conduct, that they had discovered something which they did not choose to have exposed?" Provoked by the insinuation, Henry Lee averred that he had personally been assured by Secretary Pickering that the State Department possessed no relevant correspondence with the British, which of course was patently false.[42]

House Republicans, if only by invoking the public's wrath, nearly prevailed. In a white-knuckle vote taken after a full day's debate, Federalist abstentions and two defections resulted in a tie of 46 yeas to 46 nays. It was nonetheless a moral victory, though Speaker Sedgwick broke the tie by voting to defeat the motion, thereby preventing access to copies of Pickering's correspondence with Robert Liston and, more important, Charles Lee's letter to Pickering opposing extradition of the three Trenton defendants. That invariably would have led Republicans to question the attorney general's exclusion from the Robbins case, all the while prolonging the debate into the spring. Had they been forced to settle for Pickering's pelt, that would have been good enough. As for Adams, certainly his competence, if not his motives, would have generated criticism for his failure to consult Lee on such a pressing matter.[43]

It had been over two weeks since Livingston introduced his resolution of censure on February 20. With nowhere else to turn, Republicans reconciled themselves to a vote on the merits of their case. The final act played out over the next two days, with closing speeches by each party. On Thursday the sixth, a clear day, Nicholas rose to speak, laying out, point by point, the constitutional grounds for censure. All to little effect. Immediately afterward, in its capacity as a committee of the whole, the House voted to reject the resolution 58 to 34, in a party-line vote save for a single defection from each side and Republican abstentions.[44]

Yet a second vote was required to be taken on the "committee's" decision. Undaunted, Gallatin held forth for two hours before the House adjourned. His speech, if at times plodding, was competent and clearheaded, undergirded by references to the Constitution and international law. Addressing topics from piracy to impeachment, he endeavored to persuade his peers rather than stir their passions. Only toward the close of his remarks did he grow more animated. Like Nicholas, the thirty-nine-year-old Gallatin had avoided trading on the public's anger over Robbins's extradition. More than once, he had inadvertently referred to the seaman as "Nash." But the Pennsylvania congressman's tenor abruptly changed as he turned to the consequences of Adams's inter- ference. No less alarming, he declared, was that Judge Bee, in acting upon the president's "advice and request," had surrendered a purported citizen of the United States whose only crime had been to resist British oppression. Exclaimed Gallatin, "I will insist that a citizen ought not to be surrendered for murder committed while resisting impressment, or attempting to recover his liberty." Such a construction by virtue of the British Treaty, he continued, would permit the Royal Navy to impress other Americans, only then, upon their escape, to demand their sur- render! Rising from his seat, Lee retorted that no one had claimed such a right for Britain, but Gallatin, having found his voice, noted that Bee had blithely proclaimed his indifference to the relevance of citizenship. "Jonathan Robbins was accordingly surrendered," Gallatin admonished, "without an investigation of his claim of being an impressed citizen." It was for that reason, he proclaimed shortly before adjournment, that he was "strongly impressed with the impropriety of the interference of the President, and of the decision the judge made in compliance."[45]

On a clear, cold Friday morning, at the stroke of eleven, the House debate again got under way. Only one Federalist representative rose to speak against Livingston's resolution. No ordinary congressman, John Marshall enjoyed a distinguished reputation at forty-four years of age. In December, he had been given the honor of composing the House's reply to the president's opening address to Congress. His nationalism had arisen, in part, while an officer in the Revolutionary War, serving "with brave men from different states who were risking life and everything valuable in a common cause." This, he later wrote, confirmed his "habit of considering America my country, and congress my government." Even so, he was not an orthodox Federalist, having questioned the wis- dom of the Alien and Sedition Acts. Marshall, feared a party leader from Massachusetts, was "little better" than a "half-way" Jacobin.[46]

A prominent member of the Virginia gentry, Marshall cut a com- manding figure, not unlike Washington. Congressman Hill claimed to be "charmed" by his persona and intellect—"as an orator," Hill mar-

veled, "he captivates your mind." Marshall's opening remarks paid tribute to
Republican opponents as "gentlemen of
great talents." Though he "did not flat-
ter himself with being able to shed much
new light on the subject," he spent the
remainder of the day forcefully arguing that the president enjoyed extensive authority under the Constitution
to execute the nation's treaties, which
included, in the matter of Thomas
Nash, instructing a member of the federal judiciary. After first laying out the
predicate for the treaty's execution—
Britain's jurisdiction aboard its own

Cephas Thompson, John Marshall,
1809–1810

vessels at sea—he turned the Republicans' central charge on its head.
Rather than the president being at fault for judicial interference, the
judiciary's role was limited strictly to executing his instructions. On this
point, Marshall was unyielding: "The case was in its nature a national
demand made upon the nation. The parties were the two nations. They
cannot come into court to litigate their claims, nor can a judge decide
on them. Of consequence the demand is not a case for judicial cogni-
zance." Put more broadly, Marshall insisted, "The President is the sole
organ of the nation in its external relations, and its sole representative
with foreign nations."[47]

It was a masterful defense, brimming with erudition, in which Marshall repeatedly chided Republicans and more than once mocked their
claims. "The gentleman from New York [Livingston] has asked, triumphantly asked," he declared, "what power exists in our courts to deliver
up an individual to a foreign government? Permit me, but not triumphantly, to retort the question." Not until the end of the day did Marshall conclude, putting off a final House vote on Livingston's resolution
to Saturday morning, following concluding words from Nicholas. The
tally was not close, ending in just 35 votes for censure and 61 in opposition. Federalist ranks held firm, joined by five Republicans, of whom
one, Davis of Kentucky, later professed his reluctance to express "a want

of confidence in our Chief Magistrate" on the eve of treaty negotiations with France. "We have taken the final question on Livingston's impudent resolutions, which are rejected," Harrison Gray Otis wrote his wife. That night, heavy snow blanketed the city, as if to smother any smoldering embers of opposition.[48]

The speech has justly been hailed as the greatest of Marshall's short political career. According to an anecdote repeated years later by Henry Adams, the great-grandson of John, Gallatin, when asked immediately afterward how he would respond, tartly replied, "Answer it yourselves." Criticisms contained in Gallatin's notes cast doubt on the story's credibility, but even Jefferson wrote that "Livingston, Nicholas & Gallatin distinguished themselves on one side & J. Marshall greatly on the other." "A very luminous argument," Timothy Pickering enthused to Rufus King. All this was true enough, but contrary to standard accounts, Marshall's speech did not rescue Adams from the House's censure. The tide, far from being turned, was already flowing in the president's favor, with Federalists predisposed to vote overwhelmingly against the Republicans' resolution. The tally on March 8 was nearly identical to the vote taken by the House in its capacity as a committee of the whole two days earlier. Proponents of censure gained one vote, whereas their adversaries picked up three. The most that might be said is that Marshall's eloquence deterred a few representatives from having been swayed by Gallatin's oratory.[49]

Adams's triumph in the House was bittersweet. As Jefferson had predicted, two days later, in the wake of the censure vote, Bayard moved to withdraw his resolution of approbation, fearing the reticence of moderate Federalists. With regard to more orthodox members of the party, despite their growing skepticism toward the president, there is no evidence that on this of all issues they intended to embarrass Adams or Secretary Pickering, one of their own, by voting against the resolution. Though a follower of Hamilton, Speaker Sedgwick, for one, had consistently demonstrated his loyalty to the administration during the debate over Robbins. Republicans, hopeful of defeating Bayard's measure, insisted that its withdrawal be put to a vote. The tally revealed a clear, albeit unorthodox, fault line. On Bayard's motion to kill the measure prior to a vote on its merits, as many as 62 representatives voted yea to 35 nays. In opposition, 34 Republicans were joined by a lone Federalist from Georgia, Benjamin Taliaferro, who was reelected to the Seventh Congress later that fall as a Republican. Enough Federalists planned to withhold their approbation that Bayard and other leaders foresaw the resolution's defeat. With the presidential election looming, a majority could not be marshaled to approve the chief executive's role in Robbins's extradition, Marshall's defense notwithstanding. It was a sobering blow to Adams and a source of no small revenge for his enemies. In a circular letter, a Virginia Republican informed his constituents, "Mr. Livingston's resolution being rejected, the other was withdrawn by the President's friends, as being rather too much to ask even of his devoted majority."[50]

SO ENDED REPUBLICAN EFFORTS TO censure John Adams. Tradition has it that the Robbins affair quickly faded as a campaign issue in the days following the party's defeat in the House. Certainly, Federalist newspapers were jubilant over the outcome. In a likely reference to Jefferson, a Pennsylvania paper chortled, "The Grand Conjuror of the House of Representatives, with his puppets, have labored hard to call up the spirit of poor Nash from the 'vasty deep' in order to secure his vote at the next election for Electors." Mocked another paper, "In spight of the magic influence of Seignor Galitini and his gang, poor Robbins is consigned to repose." Equally optimistic was Marshall, who wrote a Virginia confidant on March 16, "The debate was for the purpose principally of affecting the next election of President, but I believe that it has completely faild of its object." With the Electoral College due to convene in fewer than nine months, he predicted that chances ran more than two to one in favor of Adams's reelection. "Completely baffled," echoed *Jenks' Portland Gazette* in condemning attempts in the "detestable affair of Robbins" to weaken public support for Adams. "With what vociferation was it blazoned from one end of the continent to the other by these base miscreants."[51]

But, in fact, the broader controversy outside of Congress Hall showed no sign of ebbing. Quite the contrary. No matter the House's decision, Pennsylvania's *Herald of Liberty* predicted on March 17 that it would not "produce any thing like approbation in the public mind." Marshall's

speech, despite its brilliance as a constitutional defense, fell flat as a
political polemic. No shortage of questions went unanswered. However
peripheral to the Republican's central allegation, these remained of great
public interest. Thus Marshall argued strongly that the president possessed the authority to intervene in the trials convened in Trenton and
Charleston, but he did not explain the patent inconsistency of Adams's
conduct—or why Federalist politicians were unwilling to prolong the
debate for a few days to obtain additional documents. Nor did Marshall
address Judge Bee's failure to consider evidence of Robbins's citizenship
or afford time for a proper investigation of his claims. Not that the Virginia congressman was indifferent to the broader controversy. Toward
the very end of his speech, he felt forced to confront, and accept, Gallatin's argument that an impressed American, having escaped after committing a homicide aboard a British ship, should not face extradition.
"Had Thomas Nash been an impressed American," Marshall concurred,
"the homicide on board the Hermione, would, most certainly, not
have been murder." What he did not defend, nor could he, was Bee's
cavalier indifference. As for Adams's ignorance of Robbins's incendiary
claim—the chief executive bore sole responsibility for executing Article
27—Marshall offered up the limp defense that "the fact of Thomas Nash
being an impressed American, was obviously not contemplated by him
in the decision he made on the principles of the case." As Jefferson jotted in his notes during the speech, "If alleged to be a murder also, then
whether he was not an impressed American was an essential enquiry."
Finding Marshall's speech both "ingenious" and "specious," the *Aurora*
delighted, "He was compelled to admit what certainly implicates both
the President and Judge Bee . . . the executive and the judge must be
culpable for not having made an enquiry."[52]

What is surprising is not Republican criticism but that Timothy Pickering, the architect of Robbins's surrender, appears to have reached a
similar conclusion. In a letter of March 17 to Senator Benjamin Goodhue of Massachusetts, a political ally, he erroneously claimed to have
"repeatedly" warned Robert Liston that American sailors had a right
to resist British impressment without risk of extradition under Article
27. Noting, then, that Marshall had iterated the same doctrine, Pickering wondered, "If this opinion be correct, . . . was not an enquiry into

the national character of Nash pertinent, on the return of the Habeas Corpus [in Charleston]? Had there been any ground to believe him an American, I presume no order or advice for his delivery up would have been given by the Executive."[53]

Grounds there had been, which no officer of the court, including Robbins's attorneys, had bothered to probe, as Pickering, in feigning ignorance, almost certainly knew. At best, his acknowledgment to Goodhue was duplicitous; at worst, he had been grossly negligent in surrendering the seaman professing to be Nathan Robbins of Danbury, Connecticut. In either event, Federalists, John Adams foremost among them, stood to reap the whirlwind.

8

Revolution of 1800

THE REPUBLICAN CAMPAIGN TO CENSURE John Adams effectively launched the monumental presidential contest of 1800, unrivaled until the election of Abraham Lincoln for its historic importance and heart-stopping drama. Not for another sixty years would electoral politics exhibit such urgency or the stakes of a presidential campaign bulk so large. At issue in the minds of Americans in this bitterly polarized contest was nothing less than the survival of their infant republic. Absent was the comfort of George Washington's commanding presence. Unheeded were his pleas for national unity. Americans clashed over the scope and administration of government, the roles of leaders and followers—indeed, over the very words and meaning of the Constitution. The race became a battle for the country's soul, whether the people would continue to accept the guidance of a paternalistic ruling class determined to establish the supremacy of the federal government or place their trust instead in representatives striving to protect and advance liberties won in the Revolution—"friends of the people" rather than "fathers of the people."[1]

No shortage of partisans on either side feared that the election could erupt in civil war. In the dire event of a Federalist triumph, Republicans stood ready to defend the doctrine of states' rights championed in the Virginia and Kentucky Resolutions. Following their passage, Alexander Hamilton had written of moving the army toward Virginia "to act upon the laws and put Virginia to the test of resistance." Should Republicans lose the election, a state resident forecast that "chains, dungeons, transportation [to Australia], and perhaps the gibbet" would follow. Just as apocalyptic, in the eyes of Federalists mindful of the French Revolution, would be a Republican victory, dooming the country to unbridled anarchy. "The air will be rent with the cries of distress, the soil will be soaked with blood, and the nation black with crimes," predicted a Connecticut Federalist.[2]

Of the two camps, Federalists enjoyed marked advantages. The party controlled the Senate and the House of Representatives as well as the presidency; and in the summer of 1799 seats it had picked up in both houses of Congress included ten in southern states, a Republican stronghold whose political strength, it bears noting, was inflated by the three-fifths clause in the Constitution allowing a slave to be counted as three-fifths of a person for purposes of apportioning presidential electors as well as congressmen in each state. Moreover, by 1800, the Adams administration, in the spirit of redeeming national honor, had conducted an undeclared war against France, supported by appropriations for a new navy and an expanded army commanded by Hamilton himself, and laws aimed at the suppression of domestic dissent and foreign subversion—all redounding to the government's strength notwithstanding Republican protests. But Adams's reelection was scarcely a foregone conclusion, not least due to fractures in Federalist ranks stemming from the president's decision to dispatch to Paris envoys who helped to bring an end to the quasi-war with France. In October, Timothy Pickering had written bitterly of his "indignation, chagrin, and distress." Of the "eastern people," John Marshall observed to his brother-in-law, "perhaps this ill humor may evaporate before the election comes on—but at present it wears a very serious aspect."[3]

By the first months of 1800, it was widely assumed that Vice President Jefferson would again challenge Adams, his estranged friend and ally, for the presidency. As a Virginia Federalist later observed, Jefferson was "the 'rallying point,' the head quarters, the everything" of the Republican opposition. In contrast to his reluctant candidacy during the election of 1796, when supporters feared that he might not serve if elected, Jefferson's mood had stiffened. As demonstrated by the Virginia and Kentucky Resolutions, which he and Madison had authored, the Alien and Sedition Acts warranted particular condemnation. While Congress remained in session, Jefferson continued to cultivate an image

Rembrandt Peale, Thomas Jefferson, *1853. A copy of the original painted by Peale in 1800*

of detachment, appearing above the fray of electoral politics. Not only did he rarely engage in public discourse about the election, but he also desisted from mailing confidential letters for fear that Federalist postmasters might intercept and publicize the contents. All the same, he increasingly played an active role behind the scenes, deftly plotting strategy and conferring with a handful of trusted intimates, notably Madison, before leaving Philadelphia in May for his cherished mountaintop estate.[4]

Few in either party were as well informed as Jefferson about the political landscape, including the importance of a handful of swing states whose Electoral College ballots would spell victory or defeat come December 3, when state electors convened to vote. On March 8, despite the House's failure one day earlier to censure Adams, Jefferson reported in a letter to Madison that "the Feds begin to be seriously alarmed about their election next fall." He estimated that the nation's electoral votes would likely be "equally divided," except for New Jersey, Pennsylvania, and New York. Detailing different scenarios for each of the three states—Pennsylvania alone presented myriad possibilities—Jefferson concluded that New York's votes, due to be cast by a majority of the state legislature up for election in late April, would be decisive. More than that, he concluded, "All depends upon the success of the city election," which would send thirteen members to the legislature. "The election of New York, being in April," Jefferson wrote, "it becomes an early and interesting object."[5]

WITH THE PRESIDENTIAL CONTEST JOINED, anger over Robbins's extradition remained raw. "Surrendered to a gibbet," scorned the *Aurora.* Citing the past potency of the "*Robbins's* affair," an Adams supporter in mid-March lamented that Republicans "have not ceased to make a proper use of it." And use it, they did. In addition to echoing earlier complaints of executive meddling, Republican voices condemned the obstinacy of Federalist congressmen for blocking efforts to retrieve records from South Carolina and executive correspondence pertaining to the trials in Trenton, resulting in a "*whitewash.*" Noting Federalist anxiety over the election, "Simon Slim" wrote in late March, "They may conceal and endeavour to bury, they may palliate and refuse to act, but the jealous minds of the people will investigate and take up even the bones of Robbins to exhibit in more strong and vivid colours, the sacrifices made through Executive interference."[6] Federalist ire, in turn, testified to the impact of Republican barbs. The *Philadelphia Gazette* condemned "the weeks of time that have been wasted in the affair of the contemptible Robbins." A Portsmouth, New Hampshire, writer mocked the items allegedly bequeathed in Robbins's will, including a "cut-throat knife" and a hangman's noose "to be loan'd occasionally to any *friend in need.*"[7]

In the meantime, congressional Republicans did not let up. In early April, the House revisited Edward Livingston's resolution introduced in early February calling for legislation to execute future extradition requests from Britain. For nearly two months, the measure had lain in a committee during the debate over Adams's censure. But on April 2, the issue returned to the floor when John Marshall introduced a bill requiring written testimony in future instances to be transmitted to the secretary of state and laid before the president. He alone would "decide whether the matter was cognizable in any court of the United States or whether the offender should be delivered up." In a nod to Republicans, Marshall's proposal promised to avert the likelihood that protestations of American citizenship would again fall on deaf ears. But in reaffirming the supremacy of the executive in foreign policy, the bill stripped the judiciary of a voice, unless solicited by the president. And the bill offered no assurance that Americans would henceforth be tried in the United States by a jury of their peers rather than face extradition.[8]

Although John Nicholas of Virginia accepted some of Marshall's language, he insisted on two amendments. The first, sharply curtailing the executive's power, forbade the surrender of "any person for offences, for the trial of which any Courts of the United States are competent," thereby preserving "inviolable the Constitutional right of trial by jury." Narrower in scope but more politically charged was the second provision, declaring that any person apprehended under the British Treaty who professed to be an American "impressed into the British service" would be permitted to "send for testimony to prove the facts of his claim." Additionally, should it then "appear he was impressed and kept on board a British ship contrary to his desire," he would be discharged from custody.[9]

The matter stalled, while the amendments were printed and circulated, until April 28, a clear, cool Monday when the House went into a committee of the whole. Discussion of the first amendment fell to Nicholas. Any doubt that Robbins's extradition lay at the core of the controversy was quickly put to rest as the Virginian questioned the premises of Marshall's March defense of presidential authority. If late in coming, the Republican rejoinder to Marshall was no less forceful. Although, Nicholas explained, he had not intended to speak, a colleague who had planned to take the floor had fallen ill, and Nicholas was loath to let "the doctrines" of his fellow-Virginian "go unanswered," however "ingeniously arrayed and eloquently delivered." He proved up to the task. Speaking at length, Nicholas noted at the outset that Marshall had "considerably narrowed the subject" by ignoring that the United States, under international law, held concurrent jurisdiction in the Robbins case. "The slightest attention to the arguments formerly used on this subject," Nicholas chastised, "will show that his colleague's positions were wholly irrelevant." Indeed, Marshall had misinterpreted a critical legal source, Thomas Rutherforth's *Institutes of Natural Law* (1754–56), which plainly denied a nation exclusive legal jurisdiction over its ships at sea. Marshall's claim that the executive alone could execute a foreign treaty was "little more than assertion." Most important, only in American courts, Nicholas avowed, would citizens "be protected from punishment for acts which are merely an assertion of the freedom which we are bound to cherish." Other members weighed in on both sides, though Marshall remained seated throughout the protracted debate. Federalists objected on the grounds that the treaty could not be altered, but remarkably, to the embarrassment of the administration, the amendment nearly prevailed, losing 42 to 45. The House mooted Nicholas's second amendment the following day; but with no consensus likely, any chance of a vote, much less passage of a bill, died, and with it legislation designed to implement Article 27 before Congress adjourned on May 14, not to reconvene until November in the new capital of Washington.[10]

Even so, in the public mind the storm over Robbins showed no signs of flagging. Along with newspapers, circular letters from congressmen to their constituents contained full descriptions of House proceedings. Since the defeat of Livingston's resolution of censure, Republicans and Federalists alike invoked the "ghost of Robbins." "I defy the most perverted political imagination to conjure up a more wicked ghost," Congressman John Chew Thomas angrily wrote a Maryland constituent in late May.[11]

Besides possessing a life of its own, the issue had grown inseparable from other controversies, among them the Sedition Act in suppressing speech critical of the government. Already the Senate had sought in March to prosecute William Duane, the publisher of the *Aurora,* for printing congressional documents embarrassing to Federalists. One of his counselors was the republican polemicist Thomas Cooper, an Oxford-educated barrister who acquired American citizenship after emigrating in 1794 to Pennsylvania. As early as July 1799, Secretary Pickering had learned of Cooper's searing critiques of the administration, provoking Adams to exclaim that his "libels and satires" were "lawless things, indeed!" Never before had Adams read "a meaner, a more artful, or a more malicious libel. I despise it; but I have no doubt that it is libel against the whole government, and, as such, ought to be prosecuted."[12]

On a rainy Saturday, April 12, a federal circuit court in Philadelphia indicted Cooper for libeling the president. Joined by U.S. District Judge Richard Powers, the presiding judge was none other than the zealous Federalist Samuel Chase, the Supreme Court justice who had presided in Trenton two years earlier. The indictment, submitted by the U.S. Attorney for Pennsylvania, William Rawle, cited several instances of libel originating the previous summer in an article in the *Sunbury and Northumberland Gazette,* a small Republican weekly in central Pennsylvania. Worse, from the administration's perspective, the *Aurora* had given Cooper's remarks broad exposure by reprinting them in November. Included were criticisms of Adams's competence and the swollen size of military appropriations. But the most serious allegation, as all parties acknowledged upon reassembling the following Saturday, the nineteenth, was Cooper's claim that Adams had inappropriately influenced Judge Bee to extradite Robbins—"an interference without precedent, against law, and against mercy," Cooper had charged in the immediate wake of the sailor's surrender. Having written that this injustice was as yet "too little known," Cooper had vowed that "the republican citizens of this free country" should be "fully apprized before the [presidential] election." And, he added, "They shall be." In light of the ensuing controversy, it was a promise that Cooper, among others, had kept. As he himself recognized, eight months later there was no need, for the jury's sake, to "enter into all the details of evidence and argument." "This case," he noted, "has received such full and such *recent* discussion; it has been so much talked of *in* congress, and written of *out* of congress."[13]

Under Chase's heavy thumb, there was little doubt of the court's verdict, notwithstanding Cooper's impassioned defense, which lasted more than three hours. With Pickering sitting in the audience, Cooper introduced a copy of the secretary's letter of June 3, 1799, to Bee conveying the president's "advice and request" that Robbins be delivered up to the British. Further, Cooper shrewdly argued, the president did so, uncertain himself of the rectitude of his involvement. "Advice and request," Cooper declared, "is the expression of hesitation and distrust; he felt the impropriety of his conduct at the time, and his language bears the impression of his feelings." Not yet finished, Cooper averted to the three sailors from the *Hermione* tried before Judge Chase in New Jersey. It was an identical prosecution, he observed, save for the absence of presidential interference; but Chase refused to take the bait and kept silent. Equally pointed was Cooper's account of President Washington's rebuff in 1794 to French appeals urging the surrender of Captain Henry Barré for desertion. "General Washington," he quoted, "from the nature of the subject, as well as from the spirit of our political Constitution, left the judiciary department [that is, the courts] to decide the question."[14]

While Chase was outwardly accommodating, even offering to adjourn the proceedings for an hour to permit Cooper, during his defense, to "recruit" his "strength," he was unyielding in more substantive rulings, including forbidding the introduction of evidence from newspapers in lieu of official copies from the administration, which had denied defense requests. Nor was Cooper allowed to subpoena Adams and Pickering, or a clerk in the secretary's office. A Philadelphia paper reported with delight that "leading Jacobins" were observed in the courthouse "passing to and fro, with folded arms, and with countenances gloomy, sullen and lowering." Rumors spread among Republicans that the jury had been packed with "old Tories and British merchants."[15]

Chase's charge to the jurors, following the prosecution's closing remarks, made no pretense to impartiality. Despite the government's burden, according to the Sedition Act, of proving a defendant's writings false and malicious, Chase insisted otherwise. "The traverser in his defence must prove every charge he has made to be true; he must prove it to the marrow"—a virtually impossible task in light of Cooper's inability to obtain written evidence and summon witnesses. Lest there be any doubt of the gravity of the offense—or Cooper's guilt—Chase opined to the jury, "I can scarcely conceive a charge can be made against the President of so much consequence, or of a more heinous nature. But, says Mr. Cooper, he has done it: I will shew you the case in which he has done it. It is the case of Jonathan Robbins." Indeed, Chase observed, the U.S. district attorney, in his own remarks, had neglected to emphasize the defendant's initial regret that the Robbins case was, as yet, "too little known." "Here then the evident design of the traverser," declared Chase, "was to arouse the people against the President so as to influence their minds against him on the next election." The jury deliberated only twenty minutes before finding Cooper guilty, whereupon Chase sentenced him to a fine of four hundred dollars and six months in prison. The Virginia senator Stevens Thomson Mason wrote Edward Livingston, "The proceeding against Cooper was in the highest degree arbitrary, overbearing, and vindictive." Chase, he added, had sought a conviction with "all the vehemence of a well fee'd lawyer and all the rancor of a personal and implacable enemy."[16]

The administration's effort to gag public criticism paid immediate dividends. Republican papers proved reluctant at first to criticize the trial, while a column in a Federalist paper in Massachusetts applauded the verdict, hoping that it would "have the effect of producing a conviction in the minds of all that the constituted authority of the country must and will prevail." The stalwart *Herald of Liberty* in Washington, Pennsylvania, initially refrained from comment, explaining in its May 5 issue that it had "studiously avoided the insertion of any article to influence the proceedings." More boldly, it went on to assert that Cooper's honor scarcely merited "vindication against the base asperities of prints devoted to the most servile purposes." Moreover, the editor expressed confidence that Republicans could "rest completely assured" that published proceedings of the trial would have a salutary effect on "the mind of the people." In fact, by printing transcripts of the trial, papers of all persuasions, either wittingly or not, gave unprecedented attention to Cooper's allegations, and by May 15, the *Aurora* was defiantly advertising, in bold print, copies—"JUST PUBLISHED"—of *The Trial of Thomas Cooper of Northumberland* for twenty-five cents, this ad placed squarely above one for Charles Pinckney's ever-popular pamphlet, *Three Letters of a South Carolina Planter, on the Case of Jonathan Robbins . . .*[17]

By then, the Robbins controversy had also grown increasingly entwined with opposition to the Alien Friends Act. This act, empowering the president to expel noncitizens designated a threat to the United States, was due to expire on June 25. No one had yet been prosecuted under the law, nor would they be. But the extradition of Robbins, as the uncertainty of his birthplace persisted, continued to force the issue, as no other incident had, of whether foreign émigrés possessed constitutional rights. As early as 1798, Edward Livingston had expressed this conviction, which helps to explain the depth of his involvement in the Robbins case. In the doomed sailor, critics of the Alien Friends Act found a martyr. Not only had Robbins been denied his rights, but as a consequence he had been extradited and executed. "This is a new mode of judicial proceeding: first to hang a man, and then undertake to prove him guilty," averred a Virginian. Whether a citizen or not, was he not entitled to due process of law? Did the Constitution, proponents persisted, not guarantee the right to a speedy and public trial by jury "in all criminal prosecutions"? This and other rights, after all, had in 1798 been accorded the pair of aliens tried in New Jersey alongside William Brigstock, a U.S. citizen.[18]

For a growing number of Republicans there was little in the matter of Robbins to distinguish alien rights from the constitutional prerogatives of citizenship. *Greenleaf's New-York Journal, & Patriotic Register* declared, "A great deal of industry has been made use of to prove Jonathan Robbins to be a foreigner. Suppose it could be proved that he was an Irishman. Would it destroy the evil arising from the precedents?" "It is curious," remarked Simon Slim, "that because a man was born in Ireland, he does not deserve the protection of the laws and constitution. Is an Irishman not a man? Has he not the faculties of a man? Does he not hear, see, aye, and feel as sensibly as an American, even as much so as John Adams?"[19]

Robbins's death, whatever his nativity, continued to highlight the plight of Irish refugees in the United States who, like him, had suffered British oppression for their republican principles. Noting that in past centuries it was not a crime for an Englishman to kill "a mere Irishman," the case of Robbins, according to a Vermont correspondent, represented "a modern improvement over this ancient law." "It is enough," protested the writer, "to *call* a man an Irishman."[20]

For all the clamor over seditious speech and alien rights, it remained the evil of impressment that the martyred Robbins magnified most forcefully. No issue, coupled with the seizure of American ships, generated such animosity toward the Adams administration. Any number of other matters, to be sure, benefited Republicans in their quest for an electoral majority: Alien & Sedition Acts, standing army, debt, taxes, and the undeclared naval war with France, to name the most obvious. All of which, in Republican eyes, reflected the anti-republican, pro-British character of the administration. "These and a thousand other such cases I could enumerate," wrote a contributor to the *Aurora* from Kentucky on April 14. "But above all," he emphasized, "are the unavailing petitions of our fellow citizens lawlessly impressed to the British naval service, and there suffered to remain because our government will [not] actively pursue their releasement"—a "faction, who cringing to British insolence, dare[s] not assert the right of the American citizen." "Things are not long to last," he hoped, unless "the blood of Jonathan Robins has washed away our democracy."[21]

The martyred sailor continued to be an overarching symbol in the popular mind that placards, handbills, poems, and newspapers reinforced—not to mention, of course, the Royal Navy's unrelenting reliance on conscription, which under Adams had only grown more dire as newspaper reports of seized ships and pressed seamen continued to multiply. Robbins had put a face on the evil of impressment that continued to incite public fury, a threat to American lives no less than an affront to national honor. A Federalist complained that Republicans have "even represented that we were not safe in our own doors; that we were liable to be torn away from our wives and children, to be sent away like 'poor Robbins,' and hung in chains, to satiate the savage revenge of the British!" Grafted onto the memory of the mutineer was an indelible image of resistance to British tyranny. "Despicable shall we appear in the eyes of other nations," a Virginian protested, "if the idea is to go forth that an American may be robbed of liberty and held in vile bondage. . . . Shall it be said that we will deliver up to British vengeance our fellow citizen?" The poor sailor, affirmed a New Jersey paper, having "suffered years of misery" aboard a British ship—"driven to labor and battle by the lash"—had "restored himself to freedom" due to "the first law of nature" and the "true spirit of patriotism."[22]

By the middle of April, no public controversy in recent months other than the surrender of Nathan Robbins had been more thoroughly publicized and debated. None had so inflamed political passions—in Congress and the courts, at election grounds, and, most important of all, in newspapers, which, in addition to printing letters and relaying news, provided detailed coverage of the political debates in Philadelphia. Nor had any previous issue, in the short history of the Republic, brought a sitting president so close to congressional censure. That, of course, failed, but so also, remarkably, had Federalist efforts to pass a House resolution commending Adams's conduct in the Robbins affair.

On top of everything else, news broke in early spring that another member of the *Hermione*'s crew in America had been given up to the Royal Navy and executed in Jamaica. In March, a report of "this extraordinary transaction" appeared in the *Aurora*. "Was this man [John Watson] surrendered to the British government by the order of the President of the United States?" the paper demanded. "If so, from what source did Mr. Adams derive his authority for the exercise of such a power? Not we presume from the Constitution, not from any of the existing laws—nor even the *supreme law of the land,* the British Treaty itself." In the *Alex-*

andria Times, a correspondent from Norfolk wrote, "The public mind has been in a state of agitation for these three weeks past." Republican papers elsewhere faithfully recounted details, including a postscript from Norfolk that the sailor from the *Hermione* had been surrendered the preceding year by a city official.[23]

NEW YORK WAS CRUCIAL. THE first state to hold an election in a series of contests designed, directly or indirectly, to select members of the Electoral College between April and early December, the state of New York, with 12 electoral votes, was the largest jewel left in the crown. Virginia (21) and Massachusetts (16) controlled more votes, but each rallied around its native son. Meanwhile Pennsylvania's 15 ballots were yet to be apportioned because of the failure of Governor McKean and the legislature to reach a compromise. Opposition from the Federalist-dominated state senate raised the possibility that Pennsylvania would abstain from voting—a calamity for Republicans who had received all but one of the state's 15 votes in 1796. By contrast, not only was New York in play, but the outcome of the election promised the victor an important measure of momentum. Partisans on both sides shared Jefferson's appraisal of the contest's centrality, all the more since Adams's victory in New York had sealed Jefferson's narrow defeat four years earlier. Of Federalist prospects, Robert Troup, an intimate of Alexander Hamilton, in March wrote Rufus King in London, "We are full of anxiety here about the election of our members. . . . We must bring into action all our energies; if we do not . . . Jefferson will be in." Soon afterward Charles Pinckney of South Carolina expressed Republican apprehension to Edward Livingston: "We look with great anxiety to you & your election." Livingston had, in fact, just written Jefferson that "the prevalence if not the very existence of republicanism in the U States depends so much on the event of our ensuing Election."[24]

Scheduled over three days, from April 29 to May 1, the election would choose candidates from two competing slates, nominated by the parties, for the state legislature. As voters understood, the newly elected legislators—assemblymen and senators—would vote as a single body for presidential electors in December. Just a simple majority would be

Francis Guy, The Tontine Coffee House, Wall & Walter Streets, *ca. 1797.*
A popular meeting place for politicking in lower Manhattan, it appears on the left.

needed. As Jefferson had forecast, nowhere else were so many seats up
for grabs as in the densely packed neighborhoods of Manhattan, which
held the balance of power in the legislature. "It is universally acknowledged both by the federalists and jacobins, that *the election of a President,*
on either side, depends upon the city of New York," remarked a South
Carolinian.[25]

No longer the nation's capital, or even the state's, owing to its trans-
fer to Albany in 1797, New York remained the second-largest city after
Philadelphia, as well as the busiest port in the United States. By 1800, it
contained a population of more than sixty thousand, an alphabet soup
of English, Dutch, Germans, Irish, Sephardic Jews, French Huguenots,
and African Americans, both slaves and free blacks. Stretching fifteen
miles in length, Manhattan was bounded by the East River (not to be
spanned until 1883 by the Brooklyn Bridge) and the majestic Hudson,
a vital conduit of agricultural produce from northern New York and
western New England. The island was three miles across at its widest.
As trade flourished, so too had the city's infrastructure, notwithstanding
the irregular design of its grid. Many of its thoroughfares, to be sure,

were narrow, dirty, and crooked, lined with wooden houses that a passing visitor termed "mean, small, and low." Nor did this observer find shopkeepers as "civil and obliging" as in Philadelphia. But in opulent neighborhoods bordering the Hudson there were brick homes and wide streets, including Broadway, which no other "city in the world," the visitor exclaimed, could equal for elegance.[26]

The outcome of the election was anything but predictable. At first glance, fate appeared to favor the Republicans. National issues, among them furor over Robbins, had set Adams on his heels; and New York Republicans claimed a brilliant strategist in forty-four-year-old Aaron Burr, who in 1796 had like Jefferson run as a Republican for the presidency and now, four years later, hoped to boost his influence in the party, with an eye, possibly, to becoming vice president by finishing second in the electoral college. Only five feet six in height, Burr had a handsome face, natural charm, and intelligence that more than compensated for his slight stature. A native of Newark, New Jersey, he descended from a family of intellectual preeminence. His mother was the daughter of the famed New England evangelist Jonathan Edwards; whereas Aaron Burr the elder, a theologian in his own right, was the second president of the College of New Jersey, from which his son had graduated with distinction at age sixteen. In the Revolutionary War, the younger Burr served with conspicuous bravery before becoming a prominent lawyer in New York. He entered politics in 1784 as a state assemblyman and found himself at odds, professionally and ideologically, with another talented attorney, Alexander Hamilton. Their differences sharpened during Washington's presidency when Burr, as a U.S. senator from New York, joined Jefferson in opposition to administration policies, especially the British Treaty. Still and all, Burr proved not a rigid ideologue, but a pragmatist for whom politics represented a contest for power, privilege, and personal profit. Defeated in his bid for reelection, he again turned his hand to furthering Republican prospects in New York City. A visiting Englishman labeled him "a genius of singular perspicacity."[27]

By the eve of April's election, Burr had constructed the foundations of America's first political machine, complete with ward committees, rallies, and the use of his own spacious home as a campaign headquarters, well stocked with refreshments and mattresses for exhausted parti-

John Vanderlyn, Aaron Burr,
1802

sans. No less important, he had personally recruited a baker's dozen of luminous candidates identified with different factions of the party, including Horatio Gates, the hero of the Battle of Saratoga in 1777, and George Clinton, who had served six terms as governor of the state. Never again in American history would such an impressive slate compete simultaneously for seats in a state legislature.[28]

For all their troubles, Federalist leaders exuded confidence. Jefferson, in many minds, remained a radical democrat and a Francophile. Martha Washington, George's widow, thought him "one of the most detestable of mankind." While conceding the impact of Republican newspapers in spreading "atrocious lies and perverse misrepresentations," Timothy Pickering predicted that the electors selected by the state legislature would "doubtless be to a man opposed to Jefferson." Just one year earlier, the party had easily won a majority of seats in the assembly. The governor, John Jay, and most members of the senate were Federalists. Such political prowess had enabled them to block Republican efforts to hold popular elections for presidential electors, hoping instead to garner every electoral vote by keeping their legislative majorities rather than split the difference, district by district. All or nothing. Moreover, Hamilton, whose political instincts equaled Burr's, stepped forward to assume command of the campaign—reputedly "sure of success." That Hamilton despised President Adams is not to be doubted, but he yet hoped for a Federalist triumph in December. Victory in New York would boost his influence in the party, laying the groundwork perhaps for a new candidate with a strong Federalist pedigree in place of Adams.[29]

The illegitimate son of a bankrupt British trader and a French mother on the island of Nevis, Hamilton was orphaned in youth, only to come under the care of a Presbyterian minister who sent him to King's College (now Columbia University) in New York. Every bit as heroic as Burr during the war, he ascended rapidly to become Washington's senior aide-de-camp. If Hamilton's checkered childhood explained his voracious ambition, then his nationalistic spirit, like John Marshall's, was forged in the military. His subsequent success as a New York lawyer, coauthor of the Federalist Papers, secretary of the Treasury, and party leader insured that the contest for control of the legislature would be warmly fought, as did the opportunity to engage his longtime nemesis at close quarters. The legendary French foreign minister Talleyrand later ranked Hamilton above Napoleon and William Pitt as the era's greatest political figure.[30]

Anonymous, after John Trumbull,
Alexander Hamilton,
nineteenth century

In an unusual step designed perhaps to draw working-class votes, Hamilton cobbled together a slate of candidates who were equally conspicuous for nothing, including a potter, two grocers, a baker, and a ship chandler. Hamilton matched Burr's frenetic pace, which was no mean feat. Similar in height and stature, with light hair and piercing eyes, he, too, bore a reputation for perseverance and unbridled energy. In advance of the election, Federalist committees met regularly, and Hamilton, like Burr, personally took to the streets to preach the virtues of Federalism, occasionally on horseback. Scoffed a critic, "Every day he is seen in the street hurrying this way and darting that." Come the election, "runners" for both campaigns stood ready to spread the gospel from one ward to the next, while party leaders stationed themselves at polling places.[31]

It is tempting to attribute the election's outcome to planning and logistics. And yet, for all the painstaking preparation, voters would cast ballots on the basis of their deepest convictions, hatreds, and fears. Without a clarion call capable of mobilizing grassroots support, politicking alone, however well orchestrated, would not succeed. Now more than ever, in the six weeks preceding the contest the city's newspapers entered the fray, aggressively publishing columns alongside partisan articles masked as news. For ammunition, Republicans drew heavily from Adams's presidency, though the British Treaty remained a grievance that explained any number of recent ills, notably the undeclared war with France, itself the wellspring of such iniquities as the Alien and Sedition Acts, heightened taxes, and a standing army. Still, the salience of some issues threatened to ebb, thereby dampening Republican ardor. As Robert Goodloe Harper asked, "What can they [Republicans] hope to do, which is not already to be done? Will they make peace with France? It is in a train of being made. Will they reduce the army? It is reduced [very shortly, in fact, disbanded by Adams and Congress]. Will they repeal the Alien and Sedition Laws? . . . They expire of themselves next session; and the occasion for them having ceased, no body thinks of renewing them. Will they discharge the public debt? Provisions are already made for its discharge."[32]

By contrast, Robbins, the martyred symbol of British impressment, continued to generate unending attacks. "To Timothy Pickering, Judge Bee, and his advisers and requestors, I wish the ghost of Robbins may be their diurnal and nocturnal visitant," wrote Simon Slim in mid-April. Arguably, no grievance proved more powerful, as the New York election neared, than Adams's surrender of an American who had valiantly struggled, as an impressed seaman, to resist enslavement by British oppressors. Again and again Republicans castigated the administration for its betrayal of "POOR ROBBINS." Given America's reputation as an asylum from tyranny, a broadside marveled that anyone claiming "to be a citizen could be delivered to a foreign tribunal and military execution." In Newark's *Centinel of Freedom,* just days before the contest, an "Essex Whig" lashed out, "He was loaded with irons, delivered over to the bloodhounds of Britain, tried by a court-martial, condemned, and *hung in chains*!!" It did not help that weekly news of freshly impressed sailors magnified the impact of polemical attacks. In March and April, newspapers reported that three hundred Americans served aboard British ships in Kingston harbor. Despite repeated complaints, Admiral Parker refused to grant an audience to an American agent. "You must not be surprised," the diplomat reportedly remarked, "if you should hear that I was impressed!!!" "The English," declared a New York paper in late April, "have never ceased their depredations, and have lately very greatly increased them."[33]

No less powerful was a long polemic, also printed in New York just

before the election in both the *American Citizen,* the city's leading Republican daily, and the semiweekly Republican *Watch-Tower.* Addressed by
a "Republican Farmer" in the state to the citizens of New York and
five other states who stood to choose "members to their state legislatures . . . in order to secure the election of Electors of a President," the
letter touched on a variety of grievances. None loomed as large, or was
expressed as forcefully, however, as Robbins's extradition. Urging voters
to "attend to the late proceedings of the House of Representatives on
the case of Jonathan Robbins," the author declared, "The most remarkable thing in the business is that the president's friends afterwards with-
drew Mr. Bayard's motion approving his (the president's) conduct in the
affair, and the plain fact is that although a majority cannot be brought to
a censure, yet that a majority have not been brought to approve explicitly his advising and requesting a judge to act in the case of Robbins,
whose life was at stake, and who has since been executed. . . . How can
you again be ever decently called upon to support by your votes a man
against whom there have been such charges—against whom indeed suspicion of improper conduct must rest, until it is removed by a clear
unequivocal and explicit vote of approbation?"[34]

For Federalists, the timing could not have been worse for news of fresh
British malfeasance to appear in the *American Citizen.* A "stranger" had
delivered the "communication" from Jamaica to the *American Mercury*
in Hartford, Connecticut. Although the editors could "not vouch for its
authenticity," they published the missive on April 17, as did three papers
in New York City besides the *American Citizen* over the next nine days.
A forty-four-gun British frigate, the *Acasta,* was said to have seized the
American brig *Sally* of New London off the coast of Jamaica "without
the slightest pretext for condemnation." According to the captain, James
Stewart, who reached New London on April 4, the entire crew except for
himself and the cabin boy, all of whom were Connecticut natives, was
carried to Kingston and impressed "without discrimination." The British captain also confiscated $4,250 from Stewart's sea chest. Treated with
"personal incivilities and contempt," Captain Stewart returned with the
Sally, joined by the masters of other American vessels whose crews had
been pressed "with their protections in their hands."[35]

Although the report bore the ring of truth, election-eve shenanigans cannot be discounted. For inspiration New York Republicans had only to recall the damaging impact, one year earlier, of allegations of French violence on the eve of elections for the state legislature. Beginning in April 1799, scores of Federalist newspapers—"from one end of the continent to the other"—including those in New York, reported the slaughter of the American captain and crew of the ship *Ocean* by French privateers north of Cuba. Only months afterward, upon news of the vessel's safe arrival, with a full company, was the "*fabricated massacre*"—as the *Aurora* put it—uncovered. One month before the vote in 1800, a New York acquaintance wrote Albert Gallatin, "It is hoped that the crew of the Ocean will <u>not again</u> be murdered."[36]

Then also, the fate of the *Sally*'s crew was oddly reminiscent of Robbins's narrative, to say nothing of being ill timed. It was a yardarm of the *Acasta,* after all, from which Robbins, a reputed Connecticut seaman like the crew members of the *Sally,* had been hanged in August. A farrago of ill fortune or a Republican ruse designed to wreak maximum damage? By the end of April, the *Mercantile Advertiser,* which inclined Federalist, alleged that the brig was actually a Swedish ship named the *Mary* that had been captured by a French privateer before being retaken by the British. Further, no Americans had belonged to the *Mary*'s crew, all of which Republicans adamantly denied. Unfortunately, neither of the *Acasta*'s logs help to resolve the mystery, apart from placing the frigate in the vicinity of Jamaica after leaving the northern port of Montego Bay on January 30. And while the *Acasta* in late winter and early spring intercepted several American vessels, four in March alone, their names were not recorded. Nor are there references in the logs to either a Swedish ship or a French privateer.[37]

But this inflammatory news, whether true or false, was not the worst of it. The presidential election of 1800, as Joanne Freeman has written, was one in which contingent and unexpected events played a powerful role—arguably none more so than the sudden arrival of HMS *Cleopatra.* In the midst of the uproar over the *Sally* and her Connecticut crew, on April 28, the day before the polls were due to open, another British frigate, in the oddest twist of all, appeared in New York City's upper bay, just off Governors Island, a half mile south of Manhattan. The captain of the thirty-two-gun ship was Israel Pellew, the younger brother of Edward,

William Guy Wall, New York, from Governors Island, *1820*

Britain's greatest living frigate commander, whose daring feats during the French Wars made him as popular as Nelson with the British public. More than once, however, Edward, the future Viscount Exmouth, had been forced to salvage the career of his star-crossed brother, at best a mediocre commander who suffered from a lethal blend of ineptitude and arrogance. Due in part to Israel's negligence in 1796, his frigate the *Amphion* exploded off the coast of Plymouth, resulting in three hundred fatalities. The following year, not only did his next crew mutiny at Spithead, but they also insisted that Pellew be put ashore along with other "tyrannical" officers. Owing to Edward's aid, however, this humiliation did not keep Israel from receiving a third frigate, the *Cleopatra*.[38]

Assigned to the North American station at Halifax, Nova Scotia, the *Cleopatra*, like other British ships operating off New England, became notorious for confiscating American merchant vessels with contraband. But in April, she drew a different mission. Pellew was to retrieve £60,000 placed in New York City for safekeeping to finance fortifications at the Halifax garrison. It was bad enough that shortly past dawn on the twenty-third amid rain and high winds, the captain ordered the seizure of a pair of American vessels en route to Amsterdam, the *Char-*

lotte and the *Warren,* one of which was owned by a New York merchant. Having first stayed its course, the *Charlotte* hove to after the *Cleopatra* fired six guns, the final shot striking "just astern of her." On being boarded, the two prizes, each commandeered by a dozen or so British sailors, were sent to Halifax and their crews taken aboard the *Cleopatra,* all of which a mate of the *Charlotte* subsequently detailed in a sworn affidavit. What enraged residents of New York all the more was that Pellew, in the wake of seizing the vessels, was "*insolent enough,*" five days later, "*to anchor near the city*" in order to collect the garrison's funds as well as take on fresh water and provisions, all the while rejecting the owners' pleas to return their ships. It did not help that the *Cleopatra* announced her arrival by saluting the fortress on Governors Island (Fort Jay, named after the prominent Federalist governor and former Supreme Court chief justice) with seven guns. "Thus, my friends," proclaimed a freshly printed handbill, "are you robbed, almost at your own doors, of above TWO HUNDRED THOUSAND DOLLARS in property, and your Fellow-Citizens detained perhaps in chains in sight of their wives and families."[39]

Tuesday the twenty-ninth dawned fair and bright for the opening of the polls. Not for another day would the two American crews be permitted ashore, by which time confusion and fear had started to sweep the island. The *American Citizen* exhorted, "Is this not alarming in the greatest degree! The vessels in our port, nay even our market boats, are unsafe. . . . Shall we continue to cherish this viper in our bosoms? Can it be possible that the Federal party in this country are so blinded by prejudice, and actuated by party spirit, that they cannot see the danger?" "Let us go forward to the polls," urged the paper, and "give our suffrages to the men who have once released us from the tyrannical yoke of Britain, and who now come forward once more to secure you that liberty they have so hardily earned!" On Thursday, a contributor styled "Shade of Seventy-six" echoed, "Heavens, are you men, and will you suffer this? Will you this day, by giving your votes for Englishmen, Tories and Aristocrats, encourage new depredations?" Caught badly off guard, Hamilton hastily denied the *Cleopatra*'s seizure of American ships, accusing Republicans of an "electioneering trick" in attempting to rally party activists.[40]

By then, Burr, never one to miss the main chance, had swiftly sprung into action. Republicans plastered handbills and placards across the city, tapping into a deep reservoir of anti-British resentment. According to a letter in the *Philadelphia Gazette* from a distraught Federalist in Manhattan, men dressed as sailors paraded "through every street & alley, proclaiming, as they passed, that they had recently escaped from British press-gangs, and from on board the British frigate then at the watering place." Whether they were actually crew members of the *Charlotte* and *Warren,* freshly freed from the *Cleopatra,* mattered little. More alarming still, the "sailors" announced that all American seamen would henceforth be subject to impressment by the Royal Navy. Although the newspaper correspondent estimated New Yorkers to be three-fourths "decided Federalists," he despaired that "these and a thousand other lies gained belief among the too credulous citizens, and effectually turned the election." Among other rumors, one in all likelihood stemmed from Britain's desire to send agents ashore from ships docked in American ports, ostensibly to seize naval "deserters" with the cooperation of local officials. However circumscribed the navy's intentions, prospects for abuse could only have heightened fears over the appearance of press-gangs in city streets. Of the *Cleopatra*'s arrival, a Massachusetts Federalist moaned, "The people of New York are highly exasperated at this conduct."[41]

The polls closed on a rainy Thursday evening. "Republicanism Triumphant," reported a party lieutenant in a midnight letter to Gallatin in Philadelphia. By any reckoning, the results were catastrophic for Adams and the Federalists. Along with three senate seats, Republicans swept all thirteen of the city's assembly seats by a combined margin of 440 ballots, representing some 8 percent of those cast, a striking turnaround from the previous year. Prima facie evidence hints at the dramatic impact of the *Cleopatra*'s ill-timed arrival. In the city, roughly two-thirds of adult white males possessed the right to vote, which required either ownership of a freehold worth £20 or tenancy in a domicile valued at £40. Republican candidates drew especially large numbers of votes from the city's two poorest wards in northern Manhattan, the sixth and the seventh. With turnout extremely high, each of these wards recorded more than twice the number of votes cast in affluent wards at the southern end of the island. Overflowing with working-class families, the sixth and seventh wards contained not only seamen fearful of incurring the fate of Jona-than Robbins but also mechanics and laborers alarmed at the possibility, however far-fetched, of British press-gangs in Manhattan. Memories yet lingered of attempts before the Revolution to conscript New Yorkers. In August 1760, armed resistance by American seamen ended in the death of five British sailors, whereas in 1764 Manhattan rioters burned a long-boat, successfully stranding a press-gang and its five captives on shore, as the commanding officer fled for his life.[42]

The balloting virtually guaranteed the party of Jefferson all of the state's twelve electoral votes. From Philadelphia, a dejected Robert Lis-ton conveyed the disturbing news to Lord Grenville. Following Pellew's arrival, he recounted, handbills were "instantly distributed, containing the most infamous misrepresentations of the conduct of Captain Pellew, and of his intention in coming to New York." With no time for "imme-diate counteraction" from administration supporters, the "effect," Liston bluntly reported, "was decisive," with the likelihood, as a consequence, "that Mr. Adams will at all events lose his election to the Presidency."[43]

The outcome in New York did not guarantee a Republican victory come December, but at a minimum it staved off a crippling defeat, to say nothing of the boost that it gave to party morale and the distress inflicted on Federalist spirits. On receiving the news, the U.S. Senate adjourned for the day in Philadelphia. "The New York election," wrote Gallatin, "has engrossed the whole attention of us." "Exultation on our side is high; the other party are in low spirits." So upset was Hamilton that he recklessly implored Governor Jay, with the aid of a lame-duck legislature, to counter the results by selecting electors in order to prevent "an *Atheist* in Religion and a *Fanatic* in politics from getting possession of the helm of the State." Notwithstanding his own disappointment, Jay had the good sense to ignore such a drastic appeal. Meanwhile, an exhilarated Edward Livingston wrote Jefferson, "We have completely and triumphantly succeeded."[44]

Deeply disheartened, President Adams held Hamilton responsible for the loss, convinced that members of the Federalist slate had been selected not for their merit but for their fealty to the former secretary. Owing to events in New York, Adams decided to purge his cabinet of two dissident voices aligned with Hamilton. On May 5, he asked for the resignation of Secretary of War James McHenry, to whom he thundered, "Hamilton has been opposing me in New York." "He has caused the loss of the election." To the delight of Republicans, Timothy Pickering was the next to depart. After he refused to resign, Adams dismissed him. "If ever a man went out of a public station loaded with the universal execrations of an injured country, it is Mr. Timothy Pickering," declared the *Aurora*.[45]

Ever since Adams had approved negotiations with France, the administration had split into rival camps: Adams partisans versus orthodox Federalists loyal to Hamilton. "Mr. Adams and Secretary Pickering are upon the coldest terms," it was reported in early March. "The cabinet is, at present, divided into two parties, who hate each other with the utmost cordiality." To intimates, Pickering attributed Adams's animosity to his refusal as secretary to support the appointment of William Stephens Smith, Adams's son-in-law, to the rank of brigadier general. Closer to the mark, the president had long resented Pickering's patent disloyalty. More broadly, he blamed his woes on a "British faction" in the party, led by Hamilton, that was conspiring to put the staunch Federalist Charles Cotesworth Pinckney, a wartime hero of the Revolution, on the ballot with Adams (in no particular order) to save the country from "the fangs of *Jefferson*."[46]

It is not easy to make sense of Adams's behavior. Some orthodox Federalists concluded that he was deranged, others that he hoped to attract rank-and-file votes by adopting a more evenhanded approach in foreign affairs—perhaps, Pickering alleged, by running on a unity ticket to serve as Jefferson's vice president. The dismantlement in May of General Hamilton's beloved New Army, which he had assembled in the event of hostilities with France, coupled with Adams's decision later that month to pardon Jacob Fries and other leaders of the 1799 agrarian uprising in Pennsylvania, reinforced Anglo-Federalist fears—an acceptable cost, Adams may have reasoned, lest Fries's execution for treason create another martyr, particularly among the state's German Americans.[47]

Whatever else, the New York election had demonstrated to Adams the perils of entangling foreign alliances—a warning that the president, by shedding unpopular policies, seemed determined to heed. George Cabot, a former senator from Massachusetts, was appalled: "I am told he talks of his late friends as men either afraid of the English, for which they ought to be treated as cowards, or devoted to the English, for which they ought to be branded as infamous. . . . I readily conceive that Mr. Adams, by rousing the spirit of animosity against the English, which only sleeps in the bosoms of our people, may secure his re-election, and a double portion of power with it."[48]

From late spring to early fall, there was even talk that Adams had disavowed responsibility for Robbins's extradition. Pickering, not the president, was to blame for surrendering an American citizen to the "murderous myrmidons of Britain." "Mr. Adams," reported the *Aurora* in August, "is said to have denied that he had authorized this letter dictating to the judiciary, which would be a violation of the constitution." The squabbling delighted Republicans. "Since the issue of the New York election, and the divisions among the Federalists," lamented Chauncey Goodrich, a Connecticut congressman, in August, "the Democrats have taken courage to come out in open day, and very busy." In a scorching pamphlet, "Marcus Brutus" declared, 'Is it not plain to every intelligent mind, that the measures of our administration have been for several years extremely partial to England? Does not the British treaty contain concessions to that country which are now denied to France? . . . Can any man account for the closeness of the intimacy between Liston and Pickering?" "Mr. Adams," Brutus proclaimed, "has been a very good witness against himself."[49]

NEVER AGAIN, OVER THE REMAINDER of the campaign, would the specter of Jonathan Robbins loom as large in a statewide election—first in Pennsylvania the previous fall and now, more prominently, in New York. Within a matter of days, the *Philadelphia Gazette* testified to Robbins's impact by rushing into print a lengthy defense of the administration's conduct that was widely reprinted in other Federalist papers. "Considerations on the Case of Thomas Nash, falsely called Jonathan Robbins" immediately acknowledged that "much has been said and written of a JONATHAN ROBBINS," not least during a prolonged debate in Congress "with a view to the next election of a President of the United States." "It will no doubt continue a subject of discussion until that election is over." Arguing that Robbins's fate was a matter of international law, the author unabashedly defended Britain's right, as a maritime nation, to suppress naval mutinies, including the necessity of exacting punishment to deter future risings. Echoing Judge Bee's ruling, the paper deemed Nash's citizenship irrelevant, as was the possibility that he had been impressed. Adams had chosen to comply with the law of nations and, more particularly, the British Treaty by surrendering the prisoner rather than protecting Nash, "supposing him a citizen," against "the charge of murder." The alternative, the writer declared, would have exposed the country to "the resentment of Britain," which might have decided to "punish the United States, because it could not punish Nash."[50]

For all of its pragmatism, it was not an argument calculated to assuage popular animosity toward Adams or Britain. It would be hard to imagine a less persuasive rebuttal were it not for the writer's cynical dismissal of natural rights. Notwithstanding John Marshall's recent acknowledgment in Congress that the presence of pressed American citizens would, indeed, have justified violent resistance aboard the *Hermione,* the author derided Republican arguments that Nash, by "the law of nature," enjoyed the right to "use his own force to recover his liberty at any expence." How far, the paper wondered, "might this doctrine of the law of nature be carried?" "I will not suppose," the author wrote sarcastically, "a case of involuntary slavery at sea or land. I will not suppose the case of a negro, who having been kidnapped in Jamaica and sold to the Honourable Charles Pinckney in South Carolina, should there excite mutiny among the slaves of that gentleman, put him and his family to death, and escape to Jamaica." It was a powerful analogy; but, in the wake of the slave uprising on Saint Domingue, it was also one that bespoke desperation, especially for its disturbing reference to a leading Republican senator (and his family) whose impassioned polemic condemning Robbins's surrender still sold widely. In Virginia, the analogy acquired deeper resonance that August, when twenty-four-year-old Gabriel Prosser, an enslaved blacksmith, attempted to mount a massive slave rebellion in the vicinity of Richmond. That Prosser had hoped to enlist the aid of Republicans in slavery's abolition saved neither his life nor those of twenty-five followers.[51]

In the wake of their victory in New York, Republicans continued to trumpet the martyred Robbins. In response to Federalist denials of his nativity, several families were reputedly discovered not far from Danbury from whom he could have originated, among them the brood of a Joseph Robbins in the border town of Southeast, New York, whose son Jonathan had long ago left for the Susquehanna frontier. A letter, reprinted in Virginia from the *Aurora,* observed in June that Robbins's extradition had "sunk deep in the American mind, and will no doubt have great effect in the Presidential election." Federalist frustration over these and other attacks ran deep. Oliver Wolcott, Jr., secretary of the Treasury, despaired to Hamilton, "We may as well attempt to arrest the progress of fire in a mass of gunpowder, as to suppress these calumnies."[52]

June brought another prosecution under the Sedition Act, this against the incendiary journalist James Callender, who had left his native Scotland for Philadelphia in 1793. Six years later, fearful of being indicted for his anti-Federalist broadsides, he fled to Virginia, where he published *The Prospect Before Us,* a scathing critique of the Adams administration. At his trial Samuel Chase again presided, resulting in yet another conviction, in part for Callender's assertion that the president's hands were "reeking with the blood of the poor, friendless Connecticut sailor." Following July Fourth celebrations, the *Philadelphia Gazette* taunted, "Neither the feelings of Governor M'Kean nor of Mr. Jefferson are hurt by being connected in toasts, at drunken revels of the very scum of the earth, with Robbins! Callender! and Duane!!"[53]

Robbins's influence in remaining contests, if less pivotal, persisted. In July, a special election to fill the congressional seat of John Marshall afforded a harbinger. For having forcefully defended Adams in the House, he was tapped in May to replace Pickering as secretary of state (just eight months later, Adams would nominate Marshall chief justice of the Supreme Court). To Marshall's embarrassment, the district voted overwhelmingly for the Republican candidate. "To succeed me," he wrote Harrison Gray Otis, "has been elected by an immense majority one of the most decided democrats in the union." Commented another Federalist, "This is a specimen of the influence of the Secretary of State in his own district."[54]

Marginally more influential in dampening the Robbins firestorm were efforts in North Carolina to circulate copies of Marshall's House speech. "A perusal of it," Congressman William Henry Hill assured an intimate in the Carolina piedmont, "will emphatically impress you." Still, Republicans claimed eight of the state's twelve electoral votes. In Maryland, the parties split the state's ten votes, a better showing for Republicans than in 1796. Front and center in Congressman Gabriel Duvall's public letter to his fifth district constituents in August was "the case of the unfortunate Jonathan Robbins"—about which "a great deal has been said for and against the conduct of the president." Duvall, after summarizing the controversy, described at length President Washington's refusal to surrender Captain Barré to the French in 1794. "Mr. Adams," he noted dryly, "with the precedent of Washington before him, has pursued a different course." Delaware and New Jersey, on the other hand, remained firmly Federalist, notwithstanding the issue's salience. In Wilmington, "Mentor" decried "the impressment and hanging of our sailors according to the British treaty," along with the Alien and Sedition Acts, as "encroachments upon our liberty"; whereas the Republican Committee of Essex County, New Jersey, reminded voters of Adams's decision to deliver up to "British barbarity a person under the protection of the law, with the plea of American citizenship in his mouth." In September, a Connecticut Federalist railed in frustration, "President *Adams* has again and again been charged with the *murder* of Jonathan Robbins!"[55]

By late November, Jefferson and Aaron Burr trailed the Federalist slate of Adams and Charles Cotesworth Pinckney by a single vote, leaving only Pennsylvania and South Carolina to select electors. In Pennsylvania the *Aurora* in Philadelphia had continued to flay the administration over Robbins, among other issues. "There never was a more disgraceful thing done by any country which had the least claim to independence," Robert Slender declared. Invoking a common Republican argument, he demanded, "If this had not been so considered even by those opposed to republicanism in Congress, can any man of common discernment think that Congress would have dismissed the matter as they did?—If they had approved of the president's conduct, Judge Bee's behaviour, and Timothy's impartiality, would they not have agreed to Bayard's motion? Would they not have exculpated the president?" Only after protracted negotiations did Governor McKean and the Republicans garner eight of the state's fifteen electoral votes. Rather than risk casting no ballots at all in December, they grudgingly decided, Robert Liston commented, that the "superiority of a single vote was an advantage not to be despised."[56]

It was fitting, given the far-reaching impact of the Robbins affair, that South Carolina, where he had been arrested, tried, and extradited, was left to decide which of the two parties would receive a majority of electoral votes. Jefferson had claimed the state in 1796, but the popular Charles Cotesworth Pinckney was a native son, as Federalists repeatedly emphasized. "On your legislature, I believe, depends absolutely the election," John Marshall wrote to Pinckney in late November. "The issue of the election of a President," echoed Secretary Wolcott from Washington, "is, at this time, as uncertain as ever; all depends on the vote of South Carolina, and this is claimed, and expected by both parties."[57]

Prospects for Republican success fell largely to Senator Charles Pinckney, who, as party manager, boldly predicted a sweep of the state's eight votes once a freshly elected legislature convened in the capital of Columbia. That "Blackguard Charlie," a second cousin of Charles Cotesworth, still felt passionately about the Robbins affair was not to be doubted. Mocked by the Federalist press as "the friend of the pirate Robbins," he informed voters in the *City Gazette*—"in the ever-memorable case of JONATHAN ROBBINS"—"that although the *federal* majority [in the House of Representatives] would not adopt Mr. Livingston's resolutions, as going too far and looking to impeachment, yet that a majority *of even that house* could never be brought to approve the business." Upon his arrival from Philadelphia in June, a dislocated shoulder notwithstanding, Pinckney assiduously circulated copies of his writings, including his letter denouncing Robbins's extradition, for which he remained best known. Pinckney was "the man," declared an Albany, New York, paper in late October, "whose able and unanswerable writings on the fatal *British Treaty* and the ever memorable case of *Jonathan Robbins*, have justly ranked him among the highest on the list of American patriots and statesmen."[58]

In the meantime, a "Republican of St. Bartholomew's Parish" reminded South Carolinians that Jonathan's "bones are now bleaching on a gibbet at Jamaica"—"a dreadful evidence of the dishonor of his country, and the weakness of those who so disgracefully abandon an unfortunate man, who had as strong claims to protection as any of us." "Never," he implored, "let the name of the unfortunate *Jonathan Robbins* be forgotten; let his melancholy tale be handed down to your latest posterity, and they will learn from it how to protect the unfortunate."[59]

Following election results for the legislature that appeared to favor the Federalists, Pinckney decamped from his Charleston home for Columbia, 130 miles inland. Upon the opening of the assembly session in late November, he lobbied members with unsparing fervor, armed with bundles of handbills, broadsides, and newspapers dispatched by Seth Paine of the *City Gazette* to Peter Freneau, his coeditor and by now Pinckney's close ally in Columbia. On receiving a fresh batch of "letters and the papers and pamphlets," Freneau reported to Paine that everything "possible shall be made of them to assist the cause." Miraculously, after repeated meetings with legislators, Pinckney netted enough support to capture all eight electoral votes, just two days before the Electoral College was set to convene. As he boasted with justice in a letter to Jefferson, "Most of our friends believe that my exertions and influence owing to the information of federal affairs I gave them, has in great measure contributed to the decision."[60]

A New York newspaper proclaimed, albeit prematurely, "We may fairly conclude that Mr. Jefferson will be the President after the 4th of March next; that the Duke of Braintree will be permitted to retire to Quincey, where he may compose compliments to 'England's great Queen,' and chant requiems to the manes [soul] of Jonathan Robbins!" In the end, Jefferson and Burr, the two Republicans, each claimed a total of 73 votes, compared to 65 for the president and 64 for Pinckney, throwing the contest into the House of Representatives and setting the stage for Jefferson's selection on the thirty-sixth ballot and his inauguration on March 4 in the new capital of Washington.[61]

Earlier on that festive day, at the stroke of one minute past midnight, a letter arrived at the White House just hours before John Adams, unwilling to remain for the ceremony, stole away by coach for Massachusetts. Wagons overflowing with personal belongings trailed behind. For the embittered Adams, his presidency was not supposed to end this way. He left a city whose public edifices, despite their rustic surroundings, were already exciting admiration. The letter, which subsequently appeared in Republican papers, was from Congressman Matthew Lyon, a self-made Vermont farmer who as a boy had arrived from Ireland as an indentured servant. He remained best known for having been severely caned in the House in 1798 days after having spat in the face of the Federalist representative Roger Griswold. (According to Edward Livingston, "Gentlemen rose to express their abhorrence of abuse in abusive terms, and their hatred of indecent acts with indecency.") More recently, the "Spitting Lyon," as he was nicknamed, had been fined a thousand dollars and forced to spend four months in an unheated jail cell by virtue of the Sedition Act. In honor of his fortitude, not only was he reelected to Congress by two thousand ballots, but Republican colleagues had allowed him to cast the deciding vote for Jefferson in the House.[62]

Addressed to Adams, his "Fellow Citizen," Lyon's screed was unsparing in its judgment of the president's record: the XYZ Affair, the war, and the Alien and Sedition Acts. "Let me advise you," counseled Lyon, "to take water at the Federal City [Washington] and to land at the nearest port to Quincey; the condolence of your old confederates, all along from this to Quincey, and the silent contempt of the multitude, will be too hard for you to bear." Only when Lyon turned to the topic of Jonathan Robbins did he convey the full measure of his vitriol. Taunting Adams for being haunted by Robbins's ghost, he noted that Thomas Bee of South Carolina had recently been offered a "midnight" appointment as chief judge of the Fifth Circuit Court. "Your confederate in that case," Lyon wrote, "it seems you have provided well for in this world, but there is another world to which you have sent poor Jonathan, where you will both meet him. May you by sincere repentance be prepared for that awful meeting."[63]

HAD RAW MEMORIES OF the martyred Robbins, fraught with emblematic meaning, doomed Adams's reelection amid a rising tide of Anglophobia over the contentious issue of impressment? With the election still under way, Thomas Macdonald, a former British commissioner in Philadelphia, wrote Lord Grenville in late October, "Four-fifths of the people there [the United States] in good earnest believe that we are, *politically* if not morally, a most tyrannical and unprincipled nation." For an example, Macdonald cited the "exultation" in America experienced by "many persons of all descriptions" over the Spithead and Nore mutinies and "the horrible affair of the Hermione frigate." "It was said with satisfaction," he related, "that probably those and similar events were to be ascribed to the *brave* efforts of impressed American seamen, whose *right* to mutiny, and even murder British officers, was *asserted* and maintained in elaborate arguments, even in Congress."[64]

This is not to deny the consequences of dissension within Federalist ranks, including Hamilton's condemnation of Adams in the closing weeks of the campaign in a fifty-four-page diatribe to party leaders. So venomous was the invective that even orthodox Federalists were stunned—redounding possibly to Adams's benefit. Nor is it to ignore that other, in some cases entwined, grievances, notably the Alien and Sedition Acts, spurred Republican voters to the polls. But which other issues, we may ask, by unleashing and sharply accentuating simmering anti-British tensions dating at least to the British Treaty of 1794, incited such deep-seated anger over such a prolonged period prior to the election, or, for that matter, resulted in a de facto vote of no confidence in Adams on the eve of the presidential campaign, as Republican polemicists persistently reminded voters? It was the "palpable delivery of Jonathan Robbins to a British gibbet," a New England newspaper later noted—"this act of mean barbarity"—that for the public broke "the talisman of delusion—the nerve of horror vibrated from Maine to Georgia."[65]

Plainly, the Robbins catastrophe played a significant role in at least two critical swing states: Pennsylvania, by lending momentum to Governor McKean's election, which won for Republicans eight of fifteen electoral votes; and New York, by helping to net all twelve electoral votes. In New York City, which proved critical to Republican prospects, the margin of victory was narrow. As Stanley Elkins and Eric McKitrick have underscored, if "a few hundred votes" had not switched in favor of Republican assembly candidates in wards that were "hitherto safely Federalist," Adams would have been reelected president. And, of course, Robbins's spirit, with the fervid assistance of Republican newspapers, continued to haunt subsequent contests, concluding with South Carolina's surprising turnaround in December. At the very least, the extradition and execution of Jonathan Robbins profoundly reinforced popular perceptions of Adams as a cold-blooded "monarchist" indifferent to the well-being of the common man, particularly when British interests hung in the balance. Condemning impressment as an attack on "the rights of insulted humanity," a Boston writer later opined, "The too ready acquiescence of Mr. Adams to the recommendations of the British ministry in regard to points which comprehend much of our naval independence, lost him the hearts of his countrymen."[66] There was truth in that. If the Robbins affair did not render the election's outcome inevitable, it is also difficult, in its absence, to imagine the Republicans' razor-thin triumph.

9

Jonathan's Ghost

GREAT BRITAIN GREETED THOMAS JEFFERSON'S pending election
with understandable dismay. "The result is certainly unpleasant towards
this Country," the London *Times* remarked in January in anticipation of
his victory. Already relations had begun to cool once John Adams, in the
final year of his presidency, had made peace with France and war with
the "British faction" within his own party. Jefferson's rhetoric, dating
to his opposition to the British Treaty (a "millstone round our necks"),
gave London few grounds for hope, especially in light of the ever-vexing
issue of impressment. On November 28, the envoy Robert Liston wrote
Lord Grenville that only one danger immediately threatened harmoni-
ous relations between the two nations: "The perpetual and numerous
complaints of the impressment of American seamen, and of the unjust
sentences of the British Colonial Courts of Admiralty." Regrettably, he
added, "The nature of this republican government compels the members of the Administration to pay more attention than the matter in
justice deserves."[1]

All the same, relations between Britain and the United States temporarily improved upon news that the Admiralty had recalled Sir Hyde
Parker as commander in chief of the Jamaica station for a post in the
Baltic, where he briefly served as Horatio Nelson's superior at the Battle
of Copenhagen. Parker's indifference in the West Indies to American
protests had long been a source of contention. Even London had grown
exasperated with the Admiral's rapaciousness. In just four years, he had

Anonymous, James Madison,
ca. nineteenth century

reportedly reaped £200,000 in prize money. Equally pleasing to U.S. officials was word, in early 1801, that Captain Israel Pellew of the *Cleopatra* also had been recalled, following a stern complaint in January from Rufus King that Pellew had "vexed our trade upon our own Coast." His brazen appearance off Manhattan the preceding spring was but the most egregious incident. Jefferson's newly appointed secretary of state, James Madison, wrote King in July 1801, "The removal of Admiral Parker and Captain Pellew from the America station, and on the grounds assigned for it, is another indication of a juster policy toward the United States." Robert Liston, reviled by Republicans, had departed as well, pleading ill health owing to the "intemperance of the seasons" in America.[2]

But Secretary Madison yet fretted that Britain, in addition to disrupting American commerce, had over the years impressed nearly two thousand U.S. citizens, more than four-fifths of whom were reputedly native-born. If anything, the number was escalating. From his quarters in the new capital on the Potomac, he informed King, "The complaints daily arriving at this office, show that our mariners are impressed without the least respect for their legal protections, certified in the most authentic forms; that after impressment they are often menaced or maltreated into enlistments." "These wrongs," he emphasized, "have made a deep impression on the American mind," suggesting that continued depredations would cause the United States to retaliate. In October, Madison again expressed frustration to King over the boarding of American vessels, ostensibly to capture fugitives from the *Hermione* still at large:

It is now a long while since the vengeance
of that country has steadily pursued the
actors in the tragedy of the Hermione, and
many dreadful examples of their punishment
have been given. It therefore appears high

time that the scene should be closed, at
least as far as the tranquility and security
of foreingers [*sic*] and their vessels are
concerned.[3]

It was ill news to the Jefferson administration that one of the British
ships again active in the Caribbean was the forty-two-gun frigate HMS
Retribution, none other than the *Hermione* herself, a notorious scourge
to American commerce prior to the mutiny. Within days of her triumphant return to Jamaica from Puerto Cabello in November 1799, officers
of the yard at Kingston had pronounced the frigate "in every respect a fit
ship for His Majesty's Service," to the delight of Sir Hyde Parker. First
named the *Retaliation,* she had been ordered to sea as early as December 22 under the command of Captain Samuel Forster. Newly commissioned the *Retribution* the following September, she spent the next two
years harassing commercial vessels, including American shipping. Thus
the fate of the *Sea Horse,* bound from Puerto Cabello for New York,
which was captured as a prize in February 1801 and brought to Jamaica.
Soon afterward, as the *Retribution* bore down on a foreign schooner off
Santo Domingo, a gun burst, resulting in heavy damage to the larboard
deck and upward of forty deaths. Well covered in the United States,
the story prompted the *Carolina Gazette,* in recalling Jonathan Robbins's fate, to observe that the British "cannot escape the vengeance of
Heaven."[4]

Summoned from Port Royal, the *Retribution* arrived in Portsmouth,
England, in January 1802. The following month at Spithead, the execution of William Bower, a member of the *Hermione's* crew, took place on
her main deck. Not long afterward, she was deployed to help defend the
Thames from a possible French invasion. In June 1805, having changed
hands many times in the course of twenty-two years, the *Retribution* was
finally broken up at the Deptford dockyard in southeast London.[5]

Less easily laid to rest for the Admiralty was the haunting knowledge that numerous mutineers yet remained at large, their ranks thinned
but scarcely eradicated since the uprising. The "fate of the *Hermione*"
an Exeter paper attested in September 1801, remained "fresh in the
memory of the public." Along with Bower and Robbins, another four-

teen men were tried in the years after 1798, on top of the seventeen apprehended within the first fifteen months of the mutiny. Of the sixteen court-martialed after 1798, thirteen were executed. "The hand of Providence," exulted a London newspaper in late 1800, "has evidently shown itself in the punishment of these atrocious wretches, the shame of England and of humanity."[6]

Only a few fugitives were taken at sea, having long scattered across the Caribbean and North Atlantic. James Duncan, a foretopman, on reaching Denmark from the island of Saint Thomas, was imprisoned for mutiny in Helsingør's Kronborg Castle (the setting for Shakespeare's *Hamlet*) before being transferred to a British sloop. Two men, William Johnson and Hadrian Poulson, were found on Curaçao after the Dutch surrendered the island to the British in September 1800. Poulson, a Dane, was convicted of having pushed Pigot overboard. Johnson, who gave himself up, had been employed on the island as a clerk at the American consulate, notwithstanding the consul's knowledge of his checkered past. Conveyed to Portsmouth, Johnson received a pardon from the Admiralty upon the recommendation of a court-martial board. Less fortunate was a shipmate who arrived in Bristol aboard *HMS Hannibal*. Having aroused the captain's suspicion by frequently speaking of the *Hermione* in his sleep, he hurriedly disembarked, later to be seized by crew mates.[7]

Aside from Robbins, authorities netted their most infamous catch in Portsmouth. On March 10, 1802, a sixteen-gun sloop commanded by Captain Edward Kittoe arrived after three years plying the Caribbean. In the ensuing days, a bargeman by the name of Thomas Williams, a favorite of the captain, frequently slipped ashore at the Point, a tongue of land teeming with grog shops on the eastern edge of the harbor. But on the twenty-second, while passing through King James's Gate, Williams was abruptly tapped on the shoulder. "Isn't your name David Forrester?" asked John Jones, Captain Pigot's steward aboard the *Hermione*. Told no, Jones persisted. "Yes, but it was in the *Hermione!*," he exclaimed upon grabbing the seaman. Dragged to a guardhouse following the chance encounter, Forrester confessed. The following week, Jones and Master Southcott were among the witnesses at a court-martial aboard the *Gladiator*. The testimony of either man would have pro-

Thomas Rowlandson, Portsmouth Point, *1811*

duced a conviction, but Jones's recollection was particularly devastating: "David Forester came out of the cabin with a cutlass or tomahawk in his hand. . . . He tapped me on the shoulder and said, 'I have just launched your bloody master overboard.' " Justice for Forrester was swift. Three days later, minutes after describing Pigot's murder and those of two other officers in gruesome detail, he was hanged from a yardarm. "We do not recollect ever seeing so great a number of spectators assembled on such an occasion," reported the *Hampshire Telegraph & Portsmouth Gazette.*[8]

Not for four years did the final execution take place. Just twenty-five years old, Thomas Woods confessed at a Plymouth court-martial to having served aboard the *Hermione* during the mutiny, a statement that Southcott confirmed. Yet as authorities later discovered, Woods had been in Portsmouth on board the *Marlborough* at the time. On being forewarned of Southcott's testimony, rather than assert his innocence, Woods had chosen to incriminate himself, hoping the court would show mercy. In fact, as he pleaded the day before his hanging, Woods had never seen "the outside of the ship," much less served aboard it.[9]

In the annals of the Royal Navy, the mutiny on board the *Her-*

mione was not only the most violent but also one of the most successful. Despite the Admiralty's dogged pursuit, at least a hundred seamen
eluded apprehension. Still at large were such notorious figures as John
Farrel, William Turner, Patrick Foster, William Crawley, and Lawrence
Cronin. Some crew members never left Venezuela, but others, addicted
to the sea, continued to serve under British as well as foreign flags. As
many as nine Hermiones were said to have enlisted aboard the French
warship *La Brave*. Two others played a key role in the *Danae* mutiny
in 1800, in which a British post ship was carried into the French port
of Brest. And almost certainly a sizable, if indeterminate, number of
Hermiones took up new lives in America.[10]

A spate of false confessions akin to that of Thomas Woods rendered
the navy's hunt more difficult. At one time or another, as many as six
sailors boasted of striking the first blow against Pigot. All were interro-
gated and in some cases transported home from overseas, but not one, it
turned out, had served on the *Hermione*. In 1801, William Oates found
himself confined aboard the *Pompee* after bragging about cutting off
Pigot's head. Coming to his senses upon the ship's arrival at Spithead, he
escaped ashore disguised in women's clothing. Every bit as vivid was the
tale recounted by Benjamin Brewster, well known aboard the American
ship *Hero* for claiming to have thrown the boatswain overboard during the uprising. Notwithstanding "being a very violent man," Brewster
had, in fact, been freed from the *Hermione* in April 1797 as an impressed
American citizen from Preston, Connecticut—a former shipmate whom
Thomas Nash, perhaps, later chose to emulate.[11]

Apart from exacting retribution, the Royal Navy undertook modest reforms following the unrest of 1797. Once immediate fears of further violence had subsided, the mutinies, both at home and abroad,
prompted a subtle shift in attitudes toward shipboard discipline. By the
time of the Peace of Amiens in 1802, the rough paternalism of commanders had begun to give way, with the Admiralty's encouragement,
to a more enlightened style of leadership designed to afford sailors
greater dignity and respect. "Seamen are nowadays a thinking set of
people," opined a commander, "and a large proportion of them possess
no inconsiderable share of common sense." Still low by the standards
of merchant seamen, wages rose; and while flogging continued to be

employed, restraint and discrimination were expected of ship captains. In 1806, the punishment of "running the gauntlet" was abolished, and by 1811, captains were required to justify instances of corporal punishment in writing. Then, too, as N. A. M. Rodger has written, "Officers of all shades of opinion united in insisting that men were not to be worked unnecessarily, especially not for drill or show."[12]

In this new mental climate, no less a figure than Sir Edward Hamilton ran afoul of naval regulations. Profusely honored for cutting out the *Hermione* from Puerto Cabello as captain of the *Surprise*, he was summoned before a court-martial at Spithead in January 1802 for having ordered an elderly gunner and his crew strapped to the main rigging—"seized up in the shrouds"—for three hours on a bitterly cold day for having failed to clean the guns on the ship's quarterdeck. (By an odd happenstance, the *Retribution* arrived in port just as the tribunal got under way—"as if," reported a newspaper, "she had come at that particular instant to plead his cause.") Though Hamilton contended that the head injury received at Puerto Cabello had affected his judgment, the board dismissed him from the service. "Such is the close of the career of the gallant officer who cut out the *Hermione*, and who has, from the age of eight years, devoted his life to the service of his king and country," bemoaned a London magazine. "But deeds of heroism," it added, "are no longer in request."[13]

To be sure, most of these changes were a matter of degree, nor were all directly attributable to the *Hermione* or less violent uprisings. They were also the product of a broader shift in cultural attitudes during an age of reform that saw sweeping innovations in law enforcement, including the growing prominence of prisons in lieu of corporal punishment. Yet the 1797 risings, not least the shocking bloodbath aboard the *Hermione*, long weighed on reformers' minds. Even stern disciplinarians did not excuse Hugh Pigot's indiscriminate reliance on the lash—which for reformers, who shared a strong distaste for physical suffering, illustrated the catastrophic consequences of excessive punishment. Others blamed neither Pigot nor flogging but impressment as the root cause of unrest. Conscription, they contended, naturally made seamen more rebellious. Thus in London's *Morning Chronicle*, "Nauticus" reflected in 1815, "The power to inflict severe punishments may be traced to the necessity there

is to repress the ill temper occasioned by impressment, on which therefore these evils may be justly charged."[14]

IT WAS IN THE UNITED STATES, not Britain, that the ramifications
of the *Hermione* mutiny and more particularly the full force of Robbins's surrender continued to be felt most deeply. Following the election
of 1800, their influence was profound and lasting. "While Americans
retain any portion of sympathy or sensibility," declared a Trenton newspaper in July 1801, "they will never forget the order of Mr. Adams to surrender *Jonathan Robbins* to a British officer for execution on a gibbet."[15]

In the wake of his death, Robbins had become an indelible symbol
of British oppression. Again and again Republicans invoked his personal sacrifice—in poems, sermons, essays, and orations. Not since the
Boston Massacre or Lexington and Concord had an act of martyrdom
so transfixed the public. A "raw head and bloody bones story," Federalists decried, owing to the narrative's powerful impact. At a July Fourth
gathering in Wallingford, Vermont, in 1801, a squire proposed in a toast
that the yard arm from which Robbins was hung might "never rot until
every democrat in the United States is hung upon it." In Pennsylvania,
Germantown Republicans, by contrast, celebrated by singing the tune
"Robbins' Ghost." Another favorite, set to the melody of the "Galley
Slave," was "Robbins' Lament":

> By Executive influence, ROBBINS the brave,
> Was a sacrifice, borne away,
> In the hands of his foes, a sad victim
> of state as a martyr he yielded his breath;
> Ye sons of Columbia, O! I think on his fate.
> He resolv'd to have freedom or death.[16]

Following Jefferson's inauguration, a scathing sermon, "The Reign
of Terror," invoked satanic metaphors from the Book of Revelation to
castigate Robbins's oppressors. "Ah Jonathan!" it bemoaned, "thou little
knowest the gloomy fate that awaited thee! The great Beast, full of power,
who sat at the Helm of Government, favoured not thy pious intensions;

and the British Bloodhounds demanded thee back." A refrain oft voiced in Republican papers was "Who gave up Jonathan Robbins?"[17]

In *Jefferson and Liberty,* a five-act play composed in honor of Jefferson's inaugural by the satirist J. Horatio Nichols, Robbins and his ghost both played prominent roles. Other dramatis personae included Judge B., Liston, Timothy Vigilant, and the Duke of Braintree. Says Braintree to Vigilant in the second act, "Altho one murder makes a villain, / 'Tis pard'nable in a case like this, / When a nation's policy is thus involv'd, / We chuse the smaller evil; sacrifice / One vulgar man, sooner than the friendship / Of the well born few whose right is to rule, / Should be dissolved." Depicted, in turn, are Robbins's trial ("O Liberty how art thou perverted!"); Adams's dismissal of Pickering ("Who can tell but he may betray me in the affair of Robbins?"); and Jefferson's triumph at the polls. Afterward, Braintree is awakened one night by Robbins's spirit. "Be ready at a thunders call, / To know thy doom from awful heaven's tongue," Braintree is admonished before his death. "How much a traitor to all human right / Thou wast."[18]

And the issue continued to arise in Congress. In the midst of a House debate in April 1802 surrounding the return of a captured corvette to the French government, John Randolph seized on Federalist calls for an investigation of the Jefferson administration. Never allowed, he declared, was a proper review of Robbins's extradition, which the previous incumbent had blocked with allies in the House. With James Bayard of Delaware rising to protest, only the Speaker's gavel ended a testy debate, though Randolph's eruption would not be his last on the subject. "The case of Jonathan Robbins," a fellow Republican representative later observed, "excited a fermentation in this country almost beyond example."[19]

It was at election time that Robbins's memory roused the greatest ardor. The martyred sailor became a persistent fixture of Republican campaigns. Since the Revolution, there had been no more famous victim of British tyranny; and largely as a consequence, recollections of his death continued to draw droves of voters to the polls, including plenty of Irish Americans. Federalist allegations that Robbins had been a native of Waterford only magnified support among the "sons of Hibernia," first in 1800 and again in 1804. It made no difference that Jefferson's opponent during his reelection contest, Charles Cotesworth Pinckney, bore no responsibility for the Robbins debacle. Noting that "many a doleful ditty will yet be sung by the demos," a Charleston newspaper remonstrated in September 1804, "The democrats at the Northward have once more conjured up the ghost of THOMAS NASH (alias *Jonathan Robbins*) to bear witness against federalism." For Nash, "a pirate and murderer," the paper moaned, "has so long excited the sympathies of the democrats in the middle and Northern States of the Union."[20]

There was little for Federalists to do. Exasperated by the controversy, a loyalist asked, "How long shall we see men, so zealously espousing the cause of foreign outcasts, murderers, pirates, insurgents, house-breakers, and letter-stealers, whilst they persecute with unrelenting rigour, native Americans of honour and integrity who have grown grey in the service of their country?" During the War of 1812, lest the "political depravity of federalism" be forgotten, "Resuscitator," writing in upstate New York, recalled the "Reign of Terror" during the Adams administration. "First in magnitude" was "the case of the poor unfortunate Jonathan Robbins," which he revisited at length. "What American," he demanded, "can read the above account without horror and detestation! Modern federalism is a 'chip of the old block.' " A favorite target remained Timothy Pickering, who, following his tenure as secretary of state, represented Massachusetts in both the Senate (1803–11) and the House (1813–17). As late as 1814, fifteen years after Robbins's extradition, Pickering deplored that the "ghost of Jonathan Robbins has since been repeatedly conjured up; particularly when at any time it was convenient to bring a railing accusation against me."[21]

And John Adams? No one had suffered greater torment at Republican hands, returning to Quincy embittered by his rejection by American voters and the opposition press's unrelenting barbs. Fiercely proud of his accomplishments, at home and abroad, in war and in peace, he struggled to make sense of the political turmoil in 1800 that Jefferson later labeled a revolution. Before American independence, as a Boston lawyer he had famously defended victims of British oppression, among them four Irish seamen charged with the murder of a British naval officer in resisting impressment. Indeed, Adams regarded the case as more important than his storied defense one year later of British redcoats in the aftermath of the Boston Massacre. Not only did his role in *Rex v. Corbet* remain a singular source of pride, but he continued to condemn Britain's reliance on conscription. "A daring act of despotism," he wrote his son John Quincy, in 1808. But if he regretted his decision to sanction Robbins's extradition, having—a New Hampshire paper reflected in 1804—"signed the death warrant of his own dignity," he never acknowledged a twinge of remorse. Instead, both in private and in public the former president gave no quarter in defending his conduct. In the *Boston Patriot* in 1809, Adams wrote of the "hideous clamor" occasioned by the Alien and Sedition Acts and the "surrender according to the British Treaty, of the Irish murderer Nash, imposed upon the public for Jonathan Robbins." Twice in his twilight correspondence with Jefferson, he turned to the "fictitious fabricated case of a Jonathan Robbins who never existed." The unkindest cut? Adams reserved his greatest enmity for the former congressman, Edward Livingston, whose "lying Villainy," he assured Jefferson in 1812, "I have not forgotten." "Neddy is a naughty lad as well as a saucy one," he fumed. Barely a year later, Adams recalled having been threatened by Livingston with "impeachment." Only in a letter of May 13, 1812, to his close friend Benjamin Rush did his tone betray the faintest hint of resignation. Robbins he condemned as "a scandal that ought to have been killed before it died of old age"—"a more infernal, wicked, malicious, unprincipled, deliberate, and cruel scandal never stalked this earth," one that he still failed to comprehend. "Indeed," he confessed to Rush, "I know not whether it be dead yet."[22]

HAD MEMORIES OF ROBBINS BEEN confined to electioneering, they would not have had such sweeping repercussions during Jefferson's presidency. But with majorities in both the House and the Senate, Republicans paid more than lip service to the martyred seaman. In his first address to Congress, hand delivered on December 8, 1801, to be read aloud by a clerk, Jefferson, nearing fifty-eight years of age, concluded his appraisal of the Union's state by pointedly invoking America's messianic pledge to afford a haven for persecuted refugees. In stark contrast to the nativism of the Adams administration, he declared, "Shall we refuse to the unhappy fugitives from distress, that hospitality which the savages of the wilderness extended to our fathers arriving in this land? Shall oppressed humanity find no asylum on this globe?"[23]

Among other priorities, the new administration targeted the Naturalization Act, one of the three Alien laws of 1798. Although Congress retained the Alien Enemies Act, authorizing the president in time of war to deport suspicious males from hostile nations, Jefferson pardoned individuals who had been prosecuted during the conflict with France, as he did persons convicted under the Sedition Act. In the meantime, the Alien Friends Act, threatening to exile other foreign nationals from the United States, had expired on June 25, 1800, two years after its passage. But the Naturalization Act, which for prospective citizens had extended the minimum period of residence in the country from five to fourteen years, remained on the books to the dismay of Republican lawmakers and a handful of Federalists, not to mention large numbers of immigrants.[24]

Central to all three acts was the contentious issue of alien rights. While aspiring citizens awaited naturalization, their legal status under the Constitution remained at best uncertain. Many Federalists were prepared to deny aliens, even in peacetime, any safeguards at all, as was the case with European governments, where foreigners could be deported at will. In the view of Congressman Bayard, "Aliens cannot be considered as members of the society of the United States. . . . Whatever is granted to aliens is a mere matter of favor; and if it is taken away, they have no right to complain." In Boston, "Hume" affirmed in 1802, "All well governed states have placed aliens under disabilities as inhabitants, and entirely excluded them from their public councils." Meanwhile, a New Hampshire newspaper lampooned the limits of Jefferson's compassion. Conspicuous by their absence from the ranks of "unhappy fugitives" were slaves.[25]

Since its inception, the Robbins affair had drawn unprecedented notoriety to the rights of foreign nationals (if not yet to those of African Americans). Whatever the seaman's origins, Republicans relentlessly insisted that Judge Bee had not afforded him basic rights of due process, including a trial by jury as well as the opportunity to acquire evidence and confront his accusers. The *Aurora* declared, "In the view of national independence—as it relates to our character as a nation—as it relates to the character and independence of our judiciary, it is a matter of utter insignificance whether *Jonathan Robbins* was a native of the *Irish bog,* or of the rough declivities of Connecticut." Against the backdrop of rising numbers of Irish immigrants trumpeting the cause of alien rights, the alarming specter of Robbins's surrender contributed powerfully to the mounting debate. During the election of 1800, it is likely that few publications achieved wider currency than the address printed in March for the citizens of states due to elect legislators for the purpose of selecting presidential electors. Widely reprinted that spring in Republican newspapers at the behest of "a number of Republican citizens," the four-page address, signed by a "Republican Farmer," portrayed Robbins's extradition as the horrific consequence of the Alien Friends Act executed to its logical extreme:

> Every oppressed man was taught to believe
> that here he would find an asylum from tyranny
> and confusion—that the sacred right of jury
> should be preserved to him—that it should not
> depend on the will of any individual however
> important and elevated, and in whose breast
> was impenetrably locked the reason of [t]his
> procedure, to force him from this asylum, and
> banish him without the intervention of a jury.
> You did not then believe that any man found in
> your country, and claiming, whether this claim
> was true or not, to be a citizen, could be
> delivered to a foreign tribunal and military
> execution, at the request of any individual to
> a judge, without the trial or opinion of a jury.[26]

Less than a year into Jefferson's first term, the cause of alien rights acquired growing momentum. Even sundry Federalists grudgingly embraced shifting attitudes.[27] In time, shrewd members eager to right the party openly courted immigrant votes, including those of Irish Americans, who overwhelmingly voted Republican. Any doubts about their burgeoning power were laid to rest when the nativist congressman

Bayard was defeated in Delaware in 1802, reputedly by swelling numbers of Irish American voters. A delighted President Jefferson wrote the victorious Republican candidate, "Our success in defeating Bayard has mortified our *Feds* beyond expression." Six years later, however, a "Naturalized Irishman" in a Pennsylvania paper felt the necessity to remind immigrants that their interests lay not with the "enemies to the common rights of man." After citing, among other incidents, "Jonathan Robbins, delivered up by an infamous Pickering," he affirmed, "Behold the same junto, the firm supporters of these men and measures, coming forward, like crawling sycophants, to ask for your suffrages."[28]

Numbers of Americans, in grappling with Robbins's identity, more readily comprehended the meaning of their own. Assuming an unprecedented dynamic, the concept of nationality took on a richer significance. For Republicans, the possibility that Robbins had been Irish, not an American citizen, became steadily less consequential. The question of his identity, which had initially transfixed the public, in the end became more important for its irrelevance. Simon Slim averred, tongue in cheek, that he could not recall whether Robbins or Nash was his real name. Federalists understandably became irate at such indifference. Of Robbins's discredited claims, a South Carolinian complained, "The Jacobins were not to be staggered by facts; they still harped upon the old key to a new tune." If not an American by birth, Robbins was adopted posthumously. At the height of the campaign in 1800, the "Republican Farmer" proclaimed, "May the government of America never forget that the persecuted patriots of Europe have as good a right to an asylum in the woods as their forefathers had." More important than his birthplace were Robbins's republican convictions, thereby encouraging, with unparalleled power, a broader definition of citizenship and national identity, based on belief and volition, not just the vagaries of nativity. Indeed, as a young and increasingly diverse nation of immigrants or the descendants of immigrants, what bound most Americans together as a distinctive people was their common commitment to liberty. This recognition of national self-consciousness, this rebirth of the libertarian spirit of '76—recently ignited by the Alien and Sedition Acts—acquired heightened importance in Robbins's martyrdom.[29]

Drawing on John Locke, the attorney Michael Barrett argued vigorously for the right of any individual—"at liberty to pursue his own happiness"—to flee domestic oppression. In *The Reply of a Friend to Justice to a Friend to Propriety on the Fate of the Unfortunate Robbins,* Barrett continued, "If the persecutions exercised against our ancestors, and their prejudices against European governments, justified them in expelling the aborigines of America from their native soil, a slight recurrence to this fact ought to create, in an American sympathizing bosom, some degree of compassion towards those unfortunate men, fleeing to our shores for protection, from the most accursed tyranny that ever disgraced an unfortunate country [that is, Great Britain]." Robbins, he wrote, was "an immolated martyr at the shrine of American independence." No less emphatic, the moderate Federalist John Steele, Adams's comptroller of the Treasury, proclaimed in his anonymous "Letter from a Federalist": "It is of little moment whether his name was Robins, or Nash; whether he was a Citizen, or an Alien; it is enough that he was *a man* who sought asylum in an INDEPENDENT COUNTRY, whose peace he had not disturbed."[30]

Doctrinaire Federalists at first derided such fugitives as "imported" patriots. Noting Robbins's claim to citizenship, a South Carolinian lamented, "We expect soon to hear every unhung rogue of Europe, who finds an asylum on our shores, dubbing himself a whig of '76." Republicans, by contrast, continued to welcome immigrants as fellow freedom fighters. A Rhode Island paper attributed Federalist abuse of "foreigners" to "their being sworn foes to Regal Oppression and warm friends of Republican Liberty." Rumors persisted that Republicans had long known of Robbins's Irish roots. In 1809, Stephen Cullen Carpenter, author of the spurious *Memoirs of the Hon. Thomas Jefferson,* still raged, "The pirate, mutineer, and murderer was dear to them, and the more dear because the outrages he committed were against the great enemy of Jacobinism and France, and because the lives he helped to destroy of British officers. The case of Nash, had every thing in it that could recommend him to their guardian care."[31]

Apart from the acquisition of constitutional rights, which the Supreme Court under Chief Justice Marshall periodically affirmed in subsequent decades, aliens, by virtue of a new Naturalization Act on April 14, 1802, stood to become citizens in five rather than fourteen years, the same period prescribed by the Naturalization Act of 1795. A declaration of intent three years prior to naturalization was also required. The staunchest advocates urged a quicker path to citizenship of no more than two years, the original period during the Washington administration. But most Republican leaders insisted that five years would permit foreign nationals to fully adopt American values, however deep-seated their commitment to liberty. "A residence shall be required sufficient to develop character and design," as Jefferson put it. The foundation of immigration law for the remainder of the nineteenth century, the Naturalization Act of 1802, as with that of 1795, required applicants to affirm their republican convictions by swearing allegiance to the Constitution, providing written testament to their good character, and by renouncing foreign titles and former loyalties. Now more than ever, these prerequisites acquired enlarged importance. Europe, by contrast, yet embodied degradation and destitution, lords and peasants, subjects rather than citizens.[32]

Republican zealots demonized natives as well as newcomers who exhibited dubious loyalties and questionable convictions. Federalists, scolded a Boston writer, "owed their origin to the agents of the corrupt government of Great Britain." Another partisan urged that "native citizens, as well as foreigners, who abuse the blessings with which Providence has pre-eminently favored this country, ought to be divested of all public confidence and private esteem." Of fugitives from abroad, contended a New York newspaper, "They are the more ardent in asserting the principles of liberty than those who having never lived under oppression feel not the impulse of experience to make them equally active in supporting freedom"; whereas a "Citizen of the World" went further by proposing that unpatriotic citizens be stripped of the right to vote. "I would exclude," he asserted in the *Vermont Centinel* of July 16, 1801, "every foreigner, but by foreigner I include every person who is alien and foreign to the true interest of America, wherever born." One Edward Sharman, writing in the *Centinel of Freedom,* yet urged the expulsion of aliens "who are not decidedly in favor of republicanism."[33]

But most were. And lured by the prospect of Republican reforms, freedom, and prosperity, thousands of immigrants, predominantly Irish, flooded into American ports, beginning shortly after Jefferson's inauguration. New York City, Philadelphia, and the nearby port of Newcastle, Delaware, were favorite destinations. New York reported in July 1801 the arrival of nine hundred immigrants over the past month. By late 1804, twenty-seven thousand, just from Ireland alone, were said to have arrived in America during the previous year. "Emigrants from Europe," announced a Virginian, "are pouring into the United States."[34]

IN THE EARLY YEARS of the Jeffersonian ascendancy, Robbins's martyrdom continued to advance the rights of rising numbers of immigrants, including the right to citizenship by virtue of possessing republican convictions. Democratic reforms, themselves associated with the Revolution of 1800, from the "rise of universal white male suffrage" to the "switch to popular voting in presidential elections," could only have benefited from this influx of aspiring American citizens. As the nation's culture became progressively pluralistic, it also grew more democratic, however distant the achievement of a genuine democracy inclusive of women and nonwhites.[35]

Of parallel importance, the uproar over Robbins dramatically diminished the future likelihood that the United States would surrender an American citizen or, for that matter, a resident alien to a foreign power. Such had been the resistance to his extradition that Article 27 of the British Treaty fell by the wayside well before its expiration in 1806. "The fate of Jonathan Robbins," wrote a Pennsylvanian in 1807, "has at least established this principle in the feelings of the people."[36]

As a consequence, an unknown number of Hermiones who had fled to the United States no longer faced the dangers of extradition and execution. Leaving no tracks, they vanished into the vast expanses of the American backcountry or into heavily populated seaports where neither their manners, appearance, nor language set them apart—not that government authorities ever took an interest in their prosecution. The consequence was that sundry seamen, including the most culpable, owed their lives in large part to their ill-fated shipmate.

In Virginia, fueling the storm over Robbins was the growing certainty that at least one other crew member had been delivered surreptitiously to the British in 1798, much as early reports had suggested. On December 1, 1800, in a letter to the General Assembly, the Republican governor James Monroe condemned the incident, adding that he had referred all available evidence to the state attorney general. Two days later, after first casting the state's electoral votes for Jefferson, the legislature appointed a committee to investigate what a Republican paper labeled an "unparalleled act of treachery"; and by the third week of January, legislators enacted a bill criminalizing the surrender of any individual to a foreign power. Notably, the act prohibited the extradition of aliens as well as citizens on penalty of capital punishment should the subject himself be executed. "Every person concerned in such delivery shall be adjudged a felon and suffer death." In the end, the Norfolk magistrate Dr. John K. Read was absolved of having wittingly committed a crime, but he was found guilty of misusing his office. In July 1801, when Meriwether Jones, a prominent Richmond printer, sought a presidential appointment for his friend, Jefferson angrily snapped that there was not "a man in the United States who deserves countenance less than Dr. Read."[37]

Not for eight years after Robbins's surrender did Great Britain make a subsequent extradition request—notwithstanding the British Treaty's expiration. On January 4, 1807, the British minister to the United States, David Erskine, informed Secretary of State Madison that HMS *Bermuda* had commandeered an American brig months earlier with the intention of bringing her to Halifax. The American captain, however, successfully retook control of the ship with the aid of British seamen and sailed the brig to Portland, Maine. "Under the circumstances of atrocity and violence," Erskine wrote, "I can not suppose that the protection of the United States will be extended to the British seamen," who by then had reportedly fled to Boston. Three days later, Madison tersely responded that "no prerogative for the purpose in question is vested in the Executive of the United States." Moreover, "neither the law nor the practices of [our] nation imposes on them an obligation to provide for the surrender of fugitives from the jurisdiction of other powers." Of greater concern to the secretary was news that a Captain Douglas had recently detained American citizens aboard HMS *Bellona* in Norfolk harbor to force the surrender of the British seamen—an act of "illegal violence within the very harbours" of the United States, condemned Madison.[38]

Irwin John Bevan, Chesapeake vs. Leopard, *n.d.*

In the meantime, Erskine had boldly made a second request on learning that a notorious mutineer from the *Hermione,* the Belfast surgeon's mate, Lawrence Cronin, "the principal adviser of the mutiny," now worked for a druggist in Providence, Rhode Island. This fact had been deposed by Thomas Woods before his execution in Portsmouth, though at the time no one had sufficient reason to doubt his veracity. Waiting on Madison in person, Erskine asked "whether it was the determination of the American government not to interfere in any case however flagrant." Despite the government's wish to help, the secretary replied that he had no power to interfere. As for the *Bellona,* he expressed "exasperation," threatening to cut off all supplies to the ship and to resort to "some ulterior force" unless the Americans were set on land. "Of what nature," the perplexed Erskine reported to London on February 1, "he did not say."[39]

Less than five months later, on the morning of June 22, the Chesapeake Affair erupted. Intercepted off the coast of Norfolk just beyond Cape Henry by the British frigate *Leopard,* the captain of the frigate USS *Chesapeake,* James Barron, refused to heave to, lest a boarding party attempt to seize members of his crew, none of whom, he assured the British, were deserters. In response, the *Leopard* fired repeated broadsides, killing three seamen on the spot and wounding eighteen others.

Forced to surrender after managing a single blast, the *Chesapeake,* on being boarded, gave up four deserters, three of whom were Americans formerly impressed into the Royal Navy. The fourth deserter, a native of London, who on reaching Norfolk had declared America "the land of Liberty," was hanged from a British yardarm. British apologists in the United States intimated that Secretary Madison's earlier refusal to extradite deserters had led to the confrontation. A Portland paper reported that Minister Erskine, in having tried to retrieve four British seamen, had been "informed that it could not be done." Thomas Truxton, revered by Federalists for his exploits as captain of the USS *Constitution* during hostilities with France, suggested as much in a letter to Timothy Pickering. Indeed, Truxton claimed, the British had been rebuffed in their attempt to reclaim four seamen, convicted of mutinous words, who had absconded from a British sloop to sign on to the *Chesapeake.* Noting the severity of the crime of desertion, he stated that the "commander of the Chesapeake ought to have delivered those mutineers and deserters upon a proper application," adding, however, that the captain of the *Leopard* should have reported the incident rather than resort to force.[40]

If Britain's belligerence in the Chesapeake Affair resulted in part from its inability to extradite naval deserters from the United States, memories of Jonathan Robbins, in turn, exacerbated American anger, already white-hot over ongoing British depredations at sea. "Witness the three thousand of our seamen forced aboard her fleet, as if slaves, to fight her iniquitous battles," the *Centinel of Freedom* had protested the preceding year. "If the least murmur or complaint against unlawful detention is heard, the fate of the never to be forgotten, poor Jonathan Robbins is speedily executed." Republican loyalists once again cited Robbins's extradition to condemn Federalist partisans as well as the British—all the more because both had strenuously argued in 1799 that naval vessels at sea fell within their nations' territorial jurisdiction. As the *Virginia Argus* and other Republican papers delighted in reminding readers, it was precisely these grounds on which "the present chief justice of the U.S. when a member of Congress advocated the surrender of Jonathan Robbins to be tried by a British tribunal." For the "Happy Farmer," writing in October 1807 in the *True American,* the only solution short of war lay in a presidential proclamation pledging the United

States to protect not just American sailors but "all British deserters." In light of their low morale—stemming from the brutality of shipboard discipline—impressed "British seamen," he declared, "are ready whenever we give the signal to do the work of an American fleet. Which is our best policy, to give them [deserters] up as Robbins was given up?" "If men must be killed," the "Happy Farmer" insisted, "is it not as right that the oppressed on board of the British navy to kill their oppressors?" Impressment, John Adams lamented soon afterward, "will keep alive an eternal hatred between the two countries, and end in a war at last."[41]

In just a few years deteriorating relations between the United States and Great Britain climaxed in the War of 1812, caused in large measure by their inability to resolve the vexing problem of impressment. The harassment of American ships and their crews had persisted. "Friends of the country," consoled "The Ploughboy" a day after the United States declared war on June 18, "think nought of the little expences which our country will be put to in defence of blood and the rights of man. But think—alas poor Jonathan Robbins, and thousands of our brethren at present, groaning under bondage and oppression, crying out for help, to relieve them from the enemies of both God and man!"[42]

Epilogue

TO A DRAMATIC DEGREE, then, the martyrdom of Jonathan Robbins helped to widen America's open door to immigration, having contributed to a revolutionary conception of citizenship rooted, more deeply than ever, in republican principles. Of collateral significance was an equally enduring legacy, one born of those very political principles. In the future, fugitives from foreign governments, with the prospect of a safe haven, would enjoy the full promise of American independence. It had not always been so. Before Robbins's surrender, the concept of extradition, incorporated in the British Treaty, had aroused scant opposition among Americans. After his surrender, not for decades—forty-three years—would one person, citizen or alien, be given up by the federal government to another country, despite periodic requests from abroad. Nor would extradition treaties be signed or new legislation enacted. Such had been the poisonous fruit born of Robbins's fate that no branch of the government favored extradition's resumption: not Congress, by passing fresh legislation; not the judiciary, by ruling in the absence of laws or international treaties; and not, for the time being, the White House, either by negotiating accords with European powers or by exercising executive authority. Robbins had forced Americans to confront the alarming prospect of forsaking one of their own—a torchbearer of liberty—to the cruelty of foreign tyranny.

Nor would they soon forget. In 1823, a Philadelphia justice of the peace arrested an Irish immigrant, Edward Short, for having allegedly

committed a murder two years earlier in County Tyrone. Before he could
be extradited, the state supreme court heard Short's case. In his decision,
Chief Justice William Tilghman observed, "We are now in the 48th year
of our independence, and yet it is not known *that in any one instance* a
fugitive from Europe has been surrendered, except Jonathan Robbins,
whose case turned upon our treaty with Great Britain." Declaring that
the executive branch did not possess the power to act independently, he
discharged the prisoner, which provoked a Rhode Island newspaper to
exclaim, "No similar case has occurred in this country since the infamous surrender of Jonathan Robbins to the British government in the
'*reign of terror*'; and we trust none will hereafter occur!"[1]

Three years later, President John Quincy Adams, in seeking to
negotiate a treaty with Britain over a thicket of prickly issues—from
America's northeastern boundary with Canada to fishing rights and
impressment—instructed his minister in London, Albert Gallatin, now
aged sixty-five, to draft an extradition agreement. By then, following the
demise of the Federalist Party, the Democratic-Republican party had
splintered into regional factions. The irony of Gallatin's assignment,
from the son of John Adams no less, was, of course, rich. Second only to
Edward Livingston in attempting to censure the elder Adams in 1800,
Gallatin nonetheless enjoyed a civil relationship with the incumbent
president.[2]

Before embarking from New York for London, Gallatin wrote Secretary of State Henry Clay in late June. Clay in 1813 had denounced the
surrender of Robbins. "The subject of extra tradition [*sic*]," Gallatin
noted, "has ever been in practice one of the most delicate and difficult
of the law of Nations. Even when free of many abuses & confined to the
offences of murder & forgery, the surrender of a citizen will ever be odi-
ous and even that of an alien unpopular. National pride may feel interested in the question: but the difference between our penal code and
that of Great Britain and those perhaps existing in the administration
of justice to the two countries form a solid objection." Observing that
"the only attempt" to implement the extradition provision in the British
Treaty of 1794 had not been "fortunate," he urged that the administration drop the issue that had so bitterly convulsed the country. "The
excitement caused by the surrender of that man [Robbins], its effect

on popular opinion are well known. Is it
wise, is it sound policy on a question of
doubtful utility and minor importance to
awaken ancient recollections and feelings?
Perhaps to endanger a whole convention
in other respects acceptable?" With the
decision to delay negotiations with Britain on manifold fronts, save for signing
a commercial agreement, John Quincy
Adams never again pursued the issue.[3]

Anonymous, Daniel Webster,
1835

Despite foreign requests, another sixteen years would pass before an American president, John Tyler, a Whig aristo-
crat from Virginia, appeared willing to resume extradition, and then as
one element of a broader treaty with Britain necessitated by lingering
disputes with Canada, in addition to competing claims over the territory of Oregon. With good reason, as intimated by Gallatin, extradition remained controversial long after the turmoil over Robbins. Highly
charged issues, fundamental to the Constitution and America's character, had roiled national politics in the aftermath of his execution. Extradition, given the nationalistic fervor of the post-Jackson years, already
would have given politicians pause. But without a single successful
instance in over four decades, the surrender of Robbins assumed all the
more importance in the public mind. Notwithstanding the long span of
time, the affair, as a New Hampshire newspaper observed in 1835, was
"doubtless fresh in the recollection of many readers." According to a
southern jurist, "The surrender of Jonathan Robbins under a treaty, and
by order of our own courts, created a ferment which shook the government almost to its foundations." A Boston paper asserted in 1839, "No
event that ever occurred in our country has given rise to such a deep and
angry excitement." If anything, the so-called rise of the common man
in recent years only diminished prospects for an accord by glorifying
the poor sailor's struggle against British tyranny. The tragic narrative of
Jonathan Robbins, however false, acquired fresh resonance in the afterglow of Jacksonian Democracy.[4]

For some ten weeks beginning in June 1842, Secretary of State Daniel

George Peter Alexander Healy,
Alexander Baring, Lord
Ashburton, *1842*

Webster, at sixty years of age, met with Alexander Baring, 1st Baron Ashburton, to broker a treaty. Before departing London, Lord Ashburton had queried Edward Everett, America's minister to Britain, about prospects for an extradition agreement. The chances were good, Everett replied, as long as it did not "extend to treason or any other political crime." Years later, in his memoir of Daniel Webster, the former envoy, who was a fellow New Englander, noted that extradition had originally been suspended with Britain owing to the "political notoriety" of "the case of Jonathan Robbins."[5]

Most talks took place in Lord Ashburton's elegant four-story brick home on Lafayette Square in Washington, rented for $1,000 per month. Already on April 9 Webster had asked his close friend Supreme Court Justice Joseph Story to draft an article pertaining to extradition. "You can do more for me than all the rest of the world," he assured the eminent jurist. Story responded promptly, taking as his model Article 27 of the British Treaty of 1794, with two significant exceptions. First, the earlier treaty, he explained to Webster, "stops short of pointing out how the surrender is to be accomplished." Rejecting Marshall's defense of the executive prerogative, Story urged that it be "through the judicial power" to avoid "the senseless popular clamour in Johnathan Robinson's [*sic*] case." In short, the courts, not the executive branch, should rule on future requests from abroad. Equally important, Story counseled, extradition should be restricted to crimes "which most usually occur, and will be likely to call for the interposition of the Government for extradition." "I have purposely excluded," he underscored, "political offences, as involving [many] very debateable matters, not to say also, that they might hazard the ratification by our Senate from popular clamour."[6]

By then, however, relations between the two countries had grown strained. On the evening of November 7, 1841, 19 of 138 slaves en route from Hampton Roads, Virginia, to New Orleans successfully rebelled aboard the *Creole,* an American brig. Having killed a slave master on board and severely wounded the captain, first mate, and two crew members, they compelled the second mate to sail to Nassau, a British possession in the Bahamas. To the bitter disappointment of southern slaveholders and the Tyler administration, British officials stoutly refused to permit the ship to leave for America as Bahamians, black and white, began helping slaves ashore. Among slave owners in the United States, there was even talk of war.[7]

Previously, in July 1839, a slave uprising aboard the Spanish schooner *Amistad* had prompted abolitionists in the United States to invoke the Robbins affair. After the ship had been taken into custody by the USS *Washington* off the Long Island coast and escorted to New Haven, the fate of fifty-three West Africans fell to the courts. The abolitionist newspaper the *Emancipator,* published in New York, averred, "The various opinions advanced in the case of the Amistad have reminded us of Jonathan Robbins, and of the strong grounds taken in his case favorable to the proposition that a man forcibly and illegally shipped on the high seas, may master the crew and assume control of the vessel, with a high and bloody hand, in order to regain the liberty of which he is wrongfully deprived, and in doing so stand acquitted of all criminality." In support, the paper cited both Marshall and Gallatin, even though the future chief justice's argument had rested upon Robbins's citizenship ("Had Thomas Nash been an impressed American . . ."). Antislavery supporters also noted that no extradition treaty, as in the case of Robbins, required surrendering the *Amistad*'s slaves to Spain.[8]

The *Creole* crisis raised, just as forcefully, issues central to the Robbins affair. Again, abolitionists invoked the right of slaves to resist their oppressors, and the absence of a treaty with Britain was also emphasized. On the other hand, by the standard adopted in 1799 by Britain, the uprising aboard the *Creole* had occurred within the territorial jurisdiction of the United States. Nor were the slaves British citizens. At the head of abolitionists condoning the bloodshed was William Jay, a New York attorney and the son of the late Supreme Court chief justice, John Jay, whose name had become synonymous with the British Treaty of 1794. In a pamphlet published in 1842 and titled "The Creole Case, and Mr. Webster's Despatch," Jay argued passionately against the extradition of slaves aboard the *Creole* to the United States. Noting that although Gallatin and Marshall had been on opposite sides of the "vehement discussions" regarding Robbins, both had embraced "the right of a man, unlawfully held in bondage, to resist even unto death." Indeed, Jay continued, Virginia had passed a law in 1800 decreeing the death of any person guilty of delivering up a resident of the Commonwealth to a foreign power for execution. "We submit, then," he insisted, turning the law on its head, "that Virginia is estopped by her own unrepealed legislation from urging upon other nations [that is, Britain] claims analogous to those which, under penalty of death, she prohibited any compliance with on the part of her citizens." "The right of resistance," he declared, "cannot depend upon the color of the skin."[9]

For his part, Lord Ashburton dearly wished to settle the fate of the *Creole* lest it destroy any chance of a treaty. But the British were unalterably opposed to slavery, unwilling even to consider compensating the slaves' owners for their loss in order to avoid signifying support for an institution declared illegal throughout the empire in 1833. The British were all the more upset because of the unauthorized surrender in January of a runaway slave to the United States by Canada's newly appointed governor general. Nelson Hackett had made his way north from Arkansas the preceding summer to join twelve thousand free blacks already in Canada. His restoration to his former master, justified in the governor general's eyes by Hackett's theft of a beaver coat, a gold watch, and the master's fastest horse, enraged British authorities nearly as much as it did abolitionists and the free black community. Hackett had become their Jonathan Robbins.[10]

Fortunately, the United States, following Justice Story's advice, was anxious to exempt political offenses from the list of crimes for which individuals, aliens and citizens alike, could be delivered up. Included instead on the list were such common felonies as murder, robbery, arson, and forgery. The "political offense exception," as it came to be called, covered not only treason but also mutiny and desertion from the armed forces, a concession dear to American hearts owing to memories of Robbins and the continuing legality of British impressment, which London refused to negotiate.[11]

Although the Greeks granted cross-border asylum to fugitives as early as the eleventh and twelfth centuries B.C. (the word "asylum" originated from the Greek *asylos,* meaning "that which may not be seized

Charles T. Webber, The Underground Railroad, *1893*

or violated"), not until the 1790s did the notion of "political crimes" in Europe or America formally arise. Among the first to articulate the concept was Jefferson, in detailing his opposition in 1792 to a lengthy list of extraditable offenses. He believed that treason, for instance, should be exempted because most nations "do not distinguish between acts against the *Government* and acts against the *oppression of the Government.*" In Europe, however, it was not until the 1830s that the exemption of political offenders from extradition acquired popularity, and then only in France and Belgium.[12]

What emerged in early August 1842 was a compromise between Britain and the United States with critical implications both for political refugees seeking asylum in the United States and for fugitive slaves bound for Canada—or, in the case of the *Creole,* insurgents at sea. In exchange for Britain's exclusion of political offenses from extraditable crimes, among them mutiny and desertion, the Tyler administration, with grave misgivings, resigned itself to exempting fugitive slaves. In sum, due to American insistence upon the political offense exception arising from the Robbins affair, fugitive slaves, as unintended beneficiaries, stood to escape the threat of extradition to the United States. As Ashburton later explained to a gathering of abolitionists in New York, "The governor of

Canada was anxious that [military] deserters should be included," but once it was learned "that a claim would be put in [by the United States] for the delivering up of fugitive slaves, he abandoned the question of deserters from H.B.M.'s possessions." "He was also very desirous to secure the delivery of mutineers," Ashburton stated, "but did not press it, lest it should involve, on the part of his Government, the delivery of slaves situated as were those on board the Creole." As a concession to Tyler and southern slave owners, Ashburton pledged to instruct British officials overseas to avoid "officious interference" with American ships "driven by necessity, accident, or violence into British ports," though the "instruction" was never sent, nor would fugitive slaves be extradited from British territory.[13]

Moreover, as Story had urged, American courts, not the executive branch, would directly process all extradition requests from Britain, thus rejecting once and for all Marshall's central argument in 1800. Only after a court had confirmed sufficient evidence of criminality "according to the laws of the place where the fugitive or person so charged shall be found" would it certify "to a proper Executive authority, that a warrant may issue for the surrender of such fugitive." The Supreme Court justice John Catron would write ten years later in a majority opinion pertaining to a fugitive from Britain (*In Re Thomas Kaine*) that "the eventful history of Robbins's case had a controlling influence on our distinguished negotiator, when the treaty of 1842 was made . . . is, as I suppose, free from doubt." In a pointed reference to the election of 1800, Catron added, "The assumption of power to arrest, imprison, and extrude on executive warrants, and the employment of a judicial magistrate to act in obedience to the President's commands, where no independence existed, or could exist, had most materially aided to overthrow the administration of a distinguished revolutionary patriot."[14]

The "Washington Treaty" (later christened the Webster-Ashburton Treaty) was signed at the White House on the morning of Tuesday, August 9. But the draft, which among other accomplishments adjusted the border between Canada and the United States, still required ratification by two-thirds of the Senate, and Article 10, relating to extradition, was one of several provisions to foment debate. In the forefront of dissenters was the Jacksonian Democrat Thomas Hart Benton of Missouri, by all accounts a formidable foe. A number of issues had turned him against the treaty, including its inattention to impressment. Although an opponent of slavery's westward expansion, he also feared, like other slave owners, the impact of allowing the *Creole*'s slaves to elude apprehension by American authorities. Nor did Benton think it the least hypocritical to criticize the treaty for failing, explicitly, to exempt political offenses from extraditable crimes. Even Article 27 of the British Treaty of 1794, he argued, was preferable for having limited extradition just to murder and forgery. And, he hastened to add, "Mr. Jay's treaty was no favorite with the American people, and especially with that part of the people which constituted the republican party. Least of all was this 27th article a favorite with them. It was under that article that the famous Jonathan Robbins, alias Thomas Nash, was surrendered—a surrender which contributed largely to the defeat of Mr. Adams and the overthrow of the federal party in 1800!"[15]

Although Article 10 did not specifically exempt political offenses, Tyler had addressed the omission in submitting the text to the Senate, pointing out that "in the careful and specific enumeration of crimes, the object has been to exclude all political offences, or criminal charges arising from wars or intestine commotions. Treason, misprision of treason, libels, desertion from military service, and other offences of similar character are excluded." Aided by that assurance, the Senate ratified the treaty by a vote of 39 to 9 on August 20. And from that point on, virtually every extradition treaty between the United States and a foreign government contained language exempting political offenses, beginning with a Franco-American accord in 1843 barring extradition for "any crime or offense of a purely political character." Five years later, this doctrine was incorporated in Congress's first extradition law, the point at which political asylum became the express policy of the United States, a major legislative achievement toward fulfilling the American Revolution's pledge to provide "an asylum for mankind." Further, in pursuing a more energetic role in international affairs through the adoption of extradition agreements, the United States significantly promoted the doctrine of political asylum not only at home but also abroad.[16] Public debates in and out of Congress, beginning in 1799, had laid the foundations of this historic juncture, with the result that innumerable refugees, ever since, have benefited from the protracted aftershocks of the mutiny aboard the *Hermione*.

Coda

ON THE TWENTY-THIRD OF DECEMBER, 1981, a surprisingly warm Wednesday morning, a three-judge panel of the United States Court of Appeals for the Second Circuit convened in the august federal courthouse on Foley Square in lower Manhattan. Before the bench sat Desmond Mackin, a former Belfast taxi driver desperate to avoid extradition to British authorities in Northern Ireland. The request had been made of the United States by the United Kingdom pursuant to an extradition treaty signed by both countries in 1972, the successor to Article 10 of the Webster-Ashburton Treaty of 1842 and Article 27 of the British Treaty of 1794. An admitted member of the Provisional Irish Republican Army, Mackin, aged twenty-seven, had fled to the United States after being charged with attempted murder in 1978 following the shooting of a British soldier, Stephen Wooten, in Belfast. Mackin, in turn, had been shot thrice during their back-alley skirmish. Already a U.S. magistrate had ruled in Mackin's favor on the grounds of the "political offense exception." "The IRA," wrote Magistrate Naomi Rice Buchwald, "was conducting" at the time of the shooting "a political uprising" with the goal of "an independent Ireland, free of British rule, through the use of violence."[1]

In writing the majority opinion for the court of appeals, the distinguished jurist Henry Friendly affirmed Buchwald's ruling. He, too, invoked the political offense exception emanating, he detailed at length, from the momentous case of Jonathan Robbins. "Whatever we might

decide if writing on a clean slate," Friendly stated, courts had long determined the applicability of the political offense exception owing to the
consequences of the Robbins controversy. "Although the term 'political
offense' was not current at the time, and apparently was not used in the
debates surrounding the Robbins case," he noted, "the argument made
on Robbins' behalf bears many resemblances to the political offense doctrine. In both instances an otherwise extraditable crime is thought to be
rendered nonextraditable by the circumstances surrounding its commission and by the motives of the criminal. Significantly, in later years the
Robbins case came to be regarded as centering on the political offense
question." Indeed, he added, Justice John Catron had written in 1852
that "the eventful history of the Robbins's case had a controlling influence on our distinguished negotiator [Daniel Webster] when the Treaty
of 1842 was made; and," Catron emphasized, "especially on Congress,
when it passed the [Extradition] Act of 1848." "With the Robbins case
thus firmly in the legislature's mind, it is difficult to avoid the conclusion," affirmed Judge Friendly, "that when Congress charged commissioners and judges with determining whether evidence exists to 'sustain
[a] charge under the provisions of the treaty,' . . . it had no intention of
silently excepting the political offense issue from the magistrate's consideration." Were the executive branch, by contrast, to adjudge cases,
Friendly warned, in echoing early opponents of executive authority, foreign policy interests might instead predominate.[2]

With Buchwald's ruling upheld, the federal government, rather than
appeal the case further, deported Mackin to Ireland in January for an
immigration offense. "As far as I know there is nothing against me in
the Republic," Mackin volunteered upon exiting the Aer Lingus flight.
"My hope is that I can see my family in Dublin, my wife, Mary, and
5-year-old daughter and begin my life all over again."

Less pleased by Mackin's release, on top of failed attempts to extradite other IRA fugitives, were President Ronald Reagan and most
members of Congress as well as the government of Prime Minister
Margaret Thatcher. Four years later, yet a new Anglo-American accord,
the United States–United Kingdom Supplementary Extradition Treaty
of 1985, was signed and ratified, which gutted the right of American
asylum for political fugitives from the United Kingdom. "Violence

should never be deemed part of the political process," a senior senator affirmed.[3] For British fugitives, the stroke of a pen put an abrupt end to a policy honored by the United States ever since the surrender in 1799 of Desmond Mackin's kinsman-in-arms, the Irish mutineer Thomas Nash, best remembered as the martyred Jonathan Robbins.

Acknowledgments

A DECADE AGO, LIKE MOST PEOPLE, I had never heard of the benighted frigate HMS *Hermione,* Captain Hugh Pigot, or Jonathan Robbins, much less Thomas Nash. Nor, despite my background in the history of the early Republic, did I have any knowledge of the mutiny's far-reaching consequences for the United States. Encountering Dudley Pope's *The Black Ship* (1962) and Ruth Wedgwood's "The Revolutionary Martyrdom of Jonathan Robbins" in the *Yale Law Journal* (1990) helped to remedy my ignorance, setting me on a course of exploration and research that has held my fascination for the past eight years.

Instrumental in this regard have been numerous archives, libraries, and historical societies, first and foremost the British National Archives at Kew, a splendid facility whose staff was consistently helpful and efficient. I am also grateful to the National Maritime Museum in Greenwich, the Warwickshire County Record Office, the National Archives in Washington, D.C., the Library of Congress Manuscript Division, Alderman Library and the Small Special Collections Library at the University of Virginia, the New York Public Library, and the New York Historical Society. For their unfailing perseverance, special thanks are due the staff of the Massachusetts Historical Society (particularly Tracy Potter), Erin Beasley and Deborah L. Sisum at the National Portrait Gallery in Washington, D.C., Squirrel Walsh at the Princeton University Library Department of Rare Books and Special Collections, and Steve Smith at the Spartanburg County Public Libraries. Most deserving of my gratitude is the inter-library loan office in Newman Library at Virginia Tech. For all of their support and good cheer, I am very grateful to Sharon A. Gotkiewicz and members of her staff.

Research grants from the History Department and the College of Liberal Arts and Human Sciences at Virginia Tech greatly assisted my travels, whereas research leave from the university coupled with a generous fellowship from the National Endowment for the Humanities afforded a year in which to concentrate upon writing.

In light of the significance of both American and British newspapers and periodicals to this study, I am indebted to companies that make available a number of electronic databases, among them America's Historical Newspapers, American Periodical Series, Chronicling America, British Periodicals, Nineteenth-Century British Library Newspapers, and the British Newspaper Archive.

Colleagues and friends who read all or portions of the manuscript include Peter S. Onuf, James Rogers Sharp, Paul Gilje, Jon Kukla, Jeffrey Pasley, Larry Shumsky, and my nephew Jason Chung. Their comments rescued me from a number of errors. Any that yet remain are mine alone. Philip D. Morgan and David Hackett Fischer both provided invaluable assistance at a critical juncture. Dennis Hidalgo's knowledge of Caribbean history was very helpful, and I much appreciate the encouragement of Mark Barrow and Richard Hirsh. For her skills as an author and an attorney and for her background in commercial fishing off the Oregon coast, I relied upon the generosity of Michele Longo Eder. I am heavily indebted to Edward Weisband, whom I am fortunate to call both a colleague and a friend. And I am thankful for the opportunity to present an early preview of the book to faculty and students at Washington and Lee University.

I am supremely grateful to Linda Fountaine, Jan Francis, Kathy McIntyre, and Brianna Crowder, friends and colleagues all, for their help and support. The expertise of Clara Enriquez, the designer of my website and the History Department's miracle worker as computer resources manager, has been indispensable. Georges Borchardt, my stellar agent, and his colleagues, including Anne and Valerie Borchardt, Samantha Shea, and Rachel Brooke, I treasure for their kindness and exceptional wisdom. At Pantheon, I have been blessed by the sagacity and inspiration of my editor, Victoria Wilson, along with the unflagging assistance of Ryan Smernoff, Michiko Clark, and Audrey Silverman. I am deeply grateful to them all, as I am to Chris Jerome for her painstaking efforts to improve the manuscript.

My family has been a boundless source of joy and encouragement. For Alice, my amazing wife, and our marvelous children, Alexandra, Sheldon, and Christian, my love, always.

Abbreviations Used in Notes

AC:	*American Citizen* (New York)
ADM:	Admiralty, UKNA
AM:	*American Mercury* (Hartford, CT)
ANB:	American National Biography Online
Annals:	*Annals of Congress,* House of Representatives
ASP:	*American State Papers*
AT:	*Alexandria Times*
Aurora:	*Aurora* (Philadelphia)
Bee:	*Bee* (New London, CT)
Bradburn, *Citizenship:*	Douglas Bradburn, *The Citizenship Revolution: Politics and the Creation of the American Union, 1774–1804* (Charlottesville: University of Virginia Press, 2009)
British Notes:	*Notes from the British Legations in the United States to the Department of State, 1791–1906* (USNA Microfilm Publication M50, roll 3)
Brunsman, *Evil Necessity:*	Denver Brunsman, *The Evil Necessity: British Naval Impressment in the Eighteenth-Century Atlantic World* (Charlottesville: University of Virginia Press, 2013)
CA:	Commercial Advertiser (New York)
Casey, "Statement of Service":	"Statement of Service, 1789–1839, of Lt. David O'Brien Casey (1779–1853)," National Maritime Museum, Greenwich, BGR/12, United Kingdom
CC:	*Columbian Centinel* (Boston)
CF:	*Centennial of Freedom* (Newark)
CG:	*Carolina Gazette* (Charleston)
CGDA:	*City Gazette & Daily Advertiser* (Charleston)
CM:	Court-Martial
CT:	*Constitutional Telegraph* (Boston)
DA:	*Daily Advertiser* (New York)
Domestic Letters:	*Domestic Letters of the Department of State, 1784–1861* (USNA Microfilm Publication M40, roll 10)

EM:	*Evening Mail* (London)
FO:	Foreign Office, UKNA
GEP:	*General Evening Post* (London)
GNYJ:	*Greenleaf's New-York Journal, & Patriotic Register*
GUS:	*Gazette of the United States* (Philadelphia)
HL:	*Herald of Liberty* (Washington, PA)
IC:	*Independent Chronicle* (Boston)
King, *Correspondence:*	Charles R. King, ed., *The Life and Correspondence of Rufus King . . . ,* 6 vols. (New York: G. P. Putnam's Sons, 1894–1900)
LC:	*London Chronicle*
LEP:	*Lloyd's Evening Post* (London)
Letters and Opinions:	*Letters from and Opinions of the Attorneys General, 1791–1811* (USNA, Microfilm Publication T326, roll 1)
Liston Papers:	Robert Liston Papers, Library of Congress, Washington, D.C.
Livingston Papers:	Edward Livingston Papers, Princeton University, Princeton, New Jersey
Mayo, *Instructions:*	Bernard Mayo, ed., *Instructions to the British Ministers to the United States 1791–1812,* 3, Annual Report, American Historical Association 122, no. 56
MC:	*Morning Chronicle* (London)
Mends, *Narrative:*	*Captain Mends's Narrative of the Mutiny, Murder and Piracy Committed on Board His Majesty's Ship Hermione* (Mole Saint Nicholas, Saint Domingue: Sans de Vertmont, 1798)
MM:	*Massachusetts Mercury* (Boston)
"Mutineers":	"Mutineers of the Hermione, Saint John's (Antigua), 14th April 1798"
"Naval Crew":	"Information respecting the naval crew of HM Ship Hermione, as by John Brown's Confession," CR114A/330, Warwickshire County Record Office, Warwick, UK
NG:	*National Gazette* (Philadelphia)
ODNB:	*Oxford Dictionary of National Biography,* 60 vols., (Oxford, 2004)
PA:	*Public Advertiser* (London)
Parker, Dispatches I:	In Letters, Admiral's Dispatches, Jamaica, 1797–1798, ADM 1/248
Parker, Dispatches II:	In Letters, Admiral's Dispatches, Jamaica, 1799–1800, ADM 1/249
Parker, Journal I:	Journal of Sir Hyde Parker, 1797–1798, ADM 50/65
Parker, Journal II:	Journal of Sir Hyde Parker, 1799, ADM 50/33
PG:	*Philadelphia Gazette*
Pickering Papers:	Pickering Papers, F. Allis, ed. (Massachusetts Historical Society microfilm edition 1966, Boston)
Pinckney, *Three Letters:*	Charles Pinckney, *Three Letters, written, and originally published, under the Signature of A South Carolina Planter* (Philadelphia: Aurora Office, 1799)

Pope, *Ship:*	Dudley Pope, *The Black Ship* (London: Weidenfeld and Nicolson, 1963)
Pyle, *Extradition:*	Christopher Pyle, *Extradition, Politics, and Human Rights* (Philadelphia: Temple University Press, 2001)
Rodger, *Command:*	N. A. M. Rodger, *The Command of the Ocean* (New York: W. W. Norton, 2005)
Rodger, "Shipboard Life":	Nicholas A. M. Rodger, "Shipboard Life in the Georgian Navy, 1750–1800: The Decline of the Old Order," in Lewis R. Fischer et al., eds., *The North Sea: Twelve Essays on Social History of Maritime Labour* (Stavanger, Norway: Stavanger Maritime Museum, 1992), pp. 29–40.
Rodger, *Wooden World:*	N. A. M. Rodger, *The Wooden World: An Anatomy of the Georgian Navy* (New York: W. W. Norton, 1986)
SCSG:	*South Carolina State Gazette* (Charleston)
SJC:	*St. James's Chronicle: or, the British Evening-Post* (London)
Stoutenbourg, Deposition:	Deposition of Isaac Stoutenbourg, June 6, 1798, CR114A/330, Warwickshire County Record Office, Warwick, UK
UKNA:	National Archives, Kew, United Kingdom
USNA:	National Archives, Washington, D.C.
VA:	*Virginia Argus* (Richmond)
Wedgwood, "RMJR":	Ruth Wedgwood, "The Revolutionary Martyrdom of Jonathan Robbins," *Yale Law Journal* 100 (1990): 229–368.
WEP:	*Whitehall Evening Post* (London)
Wharton, *State Trials:*	F. Wharton, *State Trials of the United States during the Administrations of Washington and Adams* (Philadelphia: Carey and Hart, 1849)
Winfield, *British Warships:*	Rif Winfield, *British Warships in the Age of Sail,* 1793–1817 (London: Chatham Publishing, 2005)
Wood, *Empire of Liberty:*	Gordon S. Wood, *Empire of Liberty: A History of the Early Republic, 1789–1815* (New York: Oxford University Press, 2009)

Notes

PREFACE

1. Pope, *Ship*. See also J. D. Spinney, "The Hermione Mutiny," *Mariner's Mirror* 41 (1955): 123–36; Leonard F. Guttridge, *Mutiny: A History of Naval Insurrection* (Annapolis: Naval Institute Press, 1992), pp. 75–82. For a more recent article that attempts to place the mutiny in the broad context of maritime resistance, see Niklas Frykman, "The Mutiny on the Hermione: Warfare, Revolution, and Treason in the Royal Navy," *Journal of Social History* 44 (2010): 159–87.
2. Wedgwood, "RMJR."
3. See Wedgwood, "RMJR," esp. pp. 323–34, 354–61; Pyle, *Extradition,* passim; and for a more dated though still helpful account, Larry D. Cress, "The Jonathan Robbins Incident: Extradition and the Separation of Powers in the Adams Administration," *Essex Institute Historical Collections* 111 (1975): 99–121.

PROLOGUE

1. For the ensuing events, I have drawn from L. Kinvin Wroth and Hiller B. Zobel, eds., *Legal Papers of John Adams* (Cambridge, MA: Harvard University Press, 1965), I, pp. lii–xliv; II, pp. 275–335; Charles Francis Adams, ed., *The Works of John Adams . . .* (Boston: Charles C. Little and James Brown, 1850), II, pp. 224–25; IX, pp. 317–19; X, pp. 204–10; *Boston Evening-Post,* May 1, June 19, 1769; Hiller B. Zobel, *The Boston Massacre* (New York: W. W. Norton, 1970), pp. 113–31. For a different perspective on Thomas Hutchinson's motivation, see William Pencak, "Thomas Hutchinson's Fight Against Naval Impressment," *New England Historical and Genealogical Register* 132 (1978): 25–36. For two compelling biographies of Adams, see David McCullough, *John Adams* (New York: Simon & Schuster, 2001); James Grant, *John Adams: Party of One* (New York: Farrar, Straus and Giroux, 2005).

I   MEN-OF-WAR

1. *Felix Farley's Bristol Journal,* Sept. 7, 1782; Winfield, *British Warships,* p. 199; John Lord and Jem Southam, *The Floating Harbour: A Landscape History of Bristol City Docks* (Bristol, UK: Redcliffe Press, 1983), pp. 20–21; Grahame Farr, *Shipbuilding in the Port of Bristol* (Basildon, UK: National Maritime Museum, 1977), pp. iv, 2, map between pp. 26 and 27; Walter Minchinton, "The Port of Bristol in the Eighteenth Century," in Patrick McGrath, ed., *Bristol in the Eighteenth Century* (Newton Abbot, UK: David & Charles, 1972), pp. 131–45; Peter T. May, "Eighteenth Century Views of Bristol and Bristolians," in McGrath, ed., *Bristol,* pp. 26–27. For Teast's shipyard, see the 1760 drawing by Nicholas Pocock between pp. 53 and 54 of Marcus Rediker, *The Slave Ship: A Human History* (New York: Viking, 2007).

2. Winfield, *British Warships,* p. 199; Rodger, *Command,* pp. 417–20; David Lyon, *The Sailing Navy List: All the Ships of the Royal Navy—Built, Purchased and Captured—1688–1860* (London: Conway Maritime Press, 1993), p. 84; Madge Dresser, *Slavery Obscured: The Social History of the Slave Trade in an English Provincial Port* (London: Continuum, 2001), p. 31.

3. Homer, *The Odyssey,* Robert Fitzgerald, trans. (New York: Alfred A. Knopf, 1992), p. 53.

4. *Providence Gazette, and Country Journal,* Nov. 13, 1762; *MC,* May 28, 1794; *New-York Mercury,* Sept. 20, 1762; Thomas Mante, *The Naval and Military History of the Wars of England; including, the Wars of Scotland and Ireland . . .* (London: Lewis and Co., [1795–1807]), p. 374; "Extract of a Letter from Portsmouth, Aug. 1," *Pennsylvania Gazette,* Oct. 7, 1762; *Sussex Advertiser,* Aug. 16, 1762; *New York Gazette,* Oct. 11, 1762; *Boston Evening-Post,* Oct. 25, 1762. A London writer later reflected that the capture of the *Hermione* "was a sufficient incitement to our spirited British youths to enter into the service against the haughty Dons." *Diary of Woodfall's Register* (London), Nov. 11, 1790.

5. Jeremy Black, "Naval Power, Strategy and Foreign Policy, 1775–1801," in Michael Duffy, ed., *Parameters of British Naval Power, 1650–1850* (Exeter, UK: University of Exeter Press, 1992), pp. 106–16; Michael Duffy, *Soldiers, Sugar, and Seapower: The British Expeditions to the West Indies and the War against Revolutionary France* (Oxford: Oxford University Press, 1987), pp. 3–5.

6. *Reading Mercury,* Jan. 13, 1783; Black, "Naval Power," in Duffy, ed., *British Naval Power,* pp. 106–16; P. L. C. Webb, "The Rebuilding and Repair of the Fleet," *Bulletin of the Institute of Historical Research* 50 (1977): 194–209; "Peter Cullen, Esq., 1789–1802," in H. G. Thursfield, ed., *Five Naval Journals, 1789–1817* ([London]: Navy Records Society, 1951), p. 52.

7. Paul Webb, "British Squadrons in North American Waters," *Northern Mariner* 5 (1995): 19–34; Tom Wareham, *The Star Captains: Frigate Command in the Napoleonic Wars* (Annapolis: Naval Institute Press, 2001), pp. 10–11, 47–48.

8. Wareham, *Star Captains,* pp. 34–46; Rodger, *Command,* p. 522. One who stood to profit was Captain Josias Rogers, born in 1755, who had originally been drawn to naval service as a young boy after catching sight of a famous Spanish prize in Portsmouth (almost certainly the *Hermione* in 1762). Some thirty years later, saddled with debt, he opted to return to duty, declining the Caribbean command of a line ship in favor of a thirty-two-gun frigate. The same year the newly appointed captain of the *Phaeton* pocketed £13,000, while his crew shared over half of the winnings. William Gilpin, *Memoirs of Josias Rogers, Esq. . . . .* (London: T. Cadell and W. Davies, 1808).

9. Winfield, *British Warships*, p. 199; "Extract of a Letter from Portsmouth," *General Evening Post* (London), Oct. 16, 1783; *Morning Herald and Daily Advertiser* (London), Apr. 1, 1785; "Extract of a Letter, Dated Spanish Town, Cape Breton, Dec. 13, 1785," *PA*, Mar. 31, 1785; "Extract of a Letter from Portsmouth, Aug. 29," *GEP* (London), Aug. 27, 1785; "Extract of a Letter from Waterford, Jan. 18," *GEP*, Jan. 20, 1789; "Cullen," in H. G. Thursfield, ed., *Five Navy Journals, 1789–1817* ([London]: Navy Records Society, 1951), p. 73.

10. Winfield, *British Warships*, p. 199; *Hereford Journal*, Feb. 27, 1793; Rodger, *Command*, p. 426.

11. Duffy, *West Indies*, pp. 5–16; Rodger, *Command*, p. 426.

12. Duffy, *West Indies*, pp. 16–25, 41–58; *ODNB*, s.v. "John Jervis." As envisioned by Henry Dundas, Pitt's war minister, "This country, having captured the French West India islands and destroyed their existing fleet, may long rest in peace." Rodger, *Command*, p. 426.

13. Richard S. Dunn, *Sugar and Slaves: The Rise of the Planter Class in the English West Indies, 1624–1713* (New York: W. W. Norton, 1973), pp. 21, 43–44, 149–50; *World* (London), Sept. 28, 1793; *Sun* (London), Dec. 10, 1793; Duffy, *West Indies*, pp. 56–57, 62; Brian Lavery, *Nelson's Navy: The Ships, Men, and Organization, 1793–1815* (Annapolis: U.S. Naval Institute Press, 2000), pp. 247–51.

14. Casey, "Statement of Service," fol. 2; Duffy, *West Indies*, pp. 97–104; "Return of the Loss Sustained by his Majesty's Ships in the Attack of Port-au-Prince," *WEP* (London), July 15, 1794.

15. Casey, "Statement of Service," fol. 2v; Duffy, *West Indies*, pp. 326–37; Rodger, *Command*, p. 436. From 1793 to 1801, the British death toll in the Caribbean surpassed sixty thousand men, perhaps one-third of whom were seamen. Limited ventilation aboard cramped vessels plagued by pests and poor sanitation, a cause of dysentery, contributed to mortality rates in excess of 50 percent. Lieutenant Casey further noted that such was "the malignancy of the prevailing disease, and the extreme rapidity of putrefaction, that we were absolutely obliged to dispose of the corpse, the moment the person expired."

16. Duffy, *West Indies*, pp. 106–14; Confession of John Mason, n.d., ADM 1/248; Casey, "Statement of Service," fol. 2v.

17. *SJC*, Feb. 15, 1794; "Extract of a Letter Dated Kingston, Jamaica, 25th February 1794 to a Member of Congress," *PG*, Mar. 27, 1794; *DA*, Mar. 31, 1794, Dec. 8, 1795; *Columbian Gazetteer* (New York), May 5, 1794; *Windham Herald*, Apr. 16, 1796; Winfield, *British Warships*, p. 199.

18. *Jersey Chronicle* (Mount Pleasant), Aug. 22, 1795; "Cato—X," *GUS*, Sept. 5, 1795; *LEP*, Oct. 14, 1795: *The American Remembrancer: or, An Impartial Collection of Essays . . .* (Philadelphia: Henry Tuckniss, 1795), p. 99; *GNYJ*, July 5, 1796; Paul A. Gilje, *Liberty on the Waterfront: American Maritime Culture in the Age of Revolution* (Philadelphia: University of Pennsylvania Press, 2004), p. 157.

19. *Bell's Weekly Messenger* (London), Jan. 7, 1798; Pope, *Black Ship*, pp. 49, 52–55; *ODNB*, s.v. "Hugh Pigot" and "Hugh Pigot."

20. Nicholas Harris Nicolas, ed., *The Dispatches and Letters of Vice Admiral Lord Viscount Nelson . . .* (London: Henry Coburn, 1845), V, p. 364; Wareham, *Star Captains*, pp. 95–96; *ODNB*, s.v. "Hugh Pigot"; Rodger, *Command*, pp. 512–13.

21. Pope, *Black Ship*, pp. 33–34, 56–57; *ODNB*, s.v. "Hugh Pigot."

22. Winfield, *British Warships*, pp. 194–95; *ODNB*, s.v. "Hugh Pigot"; Wareham, *Star Captains*, pp. 18–25, 73–74, 93–95, 100–101; Rodger, *Command*, p. 511.

23. *Federal Intelligencer, and Baltimore Daily Gazette,* Nov. 16, 1795; *Massachusetts Mercury* (Boston), Dec. 18, 1795; Pope, *Black Ship,* pp. 60–62, 67, 335–37; John D. Byrn, Jr., *Crime and Punishment in the Royal Navy: Discipline on the Leeward Islands Station 1784–1812* (Farnham, UK: Scolar Press, 1989); Rodger, "Shipboard Life," p. 53. Only after the *Bounty* reached Tahiti did floggings intensify, most commonly for desertion. Greg Dening, *Mr. Bligh's Bad Language: Passion, Power and Theatre on the Bounty* (Cambridge: Cambridge University Press, 1992), pp. 127–30.

24. "De Bordes," *PG,* July 29, 1796; *PG,* Aug. 5, 1796; Pope, *Black Ship,* pp. 21–26, 28. See also *Aurora,* Oct. 2, 1799. Liston to Secretary of State, FO 5/14/90; Admiralty to Commanders-in-Chief, Oct. 7, 1797, ADM 1/2/939.

25. Pope, *Black Ship,* pp. 22–23; *PG,* Aug. 5, 1796.

26. Liston to Grenville, Aug. 13, 1796, FO 5/14; Robert Brand Hanson, ed., *The Diary of Dr. Nathaniel Ames of Dedham, Massachusetts, 1758–1822* (Camden, ME: Picton Press, 1998), p. 606; "A Yankee," *GUS,* Aug. 8, 1796; *PG,* July 22, 26, 29, 1796; *ODNB,* s.v. "Robert Liston"; Pope, *Black Ship,* pp. 25–26.

27. Grenville to Liston, Oct 7, 1796, in Mayo, ed., "Instructions," p. 122; Pope, *Black Ship,* p. 26; *ODNB,* s.v. "Sir Hyde Parker."

28. Parker to Nepean, Jan. 24, 1797, Parker, Dispatches I; Jervis to Nepean, Dec. 22, 1797, ADM 1/396; Earl Spencer to Parker, May 11, 1800, in H. W. Richmond, ed., *Private Papers of George, second Earl Spencer, First Lord of the Admiralty, 1794–1801* (London: Navy Records Society, 1924), III, 286; Court of Inquiry, Jan. 19, 1797, ADM 50/65; Pope, *Black Ship,* pp. 26–33.

29. Richard Redmond, Statement [Mar. 1799], ADM 1/5348; Winfield, *British Warships,* p. 194; Pope, *Black Ship,* pp. 33–35; Wareham, *Star Captains,* pp. 110–11.

30. Pope, *Black Ship,* pp. 78–79.

31. Statement of Richard Redmond [Mar. 1799], ADM 1/534; "Naval Crew"; Wareham, *Star Captains,* p. 52; Pope, *Black Ship,* pp. 73–75.

32. Isaac Land, *War, Nationalism, and the British Sailor, 1750–1850* (New York: Palgrave Macmillan, 2009), pp. 2, 4–25, 35. These estimates, which are rough, are based on nationalities listed for just over half of the 168 seamen in the *Hermione's* final surviving muster book (April 7–July 7, 1797), ADM 36/12011.

33. "Cullen," in Thursfield, ed., *Naval Journals,* p. 63; "Conference with Ld. Grenville, Aug. 10, 1796," in King, *Correspondence,* II, p. 617; Brunsman, *Evil Necessity,* pp. 19, 28, 163.

34. Brunsman, *Evil Necessity,* pp. 2, 7, 20–35; Nicholas Rogers, *The Press Gang: Naval Impressment and Its Opponents in Georgian Britain* (London: Continuum, 2007), pp. 3–5; Rodger, *Command,* p. 499. Noting that the "navy was their safeguard," Foreign Minister Grenville in 1796 expressed frustration over constant complaints from the Admiralty that "the navy was decaying from the embarrassment experienced in manning their ships."

35. Rogers, *Press Gang,* p. 8; Brunsman, *Evil Necessity,* pp. 2, 34–35, 61–63.

36. Rodger, *Command,* pp. 43–45; Brunsman, *Evil Necessity,* pp. 37–38, 43, 47–48. Then, also, in much the same manner as the banishment of convicts (first to America, then to Australia) allowed Britain, for much of the eighteenth century, to avoid the construction of prisons (identified, too, with tyrannical authority), impressment—the cornerstone of a strong navy—diminished the necessity of a standing army to guard against foreign invasion, yet another tool of repression in the wrong hands. Traditional British freedoms remained inviolable at home, if neither abroad nor at sea.

A. Roger Ekirch, *Bound for America: The Transportation of British Convicts to the Colonies, 1718–1775* (Oxford: Clarendon/Oxford University Press, 1987), pp. 19–21.

37. Brunsman, *Evil Necessity,* passim; Rogers, *Press Gang,* p. 37.

38. Rogers, *Press Gang,* p. 4; *Hermione* Muster-Book, April 7–July 7, 1797, ADM 36/12011; CM, John Slushing, Mar. 13–15, 1799, ADM 1/5348; John Brown, Deposition, Mar. 26, 1798, in Mends, *Narrative,* p. 21; Niklas Frykman, "The Mutiny on the Hermione: Warfare, Revolution, and Treason in the Royal Navy," *Journal of Social History* 44 (2010): 159–87, 168–69.

39. Brunsman, *Evil Necessity,* pp. 140–46; Rodger, *Command,* pp. 499–500; Rogers, *Press Gang,* pp. 12–13; Rodger, "Shipboard Life," p. 30.

40. John Howell, ed., *The Life and Adventures of John Nicol, Mariner* (Edinburgh: William Blackwood, 1822), p. 179; Rodger, *Command,* p. 167; Frykman, "Mutiny," p. 171; Linda Colley, "Whose Nation? Class and National Consciousness in Britain, 1750–1830," *Past and Present* 113 (1986): 97–117; Land, *British Sailor,* pp. 24–25, 35, 38; T. Jenks, *Naval Engagements: Patriotism, Cultural Politics, and the Royal Navy, 1793–1815* (Oxford: Oxford University Press, 2006).

41. Brunsman, *Evil Necessity,* pp. 46–47; Land, *British Sailor,* pp. 15–19, 32, 50–51; Rodger, *Command,* pp. 495–96; Byrn, *Crime and Punishment,* pp. 125–31.

42. Rodger, *Command,* pp. 57, 504–505; Brunsman, *Evil Necessity,* pp. 147–48; Gilje, *Liberty on the Waterfront,* pp. 69–80.

43. *The Tender's Hold* ([London?]: n.p., [1790?]). See also *The Naval Songster, or Jack Tar's Chest of Conviviality, for 1801 . . .* (London: John Fairburn, [1800?]), pp. 11–12.

44. Rogers, *Press Gang,* pp. 107–111; Brunsman, *Evil Necessity,* p. 198; Rodger, *Command,* pp. 444–47; James Dugan, *The Great Mutiny* (New York: G. P. Putnam's Sons, 1965); G. E. Manwaring and Bonamy Dobrée, *The Floating Republic: An Account of the Mutinies at Spithead and the Nore in 1797* (Barnsley, UK: Pen & Sword, 2004); Ann Veronica Coats and Philip MacDougall, eds., *The Naval Mutinies of 1797: Unity and Perseverance* (Woodbridge, UK: Boydell Press, 2011).

45. Rogers, *Press Gang,* pp. 107–12; Rodger, *Command,* pp. 447–50; Brunsman, *Evil Necessity,* p. 198. Cf. N. A. M. Rodger, "Mutiny or Subversion? Spithead and the Nore," in Thomas Bartlett et al., eds., *1798: A Bicentenary Perspective* (Dublin: Four Courts Press, 2003), p. 549.

2   HAND 'EM UP

1. Henry Dundas to Earl Spencer, Aug. 24, 1796, in Julian S. Corbett, ed., *Private Papers of George, second Earl Spencer, First Lord of the Admiralty, 1794–1801* ([London]: Navy Records Society, 1913), p. 318; Pope, *Black Ship,* p. 122; Michael Duffy, *Soldiers, Sugar, and Seapower: The British Expeditions to the West Indies and the War against Revolutionary France* (Oxford: Oxford University Press, 1987), pp. 268–303, 346; Pigot to Parker, Apr. 21, 1797, Parker to Nepean, July 19, 1797, Parker, Dispatches I.

2. Pigot to Parker, Apr. 15, 21, 1797, Parker, Dispatches I; *EM,* June 5, 1797.

3. R. W. Otway to Parker, May 30, 1797, Pigot to Parker, June 9, 1797, Parker to Nepean, May 30, 1797, Parker, Dispatches I.

4. *EM,* June 5, 1797.

5. *WEP,* Nov. 23, 1797; Niklas Frykman, "The Mutiny on the Hermione: Warfare, Revolution, and Treason in the Royal Navy," *Journal of Social History* 44 (2010): 167.

6. Rufus King to Timothy Pickering, June 5, 1797, in King, *Correspondence*, II, p. 184; *Star* (London), June 9, 1796; Frykman, "Mutiny," passim.

7. A. Beckford Bevan and H. B. Wolryche-Whitmore, eds., *A Sailor of King George: The Journals of Captain Frederick Hoffman, RN, 1793–1814* (Annapolis: Naval Institute Press, 1998), p. 78; Tom Wareham, *The Star Captains: Frigate Command in the Napoleonic Wars* (Annapolis: Naval Institute Press, 2001), pp. 52–53, 227. During a troubled period in 1783, Horatio Nelson attributed low morale among seamen "to the infernal plan of turning them over from ship to ship, so that men cannot be attached to their officers, or the officers care two-pence about them." Rodger, "Shipboard Life," pp. 30–32.

8. Richard Redmond, Statement [Mar. 1799], ADM 1/5348.

9. Casey, "Statement of Service," fols. 5r–7r.

10. Ibid., fols. 7r–8v.

11. Ibid., fols. 8v–9r.

12. Parker to Nepean, Oct. 8, 1797, Parker, Dispatches I.

13. "Mutiny in the Hermione," *Hereford Journal*, Dec. 9, 1835; Pope, *Black Ship*, pp. 141–42; Casey, "Statement of Service," fol. 94; Rodger, *Command*, p. 55.

14. Mends, *Narrative*, p. 2; Pope, *Black Ship*, p. 152.

15. CM, James Irwin, John Holford the Elder, and John Holford the Younger, May 23, 1798, ADM 1/5344; CM, Henry Croaker, Thomas Leedson, and Peter Stewart, Jan. 15, 1799, ADM 1/5348; CM, Henry Croaker, Thomas Leedson, and Peter Stewart, Jan. 15, 1799, ADM 1/5348; "Mutineers," pp. 2, 3, 8–9; Casey, "Statement of Service," fols. 6v–7r.

16. CM, John Brown, William Benives, William Herd, John Hill, May 5, 1798, ADM 1/5344; CM, James Irwin, John Holford the Elder, and John Holford the Younger, May 23, 1798, ADM 1/5344; John Holford the Elder, Deposition, Apr. 23, 1798, CR 114a/330, Warwickshire Record Office, Warwick, UK; Casey, "Statement of Service," fol. 7r; "Mutineers," p. 2.

17. CM, David Forrester, Mar. 30, 1802, ADM 1/5360; *Columbian Minerva* (Dedham, MA), Nov. 4, 1800; "Domestic Intelligence," *European Magazine & London Review* (1800), p. 155; CM, John Watson and James Allen, July 30, 1800, ADM 1/5353; CM, James Irwin, John Holford the Elder, and John Holford the Younger, May 23, 1798, ADM 1/5344; CM, Henry Croaker, Thomas Leedson, and Peter Stewart, Jan. 15, 1799, ADM 1/5348; *Georgia Gazette* (Savannah), Dec. 8, 1797; Joseph Mansell's Confession, n.d., Parker, Dispatches I; "Mutineers," pp. 3, 8.

18. CM, Thomas Leach, William Mason, May 1, 1798, ADM 1/5344; CM, John Watson and James Allen, July 30, 1800, ADM 1/5353; CM, James Irwin, John Holford the Elder, and John Holford the Younger, May 23, 1798, ADM 1/5344; CM, John Williams, John Slenison, James Parrott, John Redmond, and Jacob Felhard, Mar. 13–15, 1799, ADM 1/5348; John Holford the Elder, Deposition, Apr. 23, 1798, CR 114a/330, Warwickshire Record Office, Warwick, UK; John Brown, Deposition, Mar. 26, 1798, in Mends, *Narrative*, pp. 21–24; Casey, "Statement of Service," fol. 10r.

19. John Holford the Elder, Deposition, Apr. 23, 1798, CR 114a/330, Warwickshire Record Office, Warwick, UK; CM, William Johnson and Adiel Powelson, July 2, 1801, ADM 1/5357; CM, Henry Croaker, Thomas Leedson, and Peter Stewart, Jan. 15, 1799, ADM 1/5348; CM, James Irwin, John Holford the Elder, and John Holford the Younger, May 23, 1798, ADM 1/5344.

20. CM, John Williams, John Slenison, James Parrott, John Redmond, and Jacob Felhard, Mar. 13–15, 1799, ADM 1/5348; Casey, "Statement of Service," fol. 10r.

21. Casey, "Statement of Service," fols. 10r–10v; CM, Thomas Leach, William Mason, May 1, 1798, ADM 1/5344; CM, John Williams, John Slenison, James Parrott, Richard Redmond, and Jacob Tollard, Mar. 13–15, 1799, ADM 1/5348; Pope, *Black Ship,* pp. 338–40.

22. CM, John Watson and James Allen, July 30, 1800, ADM 1/5353; CM, William Johnson and Adiel Powelson, July 2, 1801, ADM 1/5357; Casey, "Statement of Service," fol. 10r.

23. CM, John Williams, John Slenison, James Parrott, John Redmond, and Jacob Felhard, Mar. 13–15, 1799, ADM 1/5348; Stoutenbourg, Deposition; CM, Henry Croaker, Thomas Leedson, and Peter Stewart, Jan. 15, 1799, ADM 1/5348; "Mutiny in the Hermione," *Hereford Journal,* Dec. 8, 1835.

24. John Mason, Confession, n.d., ADM 1/248.

25. *Oxford Journal,* Dec. 23, 1797.

26. CM, Thomas Leach, William Mason, May 1, 1798, ADM 1/5344; CM, John Williams, John Slenison, James Parrott, John Redmond, and Jacob Felhard, Mar. 13–15, 1799, ADM 1/5348.

27. CM, John Watson and James Allen, July 30, 1800, ADM 1/5353; Casey, "Statement of Service," fol. 10v; Stoutenbourg, Deposition; CM, John Williams, John Slenison, James Parrott, John Redmond, and Jacob Felhard, Mar. 13–15, 1799, ADM 1/5348.

28. CM, William Johnson and Adiel Powelson, July 2, 1801, ADM 1/5357; CM, Anthony Mark, John Elliot, Joseph Mansell, and Peter Delany, Mar. 17, 1798, ADM 1/5343; CM, Thomas Leach, William Mason, May 1, 1798, ADM 1/5344; "Statement of Service," fol. 11; CM, John Williams, John Slenison, James Parrott, John Redmond, and Jacob Felhard, Mar. 13–15, 1799, ADM 1/5348; Deposition, John Holford the Elder, Apr. 23, 1798, CR 114a/330, Warwickshire Record Office, Warwick, UK; CM, James Irwin, John Holford the Elder, and John Holford the Younger, May 23, 1798, ADM 1/5344.

29. CM, Henry Croaker, Thomas Leedson, and Peter Stewart, Jan. 15, 1799, ADM 1/5348; CM, Thomas Leach, William Mason, May 1, 1798, ADM 1/5344; William Johnson and Adiel Powelson, July 2, 1801, ADM 1/5357; CM, John Watson and James Allen, July 30, 1800, ADM 1/5353; "Naval Crew"; Confession of John Mason, n.d., ADM 1/248; CM, John Williams, John Slenison, James Parrott, John Redmond, and Jacob Felhard, Mar. 13–15, 1799, ADM 1/5348; CM, John Barton, July 23, 1799, ADM 1/5350.

30. CM, David Forrester, Mar. 30, 1802, ADM 1/5360; Stoutenbourg, Deposition; Deposition, John Holford the Elder, Apr. 23, 1798, CR 114a/330, Warwickshire Record Office, Warwick, UK; CM, John Watson and James Allen, July 30, 1800, ADM 1/5353.

31. CM, William Johnson and Adiel Powelson, July 2, 1801, ADM 1/5357; Pope, *Black Ship,* p. 190; CM, John Pearce, Aug. 25, 1801, ADM 1/5357. See also CM, John Watson and James Allen, July 30, 1800, ADM 1/5353; CM, John Williams, John Slenison, James Parrott, John Redmond, and Jacob Felhard, Mar. 13–15, 1799, ADM 1/5348.

32. Casey, "Statement of Service," fol. 11r; Stoutenbourg, Deposition; CM, David Forrester, Mar. 30, 1802, ADM 1/5360; CM, John Watson and James Allen, July 30, 1800, ADM 1/5353; "Mutineers," p. 6.

33. H. Michael Tarver and Julia C. Frederick, *The History of Venezuela* (Westport, CT: Greenwood Press, 2005), pp. 1–6, 41–42; CM, Thomas Leach, William Mason, May 1, 1798, ADM 1/5344; Pope, *Black Ship,* p. 197.

34. CM, Thomas Leach, William Mason, May 1, 1798, ADM 1/5344; CM, William Johnson and Adiel Powelson, July 2, 1801, ADM 1/5357; Stoutenbourg, Deposition.

35. Stoutenbourg, Deposition; Mends, *Narrative,* p. 2.

3   DRAGNET

1. Master's Log, *Diligence,* Oct. 20, 1797, ADM 52/2935; Mends, *Narrative,* p. 1.

2. Mends, *Narrative,* pp. 1–2. For Mends, see *ODNB,* s.v. "Robert Mends."

3. Mends, *Narrative,* pp. 2–3; Master's Log, *Diligence,* Sept. 22, 1797, ADM 52/2935.

4. Parker to Nepean, Oct. 29, 1797, ADM 1/248; Captain's Log, *Diligence,* Oct. 31, 1797, ADM 51/1215.

5. Parker, Journal I, Oct. 31, 1797.

6. Parker to Nepean, Nov. 15, 1797, ADM 1/248; *GUS,* Nov. 21, 1797; *Claypoole's American Daily Advertiser* (Philadelphia), Nov. 22, 1797; *The Diary; or, Loudoun's Register* (New York), Nov. 24, 1797.

7. Parker, Journal I, Nov. 16, 1797.

8. *London Packet, or New Lloyd's Evening Post,* Dec. 15, 22, 1797; *True Briton* (London), Dec. 20, 1797; *Application of Barruel's Memoirs of Jacobinism . . .* (London: E. Booker, 1798), p. 42; *Hereford Journal,* Dec. 22, 1797, *Express and Evening Chronicle,* Feb. 24, 1798. See also, for example, *WEP,* Dec. 28, 1797, July 3, 1798; "Extract of a Letter from an Officer under Lord St. Vincent's Command," *Aberdeen Journal,* Feb. 27, 1798.

9. *E. Johnson's British Gazette and Sunday Monitor,* Dec. 24, 1797; *LEP,* Jan. 1, 1798; *WEP,* Dec. 28, 1797; *Morning Post and Gazetteer,* Dec. 16, 1797; *Hereford Journal,* Dec. 27, 1797, Jan. 24, 1798; *Leeds Intelligencer,* Mar. 12, 1798. See also *London Packet or New Lloyd's Evening Post,* Dec. 15, 22, 1797; *Weekly Register* (London), May 30, 1798.

10. *TB,* Dec. 20, 1797; *LC,* Dec. 12, 19, 1797; *Hereford Journal,* Dec. 27, 1797; *London Packet, or New Lloyd's Evening Post,* Dec. 13, 1797; *EEC,* Jan. 18, Feb. 24, 1798.

11. Caroline Alexander, *The Bounty: The True Story of the Mutiny on the Bounty* (New York: Viking, 2003), p. 203; *SJC,* Dec. 21, 1797; *Oracle of the Day* (Portsmouth, NH), Apr. 7, 1798. No evidence exists that the dock was destroyed or the monument constructed.

12. Josiah Woodward, *The Seaman's Monitor . . .* (London: J. Downing, 1723), pp. 69–70; "Seaman's Friend," *An Address to the Seamen in the British Navy* (London: W. Richardson, 1797), p. 8; Clare Anderson et al., eds., *Mutiny and Maritime Radicalism in the Age of Revolution: A Global Survey* (Cambridge: Cambridge University Press, 2014), pp. 2–3; Martin Hubley, "Desertion, Identity and the Experience of Authority in the North American Squadron of the Royal Navy, 1745–1812" (Ph.D. diss., Univ. of Ottawa, 2009), p. 383; John Delafons, *Treatise on Naval Courts Martial* (1805; reprint ed., Cambridge: Cambridge University Press, 2012), pp. 260–63; Brian Lavery, *Nelson's Navy: The Ships, Men, and Organization, 1793–1815* (Annapolis: U.S. Naval Institute Press, 2000), p. 217.

13. *Thirty Years from Home, or a Voice from the Main Deck: Being the Experience of Samuel Leech . . .* (1843; rpt. ed., New York: William Abbatt, 1909), pp. 38–39; Frykman, "Mutiny," p. 173; John D. Byrn, Jr., *Crime and Punishment in the Royal Navy: Discipline on the Leeward Islands Station 1784–1812* (Farnham, UK: Scolar Press, 1989), p. 171; Delafons, *Naval Courts Martial,* p. 271. See also John Howell, ed., *The Life and Adventures of John Nicol, Mariner* (Edinburgh: William Blackwood, 1822), p. 50.

14. *Hampshire Chronicle,* Dec. 16, 1797; *Memoirs of the Lady Hester Stanhope as Related by Herself . . .* (London: Henry Colburn, 1846), I, p. 282; G. L. Newnham Collingwood, *A Selection from the Public and Private Correspondence of Admiral Lord Collingwood . . .* (London: James Ridgway, 1828), p. 49; Rodger, *Wooden World,* pp. 237–39; Rodger, *Command,* pp. 322, 403–4, 444, 451–52; Timothy Jenks, *Naval Engagements:*

Patriotism, Cultural Politics, and the Royal Navy, 1793–1815 (Oxford: Oxford University Press, 2006), pp. 88–99.

15. Translation of Carbonell letter, included in Parker to Nepean, Feb. 4, 1798, ADM 1/248; *CGDA*, Feb. 6, 1798; *Leeds Intelligencer*, Dec. 25, 1797.

16. Parker to Nepean, Feb. 4, 1798, ADM 1/248; "Proclamation," *AT*, Feb. 14, 1798; Henry Harvey to Nepean, Mar. 10, 1798, in Letters, Admiral's Dispatches, Leeward Islands, 1798, ADM 1/321; *AT*, Feb. 14, 1798; *LEP*, Apr. 6, 1798; *CA*, Feb. 6, 1798.

17. CM, John Williams, John Slenison, James Parrott, John Redmond, and Jacob Felhard, Mar. 13–15, 1799, ADM 1/5348; *Aurora* (Philadelphia), Apr. 24, 1798; Casey, "Narrative," fol. 11v; "The Hermione Frigate," *Reading Mercury*, Mar. 12, 1798; CM, John Barton, July 23, 1799, ADM 1/5350.

18. Stoutenbourg, Deposition; CM, Henry Croaker, Thomas Leedson, Peter Stewart, Jan. 15, 1799, ADM 1/5348.

19. "Naval Crew"; CM, John Barton, July 23, 1799, ADM 1/5350; Stoutenbourg, Deposition; Southcott, Deposition; Holford, Deposition; Tarver and Frederick, *History of Venezuela*, pp. 39–45; CM, Anthony Mark, John Elliot, Joseph Mansell, Peter Delany, Mar. 17, 1798, ADM 1/5343; *Aurora*, Apr. 24, 1798.

20. "Naval Crew."

21. Valentin Groebner, *Who Are You?: Identification, Deception, and Surveillance in Early Modern Europe* (New York: Zone Books, 2007); Julius S. Scott, "Crisscrossing Empires: Ships, Sailors, and Resistance in the Lesser Antilles in the Eighteenth Century," in Robert. L. Paquette and Stanley L. Engerman, eds., *The Lesser Antilles in the Age of European Expansion* (Gainesville: University Press of Florida, 1996), pp. 128–43; Charles R. Foy, "Seeking Freedom in the Atlantic World, 1713–1783," *Early American Studies* 4 (Spring 2006): 63; Ernest Bassi, "Geography, Geopolitics, and the Geopolitical Imagination: Seeing the Atlantic from South America's Caribbean Coast, 1780s–1810s," Omohundro Institute of Early American History and Culture Colloquium, Williamsburg, VA, Feb. 5, 2013; Brunsman, *Evil Necessity*, pp. 173, 189.

22. Brunsman, *Evil Necessity*, pp. 178, 182; Henry Harvey to Nepean, March 10, 1798, in Letters, Admiral's Dispatches, Leeward Islands, 1798, ADM 1/321; *St. George's Chronicle and Grenada Gazette*, May 4, 1798.

23. St. Vincent to Nepean, Feb. 4, 1798, ADM 1/284; *LEP*, Feb. 16, 1798; CM, John Williams, John Slushing, James Perrett, Richard Redman, Jacob Fulga, Mar. 13–15, 1799, ADM 1/5348; *Derby Mercury*, Feb. 22, 1798.

24. Parker to Nepean, Apr. 21, 1798, ADM 1/248; CM, Anthony Mark, John Elliot, Joseph Mansell, Peter Delany, Mar. 17, 1798, ADM 1/5343; Stoutenbourg, Deposition; *SJC*, Apr. 26, 1798.

25. John Mason, Confession, [1798], ADM 1/248; "Naval Crew"; Linda M. Rupert, *Creolization and Contraband: Curaçao in the Early Modern Atlantic World* (Athens: University of Georgia Press, 2012), pp. 172–73, 245.

26. John Mason, Confession, [1798], ADM 1/248.

27. CM, Anthony Mark, John Elliot, Joseph Mansell, Peter Delany, Mar. 17, 1798, ADM 1/5343; "Letters from the Lower Deck," in H. G. Thursfield, ed., *Five Naval Journals, 1789–1817* ([London]: Navy Records Society, 1951), p. 357; Joseph Montell, Confession, Parker to Nepean, Mar. 19, 1798, Parker, Dispatches I; Delafons, *Naval Courts Martial*, pp. 207–8.

28. Parker to Vasquez, Apr. 8, 1798, ADM 1/248; "Extract of a Letter from Halifax, Nova Scotia," *LC*, May 24, 1798; *AT A COURT MARTIAL Assembled and held on Board*

His Majesty's Ship York, Mole St. Nicholas, on the Seventeenth Day of March 1798,
Parker, Dispatches I.

29. Parker to Nepean, Mar. 19, 1798, ADM 1/248; "Extract of a Letter from an Officer
of His Majesty's Ship Renommee . . . ," *Evening Mail* (London), June 15, 1798; *LC,*
May 8, 1798.

30. CM, Thomas Leach, John Mason, May 1, 1798, ADM 1/5344; Casey, "Narrative,"
fols. 12r–12v; Harvey to Nepean, May 13, 1798, in Letters, Admiral's Dispatches, Leeward Islands, 1798, ADM 1/321.

31. "Mutineers."

32. Ibid.

33. Ibid.; Groebner, *Who Are You,* pp. 97–115.

34. CM, James Irwin, John Holford the Elder, and John Holford the Younger, May 23,
1798, ADM 1/5344; Holford, Deposition; *London Packet, or New Lloyd's Evening Post,*
June 27, 1798; "Naval Crew"; CM, John Brown, William Benives, William Hard,
John Hill, May 5, 1798, ADM 1/5344.

35. CM, John Williams, John Slenison, James Parrott, Richard Redmond, and Jacob
Tollard, March 13–15, 1799, ADM 1/5348: CM, John Coe, Dec. 8, 1798, ADM 1/5347;
Weekly Register (London), July 25, 1798.

36. CM, John Williams, John Slenison, James Parrott, Richard Redmond, and Jacob
Tollard, March 13–15, 1799, ADM 1/5348.

37. Parker to Nepean, July 18, 1798, Parker, Dispatches I; Thomas Charlton's Examina-
tion, June 6, 1798, CR 114A/330, Warwickshire Record Office, Warwick, UK.

38. "Extract of a Letter from an Officer of His Majesty's Ship Renommee . . . ," *Evening
Mail,* June 15, 1798; *Evening Courier* (Charleston), Oct. 12, 1798; *Newcastle Courant,*
Apr. 28, 1798.

39. *LEP,* June 25, 1798; *SJC,* June 28, 1798.

40. Parker to Nepean, May 28, 1798, Parker, Dispatches I; Michael Duffy, *Soldiers, Sugar,
and Seapower: The British Expeditions to the West Indies and the War against Revolutionary France* (Oxford: Oxford University Press, 1987), pp. 306–11.

41. Parker to Nepean, Nov. 15, 1797, Feb. 14, 1798, Parker, Dispatches I.

4   RECEIVE THE FUGITIVE

1. A. Roger Ekirch, *Bound for America: The Transportation of British Convicts to the Colo-
nies, 1718–1775* (Oxford: Clarendon/Oxford University Press, 1987), pp. 7–8; Marilyn
C. Baseler, *"Asylum for Mankind": America, 1607–1800* (Ithaca, NY: Cornell University
Press, 1998), passim.

2. Bernard Bailyn, *The Ideological Origins of the American Revolution* (Cambridge, MA:
Belknap/Harvard University Press, 1967), pp. 138–43; Baseler, *"Asylum for Mankind,"*
pp. 7, 12, 131–34.

3. Sylas Neville of London wished that America "may be an asylum to those Englishmen
who have spirit and virtue enough to leave their country, when it submits to domestic
or foreign tyranny." Bailyn, *Ideological Origins,* pp. 140–43; Baseler, *"Asylum for Mankind,"* pp. 134–37. Echoed William Hooper of North Carolina, "Yes, Britain, it is the
criterion of thy existence; thy greatness totters. Luxury & wealth with every vice in
their train, are hurrying thee down the precipice, & liberty shuddering at thy fate is
seeking an Asylum westward." Hooper to James Iredell, Jan. 6, 1776, in Don Higgin-

botham, ed., *The Papers of James Iredell* (Raleigh: North Carolina Office of Archives & History, 1976), I, p. 339.

4. "The Former, Present, and Future Prospects of America," *Columbian Magazine,* Oct. 1786, p. 84; Aristide R. Zolberg, *A Nation by Design: Immigration Policy in the Fashioning of America* (Cambridge, MA: Harvard University Press, 2006), pp. 51–84 passim; Wood, *Empire of Liberty,* p. 248.

5. James H. Kettner, *The Development of American Citizenship. 1608–1870* (Chapel Hill: University of North Carolina Press, 1978), pp. 235–39; Hans-Jürgen Grabbe, "European Immigration to the United States in the Early National Period, 1783–1820," in Susan E. Klepp, ed., *The Demographic History of the Philadelphia Region, 1600–1860* (Philadelphia: American Philosophical Society, 1989), p. 194; Baseler, *"Asylum for Mankind,"* pp. 242–61; Zolberg, *Nation by Design,* pp. 86–87.

6. Zolberg, *Nation by Design,* pp. 87–91; Baseler, *"Asylum for Mankind,"* pp. 261–67; Bradburn, *Citizenship,* pp. 133–37.

7. Baseler, *"Asylum for Mankind,"* pp. 260–64; Zolberg, *Nation by Design,* pp. 87–92.

8. Baseler, *"Asylum for Mankind,"* pp. 267–71; Zolberg, *Nation by Design,* pp. 91–92; Bradburn, *Citizenship,* pp. 160–62.

9. Joseph Gerrald, *A Convention the Only Means of Saving Us from Ruin. In a Letter Addressed to the People of England* (London: D. I. Eaton, 1793), pp. 71–73; Pyle, *Extradition,* pp. 22–23; Joseph Montell, Confession, Parker to Nepean, Mar. 19, 1798, Parker, Dispatches I. See also, for example, John Mason, Confession, [1798], Parker, Dispatches I; CM, James Irwin, John Holford the Elder, and John Holford the Younger, May 23, 1798, ADM 1/5344. When an English privateer, half of whose crew had mutinied over the distribution of seized goods, arrived in La Guaira in March 1798, the mutineers negotiated payment for their schooner with the added condition that they would "be free to go to North America." Pope, *Black Ship,* pp. 236–37.

10. Robert Liston to Timothy Pickering, Feb. 19, 1798 (with enclosed deposition), in *British Notes;* Liston to Lord Grenville, June 5, 1798, FO 5/22/86–88; John Melish, *Travels Through the United States of America in the Years 1806 & 1807, and 1809, 1810, & 1811 . . .* (London: G. Cowie, 1818), p. 36; François-Alexandre-Frédéric, duc de La Rochefoucauld-Liancourt, *Travels through the United States of America . . .* (London: R. Phillips, 1799), II, pp. 245–66. Among other American papers, New York's *Commercial Advertiser* reported on Jan. 18, 1798, that Martin blamed "the great severity of Capt. Pigot, who was constantly flogging the men."

11. Bradford Perkins, "A Diplomat's Wife in Philadelphia: Letters of Henrietta Liston, 1796–1800," *William and Mary Quarterly,* 3rd Ser., 11 (1954), pp. 592–99; Robert Liston to Timothy Pickering, Feb. 19, 1798 (with enclosed deposition), in *British Notes;* ODNB, s.v. "Sir Robert Liston."

12. ANB, s.v. "Timothy Pickering"; Gerard H. Clarfield, *Timothy Pickering and American Diplomacy, 1795–1800* (Columbia: University of Missouri Press, 1969), pp. 1–89.

13. Pickering to Thomas Pinckney, May 2, 1796, roll 36, Pickering to Liston, June 25, 1796, Aug. 11, 1797, roll 7, Pickering to King, Sept. 10, 1796, roll 36, Pickering Papers. See also, for example, Pickering to Liston, Sept. 7, 1797, roll 37, Oct. 9, 1797, roll 11, Jan. 4, 1798, roll 37, Pickering to King, Oct. 26, 1796, roll 36, Oct. 3, 1797, roll 7, Pickering to David Lenox, Oct. 31, 1797, roll 7, Pickering Papers; Pickering to Liston, July 3, 1797, in *Domestic Letters; PG,* July 6, 1797; Clarfield, *Timothy Pickering,* pp. 80–89; Gerard Clarfield, "Postscript to the Jay Treaty: Timothy Pickering

and Anglo-American Relations, 1795–1797," *William and Mary Quarterly* 23 (1966): 106–20.

14. Perkins, "Diplomat's Wife," p. 614; Pickering to Liston, Mar. 13, 1798, roll 8, Pickering Papers; Clarfield, *Pickering,* pp. 82–89. In response, Grenville reprimanded Liston, "The practical impressment of sailors is not as you seem to imagine contrary either to the Letter, or Spirit of the English Statutes." Grenville to Liston, Nov. 17, 1797, in Mayo, *Instructions,* p. 143.

15. Liston to Pickering, Feb. 19, 1798, in *British Notes.*

16. Pyle, *Extradition,* pp. 10–12, 24–26; John Lafferty, "The Turning Point Approaches: The Political Offense Exception to Extradition," *San Diego Law Review* 24 (1987): 550.

17. Wedgwood, "RMJR," pp. 266–68; Jefferson, "Enclosure II: Considerations on a Convention with Spain," Mar. 22, 1792, in Charles T. Cullen, *The Papers of Thomas Jefferson* (Princeton, NJ: Princeton University Press, 1990), XXIII, p. 328; Jefferson to Edmond Charles Genet, September 12, 1793, in John Catanzariti, ed., *The Papers of Thomas Jefferson* (Princeton, NJ: Princeton University Press, 1997), XXVII, pp. 97–99.

18. Pickering to Liston, Feb. 21, 1798, roll 8, Pickering Papers; Pickering to Robert Morris, Mar. 29, 1798, in *Domestic Letters*; Liston to Lord Grenville, June 5, 1798, FO 5/22/87.

19. Circuit Court of the United States, Middle Circuit of the New-Jersey district. The United States, (a.) William Brigstock, other-wise called John Johnston. Indictment for murder . . . (United States: s.n. 1800; Liston to Lord Grenville, June 5, 1798, FO 5/22/87–88; *GUS,* Mar. 13, 1798; Kenneth Roberts and Anna M. Roberts, eds. and trans., *Moreau de St. Méry's American Journey [1793–1798]* (New York: Doubleday, 1947), pp. 108–109; Rochefoucauld-Liancourt, *Travels,* I, pp. 363–64, II, pp. 434–35; Isaac Weld, *Travels Through the States of North America . . . 1795, 1796, 1797* (London: J. Stockdale, 1807), I, pp. 58, 260; John Melish, *Travels Through the United States of America, in the Years 1806 & 1807, and 1809, 1810, & 1811 . . .* (London: G. Cowie, 1818), pp. 293, 310.

20. "Important," *Sun* (New York), Mar. 28, 1796; Liston to Lord Grenville, June 5, 1798, FO 5/22/87–88; "Naval Crew"; Brigstock to Livingston, Apr. 23, 1798, Livingston Papers.

21. Liston to Pickering, Mar. 29, 1798, in *British Notes;* Pickering to Lee, Mar. 13, 1798, roll 8, Pickering Papers.

22. Lee to Pickering, Mar. 14, 1798, in *Letters and Opinions;* ANB, s.v. "Charles Lee."

23. Jeffrey L. Pasley, *"The Tyranny of the Printers": Newspaper Politics in the Early American Republic* (Charlottesville: University of Virginia Press, 2001).

24. Matthew Rainbow Hale, "American Hercules: Militant Sovereignty and Violence in the Democratic-Republican Imagination, 1793–1795," in Patrick Griffin et al., eds., *Between Sovereignty and Anarchy: The Politics of Violence in the American Revolutionary Era* (Charlottesville: University of Virginia Press, 2015), p. 249; *CGDA,* Dec. 7, 1797; *Bee,* Dec. 13, 1797. See also *Aurora,* Mar. 16, 27, 1798; "Matthew Lyon," *VA,* Oct. 18, 1799. For early coverage, see, for example, *GUS,* Nov. 15, 1797, *PG,* Nov. 15, 16, 1797; *DA,* Nov. 17, 1797.

25. "From a Correspondent," *Aurora,* Mar. 16, 1798; Pasley, *"Tyranny of the Printers,"* pp. 79–104. For a stinging Federalist reply, see "A.B." *GUS,* Mar. 20, 1798, which was answered in turn in the *Aurora* of Mar. 27, 1798.

26. Weld, *Travels,* I, p. 259; Roberts and Roberts, eds. and trans., *American Journey,* pp. 108–109.

27. Circuit Court of the United States, Middle Circuit of the New-Jersey district. The United States, (a.) William Brigstock, other-wise called John Johnston; Liston to Pickering, Apr. 7, 1798, in *British Notes; New York Gazette,* Apr. 14, 1798.

28. ANB, s.v. "Samuel Chase"; Mark Edward Lender, *"This Honorable Court": The United States District Court for the District of New Jersey, 1789–2000* (New Brunswick, NJ: Rutgers University Press, 2006), pp. 22–31; Rochefoucauld-Liancourt, *Travels,* II, p. 540.

29. "Copy of Minutes," *Spectator* (New York), Apr. 8, 1800; "From our Correspondent in New-York," *AT,* Apr. 23, 1798.

30. Pickering to Liston, Apr. 13, 1798, in *Domestic Letters;* Liston to Lord Grenville, June 5, 1798, FO 5/22/88–90.

31. Wedgwood, "RMJR," p. 278; Liston to Lord Grenville, June 5, 1798, FO 5/22/90.

32. Brigstock to Livingston, Apr. 23, 1798, Livingston Papers; *Annals,* Feb. 18, p. 344, Feb. 29, 1796, pp. 382–94, Mar. 28, 1796, pp. 802–20; *Report of the Committee Appointed to Enquire into the Operation of the Act for the Relief and Protection of American Seamen . . . , Feb. 28, 1797* ([Philadelphia]: n.p., [1797]); Nathan Perl-Rosenthal, *Citizen Sailors: Becoming American in the Age of Revolution* (Cambridge, MA: Harvard University Press, 2015), pp. 173–91.

33. Rochefoucauld-Liancourt, *Travels,* II, p. 467; Charles Adams to John Quincy Adams, June 8, 1797, Founding Era Collection, University of Virginia; ANB, s.v. "Edward Livingston"; Charles Hawes Hunt, *Life of Edward Livingston* (New York: Appleton & Co., 1864).

34. Brigstock to Livingston, Apr. 23, 1798, Livingston Papers; Rochefoucauld-Liancourt, *Travels,* II, p. 429; John E. O'Connor, "Legal Reform in the Early Republic: The New Jersey Experience," *American Journal of Legal History,* 22 (1978), pp. 99–100.

35. Pickering to Lucius Horatio Stockton, June 8, 1798, in *Domestic Letters;* Liston to Lord Grenville, June 5, 1798, FO 5/22/90–91; *New-Jersey Journal* (Elizabeth-Town), Aug. 14, 1798.

36. *GUS,* Aug. 14, 1798.

37. *Richard E. Lee's Letter, the Attorney General's Opinion . . . Relative to the Conduct of Doctor John K. Read, a Magistrate of the Borough of Norfolk* (Richmond, VA: Meriwether Jones, 1800); "Alexander Jordan," *Genius of Liberty,* Apr. 24, 1800; CM, John Watson and James Allen, July 30, 1800, ADM 1/5353.

38. John Buchanan, *The Road to Guilford Courthouse: The American Revolution in the Carolinas* (New York: John Wiley & Sons, 1997), p. 164; Louise V. North, *The Travel Journals of Henrietta Marchant Liston: North America & Lower Canada, 1796–1800* (Lanham, MD: Lexington Books, 2014), p. 24; Rochefoucauld-Liancourt, *Travels,* II, pp. 2–14; Weld, Travels, I, p. 62, 170–77; Adele Hast, *Loyalism in Revolutionary Virginia: The Norfolk Area and the Eastern Shore* (Ann Arbor, MI: UMI Research Press, 1982), pp. 92–93; Thomas C. Parramore, *Norfolk: The First Four Centuries* (Charlottesville: University Press of Virginia, 1994), pp. 94–107.

39. *Lee's Letter,* pp. 29–30.

40. *Genius of Liberty* (Morristown, NJ), Apr. 17, 1800; *Lee's Letter,* pp. 29–30.

5   *UNITED STATES V. NATHAN ROBBINS*

1. Jack P. Greene, "Colonial South Carolina and the Caribbean Connection," *South Carolina Historical Magazine* 88 (1987): 192–210; Matthew Mulcahy, *Hurricanes and Society in the British Greater Caribbean, 1624–1783* (Baltimore: Johns Hopkins University Press, 2006).

2. Wharton, *State Trials*, p. 393.

3. Ibid.

4. *Hampshire Telegraph* (Portsmouth), Sept. 13, 1802.

5. Parker, Journal II, Mar. 24, 1799; *CA*, Apr. 27, 1799; Wharton, *State Trials*, 393; Robert Liston to Timothy Pickering, May 23, 1799, *British Notes*.

6. N. Louise Bailey, *Biographical Directory of the South Carolina Senate, 1776–1985* (Columbia: University of South Carolina Press, 1986), pp. 120–22; Hamilton to Washington, Nov. 5, 1795, in Harold C. Syrett, ed., *The Papers of Alexander Hamilton* (New York: Columbia University Press, 1973), XIX, pp. 395, 397.

7. *Connecticut Courant*, Aug. 19, 1799; Pinckney, *Three Letters*, p. 9; Benjamin Moodie to Sir Hyde Parker, Apr. 23, 1799, Parker, Dispatches II; Pickering to John Adams, May 15, 1799, roll 37, Pickering Papers; *Star* (London), July 22, 1799.

8. Parker to Nepean, May 19, 1799, Parker, Dispatches II.

9. Pickering to Adams, May 15, 1799, roll 37, Pickering Papers; Liston to Pickering, May 23, 1799, *British Notes*. For Pickering's low opinion of Lee, see his letter of June 9, 1800, to Christopher Gore, roll 13, Pickering Papers.

10. James Grant, *John Adams: Party of One* (New York: Farrar, Straus and Giroux, 2005), p. 175; Uriah Forrest to John Adams, Apr. 28, 1799, in Charles Francis Adams, ed., *The Works of John Adams* (Boston: Little, Brown and Company, 1853), VIII, p. 637; Robert Troup to Rufus King, June 5, 1799, in King, ed., *King, Correspondence*, III, p. 35; Pickering to Adams, May 15, 1799, roll 37, Pickering to Charles Adams, July 25, 1798, roll 37, Pickering to Rufus King, Mar. 12, 1799, roll 10, Pickering Papers; Wood, *Empire of Liberty*, pp. 55, 272–73; Eve Kornfeld, "Crisis in the Capital: The Cultural Significance of Philadelphia's Great Yellow Fever Epidemic," *Pennsylvania History* 51 (1989): 189.

11. Pickering to Adams, May 15, 1799, roll 37, Pickering Papers.

12. Ibid.

13. Ibid.

14. Pickering to Rufus King, June 16, 1800, roll 13, Pickering Papers; Pyle, *Extradition*, pp. 30–31.

15. Adams to Pickering, May 21, 1799, Adams to Secretary of the Navy, May 21, 1799, Adams Papers, #394; Grant, *John Adams*, pp. 380–81.

16. John Adams to Lord Carmarthen, Oct. 3, 1787, in Adams, ed., *Works of John Adams*, VIII, pp. 455–56; Wood, *Empire of Liberty*, pp. 272–73; David McCullough, *John Adams* (New York: Simon & Schuster, 2001), p. 524.

17. Pickering to Thomas Bee, June 3, 1799, roll 11, Pickering Papers.

18. Parker to Nepean, July 14, 1799, Parker, Dispatches II.

19. John Davis, *Travels of Four Years and a Half in the United States of America; During 1795, 1799, 1800, 1801, and 1802* (London: B. Edwards, 1803), pp. 94–95, 112, 115; François-Alexandre-Frédéric, duc de La Rochefoucauld-Liancourt, *Travels through the United States of America . . .* (London: R. Phillips, 1799), I, pp. 417, 374–80, 426; Pierce Butler to John Rea, Nov. 18, 1791, in Terry W. Lipscomb, ed., *The Letters of*

Pierce Butler, 1790–1794: Nation Building and Enterprise in the New American Republic (Columbia: University of South Carolina Press, 2007), p. 145. In her travel journal, Henrietta Liston remarked in late 1797, "Charleston is most remarkable for the polished society it affords." Louise V. North, *The Travel Journals of Henrietta Marchant Liston: North America & Lower Canada, 1796–1800* (Lanham, MD: Lexington Books, 2014), p. 30.

20. Carl R. Lounsbury, *From Statehouse to Courthouse: An Architectural History of South Carolina's Colonial Capital and Charleston County Courthouse* (Columbia: University of South Carolina Press, 2001), passim; "Preservation Society of Charleston," http://www.halseymap.com/Flash/window.asp?HMID=11.

21. *GNYJ,* Feb. 15, 1800; Parker, Journal II, May 20, 29, June 3, 1799.

22. Abraham Sasportas to Freneau & Paine, *CGDA,* Dec. 5, 1799; Alex. Moultrie to Benjamin Moodie, *CGDA,* Dec. 4, 1799.

23. Minutes, Circuit Ad District Courts, District of South Carolina, 1789–1849 (National Archives Microfilm Publication M1181, roll 1); ANB, s.v. "William Johnston."

24. Moultrie to Moodie, *AT,* Dec. 31, 1799; *Sun* (Dover, NH), Aug. 21, 1799; John Belton O'Neall, *The Annals of Newberry, Historical, Biographical, and Anecdotal* (Charleston, SC: S. G. Courtenay & Co., 1859), pp. 106–7.

25. ANB, s.v. "Alexander Moultrie"; Maeva Marcus et al., eds., *The Documentary History of the Supreme Court of the United States, 1789–1800* (New York: Columbia University Press, 1994), V, p. 502 n. 36; Christopher Shortell, *Rights, Remedies, and the Impact of State Sovereign Immunity* (Albany: State University of New York Press, 2008), pp. 50–54.

26. Wharton, *State Trials,* pp. 394–95; Nathan Perl-Rosenthal, *Citizen Sailors: Becoming American in the Age of Revolution* (Cambridge, MA: Harvard University Press, 2016), passim. For the use of American protection certificates, see also Paul A. Gilje, *Liberty on the Waterfront: American Maritime Culture in the Age of Revolution* (Philadelphia: University of Pennsylvania Press, 2004), pp. 158–59.

27. Wharton, *State Trials,* pp. 395–96.

28. Ibid., pp. 397–400.

29. Ibid., p. 400.

30. Ibid., p. 396; Perl-Rosenthal, *Citizen Sailors,* p. 198.

31. Ibid., pp. 401–4; *New Hampshire Gazette,* Sept. 3, 1799.

32. *PG,* Aug. 12, 1799; *Daily Advertiser* (New York), Aug. 16, 1791, Nov. 5, 1794, Dec. 11, 1798; *New Hampshire Gazette* (Portsmouth), Sept. 3, 1799; *Mercantile Advertiser* (New York), Aug. 6, 1799.

33. Diary of Thomas Rodney's Notes, Mar. 8, 1781, in Paul H. Smith *et al.,* eds., *Letters of Delegates to Congress* (Washington, DC: Library of Congress, 1996), XVII, p. 38.

34. *Georgia Gazette* (Savannah), Aug. 8, 1799; *Independent Chronicle* (Boston), Oct. 3, 1799; John D. Byrn, Jr., *Crime and Punishment in the Royal Navy: Discipline on the Leeward Islands Station 1784–1812* (Farnham, UK: Scolar Press, 1989), p. 56.

35. Byrn, *Crime and Punishment,* pp. 31–63 passim; John McArthur, *A Treatise of the Principles and Practice of Naval Courts-Martial* (London: Whieldon and Butterworth, 1792), p. xxiii.

36. Byrn, *Crime and Punishment,* pp. 33–41.

37. McArthur, *Naval Courts-Martial,* p. 58; John Delafons, *Treatise on Naval Courts Martial* (1805; reprint ed., Cambridge: Cambridge University Press, 2012), pp. 179–80; Byrn, *Crime and Punishment,* pp. 41–42, 55–56; Rodger, *Wooden World,* p. 224.

38. CM, Thomas Nash, Aug. 17, 1799, ADM 1/5350.

39. Ibid., ADM 1/5350.

40. Ibid.

41. Ibid.

42. Ibid.; Byrn, *Crime and Punishment*, p. 53.

43. Parker, Journal II, Aug. 19, 1799; *AT,* Sept. 30, 1799; *Columbian Museum & Savannah Advertiser,* Oct. 11, 1799; Samuel Robinson, *A Sailor Boy's Experience Aboard a Slave Ship in the Beginning of the Present Century* (1867, Hamilton, Scotland; reprint ed., Broughton Gifford, UK: Cromwell Press, 1998), p. 100.

6   MARTYR TO LIBERTY

1. Increase N. Tarbox, ed., *Diary of Thomas Robbins, D.D., 1796–1854* (Boston: Thomas Todd, 1886), I, pp. 118, iii–iv.

2. Charles Francis Adams, ed., *The Works of John Adams, Second President of the United States . . .* (Boston: Little, Brown and Company, 1856), X, p. 117; François-Alexandre-Frédéric, duc de La Rochefoucauld-Liancourt, *Travels through the United States of America . . .* (London: R. Phillips, 1799), II, p. 79; Robert Liston to J. Jackson, Dec. 11, 1799, Liston Papers, University of Virginia; Wood, *Empire of Liberty,* p. 256.

3. Wood, *Empire of Liberty,* pp. 140–212; Paul A. Gilje, *Liberty on the Waterfront: American Maritime Culture in the Age of Revolution* (Philadelphia: University of Pennsylvania Press, 2004), pp. 142–43.

4. Wood, *Empire of Liberty,* pp. 158–60, 210–11.

5. Merrill D. Peterson, *Thomas Jefferson and the New Nation: A Biography* (New York: Oxford University Press, 1970), p. 298; James Roger Sharp, *American Politics in the Early Republic: The New Nation in Crisis* (New Haven: Yale University Press, 1995), pp. 158–62. For Jefferson, see Jon Meacham, *Thomas Jefferson: The Art of Power* (New York: Random House, 2012); Annette Gordon-Reed and Peter S. Onuf, *"Most Blessed of the Patriarchs": Thomas Jefferson and the Empire of the Imagination* (New York: W. W. Norton, 2016).

6. Daniel Sisson, *The American Revolution of 1800: How Jefferson Rescued Democracy from Tyranny and Faction—and What This Means Today* (San Francisco: Berret-Koehler Publishers, 2014), pp. 361–63; Wood, *Empire of Liberty,* pp. 213, 241–68; Edward J. Larson, *A Magnificent Catastrophe: The Tumultuous Election of 1800, America's First Presidential Campaign* (New York: Free Press, 2008), p. 32; *Federal Gazette & Baltimore Daily Advertiser,* Nov. 10, 1798; Gerald L. Neuman, *Strangers to the Constitution: Immigrants, Borders, and Fundamental Law* (Princeton, NJ: Princeton University Press, 1996), p. 52; Rogers M. Smith, *Civic Ideals: Conflicting Visions of Citizenship in U.S. History* (New Haven, CT: Yale University Press, 1997), pp. 162–63; Terri Diane Halperin, *The Alien and Sedition Acts of 1798* (Baltimore: Johns Hopkins University Press, 2016); James Morton Smith, *Freedom's Fetters: The Alien and Sedition Laws and American Civil Liberties* (Ithaca, NY: Cornell University Press, 1956); Bradburn, *Citizenship,* pp. 163–67.

7. "Report of the Secretary of State, on the Communications from the Agents Employed under the Act for the Relief and Protection of American Seamen," FO 5/29B/16–22; Robert Liston to Lord Grenville, Apr. 11, 1798, FO 5/22/48; Gilje, *Liberty on the*

Waterfront, pp. 158–59; Nathan Perl-Rosenthal, *Citizen Sailors: Becoming American in the Age of Revolution* (Cambridge, MA: Harvard University Press, 2015), passim.

8. Pickering to Liston, May 7, 1799, roll 37, Liston Papers; Liston to Grenville, Sept. 30, 1799, FO 5/25/181–82; Pickering to King, June 14, 1799, in King, ed., *King Correspondence*, III, p. 47; *AT*, Sept. 30, 1799. Were it not for the "impulse of popular opinion," Liston assured Lord Grenville in June 1798, Pickering would "take sterner steps against fraudulent protections." Robert Liston to Lord Grenville, Apr. 11, 1798, FO 5/22/48. By October, such was Rufus King's own frustration that he complained to Grenville, "The conflicting claims of the two countries, in regard to the seamen in their respective service, continue to be the occasion of unceasing injury to our citizens, and of embarrassment to our Government. King to Grenville, Oct. 7, 1799, in King, ed., *King Correspondence*, III, p. 120.

9. *CGDA*, July 27, 30, 31, Aug. 1, 1799; Terry W. Lipscomb, ed., *The Letters of Pierce Butler, 1790–1794: Nation Building and Enterprise in the New American Republic* (Columbia: University of South Carolina Press, 2007), p. 213, n. 1.

10. ANB, s.v. "William Duane," "Benjamin Bache"; Donald H. Stewart, *The Opposition Press of the Federalist Period* (Albany: State University of New York Press, 1969), passim; Jeffrey L. Pasley, *"The Tyranny of the Printers": Newspaper Politics in the Early American Republic* (Charlottesville: University Press of Virginia, 2001), pp. 1–47; Wood, *Empire of Liberty*, pp. 250–58.

11. *Aurora*, Aug. 6, 12, 13, 1799.

12. "The Case of Jonathan Robbins, Candidly Considered," *GUS*, Aug. 2, 1799; *AT*, Aug. 17, Sept. 30, 1799; *AM*, Aug. 22, 1799; Pasley, *"Tyranny of the Printers*," p. 174; Robert Slender, *Letters on Various Interesting and Important Subjects . . .* (Philadelphia: Press of Dr. Hogan, 1799), p. 124, passim; "Robert Slender," *Aurora*, Aug. 24, Sept. 3, Oct. 2, 1799; *CF*, Aug. 27, Sept. 10, 1799; *GNYJ*, Aug. 28, Sept. 7, 1799; *Bee*, Sept. 4, 1799; ANB, s.v. "Philip Freneau"; Stewart, *Opposition Press*, pp. 497–500. See also "Reflections on the Case of Robins," reprinted from the *New-York Argus* in the *Aurora*, Aug. 19, 1799; "Veritas," *Aurora*, Aug. 20, 1799; "Robbins," *Aurora*, Aug. 22, 1799.

13. Stewart, *Opposition Press*, p. 630, passim; Pasley, *"Tyranny of the Printers*," pp. 1–257, esp. 153–69.

14. Pasley, *"Tyranny of Printers*," p. 6, passim; *American and Daily Advertiser*, Dec. 28, 1799; *Historical Manuscripts Commission: Report on the Manuscripts of J. B. Fortescue, Esq. preserved at Dropmore* (London: H.M.S.O., 1908), VIII, p. 359; Wood, *Empire of Liberty*, pp. 250–58; Jeffrey L. Pasley, "1800 as a Revolution in Political Culture: Newspapers, Celebrations, Voting, and Democratization in the Early Republic," in James Horn, Jan Lewis, and Peter Onuf, eds., *The Revolution of 1800: Democracy, Race, and the New Republic* (Charlottesville: University of Virginia Press, 2002), pp. 121–52; Marcus Daniel, *Scandal & Civility: Journalism and the Birth of American Democracy* (New York: Oxford University Press, 2010), passim; Stewart, *Opposition Press*, passim.

15. *CGDA*, Sept. 6, 1799; Liston to Grenville, Feb. 5, 1800, FO 5/97–100; Charles Pinckney, *Three Letters, Addressed to the People of the United States, Which Have Lately Appeared Under the Signature of A South Carolina Planter* (Charleston, SC: T. C. Cox, 1799). Whereas the first "letter" addressed "The Case of Jonathan Robbins," the second focused "On the Recent Captures of the British Cruisers, and the Right of a Citizen to Expatriate Himself," and the third "On the Claims of the British Creditors, and the Proceedings of the British Commissioners Under the Sixth Article of Mr. Jay's Treaty."

16. Marty D. Matthews, *Forgotten Founder: the Life and Times of Charles Pinckney* (Columbia: University of South Carolina Press, 2004), pp. 1–96; ANB, s.v. "Charles Pinckney."

17. *CGDA,* Sept. 6, 1799.

18. Ibid.

19. Ibid.

20. Ibid.

21. Ibid.

22. Ibid.

23. Pinckney to James Madison, Sept. 30, 1799, Robert J. Brugger *et al.,* eds., *The Papers of James Madison: Secretary of State Series* (Charlottesville: University Press of Virginia, 1986), I, pp. 229–30; Jefferson to Pinckney, Oct. 29, 1799, American Memory, Library of Congress, http://hdl.loc.gov/loc.mss/mtj.mtjbib009227; *AT,* Oct. 31, 1799; Pinckney to [James Madison], May 26, 1801, J. C. A. Stagg, ed., *The Papers of James Madison Digital Edition* (Charlottesville: University of Virginia Press, Rotunda, 2010); *Aurora,* Oct. 9, 26–28, 1799; *Telegraphe and Daily Advertiser* (Baltimore), Oct. 28, 1799.

24. Liston to Grenville, Sept. 5, 1799, FO 5/25/164–65; Wharton, *State Trials,* p. 413; Jefferson to Callender, Sept. 6, 1799, in Barbara B. Oberg *et al.,* eds., *The Papers of Thomas Jefferson* (Princeton, NJ: Princeton University Press, 2004), XXXI, p. 180; "Copy of a Letter from a Gentleman in Richmond to His Friend in Goochland County," *National Magazine,* Sept. [11?], 1799; *Centinel of Liberty,* Nov. 8, 1799; *CGDA,* Nov. 20, 1799. See also *Vermont Gazette* (Bennington), Aug. 29, 1799; Robert Brand Hanson, ed., *The Diary of Dr. Nathaniel Ames of Dedham, Massachusetts, 1758–1822* (Camden, ME: Picton Press, 1998), I, p. 693. "The Case of Jonathan Robbins," reported the *Alexandria Times,* "has deservedly excited universal attention and the indignation of the American People." *AT,* Oct. 31, 1799.

25. *Virginia Federalist,* Sept. 7, 1799; ANB, s.v. "John Marshall."

26. "A Friend to Propriety," *South-Carolina State Gazette,* Dec. 22, 1799; *Hudson Gazette,* Sept. 3, 1799.

27. James Wilkinson to Alexander Hamilton, Nov. 21, 1799, in Harold C. Syrett, ed., *The Papers of Alexander Hamilton Digital Edition* (Charlottesville: University of Virginia Press, Rotunda, 2011). Though innocent of exceeding Adams's instructions, his growing friendship with Liston seriously compromised Pickering's loyalties to the president. Alarmed by Adams's decision in the fall to dispatch a full diplomatic mission to France, he divulged to Liston the envoys' confidential instructions pertaining to "the interests of Great Britain"—as Liston informed Grenville in early November. Liston to Grenville, Nov. 4, 1799, FO 5/25/189.

28. [John Steele], "Letter From a Federalist," in H. M. Wagstaff, ed., *The Papers of John Steele* (Raleigh, NC: Edwards & Broughton, 1924), pp. 851–54; *Virginia Federalist,* Oct. 30, 1799, reprinted in *CGDA,* Nov. 18, 1799; "John Steele," in William S. Powell, *Dictionary of North Carolina Biography* (Chapel Hill: University of North Carolina Press, 1994), V, pp. 432–34.

29. Liston to Grenville, June 25, 1798, FO 5/22/109–12; Wedgwood, "RMJR," p. 329; *ODNB,* s.v. "William Cobbett." A Baltimore newspaper asserted, "America at this day does not probably contain a single person so grossly ignorant, as to entertain the slightest doubt of Cobbett's being a British emissary in British pay." *American and Daily Advertiser,* Nov. 20, 1799. See also *AT,* Dec. 31, 1799.

30. ANB, s.v. "James Ross" and "Thomas McKean."

31. Larson, *Magnificent Catastrophe,* p. 58; Liston to Grenville, Sept. 30, 1799, FO 5/25/178; *GUS,* Mar. 5, 1799; Kenneth W. Keller, *Rural Politics and the Collapse of Pennsylvania Federalism* (Philadelphia: American Philosophical Society, 1982), pp. 28–57; Harry Marlin Tinkcom, *The Republicans and Federalists in Pennsylvania, 1790–1801: A Study in National Stimulus and Local Response* (Harrisburg: Pennsylvania Historical and Museum Commission, 1950), pp. 221–41. See also William Bingham to Rufus King, Sept. 2, 1799, King, ed., *King Papers,* III, pp. 93–94.

32. Larson, *Magnificent Catastrophe,* p. 59; Liston to Grenville, Sept. 30, 1799, FO 5/25/178; Keller, *Rural Politics,* pp. 32–36; Tinkcom, *Republicans and Federalists,* pp. 230–38. For the growing importance of national issues in state and local elections, see David Waldstreicher, *In the Midst of Perpetual Fetes: The Making of American Nationalism, 1776–1820* (Chapel Hill: University of North Carolina Press, 1997), pp. 184–93, 246.

33. "An American," *HL,* Sept. 2, 30, 1799; "Matthew Huston," *Claypoole's American Daily Advertiser,* Sept. 28, 1799; Slender, *Letters,* p. 142. See also *Aurora,* Aug. 16, 1799; *CF,* Sept. 10, 1799.

34. *Aurora,* Oct. 5, 1799.

35. Larson, *Magnificent Catastrophe,* pp. 56–61; Keller, *Rural Politics,* pp. 40–55; Tinkcom, *Republicans and Federalists,* pp. 238–41.

36. Jefferson to Pinckney, Oct. 29, 1799, American Memory, Library of Congress, http://hdl.loc.gov/loc.mss/mtj.mtjbib009227; Liston to Grenville, Nov. 5, 1799, FO 5/25/194–97.

37. *Aurora,* Nov. 9, 12, 19, Dec. 12, 1799; Jeffrey L. Pasley, "The Cheese and the Words: Popular Political Culture and Participatory Democracy in the Early American Republic," in Jeffrey L. Pasley, Andrew W. Robertson, and David Waldstreicher, eds., *Beyond the Founders: New Approaches to the Political History of the Early American Republic* (Chapel Hill: University of North Carolina Press, 2004), p. 40; *Carlisle Gazette,* Nov. 13, 1799.

38. Hanson, ed., *Ames Diary,* I, p. 693; *Virginia Argus,* Nov. 11, 1799; *GUS,* Nov. 15, 1799; *Daily Advertiser* (Charleston), Dec. 3, 1799; *Constitutional Diary and Philadelphia Evening Advertiser,* Dec. 20, 1799.

39. *AT,* Nov. 15, 1799; *CF,* Oct. 22, 1799; Wood, *Empire of Liberty,* pp. 412–13, 418. Attacking Republicans who defended Robbins's right to mutiny, Cobbett decried, "[W]hat a bloody hag must that be, who says that *the mode in which he effected his escape was such as all Americans in a like situation, should make use of?*" Wedgwood, "RMJR," pp. 329, 355. See also, for example, "Remarks," *HL,* Dec. 9, 1799; "The Republican Litany," *Constitutional Diary,* Dec. 17, 1799. The *Philadelphia Gazette* of Nov. 20, 1799, remarked, "The Judiciary of the United States has been loaded with terms of opprobrium and execration by the Jacobin prints. It has been called the servile tool of presidentive despotism, and the corrupt instrument of promoting foreign schemes of influence."

40. "Thoughts on the Judiciary of the United States," *AT,* Nov. 15, 1799. See also *CT,* Oct. 19, 27, 1799; "The People," *VA,* Nov. 8, 1799; *Carlisle Gazette,* Nov. 13, 1799; *AT,* Nov. 14, 1799; *GNYJ,* Nov. 2, 1799.

41. "Robert Slender," *CF,* Sept. 10, 1799; "A Lover of Justice," *AT,* Oct. 10, 1799; *CT,* Oct. 19, 1799; "Matthew Lyon," *VA,* Oct. 18, 1799. See also *CT,* Nov. 9, 16, 1799; *Russell's Gazette,* Nov. 25, 1799; *GNYJ,* Nov. 2, 1799.

42. *CF,* Sept. 3, 1799; *HL,* Dec. 9, 1799; *GUS,* Nov. 16, 1799. See also Liston to Grenville,

Sept. 5, 1799, FO 5/25/164–65; *CT*, Oct. 5, 1799; *CF*, Sept. 10, 1799; Michael Barrett, *The Reply of a Friend to Justice, to a Friend to Propriety, on the Fate of the Unfortunate Robbins* (n.p.: n.d. [1799–1800]), p. 15.

43. Pickering to Clarke, Sept. 5, 1799, roll 12, Pickering Papers.

44. *DA*, Nov. 19, 1799; *CGDA*, Nov. 27, 1799; *Massachusetts Mercury*, Nov. 26, 1799; *Columbian Museum & Savannah Advertiser*, Dec. 10, 1799. For the affidavits and Parker's letter, see, for example, *Claypoole's American Daily Advertiser*, Nov. 16, 1799. The *Philadelphia Gazette* of Nov. 26, 1799, opined: "It is confidently, and we believe truly, asserted that William Duane, Editor of the Aurora, is just such an American as Jonathan Robbins alias Nash alledged himself to be. We hope the Parish Register of this worthy *Gentleman's* birth will be called for, and if not forth-coming that he will be forthgoing from the United States."

45. "A Lover of Justice," *AT*, Oct. 10, 1799; *HL*, Dec. 9, 1799; *Constitutional Diary*, Dec. 3, 1799; *VA*, Nov. 29, 1799; *CT*, Dec. 18, 1799. See also *Bee*, Mar. 18, 1800.

46. Elijah Ellsworth Brownell, comp., *1790: First Federal Census of all Dutchess County, New York* (Philadelphia: n.p., 1938), pp. 44, 52; Hermione Muster-Books, Oct. 31–Feb. 10, 1797, ADM 36/12009–12011; "Naval Crew." In addition, a Jonathan Robbins, Jr., aged sixteen, worked as an apprentice to a shoemaker in Wethersfield, Connecticut, sixty miles to the east of Danbury. Kathy A. Ritter, *Apprentices of Connecticut, 1637–1900* (Salt Lake City: Ancestry Publishing, 1986), p. 109. Some Republicans had no doubt that Parker had falsified Nash's disavowal of American citizenship. "It now comes out by British acc't of Jonath Robbin's trial & execution," Nathaniel Ames jotted in his diary, "that he never confessed himself an Irishman—but a true American—& Judge Bee of So Carolina guilty of his murder by delivery up to British trial!" Hanson, ed., *Ames Diary*, I, p. 695.

47. "Benjamin Moodie," *City Gazette and Daily Advertiser*, Dec. 4, 1799.

48. *CF*, Aug. 27, Oct. 22, 1799; *AT*, Dec. 31, 1799; *A Letter From Manlius to John Marshall . . .* (Richmond, VA: Samuel Pleasants, Jr., 1800), p. 17; Barry Alan Shain and Rogers M. Smith, "Introduction," in Barry Alan Shain, ed., *The Nature of Rights at the American Founding and Beyond* (Charlottesville: University of Virginia Press, 2007), pp. 2–3; Bradburn, *Citizenship*, pp. 22–29; Samuel Moyn, *The Last Utopia: Human Rights in History* (Cambridge, MA: Harvard University Press, 2010), pp. 20–25.

49. *American* (Baltimore), Oct. 5, 1799; *Aurora*, Oct 5, 1799.

50. Barry Alain Shain, ed., *The Declaration of Independence in Historical Context: American State Papers, Petitions, Proclamations, and Letters of the Delegates to the First National Congresses* (New Haven, CT: Yale University Press, 2014), p. 318; *The Plea of Erin, or the Case of the Natives of Ireland in the United States* (Philadelphia: n.p., [1798]). Jefferson, in recommending a young schoolteacher to James Monroe, wrote in 1800, "He is a United Irishman, and therefore was obliged to leave Ireland. He is of course a good republican." Jefferson to Monroe, Feb. 16, 1800, Barbara B. Oberg and J. Jefferson Looney, eds., *The Papers of Thomas Jefferson Digital Edition* (Charlottesville: University of Virginia Press, Rotunda, 2008).

51. David A. Wilson, *United Irishmen, United States: Immigrant Radicals in the Early Republic* (Ithaca, NY: Cornell University Press, 1998), passim; Margaret McAleer, "In Defense of Civil Society: Irish Radicals in Philadelphia during the 1790s," *Early American Studies* 1 (Spring 2003): pp. 176–97; Michael Durey, *Transatlantic Radicals and the Early American Republic* (Lawrence: University Press of Kansas, 1997).

52. *Massachusetts Mercury*, Nov. 29, 1799; *Albany Centinel*, Nov. 22, 1799.

7 SEIGNOR GALATINI AND HIS GANG

1. *Aberdeen Journal,* July 10, 1798; Sept. 17, 1799, ADM 50/65.
2. *ODNB,* s.v. "Sir Edward Hamilton"; Pope, *Black Ship,* pp. 303–4, 308–9.
3. Pope, *Black Ship,* pp. 303–10.
4. Ibid., pp. 309–12.
5. Ibid., pp. 312–24; Parker to Evan Nepean, Nov. 4, 1799, Parker, Dispatches, II; "The Story of the Hermione," *Wilkes-Barre Times,* July 7, 1799; Parker, Journal II, Nov. 3, 1799.
6. Parker to Nepean, Nov. 4, 1799, Parker, Dispatches, II; *Caledonian Mercury* (Edinburgh), Feb. 3, 1800; *WEP,* Jan. 7, 1800. Hamilton's return to London was interrupted when the French seized the packet ship that he had boarded in Jamaica. Sent to Paris, he was exchanged, with Napoleon's blessing, for four French midshipmen imprisoned in England. Pope, *Black Ship,* pp. 326–29.
7. *PG,* Nov. 27, 1799; *Augusta Herald,* Dec. 18, 1799; *CGDA,* Dec. 6, 1799; *Bee,* Dec. 4, 1799. For Federalist coverage, see, for instance, *Salem Gazette,* Nov. 26, 1799; *Newburyport Herald,* Nov. 29, 1799; *Massachusetts Mercury* (Boston), Nov. 29, 1799; *CA* (New York), Dec. 4, 1799; *Federal Observer* (Portsmouth, NH), Dec. 6, 1799.
8. "Eulogy on the Death of Washington," *Aurora,* Jan. 2, 1800; Robert Brand Hanson, ed., *The Diary of Dr. Nathaniel Ames of Dedham, Massachusetts, 1758–1822* (Camden, ME: Picton, 1998), I, p. 695; G. D. H. Cole, ed., *Letters from William Cobbett to Edward Thornton Written in the Years 1797–1800* (Oxford: Oxford University Press, 1937), p. 38.
9. *Aurora,* Aug. 22, 1799; Robert Slender, *Letters on Various Interesting and Important Subjects . . .* (Philadelphia: Press of Dr. Hogan, 1799), p. 127.
10. François-Alexandre-Frédéric, duc de La Rochefoucauld-Liancourt, *Travels through the United States of America . . .* (London: R. Phillips, 1799), I, pp. 363–64, II, pp. 376–87; Kenneth Roberts and Anna M. Roberts, eds. and trans., *Moreau de St. Mérys American Journey [1793–1798]* (New York: Doubleday, 1947), pp. 258–65, 336–63.
11. *Congress Hall, Capitol of the United States, 1790–1800, Independence National Historical Park, Pennsylvania* (Washington, DC: National Park Service, 1990); http://www.nps .gov/inde/learn/historyculture/places-congresshall.htm.
12. Stephen F. Miller, *The Bench and Bar of Georgia: Memoirs and Sketches* (Philadelphia: J. P. Lippincott, 1858), p. 407; Matthew Lyon to Andrew Jackson, Feb. 28, 1800, in Sam B. Smith and Harriet Chappell Owsley, eds., *The Papers of Andrew Jackson* (Knoxville: University of Tennessee Press, 1980), I, pp. 228–29; James Roger Sharp, *The Deadlocked Election of 1800: Jefferson, Burr, and the Union in the Balance* (Lawrence: University Press of Kansas, 2010), I, pp. 73–82; Stanley Elkins and Eric McKitrick, *The Age of Federalism* (New York: Oxford University Press, 1993), pp. 726–28; history.house.gov/Congressional-Overview/Profiles/6th/.
13. *Annals,* Dec. 3, 1799, pp. 188–91; Elaine Forman Craine et al., eds., *The Diary of Elizabeth Drinker* (Boston: Northeastern University Press, 1991), II, p. 1243.
14. David Stone to [John Steele], Jan. 10, 1800, John Steele Papers, Southern Historical Collection, University of North Carolina, Chapel Hill; Harrison Gray Otis to Mrs. Otis, Jan. 11, 1800, Otis Papers; *Annals,* Dec. 4, 1799–Jan. 13, 1800, pp. 191–369.
15. Harrison Gray Otis to Mrs. Otis, Feb. 11, 8, 13, n. 16, Jan. 29, 1800, Harrison Gray Otis Papers, Massachusetts Historical Society, Boston; Henrietta Liston to Uncle, March 13, 1800, Liston Papers, University of Virginia.

16. *Annals*, Feb. 4, 1800, pp. 511–12; *Raleigh Register, and North Carolina Weekly*, Mar. 18, 1800; *Drinker Diary*, II, p. 1273.

17. James Madison to Thomas Jefferson, Mar. 6, 1796, note 5, and Jefferson to Madison, Feb. 5, 1799, in Stagg, ed., *The Papers of James Madison Digital Edition* (Charlottesville: University of Virginia Press, Rotunda, 2010); "A View of Congress-Hall," *CF*, April 2, 1799.

18. W. H. Hill to Duncan Cameron, Feb. 11, 1800, Cameron Papers, Southern Historical Collection, University of North Carolina, Chapel Hill; ANB, s.v. "John Nicholas"; "The Two John Nicholases: Their Relationship to Washington and Jefferson," *American Historical Review* 45 (1940): 338–53; Nicholas Dungan, *Gallatin: America's Swiss Founding Father* (New York: New York University Press, 2010).

19. *Speech of Edward Livingston in the House of Representatives . . . on the Alien Bill, June 21, 1798* (Albany, NY: Barber & Southwick, [1798]); ANB, s.v. "Edward Livingston."

20. Noble E. Cunningham, Jr., *The Jeffersonian Republicans: The Formation of Party Organization, 1789–1801* (Chapel Hill: University of North Carolina Press, 1957), p. 175; David Ramsay to Rufus King, Jan. 28, 1800, in Robert L. Brunhouse, ed., *David Ramsay, 1749–1815: Selections from His Writings* (Philadelphia: American Philosophical Society, 1965), p. 150; Jefferson to Thomas Mann Randolph, Feb. 2, 1800, Thomas Jefferson Papers, American Memory, Library of Congress.

21. Lyon to Jackson, Feb. 28, 1800, in Smith and Owsley, eds., *Jackson Papers*, I, pp. 228–29.

22. Wood, *Empire of Liberty*, p. 60; François-Alexandre-Frédéric, duc de La Rochefoucauld-Liancourt, *Travels through the United States of America . . .* (London: R. Phillips, 1799), II, p. 666.

23. *Annals*, Feb. 20, 1800, pp. 532–33.

24. *Litchfield Monitor* (Connecticut), Apr. 9, 1800.

25. Wood, *Empire of Liberty*, p. 60; *Annals*, Feb. 7, 17, 1800, pp. 515–18, 526.

26. *Annals*, Feb. 26, p. 552; Peter Charles Hoffer and N. E. H. Hull, *Impeachment in America, 1635–1805* (New Haven, CT: Yale University Press, 1984), pp. 109–63; Buckner F. Melton, Jr., *The First Impeachment: The Constitution's Framers and the Case of Senator William Blount* (Macon, GA: Mercer University Press, 1998).

27. *Aurora*, Oct. 11, 1799; Barber & Southwick to Livingston, Feb. 21, 1800, Livingston Papers.

28. *Annals*, Mar. 5, 1800, p. 590; Leven Powell to Major Burr Powell, Mar. 5, 1800, in "Correspondence of Leven Powell," *The John P. Branch Historical Papers of Randolph-Macon College*, (1903), III, 238; Abigail Adams to Sister, Mar. 5, 1800, in Stewart Mitchell, ed., *New Letters of Abigail Adams, 1788–1801* (Boston: Houghton Mifflin, 1947), p. 237.

29. *Annals*, Feb. 25, 1800, pp. 541–45; Hill to Cameron, Feb. 11, 1800, Cameron Papers.

30. *Annals*, Feb. 25, 1800, pp. 545–47; Hill to Cameron, Feb. 11, 1800, Cameron Papers.

31. *Annals*, Feb. 26, 1800, pp. 548–53. Of the gallery, Otis wrote his wife, "It has become quite fashionable for the ladies to attend the debates, a circumstance which does not contribute to shorten them." Otis to Mrs. Otis, Mar. 5, 1800, Otis Papers.

32. *Annals*, Feb. 26, 1800, pp. 548–57.

33. Ibid., Feb. 27, 1800, pp. 558–59.

34. Ibid., Feb. 27, 1800, pp. 559–61; ANB, s.v. "Samuel Smith."

35. In Marshall's opinion, "To leave the charge unexamined, hanging over the President

of the United States, until a distance of time, how long it is impossible to say, but certainly long enough to work a very bad effect." *Annals,* Feb. 27, 1800, pp. 561–78.

36. Ibid., pp. 561–62, 567–570, 574–76.

37. Ibid., pp. 576–77.

38. Ibid., pp. 577–78.

39. Ibid., Mar. 3, 1800, pp. 583–84; "Delivery of Jonathan Robbins," *Universal Gazette.* For Livingston's extensive notes, see "Nash als. Robbins: Notes for Speech," Liston Papers.

40. Jefferson to Madison, Mar. 4, 1800, in J. C. A. Stagg, ed., *The Papers of James Madison Digital Edition* (Charlottesville: University of Virginia Press, Rotunda, 2010); James F. Simon, *What Kind of Nation: Thomas Jefferson, John Marshall, and the Epic Struggle to Create a United States* (New York: Simon & Schuster, 2003), pp. 118–20; Cunningham, *Jeffersonian Republicans,* p. 162.

41. *Annals,* Mar. 4–5, 1800, pp. 584–94.

42. Ibid., pp. 584–93.

43. Ibid., Mar. 5, pp. 594–95.

44. Ibid., Mar. 6, p. 595; *Universal Gazette,* Apr. 17, 1800.

45. *Annals,* Mar. 6, 1800, p. 596; *Universal Gazette,* Apr. 17, 24, 1800.

46. R. Kent Newmyer, *John Marshall and the Heroic Age of the Supreme Court* (Baton Rouge: Louisiana State University Press, 2007), p. 27; Elkins and McKitrick, *Age of Federalism,* pp. 558–59; B. Goodhue to Pickering, Oct. 26, 1798, roll 27, Pickering Papers; *Annals,* Mar. 7, 1800, p. 596; Elaine Forman Crane et al., eds., *Drinker Diary,* II, p. 1280. For Marshall, see also Jean Edward Smith, *John Marshall: Definer of a Nation* (New York: Holt, 1998); Simon, *What Kind of Nation.*

47. Hill to Cameron, Feb. 11, 1800, Cameron Papers; *Annals,* Mar. 7, 1800, pp. 596–618. For a complete version of the speech see *Speech of the Hon. John Marshall, Delivered in the House of Representatives of the United States, on the Resolution of the Hon. Edward Livingston, relative to Thomas Nash, Alias Jonathan Robbins* (Philadelphia: Office of "The True American," 1800).

48. *Annals,* Mar. 8, 1800, pp. 618–20; Noble E. Cunningham, Jr., ed., *Circular Letters of Congressmen to Their Constituents, 1789–1829* (Chapel Hill: University of North Carolina Press, 1978), I, pp. 183–84; Otis to Mrs. Otis, Mar. 10, 1800, Otis Papers; Crane et al., eds., *Drinker Diary,* II, p. 1281.

49. Wedgwood, "RMJR," p. 354; Jefferson to James Madison, Mar. 4, 1800, in J. C. A. Stagg, ed., *The Papers of James Madison Digital Edition* (Charlottesville: University of Virginia Press, Rotunda, 2010); Pickering to King, Mar. 10, 1800, roll 38, Pickering Papers; *Annals,* Mar. 8, 1800, pp. 619–20.

50. *Annals,* Mar. 10, p. 621; Cunningham, ed., *Circular Letters,* I, p. 196.

51. *PG,* Mar. 10, 13, 1800; Marshall to Reuben George, Mar. 16, 1800, in Charles T. Cullen and Leslie Tobias, eds., *The Papers of John Marshall: Volume IV: Correspondence and Papers, January 1799–October 1800* (Chapel Hill: University of North Carolina Press, 1984), p. 114; *Jenks' Portland Gazette,* Mar. 17, 1800.

52. *HL,* Mar. 17, 1800; *Annals,* Mar. 7, 1800, p. 617; "Notes on John Marshall's Speech," [after March 7, 1800], Barbara B. Oberg and J. Jefferson Looney, eds., *The Papers of Thomas Jefferson* (Charlottesville: University of Virginia Press, 2004), XXXI, p. 421; *Aurora,* Mar. 10, 1800.

53. Pickering to Benjamin Goodhue, Mar. 17, 1800, roll 13, Pickering Papers.

8   REVOLUTION OF 1800

1. Jeffrey L. Pasley, "1800 as a Revolution in Political Culture: Newspapers, Celebrations, Voting, and Democratization," in James J. Horn, Jan Ellen Lewis, and Peter S. Onuf, eds., *The Revolution of 1800: Democracy, Race, and the New Republic* (Charlottesville: University Press of Virginia, 2002), p. 126, and Joanne B. Freeman, "Corruption and Compromise in the Election of 1800: The Process of Politics on the National Stage," in ibid., pp. 87, 97–99; James Roger Sharp, *The Deadlocked Election of 1800: Jefferson, Burr, and the Union in the Balance* (Lawrence: University Press of Kansas, 2010), pp. 226–27; Daniel Sisson, *The American Revolution of 1800: How Jefferson Rescued Democracy from Tyranny and Faction—and What This Means Today* (San Francisco: Berret-Koehler Publishers, 2014), p. 344.

2. James Roger Sharp, *American Politics in the Early Republic: The New Nation in Crisis* (New Haven, CT: Yale University Press, 1995), p. 188; Michael A. Bellesiles, " 'The Soil Will be Soaked with Blood': Taking the Revolution of 1800 Seriously," in Horn, Lewis, and Onuf, eds., *Revolution of 1800*, p. 59; Sharp, *Deadlocked Election*, p. 227; Morgan Lewis to Edward Livingston, Feb. 23, 1799, Livingston Papers.

3. Pickering to William Vans Murray, Oct. 25, 1799, in Worthington Chauncey Ford, ed., *Letters of William Vans Murray to John Quincy Adams* (Washington, DC: American Historical Association, 1914), p. 610; Stanley Elkins and Eric McKitrick, *The Age of Federalism* (New York: Oxford University Press, 1993), pp. 726–28; James H. Broussard, *The Southern Federalists, 1800–1816* (Baton Rouge: Louisiana State University Press, 1978), pp. 14–15.

4. Sean Wilentz, *The Rise of American Democracy: Jefferson to Lincoln* (New York: W. W. Norton, 2005), p. 85; Sisson, *American Revolution of 1800*, p. 353; Noble E. Cunningham, Jr., *The Jeffersonian Republicans: The Formation of Party Organization, 1789–1801* (Chapel Hill: University of North Carolina Press, 1957), p. 199; James F. Simon, *What Kind of Nation: Thomas Jefferson, John Marshall, and the Epic Struggle to Create a United States* (New York: Simon & Schuster, 2002), p. 119.

5. Jefferson to Madison, Mar. 4, 8, 1800, in Barbara Oberg et al., eds., *The Papers of Thomas Jefferson* (Princeton, NJ: Princeton University Press, 2004), pp. 408–9.

6. *Aurora*, Mar. 7, 8, 1800; *Jenks' Portland Gazette*, Mar. 17, 1800; "Simon Slim," *HL*, Mar. 31, 1800. See also *Aurora*, Mar. 8, 1800; "Mammoth," *Salem Gazette*, Mar. 11, 1800; *IC*, Mar. 17, 1800; *HL*, Mar. 17, 24, 1800; *CF*, Mar. 25, 1800; "Billy Trim," *Carlisle Gazette*, Apr. 9, 1800.

7. *PG*, Mar. 28, 1800; "Robbins' Will," *United States Oracle* (Portsmouth, NH), Mar. 29, 1800. In response to an *Aurora* column listing five reasons not to reelect Adams, the *Political Repository* in Massachusetts castigated the final justification as the most absurd—the extradition of Robbins, a "proved pirate and murderer"—"in other words," it continued, because Adams "did not render his country the hiding hole of every guilty wretch." *Political Repository*, Apr. 29, 1800.

8. *Annals*, Apr. 2, 1800, p. 654.

9. Ibid., pp. 654–55.

10. *Federal Gazette & Baltimore Daily Advertiser*, May 5, 1800; *Annals*, Apr. 28–29, 1800, p. 691; Elaine Forman Crane et al., eds., *The Diary of Elizabeth Drinker* (Boston: Northeastern University Press, 1991), II, p. 1295.

11. "Simon Slim," *HL*, Apr. 14, 1800; John Chew Thomas, *CC*, June 28, 1800; "An Essex Whig," *CF*, Apr. 22, 1800.

12. Simon, *What Kind of Nation*, p. 111; Pasley, "Tyranny of the Printers," pp. 176–90; Marcus Daniel, *Scandal & Civility: Journalism and the Birth of American Democracy* (New York: Oxford University Press, 2009), pp. 234–74.

13. Thomas Cooper, *An Account of the Trial of Thomas Cooper, of Northumberland; on a Charge of Libel Against the President of the United States* . . . (Philadelphia: John Bioren, 1800), pp. 7–30; Crane *et al.*, eds., *Drinker Diary,* II, p. 1291.

14. Cooper, *Account of Trial*, pp. 30–31, 40.

15. *Jenks' Portland Gazette,* May 5, 1800; Cooper, *Account of Trial,* pp. 31–33, 9–12; Stevens Thomson Mason to Edward Livingston, Apr. 15, 1800, Livingston Papers.

16. Cooper, *Account of Trial,* pp. 42–52; *Sun* (Dover, NH), Apr. 30, 1800; Stevens Thomson Mason to Livingston, Apr. 21, 1800, Livingston Papers; *Derby Mercury* (Derby, UK), June 26, 1800.

17. *Greenfield Gazette* (Massachusetts), May 10, 1800; *HL,* May 5, 1800; *Aurora,* May 15, 1800.

18. *AT,* Apr. 23, 1800; *Speech of Edward Livingston, in the House of Representatives of the United States, on the third reading of the Alien Bill, June 21, 1798* (Albany, NY: Barber & Southwick, 1798). See also Marilyn Baseler, *"Asylum for Mankind": America, 1607–1800* (Ithaca, NY: Cornell University Press, 1998), pp. 286–87.

19. *GNYJ,* Feb. 26, 1800; "Simon Slim," *HL,* Mar. 31, 1800.

20. *Vermont Gazette,* July 28, 1800.

21. "Extract of a Letter from a Gentleman in Kentucky, to his Friend in this City, dated April 14, 1800," *Aurora,* May 3, 1800.

22. *Jenks' Portland Gazette,* Mar. 17, 1800; *AT,* Mar. 13, 1800; "An Essex Whig," *CF,* Apr. 22, 1800. Republicans in Fairfax County, Virginia, were reminded that Robbins had been executed "for taking the life of those tyrants who opposed his regaining that liberty" which "British violence had deprived him." "A Citizen," *AT,* Apr. 23, 1800.

23. "Norfolk, April 3," *HL,* May 5, 1800; "Alex. Jordan," *CF,* Apr. 29, 1800.

24. Elkins and McKitrick, *Age of Federalism,* p. 733; Charles Pinckney to Edward Livingston, Apr. 14, 1800, Livingston Papers; Livingston to Thomas Jefferson, Apr. 11, 1800, in Barbara B. Oberg and J. Jefferson Looney, eds., *The Papers of Thomas Jefferson Digital Edition* (Charlottesville: University of Virginia Press, Rotunda, 2008); James Roger Sharp, *American Politics in the Early Republic: The New Nation in Crisis* (New Haven, CT: Yale University Press, 1995), pp. 243–46; Edward J. Larson, *A Magnificent Catastrophe: The Tumultuous Election of 1800, America's First Presidential Campaign* (New York: Free Press, 2008), p. 109.

25. *CG,* Apr. 23, 1800; Elkins and McKitrick, *Age of Federalism,* p. 732.

26. Rochefoucauld-Liancourt, *Travels,* II, pp. 453–59; Edward G. Burroughs and Mike Wallace, *Gotham: A History of New York City to 1898* (New York: Oxford University Press, 2000), pp. 333–34; Ira Rosenwake, *Population History of New York City* (Syracuse, NY: Syracuse University Press, 2105), p. 16; Larson, *Magnificent Catastrophe,* p. 88. See also Kenneth Roberts and Anna M. Roberts, eds. and trans., *Moreau de St. Méry's American Journey [1793–1798]* (New York: Doubleday, 1947), pp. 146–66.

27. John Davis, *Travels of Four Years and a Half in the United States of America* . . . (London: B. Edwards, 1803), p. 23; Nancy Isenberg, *Fallen Founder: The Life of Aaron Burr* (New York: Viking, 2007), pp. 1–196; Wood, *Empire of Liberty,* p. 279.

28. Isenberg, *Fallen Founder,* pp. 196–99; Cunningham, *Jeffersonian Republicans,* pp. 176–80.

29. Sharp, *Deadlocked Election,* p. 104; Pickering to John Pickering, Mar. 7, 1800, roll

13, Pickering Papers; Cunningham, *Jeffersonian Republicans,* pp. 177, 182; Elkins and McKitrick, *Age of Federalism,* pp. 732–33.

30. For an excellent biography of Hamilton, see Ron Chernow, *Alexander Hamilton* (New York: Penguin Press, 2004).

31. Freeman, "Corruption and Compromise," in Horn, Lewis, and Onuf, eds., *Revolution of 1800,* pp. 98–99; Burrows and Wallace, *Gotham,* p. 328; *New-York Gazette,* Apr. 30, 1800; Susan Dunn, *Jefferson's Second Revolution: The Election Crisis of 1800 and the Triumph of Republicanism* (Boston: Houghton Mifflin,2004), pp. 179–80.

32. Harper to His Constituents, May 15, 1800, in Elizabeth Donnan, ed., *Papers of James A. Bayard, 1796–1815* (Washington, DC: American Historical Association, 1915), II, pp. 107–8.

33. "Simon Slim," *HL,* Apr. 14, 2015; *Carlisle Gazette,* Apr. 9, 1800; "Essex Whig," *CF,* Apr. 22, 1800; *Mercantile Advertiser* (New York), Mar. 24, 1800; *CT,* Apr. 2, 1800; *Norwich Courier* (Connecticut), Apr. 9, 1800; "A Friend to the Constitution," *AC,* Apr. 29, 1800. See also "A Republican Farmer," *Republican Watch-Tower* (New York), Apr. 22, 1800; *Thoughts, on the Subject of the Ensuing Election, Addressed to the Party in the State of New-York . . . Apr. 1, 1800* (Albany, NY: Barber & Southwick, [1800]); *Mercantile Advertiser* (New York), Apr. 28, 1800; "To the Citizens of New York," *AC,* Apr. 29, 1800; "More British Captures," *AC,* Apr. 29, 1800; "For the AMERICAN CITIZEN," *AC,* Apr. 29, 1800; *HL,* Apr. 28, 1800; *Aurora,* May 3, 23, 1800.

34. "A Republican Farmer," *CF,* May 6, 1800. Although it was reprinted from the *American Citizen* before April 29, I was unable to locate the remonstrance in surviving issues for the month of April. In all likelihood, it appeared in the April 29 issue of the *Citizen,* which is among the few issues missing for the month. It appeared in the *Republican Watch-Tower* on April 22. The text originated as a four-page address printed in New York, at the urging of "a number of Republican citizens," in March. "A Republican Farmer," *To the Citizens of the United States, and particularly the Citizens of New-York, New-Jersey, Delaware, and Pennsylvania, Maryland and North-Carolina, on the propriety of choosing republican members to their State Legislatures, at the ensuing elections, in order to secure the election of Electors of a President, at the approaching election for that important office* (New York: N.p., March 8, 1800).

35. "Communication," *AM* (Hartford), April 17, 1800; *AC,* Apr. 24, 1800; *CA* (New York), Apr. 23, 1800; *Weekly Museum* (New York), Apr. 26, 1800; *Mercantile Messenger* (New York), Apr. 28, 1800.

36. *Aurora,* May 4, 1799; Matthew L. Davis to Albert Gallatin, Mar. 29, 1800, Albert Gallatin Papers, New York Historical Society, New York City; *GNYJ,* Feb. 2, 1800; *Mercantile Advertiser,* Apr. 28, 1800. The *Commercial Advertiser* of Apr. 18, 1799, claimed that the falsehood had afforded an "excellent opportunity for disgorging a load of calumny, abuse, and scurrility upon innocent men for the purpose of injuring republicans and promoting the election of old and inveterate tories." See also *AC,* May 3, 1800.

37. *Mercantile Advertiser,* Apr. 28, 1800; Captain's log, *Acasta,* 1800, ADM 51/1382; Master's log, *Acasta,* Feb. 1–Apr. 15, 1800, ADM 52/2612; Captain's log, *Acasta,* Feb. 1–Apr. 15, 1800, ADM 51/1382; Master's log, *Acasta,* Feb. 1–Apr. 15, 1800, ADM 52/2612.

38. Freeman, "Corruption and Compromise," in Horn, Lewis, and Onuf, eds., *Revolution of 1800,* p. 89; Stephen Taylor, *Commander: The Life and Exploits of Britain's Greatest Frigate Captain* (New York: W. W. Norton, 2012), pp. 42, 46, 62, 134–35, 137–38; *ODNB,* s.v. "Sir Isaac Israel Pellew."

39. Master's log, *Cleopatra*, Apr. 23–29, 1800, ADM 52/2863; "HAND-BILL !!!," *CT*, May 10, 1800; *AC*, Apr. 30, 1800; Robert Murray to Evan Nepean, Apr. 26, 1800, in Letters, Admiral's Dispatches, North America, 1800–1804, ADM 1/495; *PG*, June 20, 1800.

40. "Fellow Citizens," *AC*, Apr. 29, 1800; "Shade of Seventy-six," *AC*, May 1, 1800; "British Robbery Detected," *Eastern Herald* (Portland, ME), May 19, 1800; Diary of Elizabeth DeHart Bleeker, 1799–1806, New York Public Library, Apr. 29, 1800. See also "Fellow-Citizens," *AC*, Apr. 30, 1800; "April 30," *Providence Journal*, May 7, 1800.

41. "Extract of a letter from New-York," *PG*, May 6, 1800; *Salem Gazette* (Massachusetts), May 6, 1800; Robert Liston to Robert R. Murray, July 5, 1800, Murray to Liston, July 22, 1800, in Letters, Admiral's Dispatches, North America, 1800–1804, ADM 1/495. For the emergence of electioneering "spectacles" by young men, see Andrew W. Robertson, "Voting Rites and Voting Acts: Electioneering Ritual, 1790–1820," in Jeffrey L. Pasley, David Waldstreicher, and Andrew W. Robertson, eds., *Beyond the Founders: New Approaches to the Political History of the Early American Republic* (Chapel Hill: University of North Carolina Press, 2004), p. 75.

42. Larson, *Magnificent Catastrophe*, pp. 103–4; *Aurora*, May 5, 1800; Bleeker, Diary, May 1, 1800; "To the Inspectors," *Spectator*, Apr. 30, 1800; Chilton Williamson, *American Suffrage: From Property to Democracy, 1760–1860* (Princeton, NJ: Princeton University Press, 1960), p. 111; Alexander Keyssar, *The Right to Vote: The Contested History of Democracy in the United States* (New York: Basic Books, 2000), p. 17; Jessee Lemisch, *Jack Tar vs. John Bull: The Role of New York's Seamen in Precipitating the Revolution* (New York: Garland Publishing, 1997), pp. 13–49.

43. Liston to Grenville, May 6, 1900, FO 5/29A/233. See also Joseph Hale to Rufus King, May 13, 1800, in King, ed., *King Correspondence*, III, p. 240.

44. Larson, *Magnificent Catastrophe*, p. 104; Hamilton to John Jay, May 7, 1800, in Harold C. Syrett, ed., *The Papers of Alexander Hamilton* (New York: Columbia University Press, 1976), XXIV, pp. 464–67; Livingston to Jefferson, [before May 3, 1800], in Barbara B. Oberg and J. Jefferson Looney, eds., *The Papers of Thomas Jefferson Digital Edition* (Charlottesville: University of Virginia Press, Rotunda, 2008).

45. Simon, *What Kind of Nation*, p. 102; *Aurora*, May 9, 1800; Sharp, *Deadlocked Election*, p. 92. Robert Liston attributed Pickering's dismissal to the "personal feelings of the President of the United States. Mr. Adams is remarkable for a high opinion of his own knowledge and ability in political affairs, for a perseverance in sentiments once adopted, and for an extreme impatience of contradiction." Liston to Grenville, May 29, 1800, FO 5/29a, 250.

46. *Aurora*, Mar. 6, 1800; Sharp, *Deadlocked Election*, pp. 88–92; Elkins and McKitrick, *Age of Federalism*, pp. 736–38; Pickering to Charles Cotesworth Pinckney, May 25, 1800, roll 13, Pickering Papers; Larson, *Magnificent Catastrophe*, pp. 95–96. Five months before Pickering's dismissal, Abigail Adams had written, "There is a man in the cabinet whose manners are forbidding, whose temper is sour and whose resentments are implacable, who neverless would like to dictate every measure." Phyllis Lee Levin, *Abigail Adams: A Biography* (New York: St. Martin's Press, 1987), p. 376.

47. George Gibbs, *Memoirs of the Administrations of Washington and John Adams, Edited from the Papers of Oliver Wolcott, Secretary of the Treasury* (New York: n.p., 1846), II, pp. 379, 384; Wood, *Empire of Liberty*, pp. 273–74; Pickering to Timothy Williams, May 19, 1800, roll 13, Pickering Papers.

48. Gibbs, *Memoirs of the Administrations*, II, pp. 394–95, 383–84; Pickering to Benjamin

Goodhue, May 26, 1800, roll 13, Pickering Papers; Sharp, *Deadlocked Election*, pp. 92, 94, 114; Elkins and McKitick, *Age of Federalism*, pp. 714–19.

49. *Vermont Gazette*, Sept. 22, 1800; *Aurora*, Aug. 22, 1800, May 23, 1800; Gibbs, *Memoirs of the Administrations*, II, p. 411; "Marcus Brutus," *Serious Facts, opposed to 'Serious considerations'*... (N.p.: n.p., October 1800).

50. "CONSIDERATIONS on the Case of *THOMAS NASH*, falsely called *JONATHAN ROBBINS*," *PG*, May 13, 1800.

51. "CONSIDERATIONS," *PG*, May 13, 1800; Douglas R. Egerton, *Gabriel's Rebellion: The Virginia Slave Conspiracies of 1800 and 1802* (Chapel Hill: University of North Carolina Press, 1993), pp. 34–49.

52. *AT*, June 24, 1800; *Aurora*, July 12, Aug. 20, 1800. See also *CT*, May 14, June 4, Aug. 16, 1800; "Serious Considerations, Why John Adams Should Not be Elected President," *National Magazine*..., Sept. 1, 1800, p. 235. No more hopeful, the Connecticut journalist Noah Webster wrote Oliver Wolcott in June, "The falsehoods circulating through the Jacobin prints, make a good impression on the minds of people at a distance, especially when asserted with confidence." Gibbs, *Memoirs of the Administrations*, pp. 373, 418.

53. Simon, *What Kind of Nation*, pp. 115–16; *PG*, July 11, 1800. See also J. H. Imlay to Wolcott, Aug. 25, 1800, Oliver Wolcott Papers, ca. 1759–1837, Manuscripts, Library of Congress; Robert Liston to Grenville, August 1800, FO 5/29A/283.

54. Marshall to Harrison Gray Otis, Aug. 8, 1800, Otis Papers; Gibbs, *Memoirs of the Administrations*, p. 404; Simon, *What Kind of Nation*, pp. 133–34.

55. William Henry Hill to Duncan Cameron, Apr. 22, 1800, Cameron Papers, Southern Historical Collection, University of North Carolina at Chapel Hill; "To the Freemen of the Fifth District of Maryland," *Maryland Gazette*, Aug. 14, 1800; "Mentor," *Mirror of the Times* (Wilmington), Sept. 17, 1800; "The Committee of Essex County to the People," *HL*, Sept. 29, 1800; *Connecticut Gazette*, Sept. 10, 1800; Bernard A. Weisberger, *America Afire: Jefferson, Adams, and the Revolutionary Election of 1800* (New York: William Morrow, 2000), pp. 246–55. See also "An Address to the Citizens of North-Carolina . . . July 1800" ([Raleigh?]: N.p., 1800); "A Federal Bore," *PG*, July 3, 1800; "An American," *Stewart's Kentucky Herald* (Lexington), Oct. 28, 1800.

56. "Robert Slender," *Aurora*, Oct. 2, 1800; Liston to Grenville, Dec. 6, 1800, FO 5/29A/358; Cunningham, *Jeffersonian Republicans*, p. 231.

57. Simon, *What Kind of Nation*, p. 127; Gibbs, *Memoirs of the Administrations*, p. 449.

58. "Jonathan Robbins," *SCSG*, Oct. 14, 1800; "A Republican," *CG*, Oct. 13, 1800; "Pinckney to Madison, Oct. 26, 1800, in the Presidential Election of 1800," *American Historical Association* 4 (1898): 117; *Albany Register*, Oct. 31, 1800; Marty D. Matthews, *Forgotten Founder: The Life and Times of Charles Pinckney* (Columbia: University of South Carolina Press, 2004), pp. 96–106.

59. "A Republican of St. Bartholomews," *SCSG*, Oct. 16, 1800.

60. Peter Freneau to [Seth Paine], Nov. 28, 1800, Philip Morin Freneau and Peter Freneau Correspondence, 1800–1801, Manuscripts, Library of Congress; "Pinckney to Jefferson, December 1800, in the Presidential Election of 1800," *American Historical Association* 4 (1898): 121–22; "Presidential Election," *CT*, Dec. 3, 1800; "South Carolina in the Presidential Election," *American Historical Association* 4 (1898): 111–29; Richard B. Davis and Milledge B. Seigler, "Peter Freneau, Carolina Republican," *Journal of Southern History* 13, no. 3 (August 1947), pp. 398–400; Elkins and McKitrick, *Age of Federalism*, pp. 741–43. By contrast, a New England clergyman despaired on learning the news from Columbia, "I have never heard bad tidings on anything

which gave me such a shock." Increase N. Tarbox, ed., *Diary of Robbins, D.D., 1796–1854* (Boston: Thomas Todd, 1886), I, p. 127.

61. "Presidential Election," *CT,* Dec. 3, 1800; Cunningham, *Jeffersonian Republicans,* pp. 231–45.

62. Thomas Jefferson to James Madison, Feb. 8, 1798, note 3 of J. C. A. Stagg, ed., *The Papers of James Madison Digital Edition* (Charlottesville: University of Virginia Press, Rotunda, 2010); Bernard A. Weisberger, *America Afire: Jefferson, Adams, and the Revolutionary Election of 1800* (New York: William Morrow, 2000), pp. 214–15; Gibbs, *Memoirs of the Administrations,* p. 377; John Davis, *Travels of Four Years and a Half in the United States of America; During 1795, 1799, 1800, 1801, and 1802* (London: B. Edwards, 1803), p. 172; Elkins and McKitrick, *Age of Federalism,* pp. 709–11.

63. Matthew Lyon, *AT,* Mar. 7, 1801. Thomas Bee declined the appointment to be chief judge of the Fifth Circuit due to the "fatigue of the long journies necessary to the performance of the duties of that office." Peter Graham Fish, *Federal Justice in the Mid-Atlantic South: United States Courts from Maryland to the Carolinas, 1789–1835* (Washington, DC: Administrative Offices of the U.S. Courts, 2002), p. 111.

64. *Historical Manuscripts Commission: Report on the Manuscripts of J. B. Fortescue, Esq. preserved at Dropmore* (London: H.M.S.O., 1908), VIII, pp. 358, 360; Elkins and McKitrick, *Age of Federalism,* p. 692.

65. "Anthony Pasquin. Alias John Williams," *Dartmouth Gazette* (Hanover, NH), Feb. 3, 1804; Sharp, *Deadlocked Election,* pp. 112–15; Sharp, *American Politics,* p. 240; James Grant, *John Adams: Party of One* (New York: Farrar, Straus and Giroux, 2005), p. 398.

66. Elkins and McKitrick, *Age of Federalism,* pp. 737–38; *Independent Chronicle,* May 2, 1805.

9   JONATHAN'S GHOST

1. *Times,* Jan. 20, 1801; Liston to Grenville, Nov. 28, 1800, FO 5/29A/335. See also, for example, *Ipswich Journal,* May 30, 1801.

2. King to Secretary of State, Jan. 22, 1801, in King, *Correspondence,* III, p. 376; Madison to King, July 24, 1801, in J. C. A. Stagg, ed., *The Papers of James Madison Digital Edition* (Charlottesville: University of Virginia Press, Rotunda, 2010); Liston to Grenville, Feb. 6, 1800, FO 5/29A/110; *ODNB,* s.v. "Sir Hyde Parker" and "Sir Robert Liston." For Pellew's "undiminished" appetite "for impressing American seamen," see *Augusta Herald* (Georgia), Aug. 13, 1800. "I rejoice that your stay on the Jamaica station has proved so advantageous," Earl Spencer, the First Lord of the Admiralty, wrote in May 1800 with the slightest hint of sarcasm. Earl Spencer to Parker, May 11, 1800, in H. W. Richmond, ed., *Private Papers of George, second Earl Spencer, First Lord of the Admiralty, 1794–1801* (London: Navy Records Society, 1924), III, p. 286.

3. Madison to King, July 24, 1801, in Robert J. Brugger et al., eds., *The Papers of James Madison, Secretary of State Series* (Charlottesville: University of Virginia Press, 1986), I, pp. 464–70; Madison to King, July 24, Oct. 27, 1801, in Mary A. Hackett *et al.,* eds., *The Papers of James Madison, Secretary of State Series* (Charlottesville: University of Virginia Press, 1993), II, p. 205.

4. Parker, Journal II, July 1 to Dec. 31, 1799; *CG,* Oct. 15, 1801; *London Gazette,* Sept. 20, 1800; *Morning Post* (London), Oct. 24, 1801; Winfield, *British Warships,* p. 199; *New York Gazette and General Advertiser,* Apr. 13, 1801.

5. CM, Bower, Feb. 13, 1802, ADM 1/5360; *Freeman's Exeter Flying Post,* Feb. 25, 1802;

Caledonian Mercury (Edinburgh), Jan. 25, 1802; *Hampshire Chronicle* (Winchester), Oct. 17, 1803, June 18, 1804; Winfield, *British Warships*, p. 199.

6. *Trewman's Exeter Flying Post*, Sept. 3, 1801; *London Chronicle or Universal Evening Post*, Sept. 27,1800.

7. CM, James Duncan, July 3, 1800, ADM 1/5353; CM, William Johnson and Hadrian Poulson, July 2, 1801, ADM 1/5357; *Aberdeen Journal*, Oct. 13, 1800. See also CM, Henry Croaker, Thomas Leedson, Peter Stewart, Jan. 15, 1799, ADM 1/5348; CM, John Williams, John Slushing, James Perrett, Richard Redmond, Jacob Fulga, Mar. 13–15, 1799, ADM 1/5348; CM, John Barnett, July 23, 1799, ADM 1/5350; CM, John Watson, James Allen, July 31, 1800, ADM 1/5353; CM, John Pearce, Aug. 25, 1801, ADM 1/5357.

8. CM, David Forrester, Mar. 30, 1802, ADM 1/5360; *Hampshire Telegraph & Portsmouth Gazette*, Apr. 5, 1802; *Georgia Gazette* (Savannah), July 29, 1802. Noting that testimony had identified Forrester as "the man who murdered captain Pigot," the *Aurora* queried, "Was it not *also proven* that *Jonathan Robbins* was the identical man who murdered capt. Pigot and threw his body overboard?" *National Intelligencer and Washington Advertiser*, Sept. 8, 1802.

9. "Thomas Woods," *Lancaster Gazette and General Advertiser*, Dec. 6, 1806; CM, Thomas Woods, Oct. 6, 1806, ADM 1/5375; "Execution of an Innocent Man," *Hereford Journal*, May 20, 1840; *Derby Mercury*, Sept. 21, 1859.

10. *Exeter Flying Post*, Dec. 18, 1800; *Caledonian Mercury*, June 26, 1800.

11. "Voluntary Confessions of Crime," *Cincinnati Daily Gazette*, July 11, 1871; Robert Philpot to Evan Nepean, May 14, 1801, ADM 1/2323/6?; C. Lock to Captain O'Brien, Oct. 11, 1800, in Christopher Lloyd, ed., *The Keith Papers* (London: Navy Records Society, 1950), II, pp. 398–400; Pope, *Black Ship*, pp. 90, 282–83; *Ipswich Journal*, May 30, 1801. See also, for example, *Hampshire Telegraph*, May 3, July 26, Sept. 13, 1802.

12. Nelson in 1804 upbraided a lieutenant commander for having flogged his entire crew. "I cannot approve a measure," Nelson wrote, "so foreign to the rules of good discipline and the accustomed practice of his Majesty's Navy." Rodger, *Command of the Ocean*, pp. 489–93; Rogers, *Press Gang*, p. 117.

13. *Hampshire Telegraph*, Feb. 1, 1802; *Cobbett's Annual Register* (London), Jan. 16, 1802; *Morning Post*, Jan. 25. 1802. In June, the King reinstated Hamilton to active service. *ODNB*, s.v. "Sir Edward Hamilton."

14. "Nauticus," *Morning Chronicle*, Nov. 18, 1815; "Letters on the Evils of Impressment . . . ," *Edinburgh Review* 41 (1824): 178; William James, *The Naval History of Great Britain, From the Declaration of War by France in 1793 to the Accession of George IV* (London: Richard Bentley, 1837), II, p. 103; "Captain Elliot," *Standard* (London), Dec. 6, 1842; "The Somers Mutiny," *Albany Evening Journal*, Jan. 7, 1843; Rodger, *Command of the Ocean*, pp. 492–93; Eugene L. Rasor, *Reform in the Royal Navy: A Social History of the Lower Deck, 1850 to 1880* (Hamden, CT: Archon Books, 1976), pp. 24–25; Rogers, *Press Gang*, pp. 15, 132–33. The author of "An Inquiry into the Nature and Effects of Flogging" (1826) declared, "With such unrelenting severity has the lash been inflicted in the Royal Navy, that *mutiny* and *murder* have been resorted to in a spirit of retaliation. What was it which induced the crew of the *Hermione* to mutiny; to kill the captain (Pigot), his officers, and his marines?" John D. Byrn, Jr., *Crime and Punishment in the Royal Navy: Discipline on the Leeward Islands Station 1784–1812* (Farnham, UK: Scolar Press, 1989), p. 3.

15. *True American* (Trenton), July 7, 1801.

16. *CC* (Boston), Oct. 11, 1800; "Communication," *Vermont Gazette* (Bennington), Aug. 3, 1801; *Western Star* (Stockbridge, MA), Aug. 3, 1801; "Robbin's Lament," in *The American Republican Harmonist* (Philadelphia: Duane, 1803), pp. 43–44. See also "The Duke's Retreat to Braintree," "The Retrospect," "The Republican Triumph," "Robbins; or the Victim," in ibid., pp. 15–17, 21, 27, 90–91; "To the Editor of the Citizen," *CT,* Apr. 22, 1801; "Entertaining," *The Patriot, or, Scourge of Aristocracy,* Aug. 14, 1801; "Nolle Prosequi," *AC,* Nov. 13, 1801.

17. "The Reign of Terror," *Carlisle Gazette,* Jan. 28, 1801; *An Address Delivered at a Meeting of the Democratic Association of the County of Gloucester . . .* (Trenton, NJ: Mann & Wilson [1801?]; *True American* (Trenton), Sept. 29, 1801; *CT,* Oct. 10, 1801; *Vermont Gazette,* Oct. 26, 1801; "Detector," *Trenton Federalist,* Oct 17, 1803; *VA,* Nov. 5, 1803.

18. J. Horatio Nichols, *Jefferson and Liberty, or Celebration of the Fourth of March. A Patriotic Tragedy: A Picture of the Perfidy of Corrupt Administration in Five Acts* (N.p.: n.p., 1801). What is surprising is not the attention Robbins stirred in the wake of Jefferson's election, but rather the resonance his death possessed for years afterward. In publications ranging from political polemics to legal treatises, it was an episode that continued to exert a tremendous hold on the American consciousness. Thus, in 1802, the distinguished Pennsylvania lawyer William Barton elaborated on "the well known case of Jonathan Robbins," labeling it a "catastrophe," while a Federalist that September complained of "democratic editors [who] still continue to mourn about the unfortunate Jonathan Robbins." A Massachusetts resident even claimed that Thomas Nash, "the real murderer of the Captain of the Hermione Frigate," was still alive in the West Indies; whereas a "German Republican" in Allegheny County, Pennsylvania, regretted in 1803 that "our toryfied federalists did not die in poor Jonathan Robbins' place." William Barton, *A Dissertation on the Freedom of Navigation . . .* (Philadelphia: John Conrad & Co., 1802), p. 95; *The Wasp,* Sept. 23, 1802; *Columbian Minerva* (Dedham, MA), Nov. 23, 1802 [the paper mistakenly referred to "Jonathan Nash"]; "D.M.," *The Hornet,* Feb. 1, 1803. See also "Americanus," *Carlisle Gazette,* Apr. 14, 1802; John Wood, *The History of the Administration of John Adams, Esq., late President of the United States* (New York: N.p., 1802), p. 93; *Alexandria Advertiser,* Aug. 17, 1803; *Dartmouth Gazette* (Hanover, NH), June 1, 1804; *The Rainbow; First Series* (Richmond: Ritchie & Worsley), p. 35; *Republican Star or Eastern Shore General Advertiser* (Easton, MD), July 29, 1809.

19. *Annals,* Apr. 5, pp. 1137–38, Mar. 12, 1806, p. 756, Apr. 25, 1810, p. 1980; *Carolina Gazette* (Charleston), June 10, 1802. See also, for example, "Speech on Bill to Raise an Additional Military Force," [Jan. 8, 9, 1813], in James F. Hopkins and Mary W. M. Hargreaves, eds., *The Papers of Henry Clay* (Lexington: University of Kentucky Press, 1959), I, p. 760.

20. *Charleston Courier,* Sept. 17, 1804; "Falsehoods about Jonathan Robbins again Refuted," *New-England Palladium,* Oct. 9, 1804; Wood, *Empire of Liberty,* pp. 312–13. See also, for example, *Alexandria Expositor, and the Columbian Advertiser,* June 13, 1803; [David Daggett], *Facts are Stubborn Things, or, Nine Plain Questions to the People of Connecticut . . .* (Hartford: Hudson & Goodwin, 1803), p. 11; "To the Freeholders of Loudon, Fairfax, and Prince William Counties," *Alexandria Advertiser,* Mar. 30, 1805.

21. "Detector," *Trenton Federalist,* Oct. 17, 1803; "Resuscitator," *Ontario Messenger* (Canandaigua, NY), Mar. 30, 1813; *Mr. Pickering's Speech in the House of Representatives*

of the U. States on Saturday the 26th and Monday the 28th of February, 1814 (George-town: Robert Alleson, 1814), p. 4. For Pickering, see also, for example, *Columbian Minerva* (Dedham, MA), Nov. 23, 1802; *True American* (Trenton), Mar. 21, 1808.

22. John Adams to John Quincy Adams, Jan. 8, 1808, Founders Online, National Archives, http://founders.archives.gov/documents/Adams/99–03–02–1629; "Anthony Pasquin. Alias John Williams," *Dartmouth Gazette* (Hanover), Feb. 3, 1804; "John Adams," *Boston Patriot*, July 4, 1809; John Adams to Thomas Jefferson, May 1, 1812, June 30, 1813, in J. Jefferson Looney, ed., *The Papers of Thomas Jefferson*, Retirement Series (Princeton, NJ: Princeton University Press, 2008–2009), V, pp. 3–4, VI, pp. 253–56; John Adams to Dr. Rush, May 13, 1812, in Alexander Biddle, ed., *Old Family Letters* (Philadelphia: J. P. Lippincott, 1892), p. 459. Years later, Senator Mahlon Dickerson of New Jersey, a Republican, reflected that had Thomas Nash, in truth, been Jonathan Robbins, an American, "It would have been a source of lasting regret to Mr. Adams; and had he known precisely how the case stood before Judge Bee, sure I am he would not have interfered in the manner he did. He was governed, no doubt, by a rigid sense of justice, and a regard for the conditions of our treaty with Great Britain. But I have ever thought, and still think, the act was precipitate, and peculiarly unfortunate." *Daily National Intelligencer* (Washington, DC), Apr. 5, 1821. An excellent account of Adams's postpresidential years is Joseph J. Ellis, *Passionate Sage: The Character and Legacy of John Adams* (New York: W. W. Norton, 1994).

23. *Annals of Congress, Senate,* Dec. 8, 1801, pp. 11–16. For Jefferson's first term as president, see Jon Meacham, *Thomas Jefferson: The Art of Power* (New York: Random House, 2012), pp. 347–99.

24. Marilyn C. Baseler, *"Asylum for Mankind": America, 1607–1800* (Ithaca, NY: Cornell University Press, 1998), pp. 310–15.

25. Baseler, *"Asylum for Mankind,"* pp. 276, 288; "Hume," *CC,* Jan. 6, 20, 1802; "Charming Asylum for Oppressed Humanity," *Farmer's Weekly Museum, or Literary Gazette* (Walpole, NH), Nov. 2, 1802. Already, according to Federalist complaints, Irish aliens had illegally cast ballots in sundry elections despite the rigorous requirements of the Naturalization Act. "Forms and penalties," according to a Connecticut paper, had been disregarded by both aliens and magistrates. *Windham Herald* (Windham, CT), Feb. 18, 1802. See also "Aliens," *SCSG,* Apr. 22, 1800; *CG,* Oct. 16, 1800.

26. "From the Aurora of June 20th, 1800," *GUS,* Sept. 24, 1801; "A Republican Farmer," *CF,* May 6, 1800. Meanwhile, a writer in Boston's *Constitutional Telegraph* had observed in 1800 that most of the country's "patriotic army" was composed of Irish immigrants. "Of course," he noted derisively, "Mr. Liston, or other officers of the British government have nothing to do but to exhibit a charge against this set of fellows as being rebels, United Irishmen, and traitors, who have fled from their country to avoid punishment, and conformably to the British treaty and Judge Bee's decision upon the Irishman Jonathan Robbins, they must be delivered up at Mr. Liston's request and sent to Europe for trial." *CT,* Mar. 12, 1800.

27. "Naturalization," *Boston Gazette,* Dec. 28, 1801; Aristide R. Zolberg, *A Nation by Design: Immigration Policy in the Fashioning of America* (Cambridge, MA: Harvard University Press, 2006), p. 98.

28. Jefferson to Caesar A. Rodney, [before Nov. 4, 1802], in Barbara B. Oberg, ed., *The Papers of Thomas Jefferson* (Princeton, NJ: Princeton University Press, 2011), XXXVIII, pp. 636–39; "A Naturalized Irishman," *CG,* Sept. 16, 1808; *Salem Gazette* (Massachusetts), Oct. 18, 1802; Wood, *Empire of Liberty,* pp. 305–8. See also *The Balance, and*

Columbian Repository, Dec. 28, 1802; *Courier of New Hampshire* (Concord), Oct. 28, 1802; John Tracy Ellis, *American Catholicism* (Chicago: University of Chicago Press, 1969), p. 44.

29. "Jonathan Robbins," *SCSG,* Oct. 14, 1800; "A Republican Farmer," *To the Citizens of the United States, and particularly the Citizens of New-York, New-Jersey, Delaware, and Pennsylvania, Maryland and North-Carolina, on the propriety of choosing republican members to their State Legislatures, at the ensuing elections, in order to secure the election of Electors of a President, at the approaching election for that important office* (New York: N.p., Mar. 8, 1800); "Simon Slim," *CT,* June 25, 1800; Peter S. Onuf, *Jefferson's Empire: The Language of American Nationhood* (Charlottesville: University Press of Virginia, 2000), pp. 80–108.

30. Michael Barrett, *The Reply of a Friend to Justice, to a Friend to Propriety, on the Fate of the Unfortunate Robbins* (N.p.: [1799–1800]), pp. 13–15; [John Steele], "Letter from a Federalist," in H. M. Wagstaff, ed., *The Papers of John Steele* (Raleigh, NC: Edwards & Broughton, 1924), p. 851.

31. "Remarks," *CG,* Sept. 9, 1802; "A Republican Emigrant," *Republican Watch-Tower* (New York), Apr. 25, 1804; *SCSG,* Aug, 11, 1802; "Federal Abuse of Aliens," *Rhode-Island Republican,* Oct. 3, 1801; [S. C. Carpenter], *Memoirs of the Hon. Thomas Jefferson* . . . (New York: Thomas Hall, 1809), II, pp. 83–84. See also *Greenfield Gazette* (Massachusetts), Mar. 21, 1803.

32. *Annals of Congress, Senate,* Dec. 8, 1801, p. 6; *United States Chronicle* (Providence, RI), Apr. 7, 1803; Baseler, *"Asylum for Mankind,"* pp. 312–13, 331; James H. Kettner, *The Development of American Citizenship. 1608–1870* (Chapel Hill: University of North Carolina Press, 1978), pp. 246–47; Gerald L. Neuman, *Strangers to the Constitution: Immigrants, Borders, and Fundamental Law* (Princeton, NJ: Princeton University Press, 1996), pp. 60–61. A Connecticut Federalist scolded, "Two years is the limitation proposed by some; one year by others; but *Paddy swears* by J____s, it shall be *no year at all." Otsego Herald: or, Western Advertiser,* Mar. 10, 1803.

33. *Democrat* (Boston), Nov. 3, 1804; *Independent Chronicle,* July 22, 1805; *AC,* Oct. 28, 1802; "A Citizen of the World," *Vermont Centinel,* July 16, 1801; Edward Sharman, *CF,* Sept. 15, 1807; See also *IC,* July 23, 1801; Onuf, *Jefferson's Empire,* pp. 86, 92, 107.

34. *Alexandria Advertiser,* Sept. 13, 1803; "Benevolus," *Farmer's Weekly Museum* (Walpole, NH), July 21, 1801; "Emigrants," *Northern Post* (Salem, NY), Nov. 1, 1804.

35. Jeffrey L. Pasley, "1800 as a Revolution in Political Culture: Newspapers, Celebrations, Voting, and Democratization in the Early Republic," in James Horn, Jan Ellen Lewis, and Peter S. Onuf, eds., *The Revolution of 1800: Democracy, Race, & the New Republic* (Charlottesville: University of Virginia Press, 2002), pp. 121–52; Wood, *Empire of Liberty,* pp. 302–14.

36. *Democratic Press* (Philadelphia), Nov. 26, 1807.

37. *Albany Register,* Dec. 23, 1800; "An act in addition to the act, intituled an act, to amend the penal laws of this Commonwealth," *The Revised Code of the Laws of Virginia* . . . (Richmond: Thomas Ritchie, 1819), I, pp. 589–90; Meriwether Jones to James Madison, July 10, 1801, in Robert J. Brugger *et al.,* eds., *The Papers of James Madison, Secretary of State Series* (Charlottesville: University of Virginia Press, 1986), I, pp. 395–96; Stanislaus Murray Hamilton, ed., *The Writings of James Monroe* . . . (1898; reprint ed., AMS Press, New York, 1969), III, pp. 228–30; Richard E. Lee's Letter, The Attorney General's Opinion, and the Affidavits Accompanying the Governor's Communication to the General Assembly, Relative to the Conduct of Doctor

John K. Read, a Magistrate of the Borough of Norfolk (Richmond, VA: Meriwether Jones, 1800); "Extract of a letter from Richmond," *Albany Register,* Dec. 19, 1800.

38. David Erskine to James Madison, Jan. 4, 1807, Madison to Erskine, Jan. 7, 1807, Erskine to Howick, Feb. 1, 1807, FO 5/52.

39. Howick to Erskine, Nov. 6, 1806, Erskine to Howick, Feb. 1, 1807, FO 5/52. See also Spencer C. Tucker and Frank T. Reuter, *Injured Honor: The Chesapeake-Leopard Affair, June 22, 1807* (Annapolis: Naval Institute Press, 1996), pp. 68–72.

40. *Portland Gazette and Maine Advertiser,* Aug. 10, 1807; Thomas Truxton to Timothy Pickering, Oct. 26, 1807, roll 28, Pickering Papers; Tucker and Reuter, *Injured Honor,* p. 72.

41. *CF,* Apr. 1, 1806; "From the Virginia Argus," *National Intelligencer and Washington Advertiser,* July 27, 1807; "The Happy Farmer," *True American,* Oct. 9, 1807; Adams to Adams, Jan. 8, 1808, Founders Online, National Archives, http://founders.archives .gov/documents/Adams/99-03-02-1629. See also "Marcellus," *Independent Chronicle* (Boston), July 9, 1807; *Democratic Press* (Philadelphia), Nov. 26, 1807; "British Friendship," *Virginia Argus,* Nov. 13, 1807; John P. Kennedy, ed., *Memoirs of the Life of William Wirt, Attorney-General of the United States* (Philadelphia: Lea and Blanchard, 1850), I, p. 198.

42. "The Ploughboy," *CG,* June 19, 1812. For the War of 1812 and its origins, see Alan Taylor, *The Civil War of 1812: American Citizens, British Subjects, Irish Rebels, & Indian Allies* (New York: Alfred A. Knopf, 2010); and for the importance of impressment, especially in the eyes of American mariners, see Paul A. Gilje, *Free Trade and Sailors' Rights in the War of 1812* (Cambridge: Cambridge University Press, 2013).

EPILOGUE

1. "Opinion of Chief Justice Tilghman," *Niles Weekly Register,* Aug. 30, 1823, pp. 412–16; "Something New," *Providence Patriot, Columbia Phenix* (Phenix, RI), Aug. 30, 1823.

2. Nicholas Dungan, *Gallatin: America's Swiss Founding Father* (New York: New York University Press, 2010), pp. 135–43.

3. Albert Gallatin to Henry Clay, June 29, 1826, in James Hopkins and Mary W. M. Hargreaves, eds., *The Papers of Henry Clay* (Lexington: University Press of Kentucky, 1973), V, pp. 516–17; Clay to Gallatin, Aug. 8, 1829, ibid., V, pp. 600–601.

4. "Chief Justice Marshall," *New-Hampshire Statesman and State Journal* (Concord), July 18, 1835; "Kidnapping—Jury Trial," *Philanthropist,* Nov. 14, 1837; "The Amistad," *Emancipator,* Oct. 10, 1839. See also George Tucker, *The Life of Thomas Jefferson . . .* (Philadelphia: Carey, Lea & Blanchard, 1837), II, pp. 68–69; Peter Graham Fish, *Federal Justice in the Mid-Atlantic South: United States Courts from Maryland to the Carolinas, 1789–1835* (Washington, DC: Administrative Offices of the U.S. Courts, 2002), pp. 241–42.

5. Edward Everett to Daniel Webster, Jan. 21, 1842, in Kenneth E. Shewmaker et al., eds., *The Papers of Daniel Webster: Diplomatic Papers* (Hanover, NH: University Press of New England, 1983), I, pp. 491–92; *The Writings and Speeches of Daniel Webster* (Boston: Little, Brown and Company, 1903), I, p. 124. For the long-term impact of the Robbins crisis, see also *Speech of Mr. Levy of Florida, on the Tenth Article of the Treaty of Washington . . . Delivered in the House of Representatives of the United States, March 5, 1844* (Washington, DC: Blair and Rives, 1844), p. 9.

6. Daniel Webster to Joseph Story, Apr. 9, 1842, in Shewmaker et al., eds., *Webster Diplomatic Papers,* I, pp. 532–33; Story to Webster, Apr. 19, 1842, in ibid., I, pp. 537–38.

7. Everett to Webster, Dec. 1, 1841, in Shewmaker et al., eds., *Webster Diplomatic Papers,* I, pp. 178–79; Webster to Everett, Jan. 29, 1842, in ibid., I, pp. 177–85; Howard Jones, "The Peculiar Institution and National Honor: The Case of the *Creole* Slave Revolt," Civil War History 21 (March 1975): 28–50; Walter Johnson, "White Lies: Human Property and Domestic Slavery Aboard the Slave Ship Creole," Atlantic Studies 5, no. 2 (August 2008): 237–63.

8. "The African Captives," *Emancipator* (New York), Oct. 10, 1839; "Veto," *North American,* Jan. 1, 1841; Pyle, *Extradition,* pp. 48–55. For the rebellion, see Marcus Rediker, *The Amistad Rebellion: An Atlantic Odyssey of Slavery and Freedom* (New York: Viking, 2012).

9. [William Jay], *The Creole Case, and Mr. Webster's Despatch* (New York: New-York American, 1842), pp. 35–36; Pyle, *Extradition,* p. 57.

10. Liza Schuster, *The Use and Abuse of Political Asylum in Britain and Germany* (London: Frank Cass, 2003), pp. 63–68; Pyle, *Extradition,* pp. 56–57; Francis M. Carroll, *A Good and Wise Measure: The Search for the Canadian-American Boundary, 1783–1842* (Toronto: University of Toronto Press, 2001), pp. 284–85.

11. Pyle, *Extradition,* pp. 57, 70–71.

12. Ethan A. Nadelmann, *Borders: The Internationalization of U.S. Criminal Law Enforcement* (University Park: Pennsylvania State University Press, 1993), p. 419; David M. Lieberman, "Sorting the Revolutionary from the Terrorist: The Delicate Applications of the 'Political Offense' Exception in U.S. Extradition Cases," *Stanford Law Review* 59 (October 2006): 186–87.

13. *Speech of Mr. Levy of Florida,* p. 7; Pyle, *Extradition,* p. 57. For the treaty text, see http://avalon.law.yale.edu/19th_century/br-1842.asp. The tenth article reads: "It is agreed that the United States and Her Britannic Majesty shall, upon mutual requisitions by them, or their Ministers, Officers, or authorities, respectively made, deliver up to justice, all persons who, being charged with the crime of murder, or assault with intent to commit murder, or Piracy, or arson, or robbery, or Forgery, or the utterance of forged paper, committed within the jurisdiction of either, shall seek an asylum, or shall be found, within the territories of the other: Provided, that this shall only be done upon such evidence of criminality as, according to the laws of the place where the fugitive or person so charged, shall be found, would justify his apprehension and commitment for trial, if the crime or offense had there been committed: And the respective Judges and other Magistrates of the two Governments, shall have power, jurisdiction, and authority, upon complaint made under oath, to issue a warrant for the apprehension of the fugitive or person so charged, that he may be brought before such Judges or other Magistrates, respectively, to the end that the evidence of criminality may be heard and considered; and if, on such hearing, the evidence be deemed sufficient to sustain the charge it shall be the duty of the examining Judge or Magistrate, to certify the same to the proper Executive Authority, that a warrant may issue for the surrender of such fugitive. The expense of such apprehension and delivery shall be borne and defrayed by the Party who makes the requisition, and receives the fugitive."

14. *In re* Thomas Kaine, 55 US 103—Supreme Court 1852; Pyle, *Extradition,* pp. 96–103.

15. 12 *Congressional Globe,* 27th Congress, 3rd Session (1843), Appendix, p. 12; Pyle, *Extradition,* pp. 72–74; ANB, s.v. "Thomas Hart Benton."

16. Message of August 11, 1842, 12 *Congressional Globe,* 27th Congress, 3rd Session (1842), p. 4; Shewmaker, ed., *Webster Diplomatic Papers,* I, pp. 798–99; Pyle, *Extradition,* 74.

CODA

1. "In the Matter of the Requested Extradition of Desmond Mackin by the Government of the United Kingdom of Great Britain and Northern Ireland. United States of America, Petitioner-appellant v. Desmond Mackin, Respondent-Appellee, Desmond Mackin, Petitioner, v. George V. Grant, United States Marshal for the Southern District of New York, Respondent," 668 F.2d 122 (2d Cir. 1981), U.S. Court of Appeals for the Second Circuit; Pyle, *Extradition,* pp. 171–74.
2. Ibid.
3. Ronald Sullivan, "U.S. Court Blocks I.R.A. Extradition," *New York Times,* Jan. 13, 1982; Steven V. Roberts, "Pact with Britain on Extraditions Backed by Senate," *NYT,* July 18, 1986; Ethan A. Nadelmann, *Borders: The Internationalization of U.S. Criminal Law Enforcement* (University Park: Pennsylvania State University Press, 1993), pp. 421–22.

Index

Page numbers in *italics* refer to illustrations.

ILLUSTRATION CREDITS

A NOTE ABOUT THE TYPE

This book was set in Adobe Garamond. Designed for the Adobe Corporation by Robert Slimbach, the fonts are based on types first cut by Claude Garamond (c. 1480–1561). Garamond was a pupil of Geoffrey Tory and is believed to have followed the Venetian models, although he introduced a number of important differences, and it is to him that we owe the letter we now know as "old style."

Composed by North Market Street Graphics,
Lancaster, Pennsylvania

Printed and bound by Berryville Graphics,
Berryville, Virginia

Designed by M. Kristen Bearse

DATE DUE			

202)

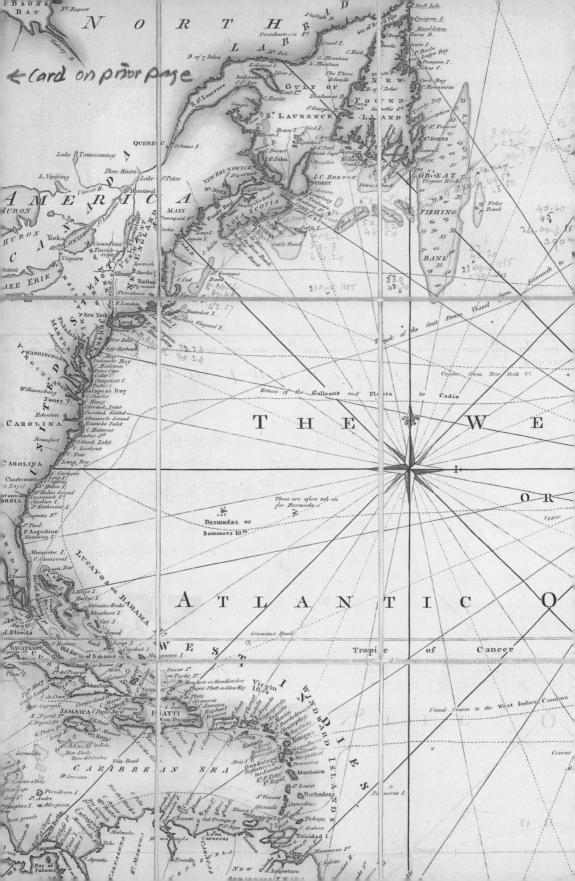